SMALL-TOWN AMERICA IN FILM

BOOKS BY EMANUEL LEVY

*The Habima—Israel's National Theater:
A Study of Cultural Nationalism*

*John Wayne: Prophet of
the American Way of Life*

*And the Winner Is . . . The History
and Politics of the Oscar Awards*

Emanuel Levy

SMALL-TOWN AMERICA IN FILM

The Decline and Fall of Community

A Frederick Ungar Book

CONTINUUM / NEW YORK

1991
The Continuum Publishing Company
370 Lexington Avenue, New York, NY 10017

Printed in the United States of America

Library of Congress Cataloging-in-Publication Data

Levy, Emanuel, 1947–
    Small-town America in film : the decline of community /
Emanuel Levy.
        p.   cm.
    "A Frederick Ungar book."
    Includes bibliographical references.
    Includes index.
    ISBN 0-8264-0484-7
    1. City and town life in motion pictures.   2. United States in
motion pictures.   I. Title.
PN1995.9.C513L4   1991
791.43′621734—dc20   90-40667
                                                            CIP

All photographs courtesy of The Museum of Modern Art/Film Stills Archive,
11 West 53rd Street, New York City

To Rob Remley

Table of Contents

Acknowledgments

The work on this book began the day my previous book, *And the Winner Is . . . The History and Politics of the Oscar Award* (1987) went into production. Unlike former books I have written, one thing was clear from the very beginning—the title of the book: It had to be called *Small-Town America*. What other title could capture the essence of that distinctly American life-style or vision? I failed to realize at the time that, along with my other books (*And the Winner Is* and *John Wayne: Prophet of the American Way of Life*), I was dealing with three of the most uniquely American symbols: the Oscar Award, John Wayne, and small-town America. To me, these three publications form some kind of logical, thematic unit, representing a decade of work on the American cinema.

I began to collect data about small-town films, not realizing their huge numbers. I subsequently decided to limit myself to the sound era and begin with that landmark film, King Vidor's *The Crowd*, a work that set forever the visual imagery of the Big City in the American cinema. During the research process, the scope of the study expanded and films about the big city and suburbia were added. The comparisons among these three ideological constructs (and life-styles) help to highlight the distinctive thematic and stylistic elements of small-town life (and films). The present book is a chronological account, decade by decade, of the portraiture of Small-Town America in films that were made over six decades, between 1927 and 1989.

Several friends and colleagues have read and commented on earlier drafts of this book and papers presented in various conferences. I would like to thank Judith Blau, Arthur Vidich, Pamela J. Riley, John Beymer, Jeanine Basinger, and Bill Shepard for providing helpful comments.

This book owes an intellectual debt to two major critics, Andrew Sarris and Pauline Kael, who have influenced my way of thinking about films. Sarris and Kael have been arguably the most influential film critics over the last thirty years. No other reviewers have, by turn, provoked, irritated, and enlightened readers as Sarris and Kael. One of the first film books I read was Sarris's *The American Cinema* (1969), the Bible of auteurism and a book that changed the direction of film criticism in America. Films were no longer evaluated in terms of their stories or ideas, but as aesthetic works; form and style became just as important as content. Kael also offered new criteria of evaluation: freshness of viewpoint, candor, wit, and context (movies as integral part of popular culture). She had no inherent prejudice against American films for their commercial aspects and mass appeal, and felt no guilt over the enjoyment of trash. Singly and jointly, Sarris and Kael could make a movie fan out of anyone.

Whether or not they qualify as auteurs, the book encompasses great films by major American directors: John Ford, Howard Hawks, Alfred Hitchcock, Orson Welles, George Stevens, King Vidor, George Cukor, Frank Capra, Preston Sturges, Joseph Loosey, Douglas Sirk, and others. And it scrutinizes the work of a younger generation of brilliant directors: Jonathan Demme, Martin Scorsese, David Lynch. I do believe one can teach the history and sociology of the American cinema by just focusing on small-town films. I am also proud that the book pays tribute to some of the finest performances ever given in American films: Katharine Hepburn (*Little Women, Alice Adams*), Jimmy Stewart (*Mr. Deeds Goes to Town, It's a Wonderful Life*), Bette Davis (*The Little Foxes*), Spencer Tracy (*Bad Day at Black Rock*), Julie Harris (*The Member of the Wedding*), James Dean (*East of Eden*), Geraldine Page (*Sweet Bird of Youth*), Paul Newman (*Hud*), Sally Field (*Norma Rae*), and so on.

Over the last decade, I have offered numerous courses dealing with film and society, ideology and politics in the American cinema, auteurism, and film genres. These courses have invariably included movies about small-town life. The best small-town films can be used in a variety of courses. For example, *The Magnificent Ambersons* or *Shadow of a Doubt* were chosen for courses dealing with classics of the American cinema, Orson Welles and Hitchcock as auteurs, expressionism in film, film noir, and so on. I would like to thank my students at Columbia University, Wellesley College, and the New School for Social Research who have contributed to this book by challenging my ideas about films.

The collection of data took place in many libraries and I would like to thank the personnel of the Margaret Herrick Library of the Academy of Motion Picture Arts and Sciences, the Lincoln Center Library for the Performing Arts, and the libraries of the American Film Institute, the Museum of Modern Art, the University of California at Los Angeles, and the University of Southern California. My special thanks to Mary Corliss and Terry Geesken of the Museum of Modern Art Film Stills Archive, for their patient guidance in selecting pictures for this book. It gives me great pleasure to thank Michael Leach and Evander Lomke of The Continuum Publishing Company for the interest they have shown in my work and for improving the manuscript—this is our third time together!

This book could not have been written without the moral support and encouragement of my late friend Nathan Waterman. I owe him my career as a writer. I dedicate this work to my friend Rob Remley, whose continuous criticism has been invaluable to the quality of my thinking and writing.

Emanuel Levy
The New School for Social Research
New York City, August 1990

Introduction

Small towns have featured so prominently in American culture that they have become a deeply rooted symbol in the country's collective consciousness. Indeed, the importance of small towns has gone beyond their historic or economic roles. The very concept of small town implies a distinct life-style with its own set of values, as sociologist Thorstein Veblen (1923) observed: "The country town is one of the great American institutions . . . in the sense that it has had a greater part than any other in shaping public sentiment and giving character to American culture." At the same time, Max Lerner (1957) astutely noted that "the phrase 'small town' has come itself to carry a double layer of meaning, at once sentimental and condescending." For many people, small towns have been an integral element of the American Way of Life. "Small-town America" has been one of the few uniquely American symbols to be continuously preeminent—despite dramatic changes in the country's history, politics, and demography.

Historians have examined the role of small towns in the nation's history, and sociologists have studied the class structure, economy, and politics of small towns.[1] However, there have been few books about the portrayal of small towns in popular culture. Broadly defined, this book aims at exploring the various manifestations of the concept "Small-Town America" in film, from the beginning of the sound era, in 1927, to the present. The book examines the symbolic representation of small-town life in feature films, attempting to answer one central question: what has the American cinema told its audiences about everyday life in small towns: work and public life; love and marriage, family and friendship; sex and leisure; politics and community life. The goal is to demonstrate the prevalence of certain myths, expressed in specific themes, stereotypes, and characters, in the cultural treatment of small towns.

The Extraordinary Preeminence of Small-Town America

It is easy to document the continuous fascination with small towns and their extraordinary preeminence in American culture. In 1986 alone,

15

more than five films, each different from the other, have explored the multifaceted small-town life, including: David Byrne's *True Stories*, David Lynch's *Blue Velvet*, and Francis Ford Coppola's *Peggy Sue Got Married*. In the same year, Pulitzer Prize–winning playwright Beth Henley was represented with two small-town films: *Nobody's Fool* and *Crimes of the Heart*. In 1989, Henley adapted to the screen another of her small-town plays, *Miss Firecracker*.

The book shows that small-town films have been a permanent staple of the American cinema from its very beginning. Their preeminence has derived from their prevalence in other cultural forms: books, short stories, and stage plays. Some of America's most esteemed artists have devoted their creative energies to the exploration of small-town life. For example, the Pulitzer Prize, one of the most prestigious awards for journalism, fiction, and drama, has honored over the years such figures as Booth Tarkington (*The Magnificent Ambersons*, 1919; *Alice Adams*, 1922), Sinclair Lewis (*Arrowsmith*, 1926), Marjorie Kinnan Rawlings (*The Yearling*, 1939), John Steinbeck (*The Grapes of Wrath*, 1939), and James Agee (*A Death in the Family*, 1958). And the Pulitzer Prize for drama has singled out plays by Thornton Wilder (*Our Town*, 1938), Robert Sherwood (*Abe Lincoln in Illinois*, 1939), William Inge (*Picnic*, 1953), and Tennessee Williams (*Cat on a Hot Tin Roof*, 1955). All of these prize-winning books and plays have been made into successful films (See Small-Town Movies by Decade).

Author Sherwood Anderson, for example, worked as a small-town editor in Marion, Virginia, before embarking on a writing career *(Winesburg, Ohio; Home Town)*. Sinclair Lewis won the Nobel Prize for literature for *Arrowsmith*, and also wrote *Babbitt* and *Elmer Gantry*, all of which have been transferred to the big screen. The best work of John Steinbeck *(East of Eden)*, William Saroyan *(The Human Comedy)*, and Carson McCullers *(The Member of the Wedding)* is set in small towns. And at present, Larry McMurtry's novels *(Horseman Pass, Lonesome Dove, Texasville)* continue to explore issues pertinent to small towns.

Furthermore, some of Hollywood's most distinguished filmmakers have made films about small towns. The notable director Frank Capra, winner of multiple Oscar Awards, devoted his entire career to the celebration of small-town virtues, admirably demonstrated in *Mr. Deeds Goes to Town* (1936), *Mr. Smith Goes to Washington* (1939), and *It's a Wonderful Life* (1946). Alfred Hitchcock, the master of suspense, directed two small-town film classics: *Shadow of a Doubt* (1943), based on Thornton Wilder's screenplay, and *The Birds* (1963), considered to be his last undisputed success. Directors and screenwriters of younger generations have also been preoccupied with small-town themes. Martin Ritt, for example, has adapted several of William Faulkner's novels to the screen, such as *The Long, Hot Summer* (1958), *The Sound and the Fury* (1960); along with other films such as *Hud* (1963), *Sounder* (1972), *Conrack* (1974), *Norma Rae* (1979), *Cross Creek* (1983), and *Murphy's Romance* (1985). Asked to explain his fascination with the South, Ritt said: "The essence of drama is change, and the South has gone through more changes than any other section of the country."[2] The literary oeuvre of Horton Foote for screen, stage, and television has been dominated by small-town stories (*Tender Mercies*, 1983; *The Trip to Bountiful* and *1918*, both in 1985; and *On Valentine's Day*, 1986).

Many screen actors were born in small towns and developed screen images that were intimately associated with small-town values. Some of America's greatest movie stars, Gary Cooper, Henry Fonda, Jimmy Stewart, have built their careers out of playing small-town heroes, be they farmers (Cooper, Fonda), lawyers (Stewart), and other countryfolk (Will Rogers). These stars functioned as much more than actors; they were folk heroes, embodying the nation's long-enduring myths. When the image of small-town heroes began to change, and they became antiheroes, a new generation of stars embodied their new values. Paul Newman, for example, played mostly Southern antiheroes in his earlier career *(Cat on a Hot Tin Roof, The Long, Hot Summer, Sweet Bird of Youth, Hud, Cool Hand Luke)*.

Theoretical Perspective

In analyzing small-town films, this book uses elements of three theoretical orientations: sociology, structuralism, and semiology. It shows points of convergence and divergence among these approaches, demonstrating how they complement each other by focusing on different aspects of film. The key concepts are context in sociology, text in structuralism, and subtext in semiology. From a sociological standpoint, cinema, like other institutions (science, politics, economy) does not operate in a social or political void. Rather, it is interrelated with the historical, cultural, and political settings in which it operates. Using structuralism, films are analyzed as cultural texts and narrative structures. And the semiological approach emphasizes that films are constructions or systems of meanings, which signify symbols (and messages) in specifically and uniquely cinematic ways.

The sociology of film uses both institutional and interactional perspectives in understanding the production and consumption of films. Films are mass products, conceived and created for the immediate viewing by large and diverse audiences. However, films often enjoy wide appeal, not because they are intrinsically interesting, but because of the historical and social timing of their release. This happens when films address timely issues in terms of occurrences outside of the film industry. Films are interwoven in a network of relationships with other institutions (family, politics, religion) and are subject to institutional (organizational, industrial, and legal) and ideological constraints that shape their thematics and stylistics. These constraints operate both within and without the film industry. For example, the kinds of films produced are determined by market considerations, which in turn are determined by demographics (the age of frequent filmgoers).

In its general use, the reflection theory (films reflect society) is not adequate. One needs to be more specific, asking what particular aspects of the film (narrative structure, thematic conventions, style) reflect what aspects of the social structure. Moreover, films may express cultural norms and social trends, but they may also reflect the personal ideology and politics of their filmmakers. For example, Capra's small-town movies can be grounded in the ideological context of the Depression, but they also reflect Capra's belief system. Along with other agencies, films perform a function of social control: By stressing consensus values, they reaffirm the status quo and exercise stabilizing effects on their viewers. To pose the question of whether films reflect *or* reaffirm *or* shape society is thus erroneous. Neither theory operates consistently, and each may be partially correct. Some films (or aspects of a film) may reflect the social structure, others reaffirm, and still others change their viewers' perception of it. This book shows that films should be analyzed in their multiple facets, as narrative, ideological, artistic, and commercial products, all conditioned by their cultural settings.

The study of small-town films challenges some of the theoretical premises of Siegfried Kracauer's pioneering and provocative treatise. Kracauer's chief assumption was that "the films of a nation reflect its mentality in a more direct way than any other artistic media," because they are the product of collaboration, thus "suppressing individual peculiarities in favor of traits common to many people."[3] But Kracauer does not take into account that collaboration does not necessarily mean equal contribution or power of every participant (producer, director, writer). Indeed, the auteur theory has assigned primary role to the director as the chief artistic force. Kracauer further assumes that because the film industry "is vitally interested in profit," it is "bound to adjust itself to the change in the mental climate."[4] but, as Andrew Bergman pointed out, how this adjustment occurs or what exactly is the nation's "mental climate" are never made clear.[5] Kracauer's work can also be faulted on methodological grounds. He dismisses the usefulness of films' box-office receipts, claiming that "what counts is the popularity of their pictorial and narrative motifs," that "persistent reiteration of these motifs marks them as outward projections of inner urges."[6] But the criteria for choosing films are not singled out, and there seems to be a confusion between important and popular films. It is possible to document that commercially successful movies are not important, ideologically or cinematically, and vice versa, that significant films are not necessarily popular with the public (Orson Welles's *The Magnificent Ambersons,* Jonathan Demme's *Citizens Band*).

This study accepts the claim that the American cinema "is primarily a commercial institution, engaged in manufacturing and selling a specific product in a capitalistic market place," but rejects the notion that the American film "is only incidentally a species of art, a political statement, a sociological document, a cultural product."[7] To claim that Hollywood's movies are commercial commodities, based on a profit motive, is not to deny they are also based on narrative conventions and embody cultural meanings. What makes American movies so fascinating a topic for the sociologist is their complex, multifaceted nature as commercial products (designed to make maximum profit), art forms (conforming to stylistic devices), and ideological constructs (embodying specific meanings), three aspects taken into account in this study.

This book attempts to understand America's small-town films in reference to the industry that has produced them, and the moviegoers who have viewed them. Made for the consumption by large audiences, films, more than other arts, need to embody values meaningful to current audiences. An analysis of films in terms of dominant themes and ideological values therefore reveals important information about the society in which they are produced and viewed. The Hollywood film has always been tailored to appeal to the largest potential audiences, which means that filmmakers have been engaged in a real and/or imagined relationship with their potential audiences.[8] To accomplish this, most movies have steered clear of controversial issues, using stories based on the lowest common cultural denominators. However, because the public's taste is, to some extent, unpredictable, there have always been unanticipated surprises (modest films that proved to be popular) and major disappointments (big-budget, all-star movies that were box-office fiascoes). The public's taste cannot be accurately predicted—otherwise there would be only successes.

The sociological perspective in this book sheds light on two concepts interrelated with "Small-Town America": the "Big City" and "Suburbia." Many films, such as Capra's populist comedies, contrasted small-town values with those of the Big City, condemning the City's corruption, greed, impersonality and dehumanization. Indeed, despite demographic facts (a growing urbanization), the Big City has almost universally featured as a "villain" in American films. Moreover, after World War II, when many Americans moved out of the cities into the suburbs, several films have dealt with suburbia. However, like the Big City, Suburbanism as a life-style has been quite consistently an object of satire and ridicule. Cycles in the production of films about Small Town, Big City, and Suburbia are described, attempting to understand them from the point of view of dominant culture. For example, small-town films have featured more prominently in the 1930s and the 1980s, but not in the 1960s or 1970s. These fluctuations derive from changes in the attitude of dominant ideology toward small towns.

Using the structuralist approach as formulated by the French anthropologist Claude Lévi-Strauss (1969), movies are analyzed as cultural myths, narratives arising from society's underlying issues and basic structures. Lévi-Strauss describes myths as transformations of *basic dilemmas* or *contradictions* that in reality cannot be resolved. Some of these contradictions have been acknowledged but suppressed by the film industry.[9] Concerned with decoding the elementary units in culture, the goal is to reveal "how the apparently arbitrary mythical representations link up into systems that link up with reality, natural as well as social, in order to reflect, obscure, or contradict it.[10] Despite manifest implausibilities and apparent contradictions, myths are coherent and logical structures. Lévi-Strauss's method seeks the underlying logic of myths, how people create cognitive order that gives meaning to cultural texts. His analysis is important, because it breaks down the most complex myths into logical categories of dialectical oppositions.[11] Based on a formal use of inversion, every category in the myth has its opposite. Indeed, the narrative structure of small-town films discloses basic, underlying conventions (see pp. 24–26).

Lévi-Strauss's analysis of myths has been criticized for being ahistorical, ignoring the specific conditions under which they arise or are reactivated. But myths endure because they are at once historical (specific) and universal (atemporal). They provide in popular fictional form (stories) both a version of concrete history and a vision of existence.[12] As collective representations, the function of myths is to preserve and legitimize the social order. Like other forms of story-telling, films are didactic, equivalent of Christian morality plays. As a group, small-town movies are pedagogical: They derive from strong moral origins, reflect moral conflicts, and offer moral solutions about human nature. This book analyzes the shape of small-town stories in both their generalized and particularized forms. The general shapes or archetypes (genre conventions) are the fundamental ways through which viewers perceive the specificities of an individual work. Archetypes determine the limits within which particular stories and characters can be used.[13]

Consisting of three basic elements, narrative, values, and hidden meanings, the survival of myths depends on two factors. First, the ability of image-makers (writers, filmmakers) to regenerate similar myths in fresh and topical way. And second, the ability of viewers to forget the weakest and most mutable examples, their willingness to suspend disbelief, to pretend they are seeing the story for the first time. The durability of *specific* myths about Small-Town America thus suggests their rich variability: Their ability to present numerous variations of formulaic conventions. At the same time, myths' influence over viewers also increase with the number of incarnations they allow for.[14] Myths associated with Small-Town America have survived for a long time—despite changes in ideology and social structure. Myths cannot easily be overthrown by contradictory reality, because viewers do not perceive reality directly, but through dominant paradigms, which determine the way they feel about specific events.

It is debatable whether Hollywood could *create* new national myths. However, because of their power, films can disseminate and popularize myths more rapidly than other cultural media (newspapers, novels, plays). The rapid transmission of images and messages, mass orientation, and visual nature, make film an immensely powerful medium. Despite the fact that the origins of cinematic myths are often in literature or drama, films portray the material of everyday life more effectively than other arts. Films are able to provide an illusion, or approximation, of reality, through the use of the "recording" camera.[15]

As myths, small-town movies are always experienced in *specific historical circumstances*. This is another point of convergence between structuralism and sociology of film. The "internal" approach of the structuralism (the inner attributes and underlying structure of films as texts) is supplemented with the sociologist's "external" approach, which grounds these attributes in their specific cultural and political settings.

Focusing on the structure of sign systems, semiology analyzes verbal as well as nonverbal symbols. Semiologists pay attention to the "meanings" of texts and the processes through which such meanings are conveyed to viewers. Socio-cultural phenomena do not contain inherent meanings; no material object has meaning in and by itself. Rather, the meanings of objects and events stem from their position in a broader system of relations. Concepts are "differential and defined, not by their positive contents, but negatively by their relations with the other terms of the system."[16] The most precise characteristic of a concept is in being what the others are not. Like structuralists, semiologists claim that the most important relationship in the production of meaning (including language) is oppositional; without such dichotomies there is no meaning (see thematic discussions below).[17] For example, in small-town films, the rich strata generate their meaning from being juxtaposed with the poor ones. But because in most texts systematic sets of polar oppositions are implied, not stated, they need to be decoded. Analyzing the language used by characters in small-town films is thus crucial since what people say (or do) is not necessarily what they mean.

The distinction among icon, index, and symbol as three aspects of signs highlights the interpretation involved in understanding signs and the conventions (codes) that guide their reading.[18] Because relationship between signifier and signified is arbitrary and unnatural, meanings must be learned. Objects and words signify similar meanings because they are based on viewers' shared conventions. Thus, separating between denotative and connotative meanings of the same object is useful, because connotation is always symbolic, i.e. arbitrary (there is no logical connection): it establishes a relationship between signifier and signified that is culturally motivated and historically conditioned. "We consider the objects solely in relation to the meaning," wrote Roland Barthes, "without bringing in the other determinants (psychological, sociological, physical) of these objects."[19] Semiologists analyze symbols for their own sake, recognizing that "the symbolic form of the message has a privileged position in the communication exchange," and that though only "relatively autonomous" in relation to the communication process as a whole, they are *determinate* moments."[20]

By contrast, in their interpretation of signs, sociologists ground them in the specificity of their contexts. For instance, the American flag generates different meanings in small-town films set in World War II and in the Vietnam War. Similarly, train whistles and train stations are used metaphorically in small-town narratives. Semiologists establish links between visual images (or colors) and emotional states. For example, in *Splendor in the Grass,* the color of the heroine's dress is used metonymically (see chapter 4). She goes from wearing white (purity, virginality) to orange to red (passion, overt sexuality). Different colors signify meanings by association; an associated detail is used to invoke an idea. The contrast between spinsterish (librarians, teachers) and sexually desirable women is often suggested in their use (or lack) of glasses and their hairstyles. These have become such established codes that most viewers can predict well in advance a romantic-sexual scene by looking at the heroine's hairdo.

The Structure of Small-Town Films

The analysis of small-town films is not based on the common practice of quantitative contents analysis, which assumes that the item that recurs most frequently is the most important. Films are complex texts, structured systems, and the place occupied by the different items (verbal or visual motifs) may be more important than the number of times they recur.[21] The qualitative analysis of small-town films segmentalizes them into their different parts, emphasizing the specific manner in which they are articulated (or not) to form a coherent (or incoherent) structured whole. Myths appear in specific forms and are marked by narrative and stylistic qualities. The structure of small-town films is analyzed in terms of five types of codes.

1. *Cultural Codes.* These are culturally shared conventions (social norms) that prevail outside the domain of film, in society at large, and are used by the media (theater, literature) to convey ideas. Artists and filmmakers borrow conventions from society's culture for their individual work.

2. *Artistic Codes.* Shared by other arts and media, these codes are not uniquely cinematic. For example, film, theater, and dance all use background music, even though they may use it in different ways.

3. *Narrative Codes.* These are textual conventions of telling a story. Small-town films share recognizable conventions: Typical conflicts and issues, a gallery of stock characters. For example, in classic small-town narratives, one may expect to find the honest doctor, the spinster–teacher (or librarian), the corrupt politician, the sensitive and misunderstood adolescent.

4. *Intertextual Codes.* Each small-town work exists within a larger system of films to which it refers by either being similar or different. As the body of this type of films continues to grow, it is impossible for filmmakers—and viewers—to perceive individual works as separate products. Rather, each film is at least in part influenced by previous films. For example, it's useful to analyze *The Last Picture Show* (1971) in relation to *Peyton Place* (1957). And it is impossible to analyze *Thieves Like Us* (1974) without reference to *They Live by Night* (1948) and *Bonnie and Clyde* (1967). Intertextuality implies self-consciousness on the part of the artist and is a matter of degree. It is important to point out the similarities and differences between individual films and the larger categories of which they are part. References to earlier works are inevitable, but may take different forms. In some cases, there is a conscious borrowing of a character or plot element, but at other times, a film provides commentary or "corrects" genre conventions (most of Robert Altman's work). Intertextuality is also enhanced by the continuity provided by specific directors and players. For example, the similarities among the various small-town films made by Capra, Hitchcock, Sirk, or Demme.

Intertextuality suggests that the meaning of a particular work derives from its relation to a larger set of films. It also means that viewers bring to the specific film watched a set of expectations, based on previous experiences, which the film may satisfy or violate. This experiential aspect of films depends to a large extent on the "tacit contract" between filmmakers and viewers.[22] But structuralists and sociologists approach intertextuality in a different manner. Structuralists tend to underplay the contextual aspects, following Oscar Wilde's dictum that "Art never expresses anything but itself. It has an independent life and develops purely on its own lines."[23] By contrast, sociologists point out the socio-historical context of intertextuality.

5. *Cinematic Codes.* These are visual and stylistic conventions that are uniquely cinematic: camera setups and movements; long shot, middle-range shots, and closeups; tracking and panning; cutting and editing; montage and mise-en-scène. These codes consist of the devices used by filmmakers in telling a story *visually.* One can compare the book *Peyton Place* to its film version in terms of plot and themes, but the perception of *Peyton Place* as a film depends on how it uses the cinematic language. Films are therefore not dealt with as just narrative structures or systems of meanings, but also as art forms. The way viewers perceive films depends as much on their visual form as on their literary values or dramatic conflicts. Stylistic conventions include all the formal attributes that set the film's texture, tone, and mood. Similar narratives can be told in different ways, employing different styles. For example, a distinction is made between attempts at harsh *(Country)* and lyrical *(The Southerner)* realism, though, realism itself is a style and a matter of choice.

Thematic Analysis of Small-Town Films

Small-town films are evaluated thematically, in terms of unit-ideas[24] that deal with basic issues: individual versus community, community versus society, nature versus culture, stability versus change, integration versus anomie, the sacred versus the profane, and the public versus the private domain. These core ideas, stated as conceptual opposites (theses and antitheses), have recurred in most films. What differs from one historical era to another, or from one film to another, are the concrete definitions of the units, the specific relation between the dichotomous values, and the ideological resolution (synthesis) suggested. Though dealing with broad issues, the substance of these unit-ideas is not universal: Their meanings change, depending on the historical and ideological contexts in which they are generated. The following taxonomy provides a partial but useful way of analyzing the narrative apparatus of small-town films.

The first core idea, *individual versus community,* is the most important one. Small-town films deal with such questions as: What should be the individuals' level of involvement and participation in communal affairs? What should be the basis of individuals' motivation: self or collective interests? How much sacrifice should the community demand—and get—from its individual members? The tension between individuals and community has persisted because each unit is associated with opposing values. The individual is associated with freedom, integrity, and self-interest, whereas the community is associated with restriction, compromise, and responsibility.

The second dichotomy, *community versus society,* is based on Ferdinand Toennis's distinction between Gemeinschaft and Gesselschaft, drawing on Max Weber's theory of rationalization and bureaucratization, Georg Simmel's Metropolis, and Émile Durkheim's anomie. In small-town films, this conceptual dichotomy takes the classical form of the Small Town versus the Big City. The ideal small town represents a primary relationship: intimate, face-to-face, personal interaction. By contrast, the Big City is based on networks of secondary relationships, signifying the ills of bureaucratic organizations: magnitude (massness), specificity, formality, impersonality, and anonymity.

The third dichotomy, *nature versus culture,* has been a perennial theme in the Western genre. But small-town works have also been preoccupied with the inherent strain between nature, a place of freer life, and culture, society's inhibitions and repressive norms. The value strain is between nature as purity and actual experience, and culture as corruption and knowledge. The tension between nature and culture may be manifested within the town itself (the escape to nature, outdoor places such as the lake, hill, barnhouse), or in the escape from the Big City to idyllic small towns or rural areas. In their search for greater freedom, individuals may be running from one town to another. In the most extreme version of this conflict, individuals become disgusted with any form of culture and subsequently turn their backs on civilization and go back to nature *(Jeremiah Johnson).*

The issue of *stability versus change* also features prominently in small-town works. Here the tension is between individuals' holding onto the present, never wanting it to change, and their acute awareness that change is ubiquitous and inevitable. Many films describe the initial resistance to technological change and the effects of such changes on the community and its individuals. This is the reason why so many films are strategically situated in transitional historical eras. For example, the turn of the century and its introduction of automobiles has been a prevalent locale *(Our Town, The Magnificent Ambersons),* or the Depression era, when motion pictures served as the nation's common cultural denominator *(Bonnie and Clyde).* Other narratives take place in the early 1950s, when movies lost their preeminent position and television took over *(The Last Picture Show).* They thus chronicle TV's contradictory effects: Isolating individuals in their private homes but, at the same time, helping disseminate a more homogenized mass culture.

The binary opposite of *integration versus isolation* also derives from classical theory, particularly Durkheim's analysis of anomie. In most small-town films, there is tension between individuals' fight to maintain their own values and the town's insistent wish to embrace and dominate them. The beginning, as well as closure, of small-town narratives differ along this dimension. During the studio system and classical Hollywood narrative, the town functioned as a coercive entity, and individuals were subjected to its moral authority. Using Robert Merton's (1938) typology of modes of adaptation to society's prescribed goals and its legitimate means to achieve them, the analysis distinguishes among individuals who are conformist, innovative, ritualistic, retreatist, and rebellious.

Durkheim's (1912) distinction between the *sacred and the profane* serves as another useful dichotomy. Every society distinguishes between these two domains and their activities. The sacred represents the less rational, more emotional values that assume religious or ritualistic meanings. By contrast, the profane represents secular attitudes or objects that gain their value from their utilitarianism or pragmatism. The narrative analysis of small-town films pays special attention to values, sentiments, objects, and places considered to be sacred or profane by the individual and community. For example, in small-town films of the 1930s and 1940s, the town meeting, military service, the American flag, are collectively deemed sacred. But these objects are no longer perceived sacred in films of the 1960s or 1970s. There may also be discrepancy between sacred and profane attitudes, as defined subjectively, by individuals, and collectively, by the town as a whole.

Finally, most narratives distinguish between the *public* and the *private* domains, a distinction that may parallel, but not always equal, the sacred and the profane. It is often manifested in the conflict between professional careerism (regarded as selfish pursuit) and selfless commitment to the town.

Organization of the Book

Because over a thousand small-town films have been made over the last six decades (See appendix 1), some criteria of selection were necessary to narrow down the number of films examined in this book.

1. The films selected are organized according to *historical decades* (the Depression in the 1930s, World War II in the 1940s, etc.). An equal representation is given to each of the six decades, from the late 1920s to the late 1980s. Within each decade, the films are discussed thematically. Each chapter begins with a description of general trends in the portrayal of small-town life, similarities in thematic concerns, prevalence of specific characters, dominant ideological attitude. A central question in each chapter is: How critical is the narrative toward small-town life?

2. The book analyzes films based on notable literary works, books by Sinclair Lewis and Booth Tarkington, or plays by Tennessee Williams and William Inge. Each film entry describes the adaptation of the literary work to the screen and the changes involved in transferring it from one medium to another; these changes (in theme and style) often have sociological foundations.

3. Following Leslie Fiedler's (1972) analysis of regional literature, the book includes films about small towns in different geographical regions: Narratives about the Midwest differ substantially from those set in the Deep South. Thematically, films about the South have been concerned with racial prejudice or political corruption, whereas films situated in the Midwest have typically dealt with family lives and social relationships. The book aims to present a comprehensive view of small towns in the American cinema.

4. Films that have been acclaimed by the critics for their originality and artistic merits. Films that have won critics' awards (*Melvin and Howard*) or have been nominated for an Oscar Award (*Mr. Deeds*) receive special attention. However, films that neglected to get their due recognition at the time of their release (*Hail the Conquering Hero, Handle with Care*) are also considered.

5. Films that were *commercially popular*, that is, widely seen by the public. The book attempts to explain the differential appeal of small-town films, and the factors responsible for their success (or failure). The films selected also include box-office failures, particularly of excellent movies that deserved to get more recognition. *The Magnificent Ambersons*, arguably Welles's best film, is a case in point: an innovative film ahead of its time.

6. The analysis of the eighty films in this book by no means represents a statistical survey of every small-town film made. Rather, the book analyzes films that have been both exemplary (typical) and seminal (innovative). The *good* small-town films have been both typical and atypical; both distinction and representativeness are characteristics of great art.[25] The essence of great popular art is in the relationships between the familiar and the surprising, the leap that viewers are asked to make from familiar generic expectations to unfamiliar transformations.[26]

7. Excluded from consideration are two genres: Westerns and musicals. Westerns are not included because they constitute a distinct genre (even though numerous Westerns are set in small towns). As for musicals, they are a stylized form that calls for a different kind of analysis. This exclusion is also based on pragmatic considerations: There have been numerous discussions of Westerns and musicals, but few of small-town films.

1

• • • • • • • •

The 1930s—
Idealism and Optimism

People talk about one another fearfully in this town, but
they don't always talk the truth. Wouldn't it be wonderful, if two people could just keep themselves to themselves?

—Alice Adams

I may not know so much of law, but I know what's right
and what's wrong.

—Young Mr. Lincoln

The decade of the 1930s was marked by the Great Depression and the
New Deal, events that had revolutionary impact on American art and
culture in that they called for a reassessment of traditional values and of
the American Dream. But this effect was selective and had differential
impact on the arts. Literature and photography were more drastically
influenced by the Depression than film. As Joseph Millichap noted,
literature in the 1930s attempted to balance harsh realism of observation
and warm emphasis on human dignity. Reflecting the new trends in
social and political thought, the arts contrasted traditional American
ideals with the bleak reality of hunger, unemployment, and poverty, best
captured in the novels of John Steinbeck.[1] Film, then the predominant
form of entertainment in America, was inspired by the Depression in
thematics more than in stylistics.

One remedy for the problems caused by the Depression was a "return
to the soil."[2] Indeed, in the early 1930s, Hollywood celebrated the
virtues of country life in a number of rural romances: *As the Earth Turns*
(1932), *Beloved* (1932), *The Life of Jimmy Dolan* (1933), *State Fair* (1933),

29

The Stranger's Return (1933), and *Our Daily Bread* (1934). Most of these films draw explicit contrasts between life in the Big City and the country.

The 1930s also provided an extremely positive portrayal of farmers and farming. This was due to dominant ideology, which favored farming and country life, but was also a reflection of the demographic and occupational structures of American society at the time. In 1930, for example, farmers and farm laborers amounted to a substantial proportion, about one-fifth (21 percent), of the labor force. In the following decades, their numbers declined dramatically,[3] though they continued to occupy an important place in the nation's mythology. An article in *Variety*[4] attempted to explain Hollywood's fascination with farmers, depicting them as "edified and glorified." Producers believed that such pictures "were demanded by the public," because "small-town atmosphere is much more wholesome than that of the metropolitan area." Glorification of the simpler rural life was not new in the 1930s. It has appeared periodically whenever the country faced major economic problems, such as the late nineteenth century, when the process of urbanization began to show its marks with the mass movement to and expansion of big cities.[5]

Back to the Soil: Agrarian Romances and Collectivist Dreams

The most popular of these agrarian romances was *State Fair*, (1933) based on Phil Stong's book of the same title.[6] A romantic idyll about the Frake family's pilgrimage from Brunswick to the Iowa State Fair, it featured an all-star cast: Will Rogers as father Abel Frake, Louise Dresser as his wife Melissa, and Janet Gaynor (at the peak of her popularity) as their daughter Margy. The two major representatives of the City are a trapeze artist, Emily Joyce (Sally Eilers), posing as the police inspector's daughter, and a newspaperman Pat Gilbert (Lew Ayres). Margy's beau, Harry, stays at home, because "his precious milk canes are more important" to him than going to the Fair. By contrast, Pat, the City person, stands for "motion and excitement," and describes himself as, "speed and sport, that's my line!" In comparison to Harry, who has never been anywhere, Pat has traveled extensively, covering races everywhere: "horses at Saratoga, automobiles in Indianapolis, airplanes at Cleveland." A city boy who is not, however, "a cheap flirt, or a drug-store cowboy," Pat wins Margy's heart.

Images of cornfields swaying in the breeze, a meadow by a brook with a dozen horses, and a well-to-do farm with a wide porch covered in Virginia creepers, introduce the locale of the Frake household. The sounds of hogs eating, hammers pounding, and saws swishing provide the audio background to the visual images. The dialogue never goes beyond the level of Margy telling her father: "I wish you loved me and Wayne the way you do Blue Boy [the hog]." Indeed, the father's major concern is for Blue Boy to win the contest. "You can call me names," he tells the superstitious storekeeper, "but don't say anything against my hog. I got faith in Blue Boy." An archetypal family entertainment, *State Fair* opened in Radio City Music Hall to mixed reviews. Richard Watts complained in the *New York Herald Tribune* that the film was not "in the rugged, embittered tradition of most American literary accounts of the sorrows of agriculture."[7] Dwight McDonald was even more critical, demanding a realistic, documentary film of American farm life.

In *The Life of Jimmy Dolan* (also 1933), a morality tale about love and redemption, the eponymous hero (Douglas Fairbanks, Jr.) is an intoxicated prizefighter who fakes a reputation as a sensitive man. When Dolan inadvertently causes the death of a reporter, he has to flee the city. Advised by his lawyer to "remain dead" for two years, he moves to Utah, living peacefully in a farm-orphanage for crippled children. His love for Peggy (Loretta Young) is the first step in his rehabilitation and, under a new name and identity, he begins a new life. The disenchanted Dolan learns to appreciate the small joys of country life: milking cows, walking in the open fields, playing with children. Challenged by a barnstorming killer to beat him for a high prize, he goes back to the ring and donates it to pay off the mortgage. Once in the country, the former hard-boiled cynicism and embitterment—associated with the Big City—disappear.

Ideological Tension: *Our Daily Bread*

If *State Fair* and *The Life of Jimmy Dolan* evoked nostalgically a simpler, decent country life, King Vidor's *Our Daily Bread* (1934) was a harsher and more important film, artistically and ideologically. Its production, exhibition, and reception are instructive in the insights they offer about the possibilities of independent filmmaking within the Hollywood studio system.

In *Our Daily Bread,* Vidor shows again[8] his belief in the rehabilitative and regenerative functions of country life. Deeply disturbed by the unemployment and low morale of the Depression, Vidor sought to channel "this nationwide unrest and tragedy into a film." "I wanted to take my two protagonists out of *The Crowd,*" recalls Vidor, "and follow them through the struggles of a typical young American couple in this most difficult period."[9] In *The Crowd* (1928), originally titled *One of the Mob,* he examined, with unprecedented realism, the predicament of two individuals in the anonymity and indifference of the Big City. To avoid melodramatic treatment, Vidor focused on the hopes and frustrations of two average people, John and Mary Sims, amidst harsh metropolitan setting. He cast the protagonists with unknown players: James Murray (an extra who happened to walk by) and Eleanor Boardman. A clerk holding a meaningless job in a huge office, John lives in a small and shabby apartment. The film was shot with seven different endings, even though Vidor opted for a grim finale, one that left John as a cipher in the crowd. Many exhibitors, however, preferred the "happy" ending; *The Crowd* was initially released with two resolutions.

The technical virtuosity of *The Crowd* is remarkable, particularly its startling opening. A beehive of activities is recorded (through hidden cameras) in the streets of Manhattan, with the camera scaling the heights of a skyscraper. The camera climbs up, gliding through a window into a large office, then stops at the hero's desk. Influenced by German Expressionism, the film displays a giant office, populated by anonymous and faceless (thus interchangeable) individuals, all sitting behind similar desks, performing similar tasks, in similar manner and pace.

Vidor found the nucleus of *Our Daily Bread*'s narrative in a *Reader's Digest* article, written by an economics professor, which proposed the organization of cooperatives as a solution to the unemployment problem. He was sure that every studio in town would be happy to produce his projected film. Vidor first turned to his friend Irving G. Thalberg, who had encouraged him to make socially conscious films. But after keeping the script for weeks, Thalberg told him it was not appropriate for MGM. "All the major companies were afraid to make a film without glamour," recalls Vidor, "even though admitting that the struggle depicted was a heroic one. . . . The fact that my characters were unemployed and down to their last few pennies seemed to scare the studios."[10] The only alternative was to raise funds by himself, though in order to get money from the banks, he needed to show a releasing contract with a distribution company. But there was a problem: the bankers were negatively portrayed; in a powerful scene, a banker forces the sheriff to make a foreclosure sale. Fortunately, Charlie Chaplin, one of the founders of United Artists, which functioned as a releasing company, came to the rescue. Committed to the project, Vidor pawned practically everything he owned. To save money, he rented an abandoned golf course outside Hollywood and shot many scenes without dialogue.

Vidor conceived of his film as a second treatment of the lives of John and Mary, "the average American man and woman." At the start of the film, the unemployed John pawns his guitar for a chicken. He claims he wants no favors, "just the chance to work." When he and Mary inherit a broken-down farm, they leave the city, determined to make it work. But John soon realizes he lacks the necessary knowledge, so he hires a Swedish farmer and advertises for workers. Many people show up, and John selects those who would be most useful to the farm. Vidor shows, in impressive long shots, the joy of people building their cooperative through various collective celebrations: constructing living quarters, plowing and planting the fields, dancing and singing. The members complement each other in skills: the carpenter builds a wooden frame for the stonemason, while the latter builds the carpenter's chimney.

The narrative, however, resorts to melodramatics in its juxtaposition of the two women: Mary, usually dressed in white, and the City girl, the outsider (Barbara Pepper), a sexy blonde dressed in black. The City (other) woman spends most of her time *indoors,* smoking and listening to jazz records. A threat to the marital union, she is soon asked to leave. Meanwhile, a drought demoralizes everybody, and John, in a moment of weakness, decides to leave the commune with the seductive woman. But his conscience bothers him and, haunted by the image of a criminal who earlier gave himself up so that the community could collect a reward, he decides to go back. In the film's climax, water comes through the ditch and the members throw themselves into the mud.

Some elements of the plot had appeared in F. W. Murnau's silent masterpiece *Sunrise* (1927), which also used conceptual types in a universal morality tale. The two major characters, "The Man" (George O'Brien) and "The Wife" (Janet Gaynor) stand in for every man and woman. Content with the security of their farm, they live a happy life, apart from the turmoil of the city. But one day a City woman (Margaret Livingston) appears in their village and seduces the husband to leave his farm. At the end, however, he repents and goes back to his wife. The three protagonists embody abstract forces: "the Man," as the strong provider; "the Wife," as the fragile and devoted wife-mother, and "the Woman from the City," as the seductress, all flesh and carnal desire.

Our Daily Bread advocates self-sacrifice and suppression of individualistic (selfish) goals for the sake of nobler collectivist ones. An escaped convict, who becomes the commune's policeman, decides to surrender so that his reward will be collected by the cooperative. Nominally, the form of government is democratic, though the film shows the members' dependency on John's charismatic leadership. A figure modeled on F. D. Roosevelt, John becomes a leader by acclamation rather than election.[11] The narrative abounds with John's patriotic speeches to his followers. In one, he uses the *Mayflower* pilgrims to rally the group: "When they arrived on the continent, what did they do? Stand around and beef about the unemployment situation or the value of the dollar? No. They set to work to make their own employment, build their own houses, and grow their own food." "If they got along without landlords and grocery bills," he concludes, "so can we. What we've got to do is help ourselves by helping others. We've got the land and we've got the strength." John is the commune's owner and leader—the film stops short of advocating collectivist ownership of the land. *Our Daily Bread* never resolves the tension between individualistic leadership and collectivist values. Every member seems to agree that John is the natural leader, as the Swedish farmer puts it: "All I know is ve got a big job, eh, and we need a Big Boss. And Yohn zims the man for the Boss."

Our Daily Bread is at once naive and utopian. In mode, the film adheres to the doctrine of socialist realism, focusing on social types, rather than individual characters, and on everyday behavior of ordinary people. Significantly, the two leads were played by actors who were not stars, and other roles featured unknown or nonprofessional actors. In visual style, *Our Daily Bread* draws on the work of Soviet filmmakers Sergey Eisenstein and Vsevolod Pudovkin. The film's climax, the construction of the irrigation system, is staged as a conscious tribute to Eisenstein's montage theory. Vidor treated the building of the ditch in a manner "a choreographer would use in plotting out the movements of a ballet,"[12] thus orchestrating every move of the barrier's opening and the rush of water. It was the longest scene to film, taking ten days of rehearsal and shooting. For sound, Vidor used a metronome and a bass drum, and composer Alfred Newman wrote rhythmical tempos.

Vidor's earnest sincerity and straightforward treatment lend the picture charm, if not credibility. Critic Maltby noted that the film's ideology was anachronistic because its pastoral fantasies were created by urbanites, not country people, and furthermore, "idealistic solutions of populist rhetoric were apolitical precisely because they were impractical."[13] The movie ignored the real conditions of agricultural production and the increasing migration of farmers to the cities. But valid as this criticism is, Vidor's humanistic idealism was still the only directorial voice in the 1930s actually to advocate cooperative farms as a radical alternative. Collectivist values and communal life-styles were seldom taken seriously by Hollywood and the dominant culture.[14]

Frank Capra's benevolent solutions (see *Mr. Deeds Goes to Town*) were less realistic than Vidor's, but conformed to Hollywood and dominant ideology of market capitalism (free enterprise, laissez-faire economy) and romantic individualism. However, Vidor and Capra shared in common deep mistrust of governmental interference in solving problems of poverty and unemployment, and a correspondingly strong belief in the puritanic ethos of hard work and self-sacrifice. Institutional authority— centralized government, planned policy and economy—were rejected, in ideology and practice, in favor of neighborliness, which took the form of communal living in *Our Daily Bread,* or the rich benefactors helping the poor in *Mr. Deeds.*

While not one of Vidor's greatest films, *Our Daily Bread* showcases his directorial strengths and weaknesses. As Andrew Sarris pointed out,

Vidor's talent was intuitive and he was better in creating great moments than great films.[15] Vidor's architectural cinema was particularly suitable for the formation of individuals against large groups. The film was well received by the critics, but not by the public. Richard Watts wrote in the *New York Herald Tribune* that it was "an adventurous, stirring, courageous film," emerging out of "idealistic materials of American existence," with none of "the glibness or smooth dexterity."[16] Andre Sennwald of the *New York Times* also singled out the film's "richness of conception," describing it as "a brilliant declaration of faith in the importance of cinema as a social instrument." As "a socially minded art of amazing vitality and emotional impact," the film was compared with the work of proletarian novelists, Albert Harper, Robert Cantwell, and William Rollins.[17] However, the Hearst press in California called the film "pinko," and the *Los Angeles Times* refused advertising layout because of the film's "too leftist" ideology.

Despite the fact that it was one of the most radical films of the entire decade, *Our Daily Bread* still conforms to Hollywood conventions. First, its anti-City bias: the characterizations of the City woman and the banker were too simplistically one-dimensional. Second, the resolution it provides is too individualistic: with all its emphasis on organized action, Tom is clearly the charismatic leader, referred to by the members as "a strong boss." In the same way that collectivist values stand in sharp opposition to American capitalism and market-oriented economy, an independent production, with strong political statements, was also not viable in Hollywood.[18] A box-office failure, the film was rescued decades later by film scholars who reexamined Vidor's career.

Small-Town Doctors

If movies of the 1930s were used as a source of information about the American occupational structure, the most prevalent screen professions, next to farmers, would be lawyers and doctors. While lawyers typically belong to the landscape of the city, doctors in movies of the 1930s were associated with small-town locales and values. During the Depression, many movies revolved around doctors: *Arrowsmith* (1931), *Dr. Bull* (1933), *Men in White* (1934), *The Story of Louis Pasteur* (1935), *The Prisoner of Shark Island* (1936), *The Country Doctor* (1936), its two sequels (*Reunion*, 1936; and *Five of a Kind*, 1938), *A Doctor's Diary* (1937), *The Citadel* (1938), *Dr. Kildare* (a film series between 1938 and 1947), and *Stagecoach* (1939).[19]

Of the three films in which John Ford examined the doctor's role in society[20] *Arrowsmith* was the most prestigious production, nominated for four Oscar Awards, including Best Picture. The film's prestige stemmed from its literary source: it was based on the novel by Sinclair Lewis, who won the 1930 Nobel Prize[21] for it, and was scripted by Sidney Howard, a Pulitzer Prize winner for drama. The film begins in a typical Ford manner, announcing it is "the story of a man who dedicated his life to science and his heart to the love of one woman." There is a good deal of irony in the title, for the film is about a man who struggles, but fails, on both fronts, in his dedication to pure science and as a husband. Martin Arrowsmith (Ronald Colman) takes after his grandmother Emmy, a woman of "pioneer and stubborn stock." The enthusiastic man is determined "not to be just an ordinary doctor. I'd rather find the cure for cancer." His mentor, Dr. Max Gottlieb (A. E. Anson), reaffirms his zealous ambition, "To be a scientist is born in a man, and in very few men." But Arrowsmith gives up a great career as research scientist to be a country doctor. He settles down with his wife Leora (Helen Hayes) in a town of 366 inhabitants in South Dakota. "Real man's country! Frontier! Opportunity!" declares Arrowsmith with excitement. Eager to concoct a serum that will save the cattle from the blackleg, his efforts are resented by the state veterinarian. "Saving cows may not be saving mankind," says Arrowsmith, "but it's a step in the right direction."

The dilemma faced by Arrowsmith is between devotion to humanistic, people-oriented medicine, or to research-oriented science. He gives up his small-town practice and moves to New York City, to work as a researcher, a more prestigious position. The brilliant Gottlieb (in a stereotypical role of a Jewish scientist) predicts a bright future for him. But after two years, he is discouraged. "I'm no good," he tells Leora, "I'm worse at science than I was at doctoring." He thus devotes his life to the combat of the bubonic plague in the West Indies. Gottlieb advises him to conduct an experiment, give the serum to only half of the population, but when the white inhabitants refuse to cooperate, Arrowsmith offers it to the entire black community. This, however, ruins his chance of conducting a scientific experiment. "I betrayed you," says Arrowsmith to Gottlieb at the end. "I didn't add to knowledge. I did the humane thing. I lost sight of science."

The film contains "message" speeches about doctors' idealism and integrity, the hallmark of many Depression films. Ford stresses the values of self-sacrifice, dedication, nobility of character, and the importance of standing above petty quarrels. For instance, in the West Indies, Arrowsmith lectures about his concern for "all continents and generations." There are two types of villains in *Arrowsmith* (and other films about small-town doctors). One is the city, bureaucratic doctor, here, the state veterinarian who opposes to Arrowsmith's serum. The other "villainous" type is more ambiguous: the research scientist who favors the progress of scientific knowledge at the expense of treatment. "Gif pills to ladies!

Deliver their babies for them! Make up their diets for them!" reflects the scientist's contempt toward country doctors.

In *Arrowsmith*, the Big City is juxtaposed with the small South Dakota town. As in *The Crowd*, Ford shoots New York's skyscrapers from a low angle, making them menacing and ominous. People are shot from a high angle—dwarfing them against the huge and anonymous buildings. The McGurk Institute is located on the twenty-sixth floor, and Ford's camera travels with the elevator up and down. Inside the Institute, Ford uses its long corridors and high ceilings to convey an impersonal, cold ambience. In the City, Arrowsmith courts Joyce Lanyon (Myrna Loy); he considers an affair with her. However, spending time with Joyce precludes him from returning home in time to save his wife. Arrowsmith is not completely devoid of vanity. "I'm off to glory," he tells Leora before departing. "If I pull this off, I'll be a great man!" This is what makes the next scene, in which Leora dies alone on the floor, so powerful.

Leora starts out as a high-spirited woman but gradually loses her self-worth and independence because of her marital devotion. They first meet at the hospital, while she is scrubbing the floors, a punishment for smoking a cigarette. On their first date, she wants to listen to soft music, but instead the jukebox is playing the "Lone Ranger" sequence from "William Tell Overture," which Tag Gallagher interprets as an alarming warning about their future marriage.[22] Later, Leora defies her narrow-minded and bigoted parents when they disapprove of her marriage, though she knows from the beginning that Arrowsmith is "self-centered and pig-headed." For a 1930s film, it is quite critical concerning the price independent women have to pay, obliterating their needs for the sake of marriage and/or husbands' careers. Leora almost apologizes for getting pregnant, "Poor Martin, you'll be tied down worse than ever now." Further, Arrowsmith is responsible for Leora's miscarriage, not being there when she needs him. "Now that I can't have a baby," Leora states tellingly, "I'll have to bring *you* up. Make a great man that everybody will wonder at!"[23] Once married, she stays at home, taking care of *his* needs. "I have no life without you," Leora says repeatedly in a sentence that resonates ambivalence.

In the end, guilt-ridden, Arrowsmith redeems himself, renouncing both pure science ("To hell with science") and the Other Woman. In an ambiguous, fantasylike closure, Arrowsmith believes he is reunited with his dead wife. Rushing after a doctor who is on his way to Vermont's backwoods, he says, "Lee and I are coming too," demonstrating that Leora's sacrifice was not in vain and that she continues to provide spiritual support.

Arrowsmith set the thematic paradigm of many films dealing with country doctors, emphasizing three basic conflicts: personal versus professional life; service (people) versus research (science) orientation; and the country doctors versus the rigid medical establishment (the city bureaucracy).

Doctors as Folk Heroes: *Dr. Bull*

Arrowsmith is a richer, darker, and more complex film than Ford's next work on a small-town doctor, *Dr. Bull* (1933), situated at the present in New Winton, Connecticut. Once again, a prologue sets the film's relaxed tone: "Doctor Bull brings his neighbors into the world and postpones their departure as long as possible. He prescribes common sense and accepts his small rewards gratefully." A busy practitioner, the middle-aged George Bull (Will Rogers) has served the town for decades. Modest, down-to-earth, without pretense or expertise, he is a doctor who identifies himself as a veterinarian; he miraculously cures a paralyzed man with experimental cattle medicine. Births and deaths are daily occurrences in Bull's work, marked by a folksy sense of humor. Asked by Louie to help his wife deliver yet another baby, Bull says: "What are you and Mussolini trying to do, fill the world with Eyetalians?" He then mumbles to himself: "You never know when another Washington is being born—or an Al Capone." And watching a patient die, Bull remarks "I've seen a hundred people die, and none of them seemed to mind it." Bull's philosophy is that "a certain percentage of people are going to die anyway," and "about all a doctor can do is make 'em think they won't." Unlike Arrowsmith, who blames himself when a patient dies ("I was a rotten doctor"), Bull believes that patients "either have the stamina to hang on and develop a resistance, or haven't got it."

After a long working day, Bull likes to visit Janet Carmaker (Vera Allen), a widow and sister-in-law of Mr. Banning, the town's obnoxious capitalist. There has been too much interest in their romance; some residents think their conduct is "a shame and a scandal to this town." "Bull's car was up at her house three nights last week," says one woman to another. "I'll tell you what they're doing up there." But in the next scene, Ford shows Bull and Janet in a most relaxed mood. He is stretched on the couch, while she is reading to him from *Alice's Adventures in Wonderland*.

Life in town is uninteresting and conversations tend to be routine. "Did you have a good Christmas?" asks the black porter of the postmistress, Helen Upjohn. "Don't be silly!" she says. "In this dull place, how could you?" And exactly the same exchange occurs at the end of the movie. This routine, cyclical life is portrayed through the visual symmetry of the film's beginning and end. Panning the train station, Ford's camera tracks an approaching train with its long whistle growing louder.

This stylistic device, of beginning a narrative with the arrival of train, and ending it with its departure, is a dominant motif of small-town films. However, trains in such films bear different meanings. In *Dr. Bull*, the train indicates the community's self-containment and isolation from the outside world.[24]

The town's hierarchy of wealth and class structure are well known. The lumber mill, owned by the greedy Banning, provides employment, but also problems. It pollutes the water supply, causing a typhoid epidemic, for which Bull is held responsible, even though he was the first to warn against the danger. Bull is accused of being against technological progress. "We know your attitude about improvements," charges Banning after announcing the construction of a new power plant. "Bull would have us riding around in a horse and buggy, if he had his way." In the next scene, Ford shows a modern car (belonging to a City expert), a status symbol and sign of progress. For Bull, this progress dehumanizes life and destroys nature: The apple tree (garden) is replaced with the plant (machinery): "Progress with its axe comes along." The film thus reaffirms the myth of the Garden versus technology's devastating effects.

As in other movies, the commonsensical knowledge of the country doctor is juxtaposed with the scientific knowledge of the City experts. "With all this machinery, you ought to keep people livin' for a hundred years," says Bull to the sophisticated Dr. Verney, who wears a sterile white coat. When Verney doubts Bull's diagnosis that it is typhoid, Bull says: "Of course, you're a specialist. I'm nothing but an old cow doctor." But the first to suggest the epidemic might be typhoid was Bull's aunt ("She smelt it!"), and the film shows the priority of commonsense knowledge, held by ordinary individuals, over scientific knowledge, created by experts in their "ivory tower." Bull's advice, to boil all drinking water and take the inoculation immediately, is rejected, because the town's corrupt leaders fear that if the news gets out there will be no tourist trade in the summer.[25]

Ungrateful and unappreciative of his service, the town wishes to get rid of Bull, and in its meeting, he is dismissed for being "grossly negligent." But the very existence of the meeting is a testament to the operation of democratic values. Further, members are allowed to voice their dissent before a final decision (based on majority vote) is made. "Bull is no longer a young man," says Janet in his defense. "If you get the State Board to take his business away from him, you'd ruin his life, there's nothing else he can do." "Sure he can," says one resident. "He can doctor cows!" True to democratic principles, Bull is permitted to speak, but he does not ask for sympathy. "You won't turn me out," he retorts. "Right here and now I quit." The town's meeting is a sacred political institution, upholding participatory democracy, even though its decisions may not reflect the best judgment. In an uncharacteristic manner of 1930s films, the town does not embrace Bull; he has to leave for the place has become too confining. But he quits as a *winner:* Having cured a man of paralysis, he becomes a celebrity, with his name all over the newspapers.

Dr. Bull belongs to Ford's favorite type of heroes: an aging, diminished man, standing for simpler, traditional values.[26] The film's initial title, *The Last Adam,* conveys Ford's intent better than *Dr. Bull.* Bull is an anachronistic hero, clinging to community life as Eden, as Garden. He fights, not against technological progress per se, but against the blind belief that new machinery will necessarily result in better life. On Bull's agenda are social ills fought by many small-town heroes: bigotry, ignorance, snobbery, and pretentiousness. He is irreverent, defying social conventions, an unredeemed individualist in a community grown too conformist and too rigid to allow for freedom of expression. For example, Bull goes to church not because he has to, but because he wants to. He derives great pleasure from singing, albeit he does it too loudly and off-key, but his singing is spontaneous and joyful. A good doctor, committed to his "old-fashioned" but proven, methods, he is not, however, an idealist in the mold of Arrowsmith. Ford directed Will Rogers in two other films, *Judge Priest* (1934) and *Steamboat 'Round the Bend* (1935), espousing in all three his brand of populism. Rogers became a typical Ford hero, an individual torn between personal and collective interests. But Bull's individualism is not excessive and therefore unharmful. When a choice needs to be made between private and social goals, Bull's (like other Ford heroes) commitment is to larger causes—at the expense of private comfort and personal interests.

In 1930s films, City doctors were often shown to be corrupt or drunk, but they usually *redeemed* their drunkenness with a heroic deed.[27] Country doctors, with the exception of *Nothing Sacred* (see below), may be in conflict with their community, but they were genuinely honest. Doctors continued to dominate small-town films in later decades, but never reached their prominence of the 1930s. The screen treatment of the medical profession has deteriorated considerably over the decades, but in the 1930s, most doctors were shown to be decent, if eccentric, practitioners. If country doctors were stock characters in movies of the 1930s and 1940s, but later disappeared, adolescents have always been prevalent in the gallery of small-town types.

Growing Pains and Family Life

Two of the best movies to explore growing pains in small towns were made by RKO, and both starred Katharine Hepburn, *Little Women* (1933) and *Alice Adams* (1935). In both, Hepburn plays an adolescent who is an outsider, a misfit. The essence of her persona is captured in both films in a dance sequence. In *Little Women*, Jo (Josephine) is standing outside the dance hall; she cannot join the other guests because there is a huge patch in the back of her dress (a result of standing in front of the fireplace). Jo promised her sisters to remain invisible. But full of energy and passion, she starts to move around and dance by herself, then dances with Laurie in the corridors outside the public eye. In *Alice Adams*, Alice, the poor girl from the wrong side of the tracks, is anxious to be invited to dance, but the "right" (rich) men ignore her. Surrounded with elegant people, both Jo and Alice stand by themselves, forcing a smile that is meant to convey they have a lovely time, but it is obvious they have a rotten one.

George Cukor's *Little Women* (1933) was the second—and best —of the many screen adaptations Louisa May Alcott's book has received.[28] Set in the Civil War in Concord, Massachusetts, the film is dominated by women. Mr. March is fighting in the war, leaving his wife, Marmee (Spring Byington), to take care of a household with four daughters, each different from the other. Jo is an ardent tomboy; Beth (Jean Parker) gentle and sweet; Meg (Frances Dee) tender and romantic; and Amy (Joan Bennett) dainty and sly. In the first part, Cukor presents the special attributes of each sister in brief vignettes. Scolded and punished for caricaturing her teacher, Amy has to stand against the wall with a sign "I'm ashamed of myself." Jo reads to her aunt; Meg takes care of Mrs. King's little children; and Beth helps at home.

All four sisters try to live up to their father's expectations, to be responsible "little women," to fit into the traditional mold of femininity and domesticity. Jo, the most eccentric, is the center of the narrative, and the superlative performance of Katharine Hepburn, singled out at the 1934 Cannes Film Festival, makes her all the more noticeable. A tomboy, Jo's manners and gestures lack femininity, but she is extremely sincere. Early on, she demonstrates her androgynous quality and stretchable personality in a performance of *The Witch's Curse*, a play she wrote. She switches smoothly from playing the mustached villain to the handsome hero—this in addition to performing all the chores backstage.

Jo is stubborn and at the same time enormously sensitive and vulnerable. In public, she pretends her physical appearance bears no importance. After cutting her long and beautiful hair—to give her mother additional money for her trip—she says, "I don't care how it looks, my head feels deliciously light and cool, and the hairman said it would soon grow out and it might come in curly." In the next scene, however, she is in her room trying to stifle her tears! Jo wants to maintain her family's unity at all costs; she is against Meg's relationship with Brooke because it threatens the family's stability. For her, love is "sickly and sentimental," and she cannot understand "why is it that things always have to change just when they're perfect." Above all, Jo is a proud girl. When Aunt March (Edna May Oliver) charges that she is like her father, "waltzing off to war and letting other people look out for his family," Jo retorts, "There's nobody looking out for us, and we don't ask any favors from anybody."

Jo and Laurie (Douglass Montgomery), the rich boy next door, fall in love. As children, they share secrets and engage in typically male pursuits, fencing in a duel, because, as Laurie says, "I forget you are a girl." By the standards of her sisters—and society—Jo uses foul language and reproachable "slang and manners." But refusing to be "elegant," she doesn't care; she likes "strong words that mean something." Her father's letter, wishing that his daughters "will fight their bosom enemies and conquer themselves," so that when he comes back he will be "fonder and prouder than ever of my little women," makes Jo vow "not to be rough and wild." But to no avail; at the party, she slides a plate of cake into her lap, messing her dress and the glove she had borrowed from Meg.

The movie conveys effectively the process by which Jo's restlessness, sorrow, and frustrations, associated with small-town life, are actively channeled into her creative career as a writer (the excitement in selling her first story). Jo declines Laurie's proposal because she is determined to make her own way as a writer. She goes to New York, to give Laurie a chance to get over his love, where she meets professor Fritz Bhaer (Paul Lukas). The shy European professor introduces her to the sophisticated world of theater and opera, lending her his volume of Shakespeare. "Look at me world, I'm Jo March, and I'm so Happy!" says Jo in a moment of genuine exhilaration. Jo has been writing weekly stories for the *Volcano*, a sensational magazine, but Professor Bhaer advises her to return to something she really understands.

While the narrative stays most of the time indoors, the film gives some sense of small-town life through its meticulous re-creation of Civil War austerity. For instance, the issue of social class is acknowledged. The March family was once rich, but lost its fortune. Amy is humiliated by the kind of school she has to attend, describing the degradation as being thrown with "ill-mannered girls, who stick their noses into refined people's business." Poverty, hunger, and infant mortality are also in the background, along with Beth's illness and death of scarlet fever. The four daughters have to sacrifice their luxurious breakfast for a starving family, living in one room with broken windows and no fire. *Little Women* is a moving film about the making of a sensitive writer and the maturation of a small-town girl who transcends her milieu and at the same time retains its heritage. This theme recurs in several small-town movies, *The Member of the Wedding* and *Peyton Place* (See chapter 3).

A Quintessential American Heroine: *Alice Adams*

Alice Adams[29] (1935), based on Booth Tarkington's 1921 Pulitzer Prize–winning novel, is remarkable for its social realism in depicting life on the other side of the tracks. Its eponymous heroine (Katharine Hepburn) is a feisty, individualistic adolescent of the lower middle class, determined to better her position in life. Alice lives in South Renford, Indiana, which, celebrating its Seventy-Fifth Jubilee Year, is described as "The Town with a Future." The town's class divisions are established right away when the camera pans along Main Street, dwelling on "Vogue," an elegant store, then crosses to "Samuels, a 5-10-15 cents store." Alice shops at "Samuels."

Alice's black-and-white dress makes her look different from anybody else. She also talks differently. Stopping at the florist, she asks for something nice to wear to a party. "The Palmer party, I suppose," says the florist, indicating that it is *the* social event in town. Upon learning that orchids cost five dollars, she says, "I wore orchids to the last party." The price of gardenias is also beyond her reach. "Oh, no!" says Alice. "Gardenias are so . . . so *ordinary,* I want something *different.*" "When one goes to a lot of parties," she explains, "it's difficult to find something new and original." Lacking money to buy any corsage, she picks some flowers at Belleview Park, despite a big sign warning "Don't Pick the Flowers."

Frustrated, but maintaining an aura of fake cheerfulness, she returns to her dilapidated house, a structure of square pillars, surrounded by ragged lawn and no flowers. The gate is sagging and needs to be lifted, and inside, the lower hall is small and crowded, the wallpaper fading, and the flowered carpet worn out. Alice's father, Virgil (Fred Stone), good-hearted if childish, is recovering from illness, spending most of the time in bed. Her mother (Ann Shoemaker) a once attractive woman, looks tired and let down; her face expresses discontent. She constantly bullies her husband: "When you get well, you mustn't go back to that old hole again" (the drug company). "If you don't owe it to *me,* at least you owe it to your children," says Mrs. Adams, urging him to make a new courageous venture, open a glue factory, for which he has a secret formula. Mrs. Adams is terribly upset when Alice has to wear a dress that is two years old. Alice is the family's moral center, the mediator and reconciliator, understanding her mother's frustrations *and* her father's weaknesses. "You are not a failure," she reassures her father, a feeling he continuously gets from his embittered wife.

Terribly embarrassed that her loutish brother, Walter (Frank Albertson), has to escort her to the Palmers' dance, she attempts to keep her dignity and pride. "I'm no society snake," says the reluctant Walter. "I'm just as liable to go to that Palmer dance as I am to eat a couple of barrels of broken glass." He believes that Alice "ought to be able to get *one* man," for "she sure tries hard enough." For her part, Mrs. Adams holds that Alice "might have any man in town if she only had money to buy decent clothes," but she is "poor and hasn't any *background*."

Alice's small bedroom has inexpensive furniture of white enamel and dotted Swiss curtains and bedspread. Standing in front of a mirror, she pretends to brush off her imaginary suitors: "Just two dances—that's all you may have, you naughty boys! Why don't you dance with the other girls?" Alice is as snobbish as the other girls. All she wants is for Frank Dowley, the fat boy, to ask her just *once,* so that she "can treat him the way the other girls do." Her fantasy is to meet "somebody new, who is tall and dark and romantic," somebody she has dreamed of all her life.

They arrive at the party in Walter's Ford Model-T roadster, a wreck with the engine already boiling. Wearing her father's old raincoat, Alice asks Walter to leave it in the men's dressing room. "Joke on us!" she tells the doorman with feigned embarrassment. "Our car broke down outside!" In a medium long shot, the dance hall reveals high ceilings and an imposing, dignified room with fine paintings and marble vases. The contrast with Alice's house and Walter's car makes it all the more elegant. Walter thinks Mildred and her parents are "frozen-faced joints," but for Alice they are "just dignified." Alice pitifully tries to attract the men's attention, but she is left alone, unattended, with people passing her right and left. She is further exposed to snotty remarks about her organdie dress, "Nobody wears organdie for evening gowns except in midsummer." Director George Stevens effectively uses high-angle long shots to accentuate Alice's isolation, spatially as well as socially. This sequence captures a most touching moment: Concerned that someone is listening, Alice makes a fake speech of what a great dancer her brother is, shaking her bouquet of flowers in his face. But her brother is as cruel as one can be. "They passed you on," he remarks scornfully, "like you had something catching."

The first invitation to dance comes, of course, from Frank Dowley, to the great disapproval of his mother. Frank is a mama's boy (a prevalent type in such films) who resents his domineering mother. Careless, Frank smashes Alice's flowers, and all she can do is drop her faded corsage, hoping no one will see it. But Arthur Russell (Fred MacMurray) picks it up and returns it to her. Alice fabricates the impression she is alone temporarily, by choice. Crossing one knee over the other, she keeps the foot swinging to the music. Once in a while she glances up casually, biting her lower lip, giving the appearance of restraining an inward smile. "I'm just waiting for my escort to return," she tells a young man. She walks to Mrs. Dresser, desperately trying to keep up a conversation, pretending the woman is her aunt. "I'd rather talk to women like you," she tells the elegant lady, "than to girls of my own age."

Her dancing with Arthur is all pretense and playacting. In sharp transition, in the next scene the camera cuts to her home, with Alice telling her mother of the "lovely" time she had. She then walks to her room, buries her face in the pillow, and sobs. Alice's ambition, like that of numerous adolescents in such films, is "to be somebody besides just a kind of nobody." "I want to go on the stage," she tells her father. "I know I can act." Her father reminds her that both her mother and aunt wanted to be actresses. The film thus reflects the mobility aspirations of many small-town girls during the Depression, all seeking glamorous careers in Hollywood, the dream factory.

Alice lives in two worlds: a dreamy world, to which she periodically escapes, and a dreary everyday life, defined by her family. In one of her greatest screen performances, Katharine Hepburn renders beautifully the mixture of desperate existence with strong hopefulness. Alice is pretentious, posing in grandiloquent manner, using French words to impress Arthur. She excels at what Erving Goffman has called impression-management,[30] orchestrating a positive image while concealing disreputable and undesirable aspects of her persona. She lies about her family's status, rattling about their nonexistent wealth. Caught by Arthur in front of the business school, she pretends to be looking for a secretary for her father. She recites (badly) scenes from Shakespeare's *Romeo and Juliet,* telling Arthur he ought to have seen her when she had "stage fever." Forgetting a line, she makes it look as if she decided to stop on purpose. When Arthur compliments her dancing, she pretends not to be surprised: "I ought to dance well, when I think of my dancing teachers, all sort of fancy instructors. I suppose that's what daughters have fathers for, isn't it? To throw money away on them."

Told that Arthur is engaged to Mildred, the strong-willed Alice dismisses the information as: "He didn't seem like an engaged man to me. Anyhow—not so terribly." Listening to Arthur talk about the "large and long dinners" at the Palmers', Alice envies him for being "in a social whirl." "Father's illness," she says, "has simply tied me to the house and everyone has to come here—that is, if they want to see me." "Most people bore me," she tells Arthur, "particularly the men in this town, and I show it." This has made her, she believes, "a terribly unpopular character!" And continuing to fabricate, she says at parties she would rather talk to a clever old woman than dance with "nine-tenth of these nonentities."

Alice is concerned—actually obsessed—with the fear that people are gossiping about her. "Didn't Mildred tell you what sort of a girl I am?" she repeatedly asks Arthur. Petrified that "something will interfere" with their relationship, Alice says, "people talk about one another fearfully in this town," but "they don't always talk the truth." "Wouldn't it be wonderful," she suggests, "if two people could just keep themselves to themselves?" But Alice is right, gossip in town is rampant and it's malicious. She is described by Mildred's mother as a "too conspicuous young woman," and "a pushing sort of girl." Mrs. Palmer holds that "every girl who meets Mildred and tries to push the acquaintance is not a *friend* of hers." For her part, Alice regards Mildred as a perfect role model. "We all adore her," she tells Arthur. "She's like some big, noble, cold statue, way above the rest of us."

"Everybody who *is* anybody in town has been asked to the Lamb's party," Mrs. Adams needles her husband. "Your daughter is being snubbed and picked on by every girl in town." The problem with Virgil is that "he had fallen behind the race;" twenty-five years ago, the people they knew weren't any better off. But while they have gone up the ladder, Virgil remained a clerk "down in that old hole!" Mrs. Adams fears that Alice will "dry up into a miserable old maid!" the ultimate fear of screen mothers. She still "has a *chance* for happiness, if she only had a father who had gumption enough to be a *man*." While the class distinctions are well-defined, the rich people in most 1930s movies are benevolent. For instance, Mr. Lamb, Virgil's employer, comes to their house after Walter has stolen money from his business, to mend differences and work together again. A sensitive man, he tells Walter, "I've lived long enough to know that circumstances can beat the best of us." In congruence to the dominant ideology during the Depression, success is attributed to differential opportunities rather than social class or individual talent.

Movies about small towns in the 1930s did not do much for ethnic minorities, either ignoring or portraying them stereotypically. In *Alice Adams,* there is a bit part, the black band conductor, but note Alice's expression of horror when her brother socializes with him. But there is also the more substantial part of Malina (Hattie McDaniel), the cook Mrs. Adams hires to impress Arthur. Fearless and outspoken, Malina differs from the stereotype of the black nanny or cook. "Ain't it pretty hot fo' soup?" she says when the menu is discussed. The hilarious dinner sequence shows that the Adams family has not rehearsed a unified line, there is not much teamwork in their presentation of collective image. Mistaking the brussels sprouts for cabbage, Mr. Adams is politely "corrected" by Alice. And he almost chokes when his daughter says: "We never have liquor in the house, father's a teetotaler." Alice and her mother work hard to present a positive and coherent facade. Mrs. Adams tells Arthur that Alice doesn't mind the heat, "but then, she's so amiable, she never minds anything." And Alice complains that they "let the servants do too much as they like," and that it is time to get new ones.

A misfit and socially displaced, Alice has several reincarnations in small-town films exploring growing pains. Alice combines romanticism with pragmatism, the belief in a better world and the ability to disassociate herself from the immediate surroundings. She is an authentic American heroine, characterized by traits of other major literary figures. Alice, like Blanche DuBois in *A Streetcar Named Desire*, feels superior to those around her, because she thinks she embodies higher standards of beauty and truth. Like Blanche, she wants "magic," not reality, but Alice is aware of her identity and efforts. "I suppose the only good in pretending," she says in a moment of truth, "is the fun we get out of fooling ourselves that we fool somebody else."

When Arthur admits he heard a good deal about her at the Palmers', she is defeated: "So they *did* talk about me." But Arthur couldn't care less, and in the film's last shot they embrace. A number of changes were made by the writers (Jane Murfin, who adapted, and Dorothy Yost and Mortimer Hoffner, who wrote the script) in translating the book to the screen. In Tarkington's novel, there is no happy ending and Arthur leaves. Tarkington is harsh on Alice, perceiving her as a victim not so much of the town, but her own pretentious snobbery. She subscribes to similar ills she presumably objects to in other people. In the book, Alice wakes up and her maturation involves disillusionment (she goes to business school to become a secretary); a keen observer of life-styles, Tarkington is all but sentimental, but his irony and subtle humor are absent from the film. Walter Kerr has defended the superimposed happy ending, claiming that Alice "had to have a man, for our sake, not for hers."[31] Made during the Depression, *Alice Adams*'s producers felt that it would be a letdown for viewers if Alice would be "punished," i.e., denied love, because of her inferior class. The film thus favored the image of an Alice who is aggressive and pretentious, but also vulnerable and capable of change.

The Small Town and the Big City: *Mr. Deeds Goes to Town* and *Theodora Goes Wild*

The juxtaposition between Country and City, in Murnau's *Sunrise* and other silent movies of the 1920s, and the condemnation of the Big City (*The Crowd*) became even more explicit in the 1930s. No director has made a more extensive use out of this conceptual contrast than Frank Capra.

In *Mr. Deeds Goes to Town* (1936), Longfellow Deeds (Gary Cooper), a quiet man from Mandrake Falls, suddenly inherits a vast fortune of twenty million dollars, which changes his life. "I don't need it," says Deeds, wondering why his uncle had left all the money to *him*. Thrust

into the cutthroat jungle of New York, Deeds is subjected to the manipulations of editors, reporters, shysters, and other parasites. At the end,
realizing that money has brought him only unhappiness, he decides to
give it up and go back to his town.

The film begins at the train station of Mandrake Falls, where attorney
Cedars and his colleagues arrive to inform Deeds of his inheritance.
They all seem nervous and impatient, victims of the fast tempo of New
York. "Small towns like this always affect me strangely," says Cedar. The
welcome sign makes them even more nervous: "Welcome to Mandrake
Falls. Where the scenery enthralls. Where no hardship befalls." It is a
friendly town, though. "Everybody knows Deeds," says an old man.
"Fine fellow. Very democratic. Talks to anybody." Deeds's housekeeper
explains that Deeds is in the park, arranging for a bazaar to raise money
for a fire engine. Proud of his greeting cards' poetry, she recites one for
which he was paid twenty-five dollars:

> When you've nowhere to turn—
> And you're filled with doubt—
> Don't stand midstream, hesitating—
> For you know that your mother's heart cries out—
> I'm waiting, my boy, I'm waiting.

Accidental death, a prominent motif of small-town films, has also been
part of Deeds's life. His parents froze to death in a storm, and his uncle
was killed in a car accident. Alone in the world, he is still unmarried and
unattached. "He's too busy," his housekeeper reasons, besides, "he's got
fool notions about saving a lady in distress." Never away from his town,
Deeds's motivation to go to New York is to see Grant's Tomb. For his
departure, the town arranges a grand farewell, with the band playing
"For He's a Jolly Good Fellow." In New York, Deeds encounters salesmen,
politicians, moochers, "all wanting something"—to exploit him. "The
world is full of pests," warns Cedar. "You need someone to keep cranks
away." Cedar's first advice concerns the press: "One must know when to
seek publicity—and when to avoid it." Indeed, before his arrival, reporters think he is "a lousy copy," a country bumpkin who has "still got hay in
his teeth." Deeds appears—but only appears—to be childish, and the
movie explores the disparity between surface appearances and real essences, a favorite theme of small-town movies. "The boy's a simpleton,"
says Cedar, "as naive as a child," and his uncle's common-law wife
describes him as "a yokel" and "a country lout."

At first he manages to elude the reporters, which infuriates editor
MacWade (George Bancroft). Deeds has been in town for three days and
what have his "numbskull" reporters brought in but "a lot of flat, unin-

teresting routine stuff, that any halfwit novice could have done better!" He thus assigns his ace reporter, sob sister Babe Bennett (Jean Arthur) to "cover" Deeds's visit. Babe is doing it, not for the challenge or interest, but for material considerations: a month's vacation with pay. In their first encounter, she pretends to be a "fainting" unemployed stenographer, but Deeds is delighted to have finally found his "lady in distress." Soon Babe's stories about "the Cinderella Man" appear on the front page, with pictures of Deeds holding up traffic and feeding horses doughnuts, and headlines like "Small Town Poet Laureate Shows Big City How to 'Cut Up.' "

As in other Capra movies *(Meet John Doe),* Babe is basically a good girl, a product of a town near Hartford. Babe has often thought of going back to her "beautiful little town," a place that always "smells as if it just had a bath." She still loves nature, reminiscing how she adored going fishing with her father. Indeed, Deeds' and Babe's romantic scene takes place in Central Park, the closest site in New York City to nature. Deeds is a nature lover: back home, he liked to take long walks, spending hours in the woods. Deeds reminds Babe of her father: He talked like him, played the drums in the band, and even advocated Deeds's philosophy: "No matter what happens, don't complain."

Babe's roommate, Mabel, is also from a small town. "They toughened us beautifully!" says Babe. "That's what they call being wise and sophisti-cated." But falling in love with Deeds has confused Babe so much that she can't make up her mind whether he is "the most imbecilic idiot" *or* the "grandest thing alive." Wholesome and fresh, Deeds looks like a "freak" in the City. "He got goodness," Babe tells Mabel. "Know what that is? No, of course, you don't. We've forgotten. We're too busy being smart alecks. Too busy in a crazy competition for nothing."

Mr. Deeds consists of encounters between Deeds and representatives of City folks. Each encounter ends with a lesson, a moral learned by Deeds and made explicit for the viewers. For example, Deeds has never met "famous people" on the caliber of writers Henobery and Morrow, but they prove to be condescending, poking fun at him. This provides an occasion for a speech about the values of cultural relativity and urban provincialism. "I know I must look funny to you," says Deeds, "but maybe if you came to Mandrake Falls you'd look just as funny to *us.*" The lesson, in Deeds's words: "All famous people aren't big people!" True to his nature, he wants to "bump" their heads together; one of Deeds's quirky habits is to beat those who displease him.

Deeds is naive but no fool. He finds that City people talk about women "as if they were cattle." "Name your poison," says Cobb, "and I'll supply it" (blond, dark, tall, or short). Though not a young man, Deeds lacks any experience with women. Told that his uncle sometimes had as many as twenty women around the house, he asks, "What'd he do with them?" "It kind of puzzles me why people want to do a lot of work for nothing," says Deeds to Cedar, when the latter wants the power to deal with the opera's board of directors. "It isn't natural." Douglas, the chair of the board, expects no difficulty in getting Deeds to put up the entire amount of the deficit. But, shocked that the opera doesn't make any money, Deeds deduces that "we must give the wrong kind of show." He rejects Douglas's argument, "You can't think of art in terms of profit and loss." "I don't see why I should keep opera alive," says Deeds, "for people who obviously don't want it." According to his logic, "If the public doesn't want our merchandise, we'll just have to change things around—or close up the business." Deeds doesn't understand "why people go around hurting each other? why don't they try liking each other once in a while?" "People here are funny," he tells Babe. "They work so hard at living, they forget to live." And he quotes Thoreau: "They've created a lot of grand palaces here, but they forgot to create the noblemen to put in them." It's an earlier, though not the only, reference to Thoreau in such movies.[32]

The movie advocates populism and egalitarianism, underlined by values of Christianity: Every person is "God's creation" and talented in his own right. Every individual possesses some talent and should do his/ her best with his/her natural gifts. "Maybe it's comical to write poems for postcards," Deeds tells the writers, "but it's the best I can do." The movie favors making the most of one's life, by choosing to live where one fits in. Objective circumstances do not count much in Capra's world; it is the subjective perception of reality that matters. When Babe says that to most people Grant's Tomb is "an awful letdown," Deeds disagrees. "It depends on what they see." Deeds sees "a small Ohio farm boy becoming a great soldier," and "the beginning of a new nation." "You're too much real," says Babe. "Go back to Mandrake Falls. You belong there!" The recurrence of such words as small and little reflect the filmmakers' populist philosophy of the "little people."

Told that he has been deceived by "a dame who took you for a sleigh ride that New York will laugh about for years," Deeds is deeply hurt. In crisis, his dreams shattered, he wants to go back home. But an unexpected meeting with a starving farmer changes his mind. The farmer can't believe that Deeds spent thousands of dollars on a party, when people are starving all around him! "Did you ever think about feeding doughnuts to human beings?"—instead of horses. At first, Deeds thinks he's a "moocher" (like the rest), but then decides to distribute his money among the poor. Deeds is now accused of possessing a "distorted mind, afflicted with hallucinations of grandeur, and obsessed with an insane desire to become a public benefactor." He has to prove his own sanity in court.

At the trial, Cedar charges that Deeds has been behaving strangely all his life, "that his derangement is neither a recent nor a temporary one." Dr. Malcolm concludes that his patient is "mentally deranged," and Dr. Fraser, an Austrian specialist, concurs; it is "purely a case of manic depressive." However, the "strongest" testimony against Deeds is provided by the two spinsterish sisters, Amy and Jane Faulkner, who describe him as "pixilated," because "he walks in the rain without his hat and talks to himself; sometimes, he even whistles and sings!" What the sisters don't tell the court is that they live in his house without paying any rent.

The debate revolves around the question of what constitutes "normal" and "abnormal" behavior. As other small-town films (See *Dr. Bull, Invasion of the Body Snatchers*), *Mr. Deeds* rejects the opinion of experts (psychiatrists), in favor of common sense. "My opinion is as good as the quack psychiatrists," says Babe. Throughout, Deeds dismisses the views of experts: managers, lawyers, writers, psychiatrists. The film cherishes individualism and eccentricity, but rejects nominal definitions of normality. Deeds plays the tuba whenever he wants to concentrate, insisting that "everybody does something silly when they're thinking. For instance, the Judge here in an O-filler, Dr. Fraser is a doodler," and others are "ear-pullers, nail-biters, or nose-twitchers." "He could never fit in with our distorted viewpoint, because he's honest, sincere and good," Babe tells the court. "If that man's crazy, Your Honor, the rest of us belong in straitjackets." The judge concurs, pronouncing Deeds "the sanest man that ever walked into this courtroom!"

Mr. Deeds proposes simplistic solutions to the Depression. What people need is "ten acres, a horse, a cow, and some seed," but they have to work for it: "If they work the farm three years, it's theirs." "No matter what system of government we have," philosophizes Deeds, "there'll always be leaders and always be followers." Using the steep hill road as a metaphor, he explains: "Every day I see the cars climbing up. Some go lickety-split up that hill on high, some have to shift into second and some shake and slip back to the bottom again. Same cars, same gasoline, yet some make it and some don't, and I say the fellers who can make the hill in high should stop once in a while and help those who can't." Deeds is in favor of benevolent neighborliness, helping "the fellers who can't make the hill in high." Deeds (and Capra) ignores the fact that the inequality begins before climbing the hill: not everyone owns a car, and not everyone has the same car; people's point of departure determines their life chances.

The movie rejects handouts by the government and supports self-help and hard work. Deeds gives up his money, because "I never earned it," and because "so far, it's brought me nothing but hard luck." The starving farmers need some "push" and encouragement; the rest will be taken care of by the Protestant ethics of entrepreneurship and hard work. While *Mr. Deeds* does not criticize the existence of an upper class and the prevalence of wealth, it does criticize rich people's lack of awareness. If one could only "open their eyes," the rich would be willing to help the starving class. The inherent benevolence of human nature is not in question, though it is the role of the underdog to humanize and sensitize the rich and powerful, who may be snobbish, childish, frivolous, and irresponsible—all correctable ills. Capra expresses his belief in a benevolent (Republican) government, though not an active one. The welfare state model is rejected in favor of "laissez-faire" economy. "Our government is fully aware of its difficulties," says Cedar, "and can pull itself out of its economic rut, without the assistance of Mr. Deeds or any other crackpot." But just about how, the film fails to specify and the government remains an abstract force. As one critic pointed out, by making specific political attitudes (New Deal policies) irrelevant, Capra diffused the issue into unarguable American generalities.[33]

Richard Boleslawsky's *Theodora Goes Wild*, based on Mary McCarthy's short story, was released in the same year that *Mr. Deeds* was. But the two films are linked together in other ways. Both films were produced by Columbia and both, particularly *Theodora*, turned out to be unexpected hits at the box office. Sidney Buchman, Harry Cohn's favorite screenwriter, also penned Capra's *Mr. Smith Goes to Washington* (1939). Irene Dunne plays Theodora Lynn, a prim New England girl who writes a titillating best-selling novel under the name of Caroline Adams. Sheltered all her life, she keeps the book a secret from her two spinsterish aunts and the other members of the "respectable" Lynn Literary Circle. This is her act of rebellion. The film describes the transformation of a supposedly plain and repressed girl into the most eccentric and fun-loving woman. And it makes a distinction between wild and silly, as Uncle John says, "A Lynn may go wild, but never silly." Theodora goes wild!

Theodora lives in Lynnfield, "The Biggest Little Town in Connecticut," boasting a population of 4,426. The town is named after the Lynn family, whose only survivors are Theodora and her two aunts, Elsie and Mary. "The two oracles," says editor Jed Waterbury (Thomas Mitchell), "ain't they gettin' tired of running this town?" No wonder the town got to be the "most benighted community"; the Lynns have been running it for seven generations. The local paper, *The Lynnfield Buggle,* is the "pulse" of the town; the residents take active interest in it. In the first scene, Mrs. Moffat complains that the installment he printed was not "fit to print." "That's just too bad," says the stubborn editor, "but *I* run this newspaper." When the telephone rings again, Jed is ready with an answer: "I know Mrs. Perry. . . . It's un-moral and not fit to print." But Jed is impressed with the fact that his readers found it "too racy" to put it down. "I want to apologize," he states scornfully, "for waking Lynnfield out of a twenty-year sleep." However, knowing his hypocritical community, Jed made sure to print out extra copies.

The printing of the serialized novel is considered so "scandalous" and "shocking," that the Literary Circle convenes at the town hall to discuss the "out and out shameless and indecent" matter. "We've kept this community clean so far," says Mrs. Perry. "There isn't a book on the shelves of our public library that isn't a credit to the good taste and morals of Lynnfield." Indeed, the members are determined not to let "sexy trash like this come right into our homes and corrupt the morals of our youth." When Jed gets his turn to speak, he accuses the community of "sticking its head in the sand," and warns against the danger of "keeping civilization out of Lynnfield forever." But believing that their duty is to keep Lynnfield "the one upstanding, God-fearing place left on earth," the circle passes a resolution to tell the publisher that "this community condemns it lock, stock and barrel." Ironically, the prim and proper Mrs. Perry doesn't know yet that her daughter has married and is pregnant in New York.

The film's tone changes when the action moves to New York. The publisher, Arthur Stevenson, a smartly dressed man in an elegant office, reads to Theodora a telegram from Lynnfield that states: "A disgrace to American morals and a sin against American youth." Theodora is so desperate she begins to believe Caroline Adams is immoral; this amuses the publisher because the book is "sweeping the country." "But not *clean*," she protests. To make the publisher understand her better, she asks him three questions: "Were you raised in a small town by two maiden aunts? Have you taught Sunday School for fifteen years? Have you played the organ in church for ten years?" Undeterred, he says: "Nobody throws away a public in the millions and a tremendous career because of a conscience! It isn't done."

Theodora's Uncle John resents his two spinsterish sisters, "the plaster saints" and "camphor balls." He is the "only Lynn black sheep in five generations, and the only *happy* Lynn." Uncle John is concerned that nobody has ever called Theodora "baby," and, what's more, "no one ever will in Lynnfield." In New York, Theodora meets Michael Grant (Melvyn Douglas), a "sophisticated" artist who has illustrated her book. Theodora contradicts his image of a writer who "ought to look like a woman that's lived," and Michael takes in on himself to emancipate her. "I'm gonna break you outta this jail," he vows, and he does. Once liberated, Theodora runs wild, surpassing Michael in pranks and audacity. She now demonstrates what he has preached to her so persuasively, "Break loose, be yourself!" She recounts with pride how she told the town off: "This is a free country. I'm over twenty-one, and what I choose to do is none of Lynnfield's business. I invite the whole town to take a jump in the lake." Indeed, Theodora courts notoriety, invoking one scandal after another. Michael is trapped in a loveless marriage (for the sake of his father's political career) and Theodora sees to it that she is named correspondent in his divorce; she also makes headlines for allegedly breaking up her publisher's marriage. Moving into Michael's apartment (he moves out), she dresses eccentrically (in feathers), ties ribbons around her dog, and grants scandalous interviews to the press. But it turns out that underneath his allegedly liberated exterior, Michael is as stifled and inhibited as she was. They take turns—now it is Theodora's role to liberate him from his bourgeois notion of propriety.

The last scene takes place at the train station, but contrary to many films wherein the protagonist leaves town, conventions are reversed with Theodora's arrival—in grand style. The whole town is on the platform awaiting her. After unloading her endless luggage, Theodora suddenly goes back. The gaping residents are horrified, and the band goes sour and trails off. A second later, Theodora comes back with a baby in her arms. There is a moment of silence: people think it is her illegitimate baby. "You'd think they'd never seen a baby in their lives," says Aunt Elsie, who is beginning to loosen up. "So help me, this town gets more narrow-minded every day." But Theodora has the final joke, placing the baby in the arms of his grandmother, the utterly shocked Mrs. Perry.

Released in 1936, comparisons with *Mr. Deeds* were inevitable, and they were not to *Theodora*'s advantage. An "inconsequential comedy" with "farcical conceits" wrote the *Herald Tribune*, but "nothing like the vitality of *Mr. Deeds*."[34] And the *Times* critic noted that "Columbia was obviously dreaming of a distaff edition of *Mr. Deeds*," but that *Theodora* "is no match for Longfellow Deeds in sound, honest homespun humor."[35] Singled out by the New York Film Critics and the National Board of Review as Best Picture, *Mr. Deeds* was nominated for five Oscar Awards, winning Capra his second directorial award. In retrospect, however, *Theodora* has aged better, qualifying as one of the best screwball comedies ever made. Moreover, the movie became the precursor of numerous romantic comedies (*The Awful Truth* and *Ninotchka*) all based on similar premise: the magical transformation of their protagonists.[36]

In their thematics, both *Mr. Deeds* and *Theodora* underline the eccentricities of small-town folk, always existent, though sometimes buried beneath solemn and prim appearances. Both works urge the viewers to look beyond exteriors and dig beneath facades to find out the "real" individuality of small-town inhabitants. Under the right circumstances and appropriate tutelage, small-town people are capable of behaving in the wildest and most idiosyncratic manner. Indeed, Theodora becomes a completely different woman, combining the best of her small-town heritage with the new Big City experiences. She is contrasted with Lynnfield's gossipy housewives and spinsters on the one hand, and New York's bourgeois, boring, and bitchy housewives (of Michael and the publisher), emerging triumphant of both comparisons.

The dominant tone in portraying small towns during the Depression was idealistic. Moreover, many small-town films had comic sensibility, using the format of screwball or romantic comedy. However, toward the end of the decade, a few movies examined serious social issues, lynching, mob behavior, discrimination and prejudice, all in the context of small towns. Capra's *Mr. Deeds* and Fritz Lang's *Fury* were released in the same year, yet one cannot find more different images of small towns than in those two movies. Capra's friendly neighborliness is replaced with Lang's stress on lust for violence, lurking behind the quietest and smallest of American towns.

Discrimination and Prejudice: *Fury*

Produced by Joseph L. Mankiewicz at MGM, a studio which was the least likely to make such grim films, *Fury* was based on Norman Krasna's Oscar-nominated story. Bartlett Cormack, assisted by Lang, fashioned a taut screenplay that probed mass psychology and mob violence in a fictional town, Strand, Illinois. Krasna was reportedly dismayed by the statistics showing, that in the last forty-nine years there have been over four thousand lynchings in the US. In the 1930s, lynching and anti-lynching legislative attempts were timely issues. Between 1930 and 1935, over seventy lynchings took place, and in the next five years, over a hundred antilynching bills were presented in Congress.[37]

As if to protect itself, *Fury* begins with a warning: "The events and characters depicted in this photoplay are fictional." The social context of the Depression is apparent from the first moments, when the two protagonists, Joe Wheeler (Spencer Tracy) and Catherine Grant (Sylvia Sydney), stand in front of a window display of elegant bedroom furniture and accessories for "the Fall Bride" (Mendelsohn's 'Wedding March' in the background), which they obviously cannot afford. Joe works in a gas station, but they are about to separate; Catherine leaves for another town to find employment. Their farewell at the train station is touching; Joe feels like the dog he finds there, "lonely and wet," but promises to join her "as soon as I have a bank account." Later, on his way to see her, Joe is arrested as a suspected member of a kidnappers' gang. Despite the fact that the evidence against him is slight, he is put behind bars.

Lang's view of small town is most condemning, taking as his chief targets ignorance, hypocrisy, bigotry, provincialism, and intolerance. The strongest aspect of *Fury* is its re-creation, almost textbooklike, of mass hysteria. Lang shows, step-by-step, the emergence of a group mind, an irrational collective that goes beyond the individuals who compose it. Individuals in a crowd lose their rationality, their behavior motivated by emotional or biological instincts. In the climax, the mob storms the county jail and sets the building on fire. In an impressive montage, Lang shows the exhilaration of violence, the burning of the jail: A woman holds up her child so that he gets a better view of the conflagration; a young boy eats his hot dog with hearty appetite; another woman kneels down in a religious ecstasy; and an adolescent sings joyfully, "I'm Popeye, the sailor man, tweet, tweet!" When Joe attempts to escape, the mob throws rocks at the window, forcing him to stay in.

It's a brilliantly executed scene, boasting the precision of a mathematical model, with each detail adding or elaborating on the previous detail. The events are not presented from a single point of view: Lang switches from the mob to the sheriff to Joe to Catherine and back to the mob. The film's viewers become integrated into the scene; later, in court, the viewers watch the mob members watch themselves on screen. The evangelist woman, who pleads innocence, is shocked to see herself whirling a firebrand. The use of a newsreel taken during the incident is shocking and innovative, because neither participants nor film viewers realize that such a newsreel exists.

Lang uses townfolks to demonstrate that the proclivity for evil is omnipresent, and that, under specific circumstances, every human being is capable of committing nasty monstrosities. With almost no exception, the protagonists are bullies, bigots, and gossips—elements most likely to support Fascist movements. The barber explains the universal potentiality for crime in the following way: "People get funny impulses. If y' resist 'em, you're sane; if y' don't, you're on the way to the nuthouse, or the pen." In the twenty years he has been "strokin' his razor across throats, there had been many a time when he has had an "impulse to cut their Adam's apples wide open." An impulse is "like an itch you got t' scratch."

The film abounds with objects of torture and acts of violence. In addition to the barber and his razor, the dim-witted Buggs (Walter Brennan) is nabbing flies while the sheriff interrogates Joe. In another sequence, Lang cuts from the jail to the hardware store, where ropes are hanging from the ceiling. A farmer tests a whip, snapping it venomously to punctuate his speech about Joe: "If *all* o' us people just had the courage o' our convictions, these vermin could vanish like spit on a hot stove!" It is a far cry from the image of friendly farmers plowing the fields.

Joe finally escapes from jail, letting the mob believe he is dead. His speech (in what was Spencer Tracy's most impressive performance to date) to his brothers, asking them to take legal action against the lynchers, shows that the experience has turned him into a criminal seeking revenge.

> I'm legally dead, and they're legally murderers. That I'm alive is not their fault. I know 'em. A lot of 'em. And they'll hang for it. But I'll give them the chance they didn't give me. They'll get a legal trial, in a legal court room. They'll have a legal defense and a legal judge, a legal sentence—and a legal death!

His brothers protest, "You're as bad as them!" and when Catherine finds out about his scheme, she also is appalled. "A mob doesn't think, doesn't know what it's doing," she says. "You might as well kill me, too, and do a good job of it!" But that is Lang's point, to show the role reversal of victim and victimizer. Joe wants his aggressors to feel the fear and panic *he* had experienced. Indeed, even the more conscientious Catherine seeks revenge, though of a different kind. "I don't want anything as blood-thirsty as an eye for an eye, or a life for a life," she states, "but I want those women to suffer, to feel what I felt. I want the woman who held up her baby to think about never seeing that baby again. I want all of them to know what it is to feel empty inside. Not to be able to cry, not to be able to think, not to want to live." Under pressure from Catherine and his own guilty conscience, Joe decides to appear in jail. In his speech, he admits that the horrendous experience has shattered his belief in justice and civility. Joe used to be proud "that this country of mine was different," but those ideals "were burnt to death with me that night." However, "the only way I could go on living, was to come here today," and his only hope is that the experience has done those people "some good."

Not one inhabitant protests the conspiracy of silence. They are all cowards and collaborators, which is demonstrated in a passage in which the "pious" women discuss the harmful consequences a lynching trial might have on the town's reputation:

> FIRST WOMAN: My husband says it's be a blessing if the community would forget what happened. It just leaves a bad taste. . . .

SECOND WOMAN: Now, don't you worry, Mrs. Garrett. Nobody's going to cut off their noses to spite their faces by naming names. . . .

THIRD WOMAN: But if any one does, what will happen?

SECOND WOMAN: Nobody's going to talk. The responsible businessmen have decided it's a community, and not an individual thing. So everybody's got to stick together against the District Attorney.

Lang condemns the manipulative press (an issue that will become more prominent in films of the 1970s) and its insatiable thirst for sensationalism. "What a shot this is," says one journalist. "We'll sweep the country with this stuff." Lang simulates the buzzing of hundreds of gossip-disseminating bees over this scene. Another citizen reports that the Chamber of Commerce has discussed "what a great publicity break our capturing this Chicago fellow's going to give our little city." *Fury* was one of the decade's few films to show that society's legitimate authority, the government/police force, is inefficient. The sheriff and his deputy are not trusted by the populace; lazy, they play cards. The politicians are corrupt demagogues using empty slogans. Will Vickery says in his campaign, "The American people, dedicated to equality and justice for all, want no Communism, Fascism, or any other such dandruff in their hair!" The governor is all too easily persuaded that dispatching the national guards would be a political mistake. By the time they are brought in, it is too late; the jail has been set on fire. The movie shows how easy it is to violate the tenets of fair play and common sense.

Teachers and education don't fare much better in this town. Jorgeson threatens the high school teacher: "If you young geniuses keep tryin' t' fill our children's heads with these radical ideas, we parents'll have to get a law!" "It's not possible to get a law that denies the right to say what one believes," says the teacher, citing the Constitution, but Jorgeson has never read—and does not care about—the Constitution. Provincial, the inhabitants are also pompous and pretentious. Asked to identify her occupation at the trial, Mrs. Hooper uses the French word couturiere, not a dressmaker.

Critics marveled at what motivated a European director to select for his first American film the topic of lynching. The director stressed the universality of the subject and his fascination with mob psychology. "*Fury* is the story of mob action," said Lang. "Lynching happened to be the result. People the world over respond in the same way." "I have been through four revolutions," he explained, "and have made an intimate study of how people act. They often start out in the best of spirits. Suddenly you realize the humor has given way to hate and violence." In

Fury, Lang wanted to show "that imperceptible line where the change comes."[38]

Lang told cinematographer Joseph Ruttenberg he didn't want "fancy photography, nothing artistic." The semidocumentary (newsreel quality) style is in harmony with the grim subject matter. As in other Lang films, the camera work is meticulously designed. "My camera setups were prepared from hundreds of continuity sketches which the MGM art department prepared from my rough drawings."[39] *Fury* combines two styles: semidocumentary, but also expressionism, in the tradition of the German cinema of the 1920s. The lengthy trial sequence uses both styles to great effect. For instance, a newsreel footage is projected as incriminating evidence against the lynchers, and Lang intercuts between freeze-frames of individual lynchers in action and their close-ups as they stand trial. And when the jury's verdict is read, Lang shows in close-up the reactions of each guilty person. To portray visually the spread of vicious gossip in town, Lang uses a nondigetic insert,[40] cutting from a scene in which the housewives gossip (about Joe's arrest), to a metaphorical shot of plucking hens in a barnyard. The women are all talking at once, their words undistinguishable under the noise of the squawking poultry.

The film was a resounding critical, but not commercial, success. "The finest original drama the screen has provided this year," wrote the *New York Times.*[41] Lang believed that MGM was not pleased with the film, because *Fury* did not receive the usual promotion accorded other studio products. *Fury* is an earlier noir film, thematically as well as stylistically. The protagonist, like many later film noir men, is an embittered loser bent on revenge. The ambiguity and obsessiveness of his character qualify him as a noir hero, a man unable to forget his harrowing past— which will continue to haunt him for the rest of his life.[42] The film was initially titled *The Mob,* then *Mob Rule,* but, concerned over their ultra-pessimistic tone, MGM opted for *Fury.* It is one of the few occasions, wherein the new title does better justice to the work. *Fury* describes two types of anger: the mob's anger (in the first part of the film) and Joe's anger (in the second), thus examining manifestations of fury on both the individual and collective levels, by parties situated on different sides of the law. In the first, more powerful and truthful, part of the narrative, there is a direct attack on lynching and a plea against mob rule. In the second, the tone becomes more sentimental and reconciliatory. Still, despite a "resolution," when Joe decides to come out of his hiding and testify, and despite a nominal "happy ending," in which Joe and Catherine are reunited, *Fury's* overall tone is grim and depressing. The film does not imply that the town's inhabitants have learned a lesson. Nor does Joe redeem himself completely of his obsessive urge for revenge.

A year after the release of *Fury*, Warners produced Mervyn LeRoy's *They Won't Forget* (1937), a film that was inspired by the Leo M. Frank trial in Atlanta and was reminiscent of other similar cases. Based on Ward Greene's novel, *Death in the Deep South*, and set in Flodden, a small Southern town, it is another tale of mob violence motivated by bigotry and prejudice. However, the political context in *They Won't Forget* features more prominently and its portrayal of public officials is even more cynical than that in *Fury*. In *Fury*, the sheriff at least tried to prevent the masses from lynching, whereas *They Won't Forget* ends on a more ambiguous note when a reporter says: "Now that it's over, I wonder if Hale really did it." "I wonder too," the prosecutor (Claude Rains) chillingly confirms his doubt. The self-seeking attorney, who wishes to become senator, sees it as an opportunity to win the voters' sympathy. But the circumstantial evidence on which the white teacher from the North is indicted is flimsy—at the end a lynching party takes care of the Yankee.

Both *Fury* and *They Won't Forget* document the fickleness of the crowd, the ease with which irrational instincts can be subversively manipulated. Both movies pose severe warnings to the democratic process, though both avoid the issue of race by featuring white protagonists as their victims. In reality, most lynch victims were blacks, but, because of the demographics of moviegoers at the time (mostly white), white victims were considered to yield better results at the box-office.[43]

Celebrating National Heroes: *Young Mr. Lincoln*

Between 1938 and 1941, Hollywood produced a cycle of films about Abraham Lincoln, described by Andrew Sarris as "obsessive reincarnation" of Lincoln in the national mythology.[44] The Depresion was ending and, with the news from Europe indicating a world war, Hollywood thought that films about national commitment and sacrifice were in order. The mythology of Lincoln in American history could be understood on many levels, particularly his embodiment of small-town values. Lincoln stood for egalitarianism and democracy, reflected in the simplicity of the Gettysburg address. He preserved the Union and helped liberate the slaves, which led to the Civil War. But as Sarris noted, there was also a personal dimension: Lincoln's triumphs commingle with many tragedies (his first love, Ann Rutledge, died), though this personal suffering made him a quintessential American hero, a martyr.

Lincoln's benevolence was evoked in MGM's *Of Human Hearts* (1938), an idyllic family saga, set in a small Ohio town. The movie deals with a "rebellious" son, Jason Wilkins (James Stewart), who, defying his minister father's restrictive code, attends medical school. Distinguishing himself as a surgeon in the Civil War, he fails to write to his mother, who thereupon thinks he is dead. But she appeals to Lincoln, who summons him from the front line and sends him home on a furlough. In John Cromwell's *Abe Lincoln in Illinois* (1940), based on Robert Sherwood's Pulitzer Prize–winning play, Lincoln was played by Raymond Massey, who re-created his stage role. But it is John Ford's epic, *Young Mr. Lincoln* (1939), an unusually effective biography, which captured the origins of Lincoln's mythology. One of the decade's most important films, it was admired by Soviet director Eisenstein because of its embodiment of the national spirit.

The narrative begins in 1832, in New Salem, Illinois, when Abe Lincoln (Henry Fonda) is introduced as a candidate for the legislature. Lincoln's speech, in favor of "a national bank, internal improvement system, and high protective tariff," is short and simple. When Abigail Clay (Alice Brady) and her two boys wish to buy flannel for shirts from him, all they can offer are books; they have no money and no credit. "Blackstone's Commentaries?" says the overwhelmed Lincoln. "Why, that's law, I could make head or tails out of it, if I set my mind to it." Lincoln is a small-town hero who can accomplish anything—once he sets his mind to it. Isolated at the river, he absorbs the contents of the book, convincing himself of the importance of defending basic rights.

His courtship of Ann Rutledge is characteristically brief and matter-of-fact. She recognizes in him the great ambitions of which he is, yet, unaware: "You've a real head on your shoulders and a way with people too." "You educated yourself," she tells the insecure Lincoln, "you read Shakespeare," reaffirming the priority of informal over formal schooling. Lincoln is a self-made man. In the next scene (a favorite of Ford), Lincoln confides in his deceased wife, "I can't make up my mind what to do." Indeed, it is Ann who decides he should become a lawyer (the stick fell toward the grave).

Structurally, the film consists of two parts: the first deals with Lincoln's rise to power; the second with the trial of the Clay brothers. Moving to Springfield, Lincoln is an attorney with John Stuart, Douglas's opponent for Congress, but he treats his clients with the same simplicity and honesty. As in other films, *Young Mr. Lincoln* abounds with communal activities that reaffirm the underlying social structure and dominant values. There is a long court sequence, which establishes Lincoln's (and the country's) legal ethics, Independence Day Celebration and its many contests: pie judging (again, having hard time to make up his mind), rail splitting, tug o'war, etc. Up to this moment, the film's mood is peaceful and progressive—small-town folks enjoying their ordinary lives. This equilibrium is suddenly disrupted by a brutal fight and murder, in which the Clay brothers are involved. Their mother, watching from afar, becomes the crucial witness and, later, the film's moral center.

Lincoln's persona is manifested in a series of confrontations. He is the idealistic lawyer, willing to volunteer his services for the cause. "Who are you?" asks Abigail. "I'm your lawyer," says Lincoln, and it is clear that he expects no remuneration. Modest, he describes himself as "a sort of jackleg lawyer without much experience in this business." Asked where his office is, he replies, "In my hat." Lincoln is not an intellectual or man of ideas, but a man of action. In a scene similar to *Fury*, albeit lacking its frightening intensity, the irrational crowds demand revenge, ready to lynch the two brothers ("what they need is a little taste of the rope"). Guarding the jail, he states unequivocally: "I am not up here to make any speeches. All I got to say is I can lick any man here, hands down." But he follows with a speech about the harmful effects of mob behavior: "When men start taking the law into their own hands, they're just as apt, in all confusion and fun, to start hanging somebody who's not a murderer as somebody who is . . . till it gets to the place where a man can't pass a tree or look at a rope without feeling uneasy." Lincoln stands for the small-town heroes obsessively committed to their mission, never considering defeat or resignation. When the judge asks if he needs a "more experienced lawyer to help him or take his place," Lincoln protests, "You suggest that I retire, take a back seat? I'm not the sort of fellow t' swap horses in the middle of the stream." Quitting is not in Lincoln's vocabulary.

Lincoln relates to Abigail as a surrogate mother. Arriving at her house, he immediately puts himself to work, chopping wood. "People used to say I could sink an axe deeper than anybody," he says. "Well, that's still not bad for a *city* fellow." Lincoln, like Abigail, experienced tragic events that ruined his life. He lost Ann, and Abigail lost her husband, killed by a drunken Indian. Once again, accidental violence and death are ubiquitous in small-town movies. Shy with women, he is described by Mary Todd as having "aversion of feminine society." Mary's elegant supper and fine dance make him feel awkward. "All the dancing I've ever done was behind a plow," he tells Mary. He is also modest about his upbringing. Asked if he is a member of that "fine family" in Massachusetts, he says, "No Lincoln I ever knew amounted to a hill of beans."

Lincoln's behavior at the trial is informal and relaxed. Feet elevated on a chair, he sits on the stairs next to the jurors. He dismisses the town's barber as a juror because he lies about a brawl that had occurred in his shop. And, conversely, he accepts men who have drunk and told lies, *only* because they have the courage to admit so. Ford draws explicit contrasts between Lincoln and the prosecutor, Felder (Donald Meek). Shorter and older, the mean-spirited prosecutor is unattractive, bald, and limping on a cane. Lincoln is tall, younger, and full of charm. Their styles of delivery could not be more different. Felder's speech is grand and bombastic, its contents pretentious. By contrast, Lincoln's is down-to-earth, replete with tales and jokes ordinary people could relate to. He possesses performance skills, acting at times like a clown. "He's a great storyteller," says Douglas, "Like all such actors, he revels in boisterous applause." Lincoln is singled out for his "ability in handling an unthinking mob;" even his enemies cannot deny he has a "certain political talent."

During the cross-examination, Abigail is at the center of the frame, signifying the film's endorsement of the mother's point of view. The camera on her side, she is seated higher than the prosecutor, who appears to be at her feet. She stands for Lincoln's mother and, by extension, all mothers. Lincoln describes her as "a simple ordinary country woman, who can't even write her name." "I've seen hundreds of women, just like her, working in the fields . . . in the kitchens. Women who say little, but do much, who ask for nothing but give all." This idealization of the matriarch as the family's moral center also figures prominently in Ford's *The Grapes of Wrath*. According to *Young Mr. Lincoln,* the most important tenet in the legal system is its conception of truth and its relation to the law. Lincoln balances the social need for law with the human desire for justice. Like Mr. Deeds, he is a firm believer in common sense: "I may not know so much of law, but I know what's right and what's wrong." Lincoln charges that the prosecutor is "willing to offer the life of one son" if Abigail would tell which one of them committed the murder. Lincoln, by contrast, would rather "lose both boys than break her heart." He is presented as a man willing to take risks, a unifier rather than family breaker.

The river assumes mythic functions: it represents nature. The earlier walks along the river with Ann convey romanticism; the river's image is forever associated with Ann, and the music heightens this feeling. "It's a mighty pretty river," Lincoln tells his companion, who cannot understand his fascination with it: "Folks would think it's a pretty woman, the way you carry on." But to Lincoln it is more than a pretty girl; it stands for everything beautiful in life. In the film's coda, Ford suggests how the legend of Lincoln originated, showing the elements that made him a myth. Lincoln expresses his wish to be left alone, and the camera pulls back as he marches on to the top of the hill, with the sounds of "Glory Hallelujah" growing louder and louder. Amidst rainstorm and lightning, the real-life Lincoln is transformed into (and frozen as) his statue in Washington DC.

Typical and Atypical Films

Typical imagery of small-town life during the Depression can be found in Warners' *Four Daughters* (1938),[45] one of the most popular films of the decade. The film contains many narrative ingredients of small-town works and a gallery of stock characters. The Lemps are a one-parent family, headed by a music professor, symbolically named Adam (Claude Rains). Adam is an "old-fashioned" patriarch, preaching to his daughters that "beauty isn't enough to justify itself, unless you do something to go with it." Protesting against "jazz and swing and crooners," Adam doubts whether Gershwin's music will survive: "That modern trash isn't, and never will be, music!"

As in *Little Women*, each of the daughters represents a different type: Emma (Gale Page) is efficient and sensible; Ann (Priscilla Lane), impulsive and easily enthusiastic; Kay (Rosemary Lane), a talented singer; and Thea (Lola Lane), the smart one. Their greatest fear is to become "old frumps, with eyeglasses and long noses." Ann, like Jo in *Little Women,* is afraid of any change; she would like them to "grow old together," and "things to go on just the way they are." But the pragmatic Aunt Etta (May Robson) thinks Ann is silly: "Can you imagine anything worse than a house full of old maids?" She expresses, like the mother in *Alice Adams,* the ultimate fear of screen women: to be spinsters. There is no worse stigma for women in American films than being old maids. Using the classic narrative structure of a state of equilibrium disrupted by an outsider, the story concerns the impact of two City men, a young orchestrator, Felix Dietz (Jeffrey Lynn), and his friend pianist, Mickey Borden (John Garfield), on the otherwise stable family. All four daughters become infatuated with Felix, "the nicest thing that's come into the house since the electric percolator."

Four Daughters is remembered today for featuring Garfield's first screen role, one of the most auspicious debuts in American films. But in addition to a stunning performance, which made Garfield an instant star, a *new* screen role was introduced, that of the "outsider," a major character and plot device in later small-town films. Borden is a brash misfit from the City, a rude, reckless person. Careless, his manner is indolent, and his expression wry and surly. He doesn't think well of himself—or of the world. With cigarette dangling from his mouth, he is the disenchanted idealist who holds grudges against society. Worse yet, Borden is a fatalist, believing he has no chance of winning the musical competition because "they" ("the fates!") won't let him. They have been at him for twenty-eight years, with "no letup." In one of the most cynical speeches in a 1930s movie, Borden expresses his philosophy:

> First they said, "Let him do without parents—he'll get along." Then they decided, "He doesn't need no education—that's for sissies." Then, for the finale, they got together on talent. "Sure," they said, "let him have talent, not enough, of course, to let him do anything on his own, anything good or great—Just enough to let him help other people—[it]s all he deserves."

In New York, Borden and Ann live in a shabby tenement, but he is too proud to accept money or favors from Felix. The scenes in New York show Borden and his friends in smoky, crowded, and sleazy restaurants, the type frequented by losers and small-time artists. Ann tries to persuade him that "a man decides his own destiny," but Borden insists that "messing things up, that's where I shine." Realizing he has come between the two lovers, Borden drives his car over a cliff. Fatally injured, he feels this incident is "more of *their* (the fates') work"; they wouldn't even "let me go out in style."

Garfield's role and performance are the only realistic elements in an otherwise sentimental film. At the end, romantic love wins and order is reestablished. *Four Daughters* presents a clear visual symmetry. The film opens on a joyous note, showing a blossoming peach tree, behind which the entire family is engaged in a rendition of Schubert's "Serenade." And it ends with the same image: the flowering peach tree and Schubert's "Serenade." This recurring motif, with the camera pulling away from a cozy family tableau, is meant to reassure the viewers of the family's harmony and continuous unity.[46] Unaccountably nominated for four Oscar Awards, it was so successful that Warners immediately made a sequel, *Daughters Courageous* (1939),[47] in which Garfield plays another misfit, an impetuous man who courts and loses. "You and me?" says Garfield. "Nah. It's not written in the book."

In most 1930s films, the contrast between the two conceptual opposites, the Small Town and the Big City, was used to highlight the positive features of small-town life. One film that deviated from this pattern was *Nothing Sacred* (1937), William A. Wellman's screwball comedy. Ben Hecht[48] changed the locale of James H. Street's story from Mount Ida, Arkansas, to Warsaw, Vermont. The movie has been interpreted as a satire on "yellow" journalism, because of Hecht's personal experience and previous scripts. There is a key line in the film, in which a New York journalist is told: "A newspaperman, huh? The hand of God reaching down into the mire couldn't elevate one of them to the depth of degradation!" Nonetheless, the movie's issues are broader than journalism, dealing with the creation of instant celebrities (a topic ahead of its time), corruption, and excessive materialism. Furthermore, it presents a counterview of the small town, a rare film to suggest that there are no significant differences between small-town and big-city folks because their conduct is shaped by similar (selfish) motivations.

The protagonist, Hazel Flagg (Carole Lombard), lives in Warsaw, a small town dominated by the Paragon Watch Company. Like many young people, she has always dreamed of visiting the glamorous city. The opportunity comes when Dr. Downer (Charles Winninger) informs her she is a victim of radium poisoning (contracted at the factory) and has only a few months to live. The story of her impending death reaches

Wally Cook (Fredric March), a down-on-his luck journalist. Cook has fallen out of favor with his cynical and dyspeptic managing editor, when he tries to pass off a poor black man as the "Sultan of Marzipan," a prospective donor of a huge amount of money for an art institute. But during the dignified banquet, the black man is exposed by his wife and kids, and Cook is demoted to writing obituaries in a small corner of the office. Anxious to get out of this rut, Cook seizes the opportunity of advertising Hazel's radium poisoning in the form of an exposé titled "The Last Days of a Courageous Girl." By exploiting her, he hopes to enhance his prestige and also increase the paper's circulation. Little does he know that, in the meantime, Dr. Downer has changed his diagnosis. "You're not going to die," he informs Hazel, "unless you're going to be run over." Extremely distressed, her plan to go to New York and "die happily," goes down the drain. Disappointed, she cries: "To be brought to life twice, and each time in Warsaw!" But shrewd and unscrupulous, Hazel persuades her doctor to maintain the story of her death.

The only scene in Warsaw occurs early on, when Cook arrives to meet Hazel. It is far from the idealized and hospitable small-town of the Capra movies. Upon arrival, the baggage man refuses to take Cook to Hazel's residence, warning him that no one in town will talk to him; the only reason *he* responded was to get his money. The drugstore lady is not much friendlier, answering his questions as laconically as possible, with yeps and nopes. She, too, is greedy, grabbing his coin. And Dr. Downer's housekeeper is just as reserved and uninviting as the others. "Tell him yourself," she tells Cook, when he asks to be announced. Walking in the town's streets is no fun either. Children on an ice wagon throw bits of ice; a maniacal child runs out after Cook and bites him on the leg. Hazel is not the innocent small-town girl, bewildered by the Big City. If anything, *she* is the manipulator and aggressor. That she and her doctor are one of a kind becomes clear when, hung over, she has misgivings about her behavior. "Why did you let me come to New York?" asks Hazel, "You were always as honest as you look!" Hazel and Downer can make themselves look innocent, demonstrating that appearances are deceptive and not to be trusted. Cook, by contrast, looks suave and shrewd, but is more innocent than Hazel.

Conclusion

During the Depression, one solution to the nation's economic problems was "the return to the soil." Indeed, most films praised the virtues of small towns and criticized urbanization and industrialization. Despite the demographic evidence (a growing urbanization from the 1920s on), the City has continued to feature as a "villain" in American films. Peter

Roffman and Jim Purdy have described the populist ideology of these films, in which "the city is an entirely negative environment, the epitome of modern progress," whereas "the country, or more directly, the soil, is the direct antithesis to the city, a symbol of the past, of self-help, rugged individualism, and good neighborliness."[49] Capra's populist comedies contrasted small towns with the Big City, condemning the City's corruption, greed, superficiality, and impersonality. *Our Daily Bread* was the only movie to propose the radical solution of establishing cooperatives, but even this movie could not reconcile the tension between collectivism as utopian ideal and individualism as reality.

Unconditional faith in the land and commitment to preserve it at all costs were two prevalent values in the Depression that continued to dominate films of later decades. For example, *Gone with the Wind* (1939) romanticized the Old South by celebrating the importance of the land, not just for the economy, but for one's identity. Broken down and desperate, Scarlett O'Hara decides to go back to Tara and save her family's land. That she succeeds, the film suggests, is a measure of her strong-willed personality. Moreover, a good cause justifies the means used: Self-absorbed and a determined Southern belle, Scarlett is a predecessor of the strong heroines in future farm movies (chapter 6). *Gone* featured a feminist heroine for its times, but propagated traditional values, such as romantic individualism and hard work.[50]

The best films of the decade, cinematically and narratively, often ran against dominant ideology. With the possible exception of *Mr. Deeds* and *Mr. Smith,* the other idealistic films have not aged well. By contrast, *Fury, Theodora Goes Wild,* and *Nothing Sacred* have assumed the status of classics because of their thematic or stylistic audacity. In the 1930s, many small-town films featured a comic sensibility; the best movies were screwball comedies *(Mr. Deeds, Theodora, Nothing Sacred).* They upheld traditional virtues of family life and almost invariably contained happy endings, in which their heroes (and heroines) were integrated, usually by marriage, into the established social order. Their narratives suggested that stability was the rule of the game, and that the most individualistic and eccentric protagonists could find their place within mainstream arrangements. Thus, the inherent tension between individual and community was resolved in a way that satisfied and benefited both individuals and society. But while towns in films of the 1930s had a clear moral center, a collective conscience, which was abiding, there was an equal emphasis on creative and rebellious personalities.

Small-town films of the Depression featured both male and female protagonists: Of the thirteen films discussed, five had female, seven male, and one both male and female characters. More importantly, women were portrayed as equal to men; in screwball comedies, they were often stronger than men. In *Mr. Deeds* (and other Capra films), it is the woman who is manipulative and the sexual aggressor. And as its title indicates, in *Nothing Sacred,* nothing is sacred, including the behavior of a small-town woman. Indeed, images of women differed among the film genres. Actresses who specialized in screwball comedies (Katharine Hepburn, Carole Lombard, Irene Dunne, Jean Arthur, Claudette Colbert) often taught men a lesson or two in courtship, romance, and lovemaking. By contrast, in melodramas and musicals, the more traditional mythology, of the good Small-town versus the bad big City, was maintained. For example, numerous narratives depicted naïve and unsophisticated small-town girls who come to the Big City (usually New York) to pursue their show-business career (*Morning Glory,* 1932; *Forty Second Street,* 1933; *Stage Door,* 1937).

The thematic unit of Depression films was the individual (usually one protagonist). The few films that dealt with larger groups centered on the nuclear family (*Little Women, Four Daughters*). The prevalence of screen names such as Adams, as either first (the father in *Four Daughters*) or last (*Alice Adams*) name is also noteworthy. The original title of *Dr. Bull* was *The Last Adam.* This was no accident: With all their eccentricities, the protagonists of these films were meant to be average and typical. Mr. Deeds and other Capra heroes were conceived as prototypes of the "little men," though they were never convincing as such—in large part a function of the performers' immense talent and charisma.

The decade of the 1930s, as I pointed out (1988), is important for launching the careers of four male movie stars associated with small-town values: Will Rogers, Gary Cooper, James Stewart, and Henry Fonda. The small-town heroes they played left such indelible images that, no matter what specific roles they later portrayed, they were forever associated with the earlier, small-town images.

Will Rogers was the most popular star during the Depression; his untimely death in 1935, in an air crash, terminated his career at its height. Rogers was much more than a movie star, he was a folk hero, an icon. Previously a vaudeville performer, newspaper columnist, and radio personality, Rogers functioned as a homespun philosopher, or as Andrew Sarris noted, "a combination of Norman Mailer and Woody Allen, from a somewhat broader base of audience identification."[51] The impressive volume of his film output (between 1930 and 1935, he appeared in nineteen films) enabled him to repeat his philosophy with a good deal of consistency. An ambassador of rural America and spokesman of common folk, Rogers was often cast as a small-town judge or doctor, professionals who lived a simple life. He cherished the American way of life with his two foremost weapons: acerbic humor and commonsensical wit.

Will Rogers embodied three symbols of the American Dream, at a time when it was increasingly hard to believe in such values: The dignity of common individuals; democracy as the guarantee of equality; and the ethics of hard work. In his films, Rogers stood against "governmental corruption, financial greed, and changes in morals."[52] These values were extremely important, when farmers were suffering a severe decline in their power (and prestige), and when farming was gradually incorporated into a vast technological market economy. At a time when the American system might have been redirected, with the old values deemed inadequate, Rogers showed that there was still vitality in the traditional values. His political commentary (in films, radio programs, newspapers) was instrumental in helping Roosevelt win the 1932 election. "There was something infectious about his humor," Roosevelt said in his eulogy, "In a time grown too solemn and somber, he brought his countrymen back to a sense of proportion."

Henry Fonda made his screen debut the year Rogers died, in 1935, in *The Farmer Takes a Wife,* and he played another farmer in his second film, *Way Down East* (same year). In *The Farmer,* a comedy of manners, Fonda repeated his stage role as Dan Harrow, a virtuous farmer on the Erie Canal whose ambition is to save enough money to buy his own land and live there peacefully with his girl (Janet Gaynor). In his screen persona, Fonda embodied the virtues of a small-town hero: shy, decent, ingenuous, and honest. At the center of his myth was the self-reliant farmer, the mainstay of American economy until industrialization. But the mythological significance of farmers continued to prevail, as evident in *Young Mr. Lincoln, Drums along the Mohawk* (1939), and in Fonda's best-known role, Tom Joad in *The Grapes of Wrath* (1940), all directed by Ford. Fonda's social background, born in the small town of Omaha, Nebraska, made his screen persona all the more credible. "I'm Midwest and proud of it," he once observed. "I've never tried hard to get away from that. When I have tried, I've felt phony."[53] He embodied the ideal common man, standing for democratic values and domestic ideals.

If Fonda epitomized farmers, James Stewart was most effectively cast as a small-town lawyer, establishing himself as another all-American hero in his films with Capra, the director of "the American Dream." Stewart usually played folks who found pleasure and fulfillment in an unglamorous, ordinary existence. His Jefferson Smith in Capra's *Mr. Smith Goes to Washington* (1939) is a naive Wisconsin senator committed to fighting graft and corruption. And his young sheriff in *Destry Rides Again* (also 1939), Thomas Jefferson Destry (note the similarity in the protagonists' names), looks soft and easygoing, as many small-town heroes, but is hard as nails when he has to fight. In Capra's masterpiece, *It's a Wonderful Life* (1946), Stewart is cast as the simple but honest George

Bailey who, all his life, has been dreaming of breaking away from his small town, doing "big things," only to realize how meaningful that small-town life was to him (See chapter 2). Capra also contributed to Gary Cooper's image as the spokesman of ordinary people and ordinary life. In *Mr. Deeds,* the movie that catapulted Cooper to national stardom, his tuba-playing country boy suddenly finds himself fighting Big City crooks and swindlers. And in another Capra film, *Meet John Doe* (1941), Cooper starts as a desperate ex–bush league pitcher, but ends up fighting a Fascist publisher and a corrupt political system. In *Sergeant York,* Cooper played a farmer turned war hero.[54]

The Depression also introduced a number of female stars to the public, stars who differed in their screen images from their predecessors. In the late 1920s and early 1930s, the popular stars embodied glamour, sophistication, and explicitly erotic sexuality, all situated in distinctly urban locales. Greta Garbo, Marlene Dietrich, Jean Harlow, and Mae West were all popular in the *early* 1930s, but declined in stature as the decade progressed. The new stars who replaced them (Janet Gaynor, Claudette Colbert, Jean Arthur, Irene Dunne, and Barbara Stanwyck) embodied a romantic, though not excessively sexual, image, and they were more down-to-earth.

2

• • • • • • • •

The 1940s—
Ambivalence and Cynicism

You're just an ordinary little girl living in an ordinary
little town filled with peaceful, stupid dreams. . . . How
do you know what the world is like? The world is a hell.
— *Shadow of a Doubt*

Kings Row. A good clean town. A good town to live in,
and a good place to raise your children.
— *Kings Row*

The early 1940s continued the dominant trend of the 1930s, that is,
portraying small-town life in an optimistic and idealistic manner. This
was particularly the case of popular film series—*Andy Hardy, Blondie,* and
Dr. Kildare—all of which began in the late 1930s and continued with
great success into the 1940s. The threat of totalitarianism and World War
II itself necessitated reaffirmation of traditional values: family love,
commitment to the land, and defense of the country. Believing that the
film industry should produce sentimental propaganda, many films em-
braced these values, as was evident in the hundreds of war movies made.
Yet considering the fact that the decade's most important historical event
was the involvement of the US in World War II (from 1941 to 1945), a
time calling for national unity and patriotic fervor, it is surprising to find
a number of small-town films that were critical of the American Dream
and dominant culture.

In her book, *Running Away from Myself* (1969), Barbara Deming examines America's "Dream Portrait" through films of the 1940s, noting that
the heroes of many movies are "products of a deep crisis of faith,"
mourning "a vision of happiness which eludes them." Deming describes
a bleak image, though notes that for the most part this vision was

subconscious for both films and audiences because it operated beneath a conventional narrative surface.[1] Indeed, a number of films examined the unexplored, dark side, of small towns.

Some of the most important films about small towns, thematically and stylistically, were produced in the 1940s, a particularly strong decade in this respect. From 1942 to 1944 alone, the following landmark pictures were made: *Kings Row, The Magnificent Ambersons, The Ox-Bow Incident, The Talk of the Town* (all released in 1942), *Shadow of a Doubt* (1943), *Hail the Conquering Hero* and *The Miracle of Morgan's Creek* (both in 1944). The themes and styles of these films were varied—each film introduced some innovations—but they shared one thing in common: a darker vision of small-town America.

Classic Americana: *Our Town*

The decade began with a particularly impressive film, *Our Town* (1940), based on Thornton Wilder's 1938 play, which won the Pulitzer Prize for drama.[2] Celebrating its fiftieth anniversary, *Our Town* proves to be one of the most enduring and most produced of American plays, but it is also one of the most misunderstood works. For some reason, it evokes ridicule in critics who charge that the play is too sentimental. While it may not be "a deadly cynical play,"[3] as playwright Lanford Wilson said, it is far from a simple, nostalgic hymn to small-town America at the turn of the century. And contrary to many interpretations, the play (and film) are a testimony to an experimental vision at work.

Set in Grover's Corners (modeled on the town of Peterborough, New Hampshire), it is meant to stand for any small town. Indeed, a postcard addressed to a little girl locates the town in "the World, the Solar System, the Universe, the Mind of God." In this abstract, minimalist work, Wilder was interested in exploring the most universal elements in everyday life. How would a randomly chosen day look and feel in a town where supposedly "nothing happens," where life is routine, a place "nobody very remarkable ever come out of." As other films, *Our Town* is strategically situated in 1901, the end of an era and just before a most significant technological invention—the car. The movie captures the inevitability of technological change and its pervasive effects on people's lives. Thus, the horse and buggy give way to the automobile, and the stable becomes a garage.

One can fault the film for ignoring the reality outside town, but this was a conscious choice by Wilder, attempting to conduct the theatrical equivalent of a laboratory experiment. Wilder examined the meanings of three fundamental principles of the life cycle: birth, marriage, and death, which also served as titles of the play's three acts. Covering a twelve-year period (from 1901 to 1913) in the life of Grover's Corner, *Our Town* illuminates the characters through a detailed attention to their humdrum lives. Of the three universals the movie examines, it is most concerned with death, or rather the influence of the dead on the living. Viewers are told, ahead of time, that Emily will die at childbirth, and that Mrs. Gibbs will die of pneumonia while visiting her daughter in Canton, Ohio. Joe, a bright boy who got a scholarship to MIT, will die in France during World War I.

By the time the film was produced, everyday life in small towns was far removed from Wilder's notion, but he wanted to evoke a bygone time and place. Stripping the essentials of life down to their most elementary principles, Wilder stressed the power of stoicism and endurance in the face of adversity, an idea not unlike Capra's *It's a Wonderful Life.* Soon after 1913, the druggist says, "The world began to shake and fidget. We shook with it, our town, I mean, but we're still here." And similarly to *Wonderful Life,* the movie hints at the restlessness of the town's inhabitants and their wish to explore different worlds. Mrs. Gibbs would love to go to Paris. "Once in your life, before you die," she says, "you ought to see a country where they don't talk in English and don't even want to." Mrs. Webb suggests that Mrs. Gibbs "keep droppin' hints" to her husband; that was how *she* got Mr. Webb to take her to see the Atlantic Ocean. This conversation reflects the innocence and isolationism of American society prior to World War I, and the fear that exposure to new ideas might produce, or increase, the level of discontent with the small town.

Maintaining the play's innovative format, the film is narrated by the town's druggist, Morgan (Frank Craven), who introduces the characters and their backgrounds. The movie is set on June 7, 1901, just before the crack of dawn. The narrator is corrected by the history professor that the town's population is not 2,640, but 2,642; the doctor has just returned from Polish town, where he helped Mrs. Goruslawski deliver twins. The town is stratified along political and religious, but *not* class lines. Most of the inhabitants (84 percent) are Republican, with few (12 percent) Democrats, and even fewer (4 percent) Socialists. Catholics are in the minority (12 percent); the vast majority are Protestants. The film acknowledges the town's ethnic diversity. "Cuttin' across Main Street, across the tracks," Morgan says, "is Polish town, foreign people that come to work." The town is run democratically, by a Board of Selection, but no resentment is expressed over the fact that only males vote.

The two households, the Gibbses and the Webbs, are friendly: their children, George Gibbs (William Holden) and Emily Webb (Martha Scott) are in love and destined to get married. George, the doctor's son, does not want to follow in his father's footsteps; he wants to be a farmer.

Family life is intimate and important; there is no competition from the mass media yet. In fact, the local newspaper, *Grover's Corner Sentinel,* edited by Mr. Webb, (Guy Kibbee) comes out only twice a week. The lack of mass media (radio, magazines, films) also means that knowledge is still transmitted orally from one generation to another. Though respectful, the town's women enjoy gossiping, here about the drinking problem of the church's organist, Simon Stimson (possibly Wilder's alter ego). But the gossip is not as malicious or harmful as in *Alice Adams* or *Fury.* "A very ordinary town," Mr. Webb says, "we've got one or two drunks, but they're always having remorse when an evangelist comes to town." By and large, "likker ain't a regular thing in the home here, except in the medicine chest . . . for snake bite."

With the exception of two digressions, the film is faithful to the play. First, it has scenery, to make the narrative more "realistic." And second, the film deviates from the play by presenting a happy ending; Emily does not die. Wilder reportedly did not mind these changes and even supported the new resolution. In the film's last scene, the narrator is on the bridge; it is eleven o'clock. "Tomorrow's another day," says the narrator, but rather than reassurance, this statement evokes an ambiguous, open-ended question: Will tomorrow be the same kind of day as today?

Sam Wood's film is as experimental and stylized as the play. Presented in brief scenes, the film does not abide by the conventions of a linear narrative text. Viewers are told the fate of the characters almost as soon as they are introduced. Shot in a stylized black and white by cinematographer William Cameron Menzies, there is good use of deep focus (before it was used by Orson Welles in *Citizen Kane*). To produce the right ambience, Wood employs creative dissolves, montages, and superimpositions; an image of Emily at present is superimposed on her as a younger woman. Flashbacks and asides are also utilized, as in the wedding scene, when the thoughts of George and Emily are conveyed (George tells himself he doesn't want to get married).

A whole generation of playwrights was influenced by Wilder's play. Arthur Miller, for example, believes that *Our Town*'s greatness lies in its focus on "the indestructibility, the everlastingness of the family and the community, its rhythm of life, its rootedness in the essentially safe cosmos despite troubles, wracks, and seemingly disastrous, but essentially temporary, dislocations."[4] "I grew up in *Our Town*," says Lanford Wilson. "It just happened to be called Ozark, Missouri."

The Dark Side of Small Towns

Hitchcock admired *Our Town* so much that he asked Wilder to write a script for him, affording the playwright an opportunity to continue his exploration of small-town life. It was "gratifying to me," Hitchcock said, "to find out that one of America's most eminent playwrights was willing to work with me and, indeed, that he took the whole thing quite seriously." Hitchcock acknowledged his gratitude to Wilder in the credits, an unusual tribute and "emotional gesture," because he was "touched by his qualities."[5] The whole project assumed special significance for Hitchcock, as he explained: "In England, I'd always had the collaboration of top stars and the finest writers, but in America things were quite different. I was turned down by many stars and by writers who looked down their noses at the genre I work in."[6] *Shadow of a Doubt* thus became one of Hitchcock's most personal films.

In *Our Town*, the druggist plays the role of an insider-outsider: Detached from the proceedings, his comic, often wry, comments examine Grover's Corners from the outside. Emily is also able to "step aside," and look back more objectively on her life and the town. The druggist and Emily provide some tension and perspective, though despite the town's divisions, it is still unified and marked by one dominant way of life. The only outsider-outcast is the church's organist who, a frustrated artist, doesn't really belong. He is a loner with a drinking problem who is not integrated into the town.[7] In *Shadow*, Wilder and Hitchcock use the character of the outsider-deviant more explicitly as a narrative and thematic device.

The Normal and the Abnormal: *Shadow of a Doubt*

Shadow of a Doubt (1943) features prominently among the decade's films about the "other side" of small towns. It probes the two faces of small towns, the bright and the dark sides. The British master of suspense surprised many of his colleagues by choosing to direct such subject matter and by his careful re-creation of small-town Americana. Based on a story by Gordon McDonnell, the screenplay was written by Thornton Wilder, Sally Benson, Alma Reville, and Hitchcock (uncredited). The film serves as a companion piece to *Our Town* for another reason: Sally Benson's collection of stories, published in the *New Yorker*, served as basis for Vincente Minnelli's MGM musical, *Meet Me in St. Louis* (1944), another slice of small-town Americana.

It was shot in Santa Rosa, chosen by Hitchcock and Wilder after careful consideration of other towns. The house's owner was so pleased with the fact that his house had been chosen that he painted it—to look better—reflecting his and the public's image of small towns as clean, neat, and beautiful. Amused by it, Hitchcock had to repaint the house "dirty" all over again.

The strategy used by Hitchcock is that of juxtaposition. The narrative contrasts two protagonists, Uncle Charlie (Joseph Cotten) and his niece

Charlie (Teresa Wright) who, blood-related, share the same name and are connected by telepathy and love. The narrative first introduces Uncle Charlie, lying in bed in his room, then switches to his niece, showing her in the same position in her bed. The young Charlie finds her family life dull and bland: "We go along and nothing happens." "A family should be the most wonderful thing in the world," charges Charlie, "but this one has gone to pieces."

The Newton family is composed of Joseph (Henry Travers), his wife Emma (Patricia Collinge), and their three children: Charlie, Ann (Edna Mae Wonacott), and Roger (Charles Bates). Ann is an unattractive and bespectacled girl, the bookish, precocious type. In 1943, she was not yet a stock character in small-town films, as she would become a decade later (see *Picnic*). Roger is more agreeable, but his character is much less developed than his sister's.

Unlike other films of the time, *Shadow of a Doubt* acknowledges explicitly the significance of social class. The best scenes take place at dinner time, when the whole family sits around the table and talks; this is prior to the age of television, which will change forever family habits of eating and socializing. Embodying aristocratic values, Uncle Charlie represents the old order, whereas the Newtons uphold more democratic, middle-class, values. There is nostalgia for the bygone era of glamour and elegance at turn-of-the-century Europe. Lehar's melodic "The Merry Widow" is played on the sound track and the image of elegantly dressed people waltzing to its tunes recurs. "Everyone was neat and pretty then, the whole world," Uncle Charlie remarks, "not like the world today." But there is also tension, caused by the intimate bond between Uncle Charlie and his sister Emma, particularly when they reminisce about their childhood. Excluded from these talks, Mr. Newton feels inferior and insecure, having come from a lower social class than his wife. Emma has clearly lost her looks and the glamour she possessed in her youth. To help support the family, she now needs to work. She is enchanted by her brother, because he reminds her of the better life she has had. Uncle Charlie is an outsider in every sense of the term. He represents a threat to the unity and happiness of this nuclear family, not only in his later attempt to kill his niece (when she finds out he is a murderer), but by his very presence, causing tension between Mr. and Mrs. Newton.

The people of Santa Rosa seem to be friendly, if slightly eccentric. Herbie Hawkins (Hume Cronyn), the Newtons' next-door neighbor, is a mother-fixated man whose hobby is to read and solve murder mysteries. The other members, the telegraph operator, the helpful policeman (Hitchcock himself), detective Jack Graham, and the librarian, all go about their routine jobs in an agreeable manner. But one also gets a notion of frustrated people, whose life in town has been anything but happy. In a crucial scene set in a cocktail bar, the waitress, who went to high school with young Charlie, observes: "I'd just die for a ring like that." She refers to the ring that Uncle Charlie had given his niece, which he has stolen from one of his victim-widows.

One of the most interesting aspects of *Shadow of a Doubt* is its image of the nuclear family, in ideology and practice. Seeking information to incriminate Uncle Charlie, detective Jack Graham (MacDonald Carey) comes into the house under the excuse of wanting to interview a "representative American family." But no one likes the idea of being an average or typical family; Emma protests that they are not a typical family. Throughout the film, the words *typical, average, ordinary,* and *representative* abound, reflecting the inherent tension between living a quiet, ordinary, but *fulfilling* middle-class life and one that is just ordinary and *bland*. The film's characters seem to associate ordinariness with blandness.

The villain in *Shadow of a Doubt* is an original. Uncle Charlie is a murderer with a (Fascist) mission, killing old and ugly widows, whom he describes as "useless women, drinking the money, eating the money, smelling of money." Handsome, intelligent, and charming, he assumes the public's sympathy, unlike other Hitchcockian villains who are disturbed and psychopathic. Significantly, unlike *Psycho*, Uncle Charlie's violent acts are never seen; they have occurred before the narrative begins. Moreover, unlike Anthony Perkins's Norman Bates, Joseph Cotten possesses the looks and manners of a suave leading man. Hitchcock refuses to portray heroes and villains in black or white, using instead shades of gray to portray both villain and heroine.

The narrative structure is symmetric, beginning with the arrival of a train (with Uncle Charlie aboard) in Santa Rosa and ending with his departure. Hitchcock uses straightforward symbolism: a huge cloud of black smoke (evil) signals the arrival of the train, whereas in its departure, the smoke is lighter, signaling a sense of relief. Though the film is set for the most part in Santa Rosa, the earlier images of urban life (Philadelphia) are quite depressing. In the first scene, Hitchcock's camera pans across huge industrial buildings to convey the City's coldness and anonymity. The two detectives wait for Uncle Charlie on a deserted street, and Uncle Charlie lives in a shabby room.

But the movie draws a more important contrast between the small town as a garden and the small town as a hell, similar to the contrast in many Western films between the garden and the desert. "You're just an ordinary little girl living in an ordinary little town filled with peaceful, stupid dreams," Uncle Charlie tells his niece. "You live in a dream. How do you know what the world is like? The world is a hell." "Do you know the world is a foul sty?" he continues. "Do you know if you ripped the fronts off houses you'd find swine?" Uncle Charlie first disrupts, then completely shatters his niece's illusions about small-town life: "You live in a dreamworld, and I have brought you nightmares."

The duplicity motif functions on many levels of the film.[8] The title itself, *Shadow of a Doubt* (a great one), bears double-edged meaning, referring to Charlie's growing suspicions that her uncle is a murderer and to Charlie's (standing in for ordinary girls) own doubts about her life. "We're sort of like twins," she observes early on. "The same blood runs in our veins," confirms her uncle. At the end, Uncle Charlie, attempting to get rid of his niece, is brought down by her, an act that symbolizes the triumph of virtue over evil *within* herself. Moreover, the film suggests that Charlie may continue to love her uncle, in spite of her knowledge about him and his attempt to kill her. This ambiguous note might have eluded audiences at the time.

The issue of duplicity becomes most explicit in the detective's observation at the end of the film: "It's not so bad, but it seems to go crazy now and then, like your Uncle Charlie." The world is basically right, Hitchcock appears to be saying, but "it just has to be carefully watched." This sequence's ironic tone is accentuated by Hitchcock, framing it in front of the church, where the minister eulogizes Uncle Charlie as a respectable citizen. But despite formal resolution, narrative closure (Uncle Charlie's death), and happy ending (Charlie's romance with the detective), the dark anxieties operating beneath the surface register more effectively than the normal facade. The film restores social order (and normality), but shows the frail and shaky bases of such an order and the great strains it takes to maintain it.

The Passing of a Tradition: *The Magnificent Ambersons*

Orson Welles's auteurist effort (as writer, director, and narrator), *The Magnificent Ambersons* (1942) is linked to *Shadow of a Doubt* thematically, showing the dark side of small town, but also in casting, using the same actor, Joseph Cotten, in the leading role. However, in Welles's film, Eugene Morgan represents social progress and change, whereas in the Hitchcock film, Uncle Charlie embodies values of the old aristocratic order. Using Booth Tarkington's novel, Welles stresses the somber aspects in the decline and decay of a great American dynasty in the Midwest. The narrative spans a whole generation, beginning in 1873, with turning points in 1890, 1894, and 1904. Like *Our Town*, most of the narrative is set at a crucial time of change, at the turn of the century.

The film is highly innovative in its use of cinematic codes. It is framed by Welles's offscreen voice-over narration, placing the story in a broader perspective. "The magnificence of the Ambersons began in 1873. Their splendor lasted throughout all the years that saw their Midland town spread and darken into a city." (Note the word *darken* to describe the evolution of the town into a city.) The tone is nostalgic, but decidedly unsentimental, emphasizing the inevitability of change precipitated by technological innovation. The first scene shows a horse and carriage on the right side of the frame, and a streetcar on the opposite side. "The only public conveyance was the streetcar," says the narrator. "Too slow for us nowadays, because the faster we're carried, the less time we have to spare. But in those days, they had time for everything!" The introduction of cars was just the first step in the privatization and automatization of life (TV would be another), but before, there were plenty of occasions for collective celebrations: "People had time for sleigh rides, balls, assemblies, cotillions, open house on New Year's, picnics in the woods, and serenades."

As *Shadow of a Doubt* hinted, the town's rich people are elegant, members of a privileged minority: "In those days, all the women who wore silk and velvet knew all the other women who wore silk and velvet." Major Amberson (Richard Bennett) built his dynasty in Midland. "The Ambersons' Mansion!" states an old citizen. "The pride of the town! Sixty thousand dollars for the woodwork alone." The town's inequality was always visible: "Against so homespun a background, the magnificence of the Ambersons was as conspicuous as a brass band at a funeral." "Everybody in town can tell when the Ambersons are out driving after dark, just by the jingle," says an old man. The beauty of the three-story house surpassed that of the White House. When the Ambersons gave parties, elegant people arrived in their carriages, and crowds of the "uninvited" stood in the snow to watch. The Ambersons also have connections to real political power. "Uncle Jack is in Congress," says George, "because the family likes to have someone there."

Despite her great love for Eugene Morgan (Joseph Cotten), Isabel Amberson (Dolores Costello) married Wilbur Minafer, an act of downward mobility for her. She rebuffed Eugene, to whom she was engaged, when he made a fool of himself (being tipsy) in front of her house. She obviously made a mistake, as a town's matron says: "Just because a man, any woman would like a thousand times better, was a little wild one night at a serenade." The wedding, however, was in grand Amberson-style, with "raw oysters floating in scooped-out blocks of ice and a band from out of town." But the town's people, used as a chorus in a Greek tragedy, predict that Isabel and Wilbur will have "the worst spoiled lot of children the town will ever see." They turn out to be right, with one exception: they had one child, George, but he was "spoiled enough for a whole carload."

As a boy, George (Tim Holt)[9] is arrogant, domineering, and rude, a brat pretending to own the whole town. He drives his dogcart at criminal speed, forcing pedestrians to retreat from crossing. In the original script, there was a scene in which George demands new elections at the club so that he can become its president. George refers to Reverend Smith as a "riffraff," one "the Ambersons wouldn't have anything to do with." If the Reverend "wanted to see any of us, he'd have to go 'round to the side door." The residents dislike George ever since he was a boy, hoping "to live to see the day, when that boy would get his comeuppance!" "Something was bound to take him down, some day," says the narrator, "and they only wanted to be there." The rest of the film describes that something.

The narrative begins when Eugene Morgan returns to town as a widower after an absence of twenty years. An outsider who was once an insider, his return affects the town, signaling a new era. Eugene is an industrious middle-class man who achieves success through talent and hard work—with no reliance on connections or aristocratic blood. The movie parallels his ascent, as a prosperous businessman, with the decline of the aristocratic Ambersons. An inventor, he is in the process of working on a new "horseless carriage." George feels sorry for him and predicts failure: "People aren't going to spend their lives lying on their backs in the road and letting grease drip in their faces."

George offends Lucy (Anne Baxter), Eugene's daughter, at their first meeting, referring to him (not knowing he is her father) as "some old widower." George is against going to college, describing it as "lots of useless guff." He is contemptuous of any line or profession. "Just look at 'em," he tells Lucy scornfully, "lawyers, bankers, politicians! What do they get out of life, I'd like to know? What do they ever know about *real* things?" His ambition is to be a yachtsman. George wonders why "all those ducks" were invited by his mother to their party for she needs not to "worry much about offending anybody in town." "It must be wonderful," says Lucy, "to be so important as that!" "Anybody that really is anybody ought to be able to do about as they like in their own town," he replies with self-assurance. When Lucy expresses her concern about George's arrogance to her father, he tells her "three things" to explain "all that's good and bad about him: He's Isabel's only child. He's an Amberson. He is a boy."

Eugene has no concern for his father's investments; he wants to make sure he will not invest in Morgan's automobile. "The automobile concern is all Eugene's," his mother corrects him, "your father's rolling mills." And offended, Aunt Fanny says: "Eugene Morgan's perfectly able to finance his own inventions these days." George is unhappy with the way his grandfather manages his houses. "He ought to keep things up better," he says. "He lets people take too many liberties: they do anything they want to." George's philosophy is based on privileged birth and spoiled upbringing, but he expects civility among those at the top: "There's a few people that birth and position put them on top, and they ought to treat each other entirely as equals."

A politician, Uncle Jack is more realistic and pragmatic than his nephew. "What puts the lines on faces?" he asks Eugene. "Age puts some, and trouble puts some, and work puts some," replies Eugene, "but the deepest wrinkles are carried by lack of faith." Welles seems to suggest that the Ambersons, still oriented toward their glamorous past, have lost their faith in the future. By contrast, upwardly mobile Eugene is a man of the future.

In adapting the book to the screen, Welles decided to eliminate the character of Fred Kinney, Lucy's boyfriend. Instead of the rivalry between him and George over Lucy, the focus is on the rivalry between Eugene and George over Isabel's attention. *The Magnificent Ambersons* offers a turbulent family portrait, with a most complex relationship between mother and son. Isabel is the devoted mother, worshiping her son, thinking, as uncle Jack says, "He's a little tin god on wheels." As for George, he is mother-fixated, with strong Oedipal feelings. Destructive and vengeful, he does everything in his power to abort her rekindled romance with Eugene, even though he knows it is based on true love.

Aunt Fanny (Agnes Moorehead) is the film's most tragic character, a spinster still in love with Eugene, and always in the shadow of Isabel's riches, beauty and grace. Utterly humorless and ultrasensitive, she seems to be on the verge of hysteria all the time. "It all began," George explains, "when we found out father's business was washed up and he didn't leave anything." "Fanny hasn't got much in her life," says uncle Jack. "Just being an aunt isn't really the great career it may sometimes seems to be." An old maid, her behavior is motivated by contradictory feelings of love and envy and frustrated emotions for Eugene.

The film conveys the declining pride of the old order and the ascent of the industrious bourgeoisie, a theme explored in many books and films.[10] The tone of the movie is elegiac: Despite the historical necessity of progress and the inevitability of change, there is a price to be paid. Welles is ambivalent toward the notion of progress. In a crucial scene, when George describes cars as "useless nonsense," it is Eugene, the propagator of change, who says: "I'm not sure Georgie is wrong about automobiles. With all their speed forward, they may be a step backward in civilization." Eugene is aware that cars may not "add to the beauty of the world or the life of men's souls," but they are an irreversible fact, and as such are going "to alter war and to alter peace." He sees change as ubiquitous, permeating every aspect of life: "Men's minds are going to be changed in subtle ways because of automobiles." But through Eugene, Welles shows the incompatibility between the positive aspects of the old aristocratic order and the modern industrial age.

Mastering the language of cinema in *Citizen Kane,* Welles devotes more attention to characterization in *The Magnificent Ambersons;* the protagonists are individual creations rather than types, as they were in *Citizen Kane.* It is a deeper, more personal, work than *Citizen Kane,* even though it lacks the latter's narrative pull. Episodic by nature of the material, it is brilliant cinema. Welles's use of the iris to end scenes serves as an effective distancing device, which is also suitable in conveying the film's nostalgic mood. His punctuating narration provides commentary on the action as it goes along, never allowing the viewers to identify completely with the characters or the story. The juxtaposition of diegetic and nondiegetic sound is also innovative, marking the transition from his (offscreen) narration to the town's people commenting on the action, and from their words to the characters themselves.[11]

Welles claims that at least forty minutes were truncated from what he intended to be an American epic film. Still, *The Magnificent Ambersons*'s cinematic language is so powerful and innovative that it is a masterpiece even in its mutilated form. However, the resolution, a reconciliation between Lucy and George, imposed by the studio, negates what precedes it. Fortunately, this happy ending does not really mitigate the narrative's elegiac tone. There is a good deal of irony in the ending: George is injured in a car accident, the very car he objected to, and the accident occurs while he returns from work, the very essence of which was deplorable to him.

The Magnificent Ambersons opened in August 1942, one year after the release of William Wyler's *The Little Foxes,* based on Lillian Hellman's stage play. Comparisons between the two films were inevitable, and, surprisingly, some critics favored the Wyler film. For example, one critic wrote that *The Little Foxes* celebrates a similar theme, but had more cumulative power than *Magnificent,* though he admitted that Wyler's film lacked the tremendous talents that Welles demonstrated in his. Interestingly, the original viciousness in the Hellman work remained intact in the film version.

Set at the same time as *The Magnificent Ambersons,* around 1900, Hellman's morality drama examines the corruption and greed of the Hubbards, a second-generation family, in the Old South. Regina Giddens (Bette Davis), a shrewd businesswoman, schemes and plots, first against her dying husband, then against her two brothers. "You'll wreck the town," charges Horace (Herbert Marshall) at his ambitious wife. "You'll wreck the country, if they let you, you and your kind." Trapped in a loveless marriage to a submissive, sickly man, she tells him, "I've always had contempt for you." "Why did you marry me?" asks the helpless Horace. "I thought you'd get the world for me," she replies, conveying her disillusionment with love and marriage. At the end, she cold-bloodedly lets him die, refusing to hand him his medicine. Regina also loses her only daughter, Alexandra (Teresa Wright), whom she truly loves. Left alone, Regina is framed behind a window, imprisoned in her own house, as her daughter leaves with David, the seamstress's poor son from the wrong side of the tracks. Regina's greedy and domineering matriarch is the opposite of Isabel's submissive and sacrificing mother in *The Magnificent Ambersons*. And Alexandra, the sensitive adolescent, stands in diametric opposition to George.

Welles's second contribution to small-town movies was *The Stranger* (1946).[12] Harper, Connecticut, is a seemingly peaceful college town but, in actuality, it serves as a hiding place for war criminals. Franz Kindler (Orson Welles), a Nazi fugitive, who lives under the disguised identity of Professor Charles Rankin, is soon joined by his colleague Konrad Meineke (Konstantin Shayne), who still believes in the ideals of Nazism. Meineke's escape from jail was engineered by a determined government agent, Wilson (Edward G. Robinson), hoping to trail him to his superiors. A taut, if conventional, narrative, *The Stranger* is a cat-and-mouse game, set during the last days of a war criminal's life. The movie shows the irrationality and fear that invade—and almost destroy—a calm New England town. The narrative is strategically situated on Rankin's wedding day to Mary Longstreet (Loretta Young), a prominent society lady, whose father is a Supreme Court justice. This marriage, the last phase in his assimilation into American life, will finally put Rankin's mind at ease.

There are a number of outsiders in *The Stranger*. On the most obvious level, the stranger is Franz, an unwanted element, invading the most peaceful of settings, a calm town, and the most sacred of institutions, the school and church; one of Franz's obsessive hobbies is to repair old church clocks. But detective Wilson also plays an outsider: His sudden arrival sets in motion events that throw the ordinary town—and the orderly relationships of the Longstreet family—out of balance. Few of the characters are ordinary small-town residents. Mr. Potter (Billy House), for example, is ordinary by occupation, the proprietor of the local grocery store. But he has dark sides: he cheats at checkers and, prejudiced against strangers, he is too susceptible to conspiracies. The relationship between Franz and Mary is strange too: They declare love for each other, but there is no indication of intimacy or familiarity. Mary gradually realizes how little she knows her husband; she gets to know him through shocking, unpredictable outbursts of violence (one against their dog).

Filmed in black and white, *The Stranger* uses the stylistics of film noir.

It is also influenced by Hitchcock's *Shadow of a Doubt* in its treatment of the duality in human nature; here, in the motif of the double. Familial (and familiar) scenes are juxtaposed with scenes conveying fear and suspicion. Truffaut has pointed out that the sequence in which Welles saws the ladder rings in the church (to kill his wife), was lifted from *Shadow of a Doubt,* wherein Uncle Charlie saws the staircase so that his suspecting niece would fall to her death.[13] Nature, represented by the town's beautiful forest, becomes the scene of the crime, where Rankin hides the body of his Nazi friend. Just before committing the crime, Rankin runs into his students who are playing in the forest. The sharp cut from the joyful boys to the fearful Rankin conveys effectively the dual use of nature. The town's river, a place for fishing, becomes the meeting place of Wilson and Mary's brother, where they plan their moves against the professor. The church, ordinarily a sacred and unifying symbol, becomes the locale for Rankin's scheme against his wife and, later, his own death. In the original script, Rankin committed suicide, but in the film, to make it more dramatic and cinematic, he gets impaled on the bronze sword of the old clock; Rankin is killed by the object he likes best.

Welles's fans dislike *The Stranger* because it is a conventional, linear narrative film, "simple" in thematics and characterization. But this was precisely the point: Welles wanted to prove that he could direct a typical Hollywood film and bring it in on time and under budget. Paradoxically, the commercial appeal of *The Stranger* surpassed the combined grosses of Welles's more original films, *Citizen Kane* and *The Magnificent Ambersons.*

Neurosis and Psychosis: *Kings Row*

Like *The Magnificent Ambersons,* Sam Wood's *Kings Row* is conveniently situated at the turn of the century. And like *Magnificent,* it takes place in a Midwestern railroad town. The narrative begins in 1890, then jumps to 1900, following its characters through 1905. Like Hitchcock's *Shadow of a Doubt,* one of *Kings Row*'s themes is the duplicity of human nature. What is different, however, is the film's style, a Hollywood melodrama, compared with *Magnificent*'s epic scale and *Shadow*'s psychological thriller. Indeed, the best way to analyze *Kings Row* is as a melodrama, marked by excessive plotting, sentimental contrivances, exaggerated emotions, improbable motivations, and catharsis through tear-jerking.[14] The film abounds in problems of all kinds, some never treated with such explicitness on the screen before: insanity, homicide, suicide, incest, euthanasia, amputation, malpractice, and embezzlement. An uncharacteristic film of the 1940s (in tone and theme, it belongs to the 1950s), it is instructive that its release was postponed by several months—it opened in February 1942—because Warners felt uncomfortable about distributing such a film shortly after Pearl Harbor. However, the commercial success of *Kings Row* surpassed any expectations.[15]

Casey Robinson took liberties in adapting Henry Bellamann's novel about small-town frustrations. Fearing the impositions of the Production Code, the incestuous relationship between Dr. Tower and his daughter was changed into insanity; in the film, Dr. Tower kills his daughter, after realizing he is incapable of treating her insanity. Second, instead of the mercy killing of Parris's grandmother, she dies of cancer. Third, in the book, Drake dies of cancer as a result of unnecessary amputation, but in the film, Drake regains faith in life due to his wife's unbounded love and Parris's friendship.

In the opening scene, the camera travels slowly, then pauses on a road sign that says: "Kings Row. A good clean town. A good town to live in, and a good place to raise your children." As in other films, the sign is ironic, the town is anything but a good place to raise children. The first part, the prologue, is set on a nice spring afternoon. Two children, Parris Mitchell and Cassandra Tower, are walking from school through the field, resting, and enjoying nature. This hill, with its beautiful trees and grass, would later serve as a meeting point for the protagonists, where important secrets would be exchanged and personal confessions made. Throughout the film, nature is depicted as a place of escape from culture's repressions, represented by the kids' parents.

The first scene establishes the crucial attributes of the dramatis personae. Parentless, Parris lives with his grandmother in the nice side of town. An upper-class kid, he plays the piano and speaks French. Cassandra's father is the prestigious Dr. Alexander Tower (Claude Rains), whose wife is insane. Neither kid (nor the other children) has two parents; they are products of one-parent families. Parris is invited to two birthday parties on the same day: one for Louise Gordon, the other for Cassandra. The housekeeper gossips about the Towers' "strangeness" and suggests that Parris go to the Gordons' party, but grandmother interrupts her sharply: "Parris will decide for himself." The film thus cherishes the values of independent judgment. Indeed, dying of cancer, Parris's grandmother instructs him: "You have to judge people by what *you* find them to be, and not by what *other* people say they are." Appearances are deceptive and gossip is a vice to stay away from.

More than other movies of this decade, *Kings Row* stresses the importance of social class. Every character is subjectively aware of his or her class membership. Of the five protagonists, only Randy Monoghan (Ann Sheridan), is of the working class, living in a shack, on the other side of the tracks. Of Irish descent, she resides with her father (she has no mother) and brother, both working for the railroad company. Attractive in a natural fashion, she is the "healthiest," or least problematic, girl. As a youngster, she behaves like a tomboy, playing with and beating the boys; as a young woman, she becomes rational and forthright. The other, upper-middle-class, children are each problematic in one way or another. Cassandra Tower (Betty Field) is locked in her house by her father, prohibiting her to see anyone. She is a frightened, hysterical girl, peering behind closed doors. Her only chance of escape is to go with Parris to Vienna, but he wishes to finish his studies first. When her father finds out about her plan, he poisons her, then shoots himself. Louise Gordon (Nancy Coleman), a pretty but frail girl, is also kept indoors by her vicious parents, Dr. Gordon (Charles Coburn) and his wife (Judith Anderson). They forbid her to go out with Drake McHugh (Ronald Reagan) because he is "wild" and beneath her class. Her father uses force to impose his wish, slapping her when she threatens to reveal who he really is.

Drake starts as a rich kid (living on inherited allowance), but moves downtown after losing his fortune in a bank embezzlement. He has to start all over again, asking Randy's father, a railroad foreman, to employ him. The film contrasts Parris and Drake as two desirable role models. Drake is the outdoor type, carefree and happy-go-lucky. He is the complete extrovert, usually seen outdoors riding his horse carriage. Parris, by contrast, is the more intellectual type, sensitive and compassionate to the needs of others. Parris teaches Drake what he needs most: spiritual strength to meet his new, painful reality (crippled, his legs were unnecessarily amputated). And Drake brings real joy to Parris's life. They are presented as two complementary facets of ideal masculinity.

This contrast between indoor and outdoor types is consistent. With the exception of Randy, the women are placed indoors, often kept there against their will. They are withdrawn from the outside world and, by implication, from themselves. Social isolation goes hand in hand with self-estrangement and alienation. The recurrent visual motif is that of a woman standing behind closed windows, looking outside. Every house is divided into frontstage and backstage, to use Erving Goffman's dramaturgical terminology. Parris is asked by Dr. Tower to use the back door; he is not allowed to go upstairs, where Dr. Tower confines his wife (and later his daughter). Imprisoned in her own home, Louise Gordon looks forlornly through the window as Drake and his new flame, Randy, ride together in his carriage. Dr. Gordon's brutal operations are also executed on the second floor; he looks through the window as the children, downstairs, gossip about his sadistic torture of patients.

By taking the children's point of view, *Kings Row* anticipates the importance of youth culture in the 1950s. With few exceptions, the villains and causes of most problems are the oppressive and insensitive parents. Moreover, no member of the established professions is portrayed favorably. The bank president is corrupt, and Dr. Gordon is engaged in malpractice; a sadist, he uses no anesthesia in his operations. Dr. Gordon's "human" record is bad, but there is one exception: Parris's grandmother, whom he treats kindly because of her privileged class position.

The narrative provides an interesting view of the medical profession and the emerging field of psychiatry. Dr. Tower is a man who sacrificed his brilliant career when he settled down in Kings Row because of his wife's insanity. Serving as a tutor to Parris (whom he regards as surrogate son), he prepares him for medical school. "Do you want to be a good doctor or one of these country quacks (the imminent carpenter)?" asks Tower. As the hero of *Arrowsmith*, Parris wants to be a doctor like "those you read in books, the legendary sort of doctor." Dr. Tower's approach to medicine is "a game in which man pits his brain against the forces of destruction and disease." Psychiatry is the new, intriguing field, and the film acknowledges the influence of Freud and psychoanalysis on American culture. Randy and Drake cannot even pronounce the word when they first learn about Parris's intentions to become a psychiatrist, a further indication of her lower-class origins and his lack of sophistication.

Like *The Magnificent Ambersons*, the film's mood is elegiac. The values of the old social order are represented by Parris's grandmother, Madame Von Elm, French by birth, aristocratic by breeding, and one of the community's pioneers. When grandmother dies, "a whole way of life passes with her, a way of gentleness and honor and dignity that may never come back to the world." Yet *Kings Row* does not prescribe regression into the past; like *Magnificent,* it shows that life must go on. As much as reality may be painful, coming to terms with the "truth" is essential for the individual as well as community's welfare. This set of values (awareness of the "truth") will recur in numerous small-town films of the 1950s (See chapter 3).

While the leading roles in *Kings Row* are played by second-rate actors (Ronald Reagan, Robert Cummings), the supporting ones are cast with Hollywood's finest character players: Claude Rains, Maria Ouspenskaya, Judith Anderson, Charles Coburn, and Henry Davenport. The film is also distinguished in its high production values: Oscar-nominated cinematography by James Wong Howe, and production design by William Cameron Menzies (of *Gone with the Wind* and *Our Town* fame). Shot in black and white, the film employs some noir elements. Long shadows are cast in the indoor confrontational scenes, and close-ups are expressions of fear and horror and thus menacing rather than reassuring. The somber cinematography and disquieting editing stress the feelings of entrapment and claustrophobia. The low-key lighting and oblique camera angles accentuate the film's distorted vision. Erich Wolfgang Korngold's music has dark and oppressive tones, just as the thematics. One critic went so far as to praise *Kings Row* as "the first penetrating psychological study of small-town life, far superior in imagination, and more honest in treatment than Wilder's pussyfooting *Our Town*."[16]

Kings Row's view of the town as a community is at best ambiguous. The town contains good and evil, but no resident can escape its coercive influence, particularly children in their formative years. The themes of paranoia and duplicity—nobody could be trusted, not even your own family—overshadow the ending that, in tune with the times, was meant to restore social order and reassurance. Graduating from medical school, Parris returns to Kings Row and his first patient is Drake, his best friend. True love, overcoming obstacles (Drake and Randy's marriage), and the sacrifice involved in maintaining friendship, are all celebrated. At the time, the homoerotic overtones in the relationship between Drake and Parris eluded the viewers—and the censors. If this film were made in the 1950s, it probably would have ended with Randy and Drake leaving town and Parris staying in Vienna, but in the 1940s there was still belief in the town's moral power over its individuals.

Ideological Summation of an Era: *It's a Wonderful Life*

In 1946, the two major contenders for the Best Picture Award were: Capra's *It's a Wonderful Life* and William Wyler's *The Best Years of Our Lives*. Both directors had established reputations by that time: Capra with his three Oscars (for *It Happened One Night*, 1934; *Mr. Deeds Goes to Town*, 1936; and *You Can't Take It with You*, 1938) and Wyler with one award (*Mrs. Miniver*, 1942) and several nominations. *Best Years* emerged as the big winner, sweeping nine Oscars. Its immense popularity (the top grossing film of the year), as I have pointed out (1987), was a reflection not just of its artistic quality, but of the timeliness of its message and the cultural context in which it was viewed. The fact that *Wonderful Life* lost in all five categories, and that it was only a moderate success at the box-office, became the greatest disappointment in Capra's professional career: it was Capra's and Jimmy Stewart's first movie after a long military service. But film history vindicated Capra: it is recognized today as his indisputable masterpiece. *Wonderful Life*'s message would have fared better during the Depression, but not in the disillusioned mood of the country after 1945. The film's most impressive element is its nightmare sequence, a bitter and harrowing evocation of life without George Bailey and his values. At the time, however, the upbeat ending must have overshadowed its more pessimistic sequences.

Many people associate *Wonderful Life* with Christmas, which is not surprising. Christian themes feature prominently in Capra's work: In *Meet John Doe* (1941), the protagonist threatens to commit suicide on Christmas Eve. Screenwriters Frances Goodrich and Albert Hackett developed the idea for *Wonderful Life* from a Christmas card (in *Mr. Deeds*, the hero is a poet of greeting cards) and the narrative concludes on Christmas Eve. Moreover, television enhanced movie culture (before the "VCR Revolution"), contributing to this movie's visibility by showing it every Christmas. In his film, Capra deals with a universal fantasy: how would life look to a person if he had never been born.[17] George Bailey (James Stewart), a deeply depressed man, wishes he had never been born. It takes a guardian angel, Clarence Oddbody (Henry Travers) to show him what the world would be like if his wish had been fulfilled. Appalled by what he sees, he regains faith in his life.

Throughout his life, George wishes "to shake off the dust of this crummy little town." He wants to do big things, explore the world, construct skyscrapers and bridges. "I couldn't face being cooped up the rest of my life in a shabby little office," he tells his father. "This business is nickels and dimes. Spending all the rest of your life trying to figure out how to save three cents on a length of pipe—I'd go crazy." Ironically, he ends up actualizing his worst fears, running his father's business, Bailey Building and Loan Company, and never setting foot outside town. And he lives in a shabby house, with its knob falling whenever he climbs the stairs, signaling that George, like the knob, is falling apart.

Similarly to Mr. Deeds, the desperate George sees no other way out but to commit suicide, drown himself in the river. "I'm not a praying man," confesses George to God, "but if you're up there and you can hear me, show me the way." A Christian morality play about the loss and renewal of faith, the sight of George crying, "I'm at the end of my rope," is heartbreaking. It is only by negating what he possesses that George is able to reassess the value and meaning of his life. But how reassuring is this message if it takes the intervention of Divinity (God himself) to prevent George from terminating his life? In *Mr. Deeds,* it was at least human intervention, his encounter with a starving farmer, that rescued the hero. Moreover, unlike *Mr. Deeds* or even *Meet John Doe, Wonderful Life* differs from other Capra movies in its utter lack of humor, a possible indication of George's deep-seated despair.

George is contrasted with two young men, his brother Harry and his schoolmate Sam Wainwright. George wants to go to war, but is exempted for medical reasons: his hearing is impaired as a result of jumping into the river to save his brother from drowning. Harry distinguishes himself as a navy flier and comes back as a war hero, decorated with a Congressional Medal. Both Harry and Sam represent the risk, adventurism, and allure of the "outside" world. Sam's ambitions take him out of town, though the film looks down on industrial products, particularly plastic, a symbol of sterility and inauthenticity.[18] Sam's rewards are materialistic (money, power, prestige) whereas George's are spiritualistic (helping poor people who cannot get loans from a bank).

In the 1940s, the opportunities of a small-town boy consisted of: going to college, joining the army, getting a job and moving out of town, or marrying a girl from another town. *Wonderful Life* illustrates the unpredictability and irony of life chances. George makes four attempts to leave town, but there is always an obstacle (a crisis) that prevents him. The first time, he is about to go to Europe, but his father dies and he has to stay home. A childhood fantasy is shattered: All his life he has read with eagerness the *National Geographic* about far and exotic places. The second time, he is about to go to college, but is informed that his father's company would dissolve without him. On the third time, he wishes to be mobilized, but is disqualified and discharged from the army. The fourth time, he waits for Harry to graduate from college and take over the company. Instead, Harry marries a City girl and accepts a position in her father's glass factory.[19] Preaching for self-sacrifice, the movie documents the heavy price George has paid in his life. As a child, he jumped into the icy river to save his brother and subsequently lost his hearing in one ear. He also saved a patient's life, when he noticed that Mr. Gower inadvertently filled a prescription with poison, but the pharmacist beats him where it hurts most, at his ear.

Unlike other small-town films, the juxtaposition is not between small town and the Big City, but between life and no life at all. Life in this town is contrasted with nonexistence: the film suggests that any life is better than no life, thus diffusing the uniqueness of small-town life. In his nightmare, Bedford Falls has become Pottersville. Main Street is now empty of people, and there are many nightclubs, flashing their industrial look and neon lights. His wife, Mary Hatch (Donna Reed), is a spinsterish librarian, and Vi (Gloria Grahame), the good-time girl, is a prostitute walking the streets.

Structurally, the film uses flashbacks to highlight crucial events in George's life from age thirteen to thirty-nine (Stewart's age when he made the movie). The narrative is composed of several crises and their (temporary) resolution, all leading to the big crisis at the end. Alternation is another structural principle, contrasting bright and sunny episodes with darker ones, showing optimism and pessimism in equal measure. For example, George's date with Mary, a funny sequence, is abruptly terminated by the news of his father's death. Visiting Mary, she is on the telephone crying; her boyfriend Sam is in New York (with another girl). "Now you listen to me," says George, "I don't want to get married . . . ever . . . to anyone . . . you understand that? I want to do what I want to do!" But in the next scene, Capra makes a sharp cut to George's wedding! The Baileys spend their honeymoon, not in Bermuda, but in a dilapidated old house; ironically, it is the same house George had earlier pointed out to Mary, telling her he wouldn't be caught in this house "as a ghost."

Despite the fact that the narrative spans a generation (from 1919 to 1945), Bedford Falls has not changed much over the years. The town not only looks the same, its economic structure and values have remained intact.[20] Technology and the mass media (magazines, radio, movies) have apparently left no imprint on the town. Moreover, George has not experienced upward mobility; his fortunes are not better than his father's a generation ago. The only change is in the extent of debts: his father had to raise five thousand dollars, compared to George's eight thousand dollars. And both father and son are at the mercy of that greedy capitalist, Henry S. Potter (Lionel Barrymore).[21]

The weakest conception of character is that of Potter, a villain right out of Charles Dickens's books, described as "the richest and meanest man in the country." Evil incarnate, Potter is not only physically crippled (sitting in a wheelchair) but emotionally too. *Wonderful Life* may possibly be the only small-town film in which the villain is not punished for his crimes. At the bank, Uncle Billy absentmindedly leaves an envelope with eight thousand dollars in a newspaper, which falls too conveniently into Potter's hands. The conflict between good and evil is drawn too schematically: Potter has no redeeming qualities, except for his perceptiveness. Still, he is the only person who really understands George's frustrations. "Now if this young man of twenty-eight was a common, ordinary yokel," says Potter, "I'd say he was doing fine." But George is not a common, ordinary yokel, "he is an intelligent, smart, and ambitious young man who hates his job, who hates the Building and Loan almost as much as I do." Potter describes George as a man "who has been dying to get out on his own ever since he was born," but *instead,* "he has to sit by and watch his friends go places, because he's trapped into frittering his life away, playing housemaid to a lot of garlic-eaters."

Overall, Capra celebrates the heroism in living an ordinary life. George is meant to be an ordinary guy who becomes extraordinary in the most ordinary circumstances. George begins as a reluctant insider and ends as a willing insider: Throughout the film, his strongest wish is to become an outsider, literally and figuratively. If he cannot leave town, at least he will not get involved in other people's problems. But the film rules out detachment or partial involvement, preaching instead impartial belongingness and total commitment to the community. Still, unlike other small-town heroes, George is not a master of his fate: The film stresses the role of accidents and unanticipated events over which he has little, or no, control. The film also urges its viewers to accept their lives for what they are, to make the most out of mundane circumstances—optimistic passivity rather than aggressive activism. The reconciliation to domesticity (the sanctity of the nuclear family) and restoration of order may have diminished George's frustrations, but they can never make them altogether disappear. Capra, like other filmmakers, uses the train's whistle as a reminder of the outside world, of potential excitement away from Bedford Falls (George is at the train station for the farewell or welcome of his brother, which is all the more frustrating). The train whistle will continue to remind George of lost opportunities and missed adventurism. In this respect, *Wonderful Life* is one of the gloomiest movies ever made.

Rural Life: Old and New Visions—*Sergeant York* and *The Southerner*

If John Ford's *The Grapes of Wrath* (1940) celebrated the tenacity of country folks and simplicity of rural life with protest and anger, *Sergeant York*, released in 1941, performed the same ideological function in a quieter, and sentimental, way.[22] Bosley Crowther provided the best advertisement when he described the film as having "all the flavor of true Americana, the blunt humor of backwoodsmen, and the raw integrity peculiar to simple folk."[23] Nominated for eleven Academy Awards, winning two (for acting and writing), *Sergeant York* became the year's top-grossing film. Based on Alvin York's diary, the film set precedent by presenting the saga of a celebrity still alive. *Sergeant York* traces its hero's life from 1916, in "the Valley of the Three Forks," to the end of World War I. It is a tale of transformation of a Tennessee mountaineer-farmer, from an obscure hillbilly to a great national hero. As such, it belongs to the genre of films about ordinary protagonists who become *extraordinary*, as a result of charismatic personality and social circumstances. The film demonstrates the democratic credo that heroes are not born, but made, and that they could come from the most remote and unlikely places.

The young Alvin York (Gary Cooper) is a fun-loving man who likes to drink and to brawl. Back home, he is reproached by his mother (Margaret Wycherly), who believes that "a little religion won't do him any harm." Similarly to Ma Joad, Mother York is another Mother Earth, a widow aged beyond her years by the hardship of mountain life. Pastor Rosier Pile (Walter Brennan) explains that the issue is not praying, but believing. However, York holds that "there ain't no use for a feller to go out lookin' for religion," to which the Pastor replies, "It'll come when you ain't even lookin' fer hit, like a bolt of lightnin'." The film cherishes historical tradition and continuity: A close-up of a pine tree's carved trunk shows: "Dan'l Boone Kilt a Bar Here 1760."

Shy with women (as *Young Mr. Lincoln*'s hero), York's courtship of Gracie Williams (Joan Lesley) is understated. He is contrasted with his rival, Zeb Andrews, a "smart," arrogant guy who talks a lot; Zeb is shown helping Gracie knitting! An inevitable brawl kicks Zeb out of the way— and out of Gracie's life. "Why did you fight?" asks Gracie. "Because I'm gonna marry you," says York. "Ye're no good, 'cept fer fightin' an' hell-raisin'," she says, but York is determined. "A piece of bottomland would make a heap o' difference. There ain't nothing I can't get if I set my min' to it," he says, repeating a familiar phrase uttered by other heroes *(Young Mr. Lincoln)*. York brings soil to his house and looks at it with fascination, but his mother says, "Folks who live at the bottom look down at folks at the top; always like that, no change." "I'm gonna get it!" he states with heroic determination. Hawks uses a montage, showing York plowing the barren land with two mules and a crude plow share—a single man pitted against nature with its vast lands and big skies.

As most heroes of this fiction, York's goal is to own *his* own land. Swindled and cheated—the land promised to him had been sold—he sets out to kill the man. "I took your word," says York, for whom a man's word is more binding than a contractual agreement. The Pastor and Gracie try to console him, "It don't make difference." "It does to me," he says. "This land was mine. Nobody's going to take it away from me." Struck by lightning during a storm, York experiences a moment of revelation and subsequently becomes deeply religious. "Give me that old-time religion," he asks the Pastor as he goes into church. Drafted for service in World War I, York registers as a conscientious objector. Major Buxton gives him an American history book that evokes the name of Daniel Boone. Isolated in nature, he absorbs its contents, coming to terms with his own feelings about defense and freedom. This scene has similar effect to the one in *Young Mr. Lincoln,* wherein Lincoln discovers the meaning of the law. In both, the hero must understand the new principles for *himself* and from *within*. The film stresses York's great conscience struggle before joining the army. "Obey your God," says the Pastor's voice, countered by Major Buxton's dictate, "Defend your country." A reconciliation of the two symbols, God and country, is required, and York reaches the conclusion that the two are in harmony because they mean the same thing. In *Young Mr. Lincoln* too, the two symbols, the Bible and the *Farmer's Almanac,* both sacred (standing for God and nature) provide the base for Lincoln's authority because they mean the same thing.[24]

As was the custom in many films of the 1940s, *Sergeant York* begins with a "message" narration: "Before America entered the World War, the people of this secluded land had lived almost wholly apart from the civilization that had flourished around them. Isolated in remote villages, rocky highlands—with few schools—untouched by railroads or highways—they had retained the customs, the tools and weapons of their colonial ancestors, their simple, hard ways of life—and their belief in God." Indeed, the community, in which the Pastor is also the proprietor of the general store, is not up to date; the newspapers are at least three days old. Its economy is rather primitive, based on barter; York exchanges eggs for a bar of soap. The film concludes with York's return to his routine life in Tennessee, observing his land. It thus goes full circle: the transformation of York from ordinary to extraordinary (international war hero) and back to ordinary citizen (peace-loving farmer).

During World War II, farming lost the urgency it had during the Great Depression. As a screen type, the American farmer was replaced with the soldier, first fighting in combat, then readjusting to civilian life. This could explain the fact that one of the best films about the rural South, *The Southerner* (1945), was directed by a foreigner, Jean Renoir, the noted French filmmaker. As an outsider, during the time he was in Hollywood in exile, Renoir showed the other, more realistic, side of country life. *Swamp Water* (1941), his first American film, set in the Okefenokee Swamp, featured striking cinematography and interesting ambience, but it was marred by a weak story and even weaker performance by Walter Brennan (miscast as a fugitive). *The Southerner* was a better film, narratively and stylistically, winning Renoir his first (and only) Academy nomination as Best Director. The lyrical realism of this film, shot entirely on location, and its meticulous attention to detail, startled critics and audiences at the time. One critic wrote that the film makes "an interesting departure from the grove of Hollywood pictures,"[25] and another stated that "it may not be entertaining in the rigid Hollywood sense."[26]

A tribute to the staunch farmer, this grim film chronicles the plight of poor white sharecroppers, fighting storms, pellagra, and other disasters. Lacking dramatic focus, the film consists of twenty-two episodes[27] in the life of a farming family: Sam Tucker (Zachary Scott), his tireless wife Nona (Betty Field), their two children, and the acidulous Granny (Beulah Bondi). The narrative follows the Tuckers' struggle to work the land in the face of immense adversities: poverty, disease, bad weather, imminent threats to foreclose the farm, and unfriendly neighbors. It begins with an offscreen narration, repeating the message of *Young Mr. Lincoln* and *Sergeant York:* "When old Sam gets an idea in that hard head of his, there ain't no room for nothin' else."

A hymn to the human spirit, which may despair but never fails, this film's beauty is in its portrayal of daily survival: plowing the land, planting the seeds, milking the cow, building shacks, mending clothes, fixing dinner, etc. *The Southerner* deviates from most rural films of the decade in its reversal of conventions and stereotypes. Unlike *York,* it refrains from sentimentalizing farmers. For example, the "villain" is not a City person (usually a banker), but a farmer, Devers (J. Carroll Naish), the embittered neighbor, who cannot stand Sam's pride and determination to succeed. When Sam goes to Devers to ask for milk for his sick child, he is not only rejected, but Devers viciously dumps gallons of milk. "I had old-fashioned ideas about neighborliness," says the disenchanted Sam. However, the film avoids easy judgments, using Devers's past as an explanation for his behavior: "The first year, my whole crop was ruined by the hail. The second year, the hoof 'n' mouth took my cow and pig. My woman caught cold and died. Two years later, one of my kids died from spring sickness. Mebbe I lost 'em both, cause I didn't have no money for doctorin'." Nasty competition, not collaboration, is the pattern: Devers can't wait for Sam to fail to buy out his land. Finley (Norman Lloyd), another farm worker, is also depicted as vindictive and stupid. By contrast, the City fellow, Tim (Charles Kemper), a close friend of the family (and the film's narrator), is more sympathetic than the country folks.

The film's central piece is a storm, a devastating spectacle, never before depicted so accurately and graphically. The cotton, on both sides of the road, is flattened by the wind and the rain, the road transforms into mud, and the house leans over precariously; part of its roof is off. Desolation is everywhere: trees, parts of the house, and debris are carried down the current. Sam is trying—in vain—to keep the cow, "Uncle Walter," from being swept away by the current. In such weak moments, Sam, as other screen farmers, considers quitting. "I gave 'em everything I had to give, honest," he says angrily, "and what do they give me back? Nothin', nothin' but trouble and misery." "I'd be crazy to stick any longer," he says. "A feller ought to know when he's beat." Granny is not the supportive type of Mother Earth, in the mold of Ma Joad or Mother York. Acidulous and irascible, she charges Sam with being "a mean criminal." She wants to quit: "I'm takin' this weary ol' body d'rect to the cemetery . . . don't even have a decent place to sit 'n wait for my call to glory." But the indomitable Nona, who keeps the family together, says, "A time like this, folks gotta stick t'gether," threatening Granny with a stick. "Ya'll stay right here with the rest o' us."

The Southerner shows nature, physical and human, in its most complex and contradictory facets. As a force, nature can be destructive as well as regenerative and healing. The film also shows the dialectical relationship between faith and failure, optimism and pessimism in *equal* measures, an uncharacteristic balance in American farm movies. The last episode, in which the Tuckers reassess their land after a violent storm, is far from a conventional, reassuring ending. Sam regains his faith: "Now that my clothes is startin' to dry, I'm beginnin' to b'lieve again." "I knowed it all 'long," says Tim, "that you'd never leave here. Man, if there was only one farmer left on this here earth, that's be you!" Full of resolve and eager to get started, Sam says in the film's last sentence: "Spring's gonna come a little early this year. I reckon we kin start our seedin' even before the Twin Days." Hitching up the mules to the plow, with Sam in the back and Nona up ahead, the Tuckers begin *once again* to work the devastated fields. But, there is good reason to believe that the nasty side of nature will strike again.

Original Vision of Small-Town America: *The Miracle of Morgan's Creek* and *Hail the Conquering Hero*

Preston Sturges also made movies about small towns during World War II but, compared with most of Hollywood's war products set in small towns (*Tortilla Flat*, 1942; *The Human Comedy*, 1943; *The Fighting Sullivans*, 1944; and *A Medal for Benny*, 1945), in their theme, wit, and style, Sturges's films seem to have been created in another country. In similar vein to Welles and Hitchcock, both intrigued with exposing the darker and invisible facets of small towns, Sturges confronted his subject matter in an original way, turning upside down established conventions of Hollywood's small-town films. But it was not originality for originality's sake: The eccentricities of Sturges's characters mean to demonstrate the more multifarious and resourceful nature of small-town folks who only *appear* to be plain and ordinary.

Sturges's comedies, beginning with *Sullivan's Travels* (1941), reflected the thematic and stylistic influence of film noir on every genre at the time, including screwball comedies. Along with Billy Wilder, whose directorial career began at the same time, Sturges's comedies embody a cynical view, exposing the downbeat side of "normal" American life. As some critics observed, Sturges incorporated into his comedies "noirish sentiments of meaninglessness and abject existentialism."[28] Flaunting a caustic and crackling dialogue, his comedies portray not winners, but losers, individuals who resort to absurd strategies to survive the day. Sturges's protagonists refuse to accept "the hand of fate" as a controlling force of their lives, attempting to overcome insurmountable obstacles; that they seldom succeed is beside the point. Moreover, unlike noir heroes, they are not weary or beaten by life, there is always hope that life might turn out better for them. Sturges's brilliant style combines sparkling situations with witty dialogue, a mixture of farce and slapstick in the tradition of crude American comedy.

In *Hail the Conquering Hero* and *The Miracle of Morgan's Creek* (both in 1944), Sturges expresses ambivalent emotions toward basic American values and institutions. *Hail* centers around an army reject, who is accidentally thought to be a war hero. *Miracle* is a satirical folktale, spoofing just about all sacred mores, including motherhood. Indeed, in his review of *Miracle*, Crowther wondered how Sturges "ever got away with such a thing, how he persuaded the Hays Office he wasn't trying to undermine all morals."[29] The truth is that the film's release *was* delayed for several months because of censorship problems, but the approved version was most satisfactory.

A young girl goes out with a soldier, and the next thing she knows she has a wedding ring and is pregnant, lacking the slightest idea as to her husband's identity or whereabouts. In despair, she turns to her childhood friend who always loved her, "trapping" him into marriage. But at the end she "redeems" herself by marrying him and giving birth to sextuplets, all boys. The film acknowledges humorously its political context. A montage of international newspapers shows the reaction of the two Fascist leaders, Hitler and Mussolini, who seem to jump off the front pages upon hearing about the sextuplets. Some viewers were apparently outraged by *Miracle*'s plot device. "Many letters have been received here," wrote Sturges, "including bitterly denunciatory ones from unalphabets who believed the sextuplets were the result of the heroine having been promiscuous with six different men." "Education," Sturges noted, "though compulsory, seems to be spreading slowly."[30]

No issue or profession is too sacred for Sturges's biting sting, least of all politicians. The Governor (Brian Donlevy) initially doesn't even recognize the town's name. "What was the town again? Is it in my state? I never heard of it." By contrast, believing that Morgan's Creek will be the most famous town in America, the newspaper's editor asks for "State Police, food, water, beds, and blankets." "You got a flood or did you strike oil, or something?" inquires the governor. "Get a map of the state and make sure Morgan's Creek is in it," he instructs. "If it isn't, we might be able to persuade them to move over or something." He then advises the political boss (Akim Tamiroff): "You better get down to Morgan's Creek and buy up a few choice corners—some hotel sites maybe . . . and the bus franchise will be very valuable." At this point, the governor announces: "This is the biggest thing that's happened to this state since we stole it from the Indians." "Borrowed," the boss corrects him.

Each character in *Miracle* is an eccentric *individual,* not a type. Sturges reverses the prevalent images of the boy and girl next door and inverts the meanings of masculinity and femininity, spoofing machoism as well as female domesticity. Trudy Kockenlocker (Betty Hutton) is anything but the innocent or repressed small-town girl. She is assertive and loves the company of men. A bit selfish, she wants to have fun, always seeking to be the center of attention. In an early scene, she is seen singing to admiring male customers in her record store. Later, surrounded by soldiers, she drives Norval's borrowed convertible. Trudy has boundless energy. "I never get tired," she boasts to her sister, and Sturges shows Trudy going from one party to another. She is also manipulative, repeatedly abusing Norval's trust. Trudy combines traits of the girl-next-door and the town's popular girl (most small-town films separate between the two types).

It is Norval (Eddie Bracken), not Trudy, who longs for conformity to conventional, middle-class, values: marriage and domesticity. Exempt from military service, with 4-F, he says: "Every time they start to examine me, I become so excited, I get the spots!" Norval lacks control over his two main goals: to fight in the war and to marry Trudy. A bank clerk, he is an orphan, living with the Johnsons, the town's lawyer and his wife. Full of doubts, all of his fears materialize in the film, including going to jail. A helpless, yet sincere, boy, his romanticism is genuine and heartfelt. It is therefore ironic that, by sheer accident, Norval becomes the symbol of virility: the father of six boys.

Trudy's widower father, officer Kockenlocker (William Demarest), is the town's constable. A severe man, his favorite recreational activity is to clean his gun on the front porch. Trudy's sister Emma (Diana Lynn), a fourteen-year-old brat, defies her father's authority, lacking any respect for him. "I think you have a mind like a swamp!" she tells her father. Contemptuous of his coarseness, Emma wishes he would be "a little more refined." Her father's aggressiveness is both verbal and physical, kicking her around, telling her she has "ladder legs," etc. But once in a while, when both are in a quiet mood, she enjoys sitting on his lap. Emma is brighter and more sophisticated than Trudy; she is the type of girl who—in a more conventional movie—would leave town for the Big City. It is Emma who gives Trudy the idea to marry Norval to save her face. "He was made to be a patsy," says Emma, "like the ox was made to eat, and the grape was made to drink."

When a soldier asks, "which church is giving the dance tonight?" the father's angry response is, "How many churches you think we got?" It is one of the few direct observations about the town as a whole. Shot on the studio lot, there are not many outdoor scenes. The town, shown when Trudy and Norval stroll along, is clean-looking with white picket fences and large yards; the residents like to sit on their front porches and observe the scene. Its landmarks are the typical institutions: the movie house, the drugstore, the gas station, the pool hall. But even here, Sturges deviates from conventions. Trudy and Norval go to the movie house, *not* to watch a film or to "neck"; she drops him there, so that she can borrow his car and have fun with other men.

There is, of course, gossip, especially when it concerns courtship and love, but the gossip is not malicious. The bank's president, Mr. Tuerck (Emory Parnell) tells Norval he heard about his engagement to Trudy from Mr. Shottish, the neighbor who spotted Norval in the morning, after presumably a wild night on the town (ironically, Norval spent the night by himself, waiting for Trudy to come back). It is none of *his* personal business, Mr. Tuerck says, "what time you get home in the morning, or how drunk you are when you do get home," but "it's the *bank's* business. A man in a bank is like a fellow crossing Niagara Falls on a tightrope; he cannot be too careful."

Desperate over her pregnancy and with no solution in sight, Trudy says she will jump into the river together. But Norval's objection is rational: It won't work because "there's not much water at this time of year." Trudy then suggests gas poisoning, but this is also unacceptable. "What's the matter with bigamy?" he asks. At the end, trapping Norval into marrying her, Trudy becomes a legitimate mother. "You're a papa now," *she* says, specifying his new obligations. "The papa gives love and protection." Norval is the ultra-adjustable type, always adapting to the needs of others, aiming to please. Viewers are told that Norval "recovered and became increasingly happy," and Shakespeare is used for the film's coda: "Some are born great, some achieve greatness, and some have greatness thrust upon them." Norval has greatness thrust upon him.

Miracle debunks many myths of small-town America. The town's normal state of being is not order, but disorder; chaos is the norm. The residents crave to achieve celebrity status, do *anything* that will alleviate them from their humdrum lives. Sturges takes the most basic events, marriage and birth, and turns them upside down, showing their comic *and* horrible effects. "No one's going to believe something good if they can believe something bad," says Emma, expressing Sturges's view of small towns. "You don't know what to expect in a town like this," she explains, "a town that can produce schnooks like Papa, always suspicious and suspecting the worst in everything."

In *Hail the Conquering Hero* Sturges's targets are both the public (the fetish of heroism) and domestic (the cult of momism) domains. He probes into society's need for heroes and the ease with which such heroes are fabricated and revered by the masses. Once again, ironies abound in the film. The hero, boasting the long and prestigious name of Woodraw Lafayette Pershing Truesmith (Eddie Bracken), is an orphan whose father was a war hero. Embarrassed over the fact that he was dismissed from service because of chronic hay fever, he lies to his mother that he has fought with the Marines, concealing the fact that he is actually working in a shipyard. A group of marines in a San Francisco bar take his story one step further, determined to make him a war hero in his own town. What his sponsors do not realize is the mass hysteria induced by the hero-worshiping crowds. The film offers a witty commentary on demagoguery and mob behavior, suggesting that as easily as a crowd could be persuaded to lynch an innocent man, it could also be susceptible to accept phonies as heroes. Practically the whole town of Oakridge is at the train station to greet Woodraw, with not one but four bands. "I'm a haunted man for the rest of my life," says Woodraw helplessly, realizing he is trapped in a position over which he has no control.

A comparison between *Miracle* and *Hail* is in order, not only because they were made in the same year and shot on the same Paramount backlot, but because they feature Sturges's great ensemble of character players. The hero in both films is played by Eddie Bracken, though his role is quite different. In *Miracle,* he is an orphan, living at the periphery of town, but ending at its center by accident, through manipulations of others. In *Hail,* Woodraw is also fatherless, but he boasts a prestigious lineage. Woodraw was reared in the shadow of his father, Hinky Dinky, a brave marine who died in action in World War I, and his Congressional Medal of Honor. "I grew up with it," says the exasperated Woodraw. "They hung it on me." His grandfather, also in the military, continued to wear his Civil War uniform for the rest of his life. Unlike *Miracle,* in *Hail,* Woodraw is not completely innocent; after all, *he* initiates the fraud. He is responsible at least in part for the mess in his life. But if Woodraw is initially a small impostor, his fraud gets bigger and bigger, reaching a point where it becomes disproportionate to the original conceit.

The reverend Dr. Upperman states at the church that the mortgage on the home of Woodraw's mother will be paid by the town. The incumbent mayor (ironically named Everett Noble) and the boss are both corrupt. The judge wishes Woodraw would run for mayor: the town needs someone who will help them "transcend their own lives and interests." He thinks Woodraw possesses two great assets, honesty and popularity and that he has a "natural flavor for politics." Honesty is not sufficient in itself. The other candidate, Doc Bissell, a veterinarian, is an honest man, but nobody would vote for him other than his brother; there are even doubts whether his wife would. Woodraw tries to explain that his medals were pinned on him by mistake, but no one will listen.

Hail shows that society needs heroes desperately—even if they are fake—and that they are not expected to substantiate their claim to celebrity. "I been a hero, you could call it that, for twenty-five years," says Sergeant Heffelinger, "and does anybody ask me what I done?" If they asked him, he could hardly tell, as he has told it "so different so many times." The statue of General Zabriski, which decorates the town's square, also suffers from obscurity. "All everybody knows is he's a hero," but no one could identify him or say why he became a hero. The only difference between Zabriski and Heffelinger is that the birds sit on the former's statue.

The most outrageous character in *Hail* is Bugsy (Freddie Steele), the marine who "got a little shot." Obsessed with mothers, he is shocked to hear that Woodraw has not visited home. "That's a terrible thing to do to your mother," he says. "You ought to be ashamed of yourself." Obsession with motherhood prevails from the very first scene, in a San Francisco bar, where a singer sings:

> *Home to the arms of Mother*
> *Safe from the world's alarms*
> *As you stood in the gloaming*
> *To welcome me home . . .*
> *Home to the arms of Mother . . .*
> *Never again to roam!*

Touching (too) familiar chords, Woodraw asks for another song, "something gay." Woodraw is also mother-fixated, his behavior motivated by a strong need to please her. "I know you meant it for me, no matter what anyone else might think," says his mother. And at the end, when he resolves to leave town, he tells his mother: "If I can find a nice place, I'll send for you."

Back in town, Woodraw has no time for himself and no privacy. Sturges pits Woodraw, the hapless individual, against the marines, the bands, the judge's delegation, the town's crowd. Sturges's frames are extremely busy, always cramped with many people. Lacking depth or background, they convey the frantic world his narratives are set in. Yet, as James Harvey noted, "no one in a Sturges's crowd fails to register his special and unique relation to it and to the others."[31] It's not an anonymous, faceless crowd, as in *Fury* or *Young Mr. Lincoln*. As a town, Oakridge is more individualized and richly characterized than Morgan's Creek: It is a close-knit community with a strong "we" feeling. With all their eccentricities and peculiarities, the characters in Sturges's film are integrated within larger contexts, as members of social groups. The interest of such groups is always superior to the individual's interest. For example, the marines who bring Woodraw back to town are unified in a camaraderie. The warm welcome they receive, particularly from Woodraw's mother, makes them want to belong. They adopt Woodraw, taking excellent care of him; Bugsy watches Woodraw while he is asleep. But the marines are outsiders and, as such, have to leave town so that order and some equilibrium could be restored. Creating chaos and precipitating a chain of events they themselves could not have foreseen, their departure is necessary. At the last scene, set at the train station, the whole town waves good-bye to them.

Woodraw is also an outsider, but temporarily so. The town is willing to do anything to embrace him—not only to make him an insider, but to crown him as its leader. When Woodraw tells his former sweetheart, Libby (Ella Raines), that he is a phony, she exclaims in disbelief, "You—a phony?" Sturges reverses another convention: In most war films, it is the girlfriend or wife who is unfaithful, dating others while their men are fighting (*A Medal for Benny, Best Years of Our Lives, Swing Shift*). But in *Hail*, Woodraw decides to release Libby from commitment to their relationship. Another strategy Woodraw considers is to start an honest life somewhere else. Standing on a platform at the political rally, Woodraw finally confesses his deception, taking the whole blame on himself. "I stole your admiration," he says. "I stole the ribbons I wore. I stole the nomination." Relieved of the burden he has carried, Woodraw feels like a "coward, at last cured of his fear." But Woodraw's revelation demonstrates that he *is* honest, making him a *real* hero. He is nominated again, this time for his true self. Woodraw thus becomes a local hero in spite of himself!

In both *Miracle* and *Hail*, Sturges's style is hyperbolic and the pace rapid. His camera moves fast, people are always on the move, there are many pratfalls. An example of Sturges's touch is the hospital sequence in *Miracle*, with the nurse running in panic in and out of Trudy's room, bringing a blanket for the first baby, then another blanket, and another. . . . The hectic speed of *Miracle* and *Hail* conveys the notion of life in constant motion, of dynamic reality, even in small towns. In *Hail*, and to a lesser extent in *Miracle*, Sturges uses the basic paradigm of balance, followed by disruption-imbalance, and then back to balance. However, Sturges's small towns never seem to be in total balance or complete equilibrium. Sturges's vision of small-town life is richer and more complex than Capra's, stressing inherent tensions, contradictions, and ironies in such life. In Capra's message-oriented films, appearances are deceiving and one has to dig deeper to reveal the genuine human essences buried underneath (most women in Capra's films begin as deceivers, but later reveal themselves to be honest). By contrast, in

Sturges's work, appearances have their own reality and logic and, as such, are just as important as the "deeper essences."

Small-Town Housewives: *Beyond the Forest*

With the exception of *Shadow of a Doubt,* most protagonists of small-town movies in the 1940s were males (adolescents or adults). The few films that examined women usually revolved around the family, such as *Kings Row* or *Miracle of Morgan's Creek.* In this context, Bette Davis's star vehicle, King Vidor's *Beyond the Forest* (1949),[32] stands out not only in focusing exclusively on a female heroine, but also in presenting a discontented housewife who challenges the sacred institutions of marriage and motherhood. Nonetheless, similarly to other films at the time, she is examined from a strictly male point of view.

The King Vidor film is an excessively plotted noir melodrama in which the heroine, Rosa Moline (Bette Davis), is a disenchanted housewife, living with her good (but dull) doctor-husband (Joseph Cotten) in Loyalton, a lumber town in Wisconsin. Bored and contemptuous of her middle-class life, Rosa throws herself into a passionate affair with a Chicago industrialist. Her motive, actually obsession, is to move to Chicago, for which purpose she has no scruples in using her husband's patient bills. But the affair is broken off when her lover informs her he is engaged to another woman. Returning to her husband, she gets pregnant. Her husband hopes that the baby will soften her and solidify their faltering marriage. But seeing no alternative, Rosa jumps off a speeding car and suffers a miscarriage. She develops blood poisoning, and, refusing to take medicine, finds her death on the way to the station, missing the train that was going to liberate her.

The film begins with a voice-over narration: "This is the story of evil. Evil is headstrong. For our soul's sake, it is salutary for us to view it in all its ugly nakedness once in a while." Viewers are given no opportunity to make up their own judgment, and the warning by an unseen male voice, not only objectifies the story, but also distances it from the viewers, making Rosa a clinical case study. Vidor frames the story in a long flashback, which begins at the court where Rosa stands trial (for shooting a neighbor, Moose, who threatens to expose her illicit affair) and which occupies most of the narrative.

Stranded and suffocated in this claustrophobic community, Rosa describes it as "a two-train-a-day town." A passionate woman, she excels in typically male pursuits: She plays pool and is good at shooting. Rosa thinks kindly only of the town's undertaker, because he can terminate her suffering. She sums up her life as "sitting in a coffin and waiting to be carried out." "What a dump," she exclaims on another occasion, making this line immortal as high camp.[33] Rosa is literally a freak, a spectacle for the town members (and the film viewers). The issue of woman as spectacle, as Mary Ann Doane has observed, is linked closely to the voyeuristic position of film viewers, particularly male.[34] Rosa's sexy, hip-swinging walk provokes laughter and whistling, and she is the object of gossip and ridicule. An outcast, Rosa is a complete outsider. She always was. "Even in high school," one woman says, "she was different from everybody else." At her trial, the women are wondering, as the narrator says, "if at last they're going to hear the secret of Rosa's life." She is presented as an enigma, a mystery that needs to be resolved. Rosa not only acts callous, she also looks mean. Wearing a wig of long black hair, Bette Davis is heavily made up, looking like a grotesque caricature.

Beyond the Forest contrasts Loyalton with Chicago. Whenever Rosa goes to—or thinks about—Chicago, the sound track plays the melodic song "Chicago, Chicago" (which Judy Garland made popular). The same tune is played when she strokes a woman's mink coat, a symbol of the City's glamour. However, neither town nor city is favorably treated by Vidor. Chicago's skyscrapers loom menacingly in the background, and in one harrowing scene, Rosa is walking in back streets. She has just been asked to leave a bar, where women "without escorts" are not welcomed. Walking in the rain in an empty street, a woman screams at her from the balcony. The film suggests that it is a nightmare to be a lonely woman in the Big City. In the City, Rosa's clothes are dark-colored, contrasted with the brighter colors she wears in town. The only peaceful scenes of nature are outside town. Rosa's tryst is carried out in an exotic lodge in the woods, surrounded by a beautiful lake. The camera crosscuts between Rosa, making love to Ned, and her husband at work, helping a woman give birth.

Vidor repeatedly cuts from Rosa, burning with unrealized sexual energy, to the blast furnace of the local mill seen from her window. Loyalton's skies are burning at night with the sawmill's flames, just like Rosa. She is trapped in a sexless marriage, the film acknowledges, though it does not approve of her need for any sexual outlet. Unable to sleep at night, Rosa is restless, smoking in bed. She asks Lewis to pull down the shades, to protect her eyes from the hot glow of sawdust in the air, but also to make her forget the outside world, a constant reminder of an alternative, more desirable life-style. Rosa is obsessive about moving to Chicago, not for the career opportunities there, but for the prospects of being independent and living a glamorous life only the Big City can offer. "Excitement, Jenny," she screams at her housekeeper, "have you never heard of excitement!" Unlike the heroine of *Mildred Pierce*, Rosa is not a career woman, but a dissatisfied housewife who defies society's conventions of happiness for women. She detests the very notion of becoming a mother, and here the film is at its most audacious. Her pregnancy is described by Rosa as "a mark of death," not as the symbol of life; being pregnant means her body is dead as a *woman*. "You're a rotten doctor," she charges her husband, resenting her pregnancy. Told by him that "all I care about is *my* baby," she retorts, "I'll kill myself first." Contemptuous of motherhood, she tells a woman who had just given birth to her eighth child: "You certainly go for mass production, don't you?" Rosa is perceived as a selfish woman. Concerned with *her* personal needs, she embodies excessive individualism. Rosa's refusal to become a mother is all the more significant because of the Baby Boom around her in the postwar years.

Dr. Lewis Moline is a good-natured, but weak and ineffectual husband; it is hard to understand what attracted Rosa to him in the first place—perhaps the prestige of his job or the security it provided. By contrast, her lover, Ned Latimer (David Brian), a high-powered Chicago operator, is a womanizer. When she finally tracks him down, he tells her he has met the woman of his dreams: "She's a book with none of the pages cut." "And nothing on them," Rosa quickly answers. Ned implies that Rosa is an old book, with many pages cut. Returning home humiliated and dejected, she presses her house's "Doctor's night bell." Using the "Doctor's bell" and submitting to Lewis makes Rosa his *patient*, not wife. Indeed, Lewis treats her kindly, as a patient, undressing her and handing her a glass of milk.

There are only two other women in the film. Karen Lost (Ruth Roman) is Moose's elegant daughter from Chicago; the mink coat belongs to her. The other woman is Rosa's Indian housekeeper, Jenny (Dona Drake), a vulgar and gum-chewing girl who is a cruder version of Rosa. Jenny is of a lower class, but she is as surly, slattern, and defiant as Rosa, refusing to take any commands. Both are antisocial "monsters," the difference between them a matter of degree.

The nominal star of *Beyond the Forest* is Rosa, but the real star is the train station. One of Rosa's routine activities is to wear her sexy clothes and walk to the station—to watch the trains leaving for Chicago. At the film's climax, Rosa drags herself out of bed and wears excessive makeup. Delirious from an attack of peritonitis, she is in a hurry to catch the next train. Vidor uses a montage of images of the furnace, and a traveling shot to convey the train station from both sides. The camera follows Rosa from behind, then moves to the other side, showing her approach the platform and drop dead.

Significantly, at the trial, Rosa is exonerated for the murder, though it is clear she has killed Moose by design. But she is punished with death for transgressing sexual mores, for being an adulterous wife and deviant mother, inducing her own abortion. Rosa is one of the first screen heroines to insist on establishing an identity that goes beyond marital or maternal obligations. As such, she is not only an outsider but an outcast, and there can be only one fate for such a status: annihilation. Following the typical closure of classic narrative cinema, *Beyond the Forest* says that if one cannot restore a woman to domesticity, one might as well exterminate her.

Conclusion

In the 1940s, the traditional ways of depicting small towns prevailed along with the more innovative movies. However, few of the experimental films, *Our Town, Shadow of a Doubt, Magnificent Ambersons,* enjoyed a wide popular success, compared to the appeal of the more mainstream films. *Grapes of Wrath* or *The Southerner* had limited appeals, compared with *Sergeant York* or *The Yearling* (1946). All four films dealt with farmers and their commitment to the land, yet the superior *Grapes* or *Southerner* lacked the more conventionally observed ideas and sentimental values that *York* and *Yearling* reaffirmed. The timing of these films' release was also crucial to their relative success. *Sergeant York* suited perfectly the nation's mood: The movie reflected dominant ideology in July 1941, just months prior to America's entry into the war. The transformation of Sergeant York from a conscientious objector to a war hero articulated the feelings of many Americans who initially had been reluctant to fight. Farming as a social issue lost its immediacy with the passing of the Depression and, after the war, Hollywood's concern with farmers declined. The success of *State Fair* (1945), a remake of the 1933 film, had more to do with its music and production values than thematic issues.

In the forties, Hollywood produced a cycle of movies about the home front during the war. *Tortilla Flat* (1942), *The Happy Land, The Human Comedy* (both in 1943), *The Fighting Sullivans* (1944), *A Medal for Benny* (1945), were all set in small towns. Functioning as morale boosters, they stressed traditional values: family unity and sacrifice for the nation. Set in Ithaca, California, the protagonist of *Human Comedy* is Homer Macauley (Mickey Rooney), a Western Union messenger whose task is to deliver death telegrams. Because Rooney was then at the height of his popularity, some people saw the film as just another episode of the *Andy Hardy* series. Dealing with loss of innocence and initiation into adulthood, Homer is another restless small-town boy, who has never been anywhere else, but hopes to go "some day, to all the great cities of the world." However, like George Bailey in *Wonderful Life,* chances are he will never set a foot outside town. In the first scene, a baby trips and falls, but immediately gets to his feet and goes on. This image serves as the movie's central symbol: the Macauleys (standing for everyman) refuse to be stopped by life's disasters, little or big. *Human Comedy* revolves around a "typical" American family, in a "typical" small town, during "atypical" (war) times. The Macauleys belong to Capra's "inspirational little people," though lacking their charm or eccentricities.

As a group, small-town films of the 1940s were more stylistically innovative than films of the previous decade. In *The Magnificent Ambersons*, Welles qualified the deep focus device with the disorienting rhetoric of expressionistic angles and ostentatious camera angles. By contrast, middle-range shots and deep focus are associated with realism, because they offer viewers the illusion of natural perspective and approximation of reality. For example, *Best Years* aimed to reflect the image of a stable world with real spatial relationships. But the different style of these movies suited their different thematics and ideologies. *The Magnificent Ambersons* dealt with a changing (declining) social order, whereas *Best Years* was concerned with the adjustment of war veterans to a preexisting world, one still believed to be able to embrace and absorb dissident members.[35]

In movies of the 1940s, the community's interests are considered to be superior to those of the individual. Continuing the tradition of the Depression, individuals are expected to forego their self-interests in the name of family and town. As was noted, despite darker tones, *Wonderful Life* still maintains that the family should serve as the primary source of identity, and that career goals should be submerged to collective goals, be they familial or communal. This is why even Sturges's anarchic and irreverent comedies and Wyler's social problem films end similarly: The successful restoration of the social order and the integration of eccentric individuals into their communities. The dominance of classical Hollywood narrative was evident in most films of the 1940s. *Wonderful Life* raises important questions concerning the validity of the nuclear family as a source of identity, the small town as a desirable place to live, and capitalism as a market system, but, at the end, the narrative restores and revalidates all three of them.[36] Nonetheless, the restoration of the patriarchal order and the rule of the town over its individual members were *not* completely satisfactory.[37] Indeed, the 1940s would be the last decade in which small-town films presented such an optimistic view of the community as a legitimate moral center.

The only strong parts for women in small-town films of the decade were in rural dramas *(The Grapes of Wrath, Sergeant York)*, in which they function as matriarchal figures and expressive leaders of their families. But compared to women's stronger roles during the Depression, small-town films in the 1940s hint about the decline in the position of women, manifested in their subjugation to domesticity. Of all films discussed in this chapter, only one, *Beyond the Forest*, featured a strong heroine, though even she was subordianted at the end to the patriarchal order. This trend will become even more prevalent in small-town films of the 1950s.

1930s

1. The impersonality of the Big City, conveyed by the anonymous and faceless employees of a giant bureaucracy, in King Vidor's *The Crowd* (1928), a film inspired by German Expressionism. (Courtesy of The Museum of Modern Art/Film Stills Archive)

2. The leader (James Murray, center) presiding over a meeting of a farmers' commune in King Vidor's agrarian utopia, *Our Daily Bread* (1934). (Courtesy of The Museum of Modern Art/Film Stills Archive)

3. Dr. Bull (Will Rogers, second from left) at church, singing loudly and off-key, in John Ford's *Dr. Bull*. Going to church functions as a major collective ritual of the town's diverse membership in films made during the Depression. (Courtesy of The Museum of Modern Art/Film Stills Archive)

4. The one-parent family in George Cukor's Civil War melodrama, *Little Women* (1933), sacrifices a luxurious breakfast (coffee and sausages) for a poor starving family. The mother (Spring Byington) at the center, tomboy Jo (Katharine Hepburn) and Beth (Jean Parker) on her left, and Amy (Joan Bennett) and Meg (Frances Dee) on her right. (Courtesy of The Museum of Modern Art/Film Stills Archive)

5. Impression management and self-delusions are the central motifs of George Stevens's *Alice Adams* (1935). Caught by the rich guy (Fred MacMurray), the poor Alice (Katharine Hepburn) pretends to be looking for a secretary for her father. (Courtesy of The Museum of Modern Art/Film Stills Archive)

6. The small-town Longfellow Deeds (Gary Cooper) and the former small-town girl, now sob sister Babe Bennett (Jean Arthur) having fun in nature: New York City's Central Park in Frank Capra's *Mr. Deeds Goes to Town* (1936). (Courtesy of The Museum of Modern Art/Film Stills Archive)

7. The bored-to-death Theodora (Irene Dunne, center), surrounded by her spinsterish aunts and respectable housewives of Lynnfield, in the screwball comedy *Theodora Goes Wild* (1936). (Courtesy of The Museum of Modern Art/Film Stills Archive)

8. A spontaneous formation of an irrational lynching mob in Fritz Lang's *Fury* (1936), one of the first films about prejudice and bigotry in small towns. (Courtesy of The Museum of Modern Art/Film Stills Archive)

9. The small-town lawyer, Abe Lincoln (Henry Fonda, left), applies himself to country work, excelling in chopping wood and practicing law, in a pastoral scene from John Ford's *Young Mr. Lincoln* (1939). (Courtesy of The Museum of Modern Art/Film Stills Archive)

10. The effects of a physical brawl between a "dying" small-town girl (Carole Lombard) and a manipulative city journalist (Fredric March, right), watched with concern by the dyspeptic publisher (Walter Connolly) in William Wellmann's *Nothing Sacred* (1937). (Courtesy of The Museum of Modern Art/Film Stills Archive)

1940s

11. Another singing in church in Sam Wood's innovative *Our Town* (1940), which uses some elements of film noir: Note the projected shadow of the alcoholic organist (possibly Thornton Wilder's alter ego), the town's outsider. (Courtesy of The Museum of Modern Art/Film Stills Archive)

12. The motif of the double was well illustrated in Hitchcock's *Shadow of a Doubt* (1943) in the complex relationship between Uncle Charlie (Joseph Cotten) and his niece, also named Charlie (Teresa Wright). (Courtesy of The Museum of Modern Art/Film Stills Archive)

13. In *The Magnificent Ambersons* (1942), Orson Welles dealt with the passing of one (aristocratic) era and the emergence of a new (technocratic) one. The entrepreneur–inventor Morgan (Joseph Cotten) is at the center of the frame, with representatives of the older (Dolores Costello and Agnes Moorehead, to his right) and younger (Anne Baxter and Tim Holt, to his left) generations. (Courtesy of The Museum of Modern Art/Film Stills Archive)

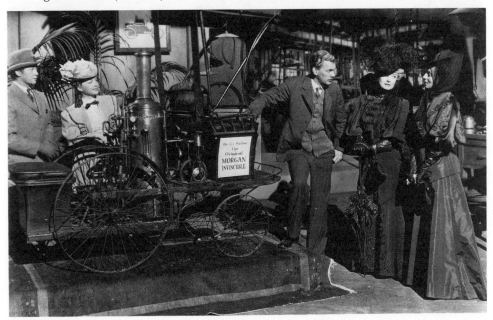

14. Generation gap was one of the issues of Sam Wood's *Kings Row* (1942), a film ahead of its time in thematics and point of view. The romantic youngsters Parris (Robert Cummings) and Cassandra (Betty Field) are watched by her rigid father Dr. Towers (Claude Rains). The staircase divides the house into frontstage and backstage; the most horrible things happen in the dark at the top of the stairs. (Courtesy of The Museum of Modern Art/Film Stills Archive)

15 and 16. Two contrasting visions of small-town life in Frank Capra's master-piece *It's a Wonderful Life* (1946). A dream: A comic, romantic scene between George (Jimmy Stewart) and Mary (Donna Reed) in Bedford Falls (15). And a nightmare: The elegantly dressed George (Stewart) standing at the empty Main Street of Pottersville, a town with industrial look, night clubs, and flashy neon lights (16). (Both courtesy of The Museum of Modern Art/Film Stills Archive)

17. A typical John Ford visual composition of community life in the Depression saga *The Grapes of Wrath* (1940). Gregg Toland's cinematography blends expressionistic and realistic elements. (Courtesy of The Museum of Modern Art/Film Stills Archive)

18. Country (land) and God are the two main symbols in Howard Hawks's inspirational biopicture *Sergeant York* (1941), embodied by the farmer turned war hero (Gary Cooper) and the pastor (Walter Brennan). (Courtesy of The Museum of Modern Art/Film Stills Archive)

19. In *The Southerner* (1945), Jean Renoir showed nature at its most cruel and devastating. Examining the wreckage are: Granny (Beulah Bondi, front center) and the young indomitable couple (on the right, Zachary Scott and Betty Field). (Courtesy of The Museum of Modern Art/Film Stills Archive)

20. A family fight in *The Miracle of Morgan's Creek* (1944), using the tradition of slapstick physical comedy. From right to left: Eddie Bracken, Betty Hutton, William Demarest, and Diana Lynn. (Courtesy of The Museum of Modern Art/Film Stills Archive)

21. In Preston Sturges's *Hail the Conquering Hero* (1944), the whole town goes to the train station to welcome its local hero (Eddie Bracken), only to find out he is a fake. (Courtesy of The Museum of Modern Art/Film Stills Archive)

22. Burning with unfulfilled sexual passion, the heroine (Bette Davis) of King Vidor's *Beyond the Forest* (1949) is contrasted with the town's sawmill's flames. (Courtesy of The Museum of Modern Art/Film Stills Archive)

3
• • • • • • • •

The 1950s—
Conformity and Repression

Stop blaming it on bad luck, you're just another guy, like
I'm just another housewife. Nothing big or wonderful is
ever going to happen to us.
                                        —*No Down Payment*

You won't stay young forever. "Did ya ever think that?
What'll become of you then?
                                        —*Picnic*

In Peyton Place, two people talking is a conspiracy. A
meeting is an assignation. Getting to know one another is
a scandal.
                                        —*Peyton Place*

I wish I had a hundred dollars and never see this town
again. . . . I wish I was somebody else except me.
                                        —*The Member of the Wedding*

The dominant attitude toward small-town life in the 1950s is better
understood in relation to its alternative life-styles. Up to the 1940s, most
films compared small towns with the Big City. But from the late 1940s
on, and more so in the 1950s, a new, alternative life-style emerged:
Suburbanism. One of the most fascinating aspects of the urbanization
process in the United States has been the rapid growth of the suburbs. In
1920, about 17 percent of the population lived in suburbs, but in the
next three decades, suburbanism increased steadily. In 1930, 19 percent
of the population lived in suburbs; in 1940, 20 percent; and in 1950, 24
percent. However, in the 1950s the growth was much more dramatic,
with practically mass flight to the suburbs. By 1960, one third (33
percent) of the population lived in suburbs.[1]

Suburbanism as a Way of Life

The flight to suburbia was motivated not only by economic but also cultural factors. As in every migration, a combination of push and pull forces accounted for this mass movement. After World War II, big cities could not accommodate the increasing demand for land, and the shortage of housing in the central city reached dramatic proportions. Correspondingly, the construction of federally subsidized highways made it easier for people to commute to the city for work. Moreover, the economy's postwar boom enabled millions of Americans, for the first time in their lives, to own their homes, due to ample mortgage opportunity from the Federal Housing Authority and the Veterans Administration.

Initially, suburbanism represented an attractive life-style, an ideal that seemed to compromise urban with rural life. There was convenient proximity to the city (if, and when, one wished to go there), but the suburb was distanced enough from the city to avoid its perceived ills and problems (density, noise, pollution, crime). In the best of American traditions, suburbanism seemed an appealing ideal to millions of people.

When the number of Americans moving into the suburbs grew considerably, Hollywood, forever searching for commercially viable topics, responded with a number of movies that dealt with the new life-style. Hollywood was afraid to lose this increasingly large suburban audience and thus made movies about suburbia. However, with few exceptions, the portrayal of suburban life was almost from the beginning an object of criticism and satire. Gradually, the tone of the movies changed, from light satire in the early 1950s to criticism in the late 1950s, to outright scorn, ridicule, and condemnation in the 1960s and 1970s.[2]

In contrast to small towns that were usually depicted as economically self-sufficient, potentially autonomous, and beautiful organic wholes, suburbs were viewed as parasites, heavily dependent on the city for employment and income. The suburbs wanted to maintain the values and intimacy of the small community without its attendant negative attributes. From the late 1950s on, the suburbs were portrayed as dull and homogeneous places, whose residents were obsessed with the neatness of their lawns, or with keeping up with the "Joneses." There was probably some truth in it, but there was a good deal of excess and exaggeration.

MGM's *Father of the Bride* (1950) was meant to describe a typical American suburban family. Director Vincente Minnelli assembled an all-star cast, headed by Spencer Tracy and Joan Bennett as the parents, Stanley and Ellie Banks, and the young Elizabeth Taylor, as their daughter Kay. Embodying a middle-class ideology, all the crucial events—courtship, engagement, and wedding—are seen consistently from the father's point of view. Surrounded by chaos, the weary father sits in his chair and narrates the chronology that led to the Big Event. Stanley Banks is a stern but sympathetic patriarch, devoted and responsible to his family, but with a tinge of jealousy and mild resentment toward losing his daughter. Beneath the expected "pleasant hysterics," however, there are serious anxieties. The film's strongest sequence features a surrealist nightmare, in which Stanley's anxieties are reflected in images of despair, failure, and inadequacy. However, because this powerful sequence stands in sharp opposition to the film's otherwise agreeable ambience, it was probably ignored (or underestimated) by viewers at the time.

The quality of writing (by Frances Goodrich and Albert Hackett) was not much above television sitcoms, but the film had charm, depicting situations and characters that were familiar to most Americans. Cashing in on its commercial appeal (*Father of the Bride* was one of the ten most popular films of the year), MGM used the same cast in a sequel, *Father's Little Dividend* (1951). It is set several months after the wedding, when Stanley Banks has at last recuperated from the wedding. He is now told that his daughter expects a baby, which at first upsets him. The "conflict" in this film concerns the problems between the paternal and maternal grandparents, but they all come to an agreement at the end. In reflecting the boom of post–World War II and the beginning of prosperity and consumerism, both films supported bourgeois, middle-class ideology concerning such sacred institutions as weddings and marriages. They idealize suburbanism, depicting it as a safe and protected life-style. Soft satires with no bite, the two *Father* movies are among the few Hollywood pictures to show the "sunny" side of suburbia.

Uniformity and Conformity: *No Down Payment*

The ultimate cinematic statement regarding suburbanism can be found in Martin Ritt's *No Down Payment* (1957), a typical Twentieth Century–Fox melodrama. One of Hollywood's most consciously sociological efforts, the film presents a myriad of four marriages, meant to be statistically representative. The narrative is set in a Los Angeles suburb, "Sun Rise Hills," with a huge sign describing it as "The Happy Ending to Your House Hunting." The background music suggests the transition from the cramped and strangling City to the spacious and sun-filled Suburbia. The score begins with harsh and unmelodic strains that gradually blend into more pleasant pastoral notes.

Revolving around leisure, not work, activities, the story begins on a Sunday morning, as members of the community leave church. Betty Kreitzer (Barbara Rush) reproaches her husband Herman (Pat Hingle) for washing his car on Sunday. What will the neighbors say? "Daddy'll go to hell and burn up," says their son. Herman believes in God, but practices a more privatized religion; he doesn't need "some mealy-mouthed reverend to speak for Him." The strain subsides as there's a lot to be done: the Kreitzers are giving a barbecue party tonight.

The outsiders-newcomers, who set the story in motion, are electronic engineer David Martin (Jeffrey Hunter) and his attractive wife Jean (Patricia Owens). They are the only couple who bought the house with no down payment. Jean sports a good eye, she selected David over Ned because she saw him as a "born leader." But David is modestly ambitious: "I don't have to outsmart or beat down anybody else to live." For Jean, however, he is still "a schoolboy at the lab," who needs a little push. As in any conversation between them, she has the last word: "Growing time is getting close. If you want to get over your new ideas, you'll have to fight." A company man, David would go as far as the rules of the game permit. "You're not playing tennis; success in the business world is not a game," says Jean in a manner that hints that if he will not fight, she will fight *him*. David's two recent promotions are not enough for Jean, wishing he would think "a little more aggressively and push a little harder." Jean has always been the more aggressive one; "if I hadn't proposed, we might never have been married." Jean outmaneuvered David: The only reason she dated Ned was "to get David to act." "It's a *man's world*," says Jean. "We have to use all the ammunition we have."

Each couple represents a different segment of the population and thus experiences different conflicts. The first is a Southern couple, transplanted Tennessee hillbillies Troy (Cameron Mitchell) and Leola (Joanne Woodward) Boone. A war hero, he works in a gas station but, upwardly mobile, he desires a better position as a police officer. Troy has spent too many years in too many places; now he wants to "buckle down in one spot, the only way to make good." However, lacking formal education, he is turned down for the job. Humiliated and depressed, Troy turns to the bottle. The uneducated Leola has desperate yearnings for motherhood, but Troy lacks respect for her, treating her like a kid. He always felt she was a tramp; when she got pregnant, he was not sure it was his baby. Troy thinks she should befriend Jean; "You can learn from her." But Leola, who lacks any self-esteem, feels "why should Jean waste time with me, a lonely, dissatisfied woman?" When Troy charges, "Why can't you run a house like any other woman?" her response is, "Why can't you act like a husband, instead of a top sergeant?" Troy runs his house as if it were "the last marine outpost on Guadalcanal." He loves "to lecture people, tell 'em what to do and how to do it." He even tells his wife how to make love!

The film reflects the increasing importance of college degrees in the

1950s. Troy believes that the Martins are "the lucky ones, everything comes easy to them." "They deserve it," says Leola, "they're both college graduates." Isabelle Flagg (Sheree North) wants her husband to work in a new line, but at thirty-five, "he's too old to start at the bottom," and "these companies prefer men fresh out of college." It is a transitional time in the occupational marketplace: of the four men, David is the only representative of the new professional class. Jerry Flagg (Tony Randall), a used car salesman, suffers from a drinking problem and, worse, grand delusions of making big money fast. A dreamer, Jerry's fantasies are fed by popular culture: he hopes his son Mike would go on a quiz show and win sixty-four thousand dollars. For Jerry, living in this neighborhood is "only a stopover," his dream is to move in a fine neighborhood, "where important people live." In the meantime, Jerry drinks because "it makes me feel I'm *somebody*."

The Kreitzers' marital union is rather stable. Herman is an amiable, rational man who manages a hardware store. He finds himself at odds with his seemingly sensitive wife, not over religion but interracial integration. Allegedly liberal, they disagree over the question of helping a Japanese-American salesman buy a home in their neighborhood. "I am a GI Joe, I qualify," claims the industrious Iko Matuko (Aki Aleong), acknowledging the exclusivity of suburbia as a white and middle-class invention, protecting itself against the intrusion of foreign elements, i.e., *any* ethnic minorities. "It's not our credit that's holding it up," says Iko, it's "lack of prestige." Herman holds that "if a guy is good enough to work here, he ought to be good enough to live here." But Betty can't bring herself to ask Leola and Isabelle to "have a Japanese for a neighbor." She did not mind going to their house for dinner, because it was "their neighborhood," but, "sitting and living next door aren't the same." The film thus shows one of the worst effects of conformity, "the fear to act," even when it is for the right cause. Overconformity is an allusion to McCarthyism and its political witch-hunting in the 1950s (director Martin Ritt was blacklisted).

All four women are housewives, though the fact that none works is not a major issue, consistent with the dominant ideology of the 1950s. Burdened with raising two children, Isabelle has tried to work, but she has no marketable skills and, more importantly, working would "crush" Jerry, damage his ego. As in *A Letter to Three Wives,* a working wife at the time was perceived as a severe blow to masculinity and patriarchal order. "Just tell me what to do," asks the helpless Jerry in a weak moment. "You're a man, you're supposed to know what to do," says Isabelle. She is a victim of oversocialization, the type of woman who believes "it's a wife's fault when a husband has to chase around."

The film abounds with "message" speeches, revealing various phobias and contradictions in dominant culture. As in *Shadow of a Doubt,* there is obsession—but ambiguity too—about being an "average American." Herman tells his wife: "We are what insurance companies call 'an average family.'" "Stop blaming it on bad luck," says Isabelle to Jerry. "You're just another guy, like I'm just another housewife. Nothing big or wonderful is ever going to happen to us." But Isabelle also blames herself: "Jerry always had big dreams and I went along, encouraging his false hopes." Now she feels guilty for "never letting him admit that we were two ordinary people who would never have much."

The four couples spend their leisure in joined barbecue parties, dancing, gossiping, and lusting after each other. Suburbia is shown to be self-imprisonment, a uniformed claustrophobic world; they very seldom go out. Conformity to the rules seems to be the name of the game. "Each group of houses set a pattern," says Jean, "and everyone living in this group has to fall in line or they're ignored." But who is the leader, who sets the pattern? Jean holds that there is one strong family in each group that sets the style and the others follow. In this group, the leaders are the Kreitzers. Herman is described as "a solid citizen," and Betty "right out of *Good Housekeeping.*" However, in a characteristic Hollywood manner, the specific ethnic background of the Kreitzers, their Jewishness, is ignored.

Every activity must be performed according to the norm. For instance, Dr. Greenspun says that it is a bad habit for children to eat in front of the TV set. Isabelle also checks with Dr. Greenspun the amounts of liquor Jerry consumes to make sure he is "strictly a social drinker." Rationality means calculating moves and planning for the future, a context in which feelings are obstacles. David used to think that producing children occurs in the "natural course of events," but is corrected by his wife, "Children don't just happen. Today's the fifteenth. I couldn't be readier!"

As in *Best Years of Our Lives,* the war heroes have become victims as soon as it was over, for many of the fighters lack education and professional skills. During the war, David worked on electric computers and promoted his own career: His outfit never saw action. By contrast, Troy, who has "enough medals to open a hock shop," laid his life on the line in combat. "Only the civilians want to forget the war," says Troy. "The guys who lived it got it tattooed." If he did not have his memories, he would "crawl in my car and turn on the exhaust pipe." The two less-successful men, Jerry and Troy, resent the pervasive trends of bureaucratization and specialization. "I don't like being an organization man," says Troy, "I like to make my own decisions," reflecting the influence of William F. Whyte's 1955 book, *The Organization Man.* But in order to succeed one has to *be* an organization man. Troy is a man of the past in other ways; he refuses to use credit cards. Jerry also rejects the benefits of a secure job with a steady paycheck. He doesn't want to be like David, because he is "a company man." Even David, the prototypical company man, feels at times "uncomfortable in a group," but his wife urges him "to spend more time with people."

The ranch houses, neat and comfortable on the outside, are really unattractive. They are so close to each other that there is no privacy at all. Indeed, the smallest domestic quarrel in one house translates into a communal affair. Along with the illusion of privacy, appearances and words are deceiving. Jean looks and talks like a "school marm, always sweet as juniberry juice," but she is aggressive. The Kreitzers are more liberal in ideology than practice. Troy wants to be the chief of police, a profession linked with assuring the safety of others, but he is the least trustworthy of men. "I guarantee," he tells Jean, "you'll be able to sleep nights with your door open." Shortly thereafter, he assaults her sexually.

If *No Down Payment* has no redeeming qualities as a work of art, it is useful as a social document, reflecting dominant culture. Despite a (superficial) happy ending, the narrative cannot conceal the anxieties generated by suburban life. But true to its format, that of melodrama, it offers quick and contrived resolutions. The brutal Troy pays with his life for the sexual assault; ironically, he dies in an accident, crushed under his own car. Unable to adjust, his wife Leola goes back to the South—the appeal of suburbanism is *not* universal. The other couples survive, readjusting themselves to another state of balance—until the next crisis. The film ends symmetrically, just as it began. It's another Sunday, but there is one difference: Iko and his wife are at church. However, to what extent they are fully integrated into the community is up to the viewers to decide.

Outsiders in Small Towns

In the 1950s, the ideological attitude toward small towns had changed and movies became more critical. In the decade's most characteristic films, life in small towns was depicted as emotionally stifling, intellectually suffocating, and sexually repressive. The major thematic paradigm in movies of the decade was that of the outsider.[3] Their narrative structure typically consists of three phases. The film begins with the arrival of the outsider in town. Prior to his arrival, the town is presumed to be in a state of balance (equilibrium), which the outsider's arrival disrupts. The second and major phase of the narrative depicts the pervasive effects of the outsider on individual residents and the town as a whole. The relationship between the outsider and the town is neither reciprocal nor symmetric: the outsider influences the town more than it affects him. The outsider functions as a catalyst, setting events and conflicts in motion. In the third phase, the conclusion, the narrative offers a resolution that usually calls for the outsider's departure and, in fewer cases, integration into town.

But this basic narrative scheme allows for many variations in thematic convention. These variations may concern the identity of the outsider, the particular role the outsider plays, the extent of the outsider's influence, and the town's reaction to the outsider. In most films, there is one outsider, but sometimes there are more. Furthermore, in the characteristic films of the decade, being outside town is both literal (arriving from other places) and figurative. In some films, the outsiders reside in town; nominally they are insiders, but their attitude toward town (its institutions or norms) makes them outsiders. The outsider is almost always a man, young or middle-aged, often attractive. For example, in *Picnic*, he is a drifter (William Holden); in *Peyton Place*, he is the new school principal (Lee Philips); in *The Long, Hot Summer*, he is also a drifter (Paul Newman); in *The Rainmaker*, he's a charming con man (Burt Lancaster); in *Rose Tattoo*, he is a simpleton truck driver (also Lancaster). The outsider's motives for arriving in (or returning to) town are also varied. In *Picnic*, *The Rainmaker*, and *The Long, Hot Summer*, the protagonists are down on their luck, hoping to start a new life. In *Peyton Place*, the outsider also begins a new life but is not running from his past.

In the few occasions the outsider is a female, she is typically an adolescent. In William Inge's *Come Back, Little Sheba* (1952),[4] a female student (Terry Moore) takes lodging with a childless couple, and her presence precipitates identity and marital crises. Doc (Burt Lancaster) and Lola (Shirley Booth) Delaney are a lonely, middle-aged couple living a monotonous and wistful life in a commonplace middle-class home. A once-attractive vamp, Lola has turned into a lazy and frumpy housewife. The highlight of her lonely day is her brief conversation with the postman. The self-pitying Lola still laments Sheba, her lost dog, which signifies her youth, beauty, and everything positive in her life. Abusing his wife, Doc resents the fact that she had trapped him into marriage (under a false alarm of pregnancy), forcing him to forsake his medical studies. Locked in a sexless marriage, he has become a weakling and alcoholic; his eager interest in their sexy lodger reflects his repressed sexuality and frustrated emotions. A violent climax, with Doc threatening Lola with a knife, leads to a (contrived) resolution: The Delaneys regain their self-respect and achieve a new balance in their marriage. The overly sentimental *Come Back* contains themes—the primacy of passion and the price of repressed sexuality—that recur in many of Inge's works: *Picnic* and *Splendor in the Grass* (chapter 4).

Repressed Sexuality: *Picnic*

Picnic (1955) is one of those rare works, a film that captures the cultural essence of the whole decade. It has assumed the status of a classic American play, continuously produced. Opening on Broadway on February 19, 1953, it was singled out as the best American play by the New York Drama Critics Circle, and won the 1953 Pulitzer Prize for Drama. Joshua Logan's film version was nominated for five Academy Awards, winning two: Best color art direction and best editing. This movie made Kim Novak a star; the stage production featured Paul Newman's Broadway debut. The movie employs thematic conventions that highlight the ideological context and subtext of the 1950s.

The narrative begins on Labor Day, thus indicating it is a special, not routine, day. Hal Carter (William Holden), a good-looking guy, jumps from a freight train in a small town on the Kansas plains. A college dropout, Carter is not a bad guy, but a bum, a man who has been searching but unable to find himself. Carter has been drifting from job to job (including the army), and from one town to another ever since he was kicked out of college, where he was admitted on a football scholarship. A screen test in Hollywood proved he was going to have a "big career" with a promising screen name, Brush Carter.[5] But "they were going to have to pull out all my teeth and get me new ones," so he "naturally refused." Hal was arrested by the police after hitchhiking in a car driven by women who wanted to party, then robbed him. "I'm telling you, women are gettin' desperate," says Hal, flash-forwarding in one sentence the movie's chief issue: desperate women. Hal hopes that his best friend from college, Alan Benson (Cliff Robertson), heir of the town's richest family, will help him find a job. Hal is an outsider who wants to become an insider, a man wishing to settle down and live a respectable middle-class life.

The bulk of the narrative deals with how this stud sets in motion an inevitable chain of events that have shattering effects on the town's residents, forever altering their lives. Heavily populated by female characters, there are five of them, each representing a social type. Mother Flo (Betty Field) is a middle-aged woman who hates Hal because he reminds her of her swaggering husband who, years back, had deserted her, leaving her the responsibility of raising two girls. Her dream now is to marry off her daughter to Benson, perceiving marriage as her daughter's only avenue for upward mobility. Madge (Kim Novak), her eldest daughter and "prettiest girl in town," is sensitive, but not too bright. Millie (Susan Strasberg), the younger daughter, is a precocious tomboy, the bookish type. Mrs. Helen Potts (Verna Felton) is the Owens's next-door neighbor, a middle-aged woman living with her sickly mother. She too has no man in her life.

Rosemary Sidney (Rosalind Russell), a high-school teacher, is a spinster who rents a furnished room at the Owens's house. Rosemary introduces herself with the following line: "Anybody mind if an old maid school teacher joins the company?" A bit neurotic, she makes her last desperate grab at marital bliss, fearing life might be passing her by. Anxious to get married, she is willing to compromise and take Howard (Arthur O'Connell), a dull and selfish traveling salesman. But so far Howard has been "just a friend-boy, not a fay friend." Her hysterical preparations for their meeting reduce her to a teenage girl waiting for her first date. She expects, by her old-fashioned morality, to be treated as a lady. By standards of dominant culture, until married, Rosemary is a failure. Unlike teachers in small-town films, Rosemary is not concerned with her career or students' education; she is never seen in a classroom. Obsessed with singlehood, she would give up her profession as soon as she gets married. Rosemary also represents conservative ethics, reproaching Mother Flo for letting her daughter read "filthy" books, such as *The Ballad of the Sad Cafe,* a book that many "wanted banned from the public library."

The introduction of each character is a field day for semiologists. Each woman is associated with an object that signifies her respective concerns: Mrs. Potts is holding a cake; Mother Flo is seen in the kitchen with eggs; Rosemary uses cream for her wrinkles; Madge carries a hair dryer (a phallic object); Millie is reading a book. In their first conversation, Millie says to Madge, "Dry your silly hair over somebody else," to which the latter replies, "Why don't you read your silly book under somebody else?" Mother Flo is horrified when Madge says, "I wish it didn't take so long to dry—I think one summer I'll cut it short." Madge's hair is the symbol of her beauty and her best asset as a woman.

The three men in *Picnic* also represent types, associated with different activities: Alan likes to play golf; Hal, to work outdoors; and Howard, to drink. Stripped to his waist for most of the film, Hal is an outdoor man who feels more comfortable in nature, by the river, far from the public eye. When Mrs. Potts offers to wash his shirt, he wonders if "anybody'd mind?" "Of course not," says Mrs. Potts. "You're a man, what's the difference?" But there is a difference, and for the rest of the story he is shirtless. Early on, Rosemary describes him as "naked as an Indian," revealing at once her sexual starvation and racial biases. "Who does he think is interested?" she asks, but she—and the other repressed women—*are* interested in him. In the film's dramatic climax, Rosemary, her inhibitions down (after a couple of drinks), makes a pass at Hal and is brutally rejected. Forcing him to dance with her, she tears his shirt; now he is naked. "You won't stay young forever," says the vengeful Rosemary, "did ya ever think that? What'll become of you then?" (Geraldine Page uses almost the same words in *Sweet Bird of Youth,* in a similar scene with her stud, Paul Newman.)[6] Hal is an uninhibited spirit, as Mrs. Potts says after his departure: "He clumped through the house like he was still outdoors. You knew there was a man in the house!" Hal and Alan complement each other: each admires the attributes of the other. Their names (Hal and Alan) are also similar. Hal was the physical type in school, excelling in football and chasing girls. Alan, the rich kid who excelled in academic studies, has always been envious of Hal's ease and success with women.

Each of the five women represents a different ideological stance toward love and marriage, demonstrating the inherent tension between the two values. The commonsensical Mrs. Potts believes in the superiority of feelings over reason. She is the only woman to give her blessings to Madge and Hal's romance from the start. Rosemary knows that marriage, even an unhappy one, will redeem her from her inferior status as spinster; a compromising (unsatisfactory) marriage is better than no marriage. Mother Flo is also more pragmatic than romantic, perceiving marriage as an economic transaction, an arrangement in which Madge's youth and beauty would be exchanged for Alan's economic security and prestige. "A pretty girl doesn't have long," she tells Madge. "Just a few years." But once married, she'll be "the equal of kings . . . she can walk out of a shanty like this and live in a palace." However, if she "loses her chance when she's young, she might as well throw all her prettiness away." Protesting that she is only nineteen, Mother Flo tells Madge: "And next summer you'll be twenty, and then twenty-one, and then forty!"

The town is ruled by the Bensons, owners of the vast grain operations. Alan tells Madge that his father is "impressed with winning," referring to her crown as the Beauty Queen, and "with people making the most of money." Having the right connections makes a difference, as one resident tells Hal, "the governor's an old sidekick of mine. That's how I got the job." The class structure is also obvious: The Owens live on the other side of the tracks. When a working-class boy courts Madge, he expresses his jealousy, saying he saw her riding around in Alan's convertible, "like you was a duchess."

The film's coda provides a resolution to its dramatic conflict, celebrating romantic love over pragmatic marriage. Mother Flo pleads with Madge to stay in town, claiming that her passionate love is transitory, that Hal is good for nothing, that he will drink and be unfaithful. But Madge is determined to leave town and, as Hal jumps on a train, she boards a bus for Tulsa. Audiences at the time saw it as happy ending, but viewed from today's perspective, this closure contains ambiguity—will Madge follow in her mother's footsteps? Weighing her alternatives, living in a repressive and boring town versus an unknown but potentially exciting future, has Madge made the right choice? Michael Wood pointed out that the film's "persistent, insidious hysteria," and its undercurrent of anxiety and loneliness, were unnoticed at the time.[7] Indeed, more than anything else, *Picnic* is about repressed sexuality and its corresponding price. No woman in the film is fulfilled, sexually or emotionally: There are either *no* men, or no *desirable* men in their lives. Hal is the only desirable male, a stud surrounded by sex-starved women.

The Small Town as Prison: *All That Heaven Allows*

As was shown, some movies underplayed the difference between small towns and the suburbs. The two life-styles seem to converge (or blur) when the image of both is negative, when life in small towns and suburbs is seen as stifling and suffocating. This is the case of Douglas Sirk's stylized melodrama, *All That Heaven Allows* (1955).[8] On the surface, Stonington, Connecticut, is a perfect town to live in, an ideal setting to raise a family. The opening overhead shot reveals a beautiful New England town with a big church, white houses, and nice trees. Cary Scott (Jane Wyman) the film's protagonist, is a middle-aged widow, living comfortably with her two children. Quiet and reserved, she has come to believe that loneliness is her fate. Sirk uses a bouquet of flowers to convey her frail beauty and mental state.

Cary falls in love with Ron Kirby[9] (Rock Hudson), a tall and sturdy man. A gardener, Ron is not uneducated; a college graduate, he also plays piano. Simple and straightforward, he lacks the superficial polish of Cary's friends. The film stresses not so much the class as their age (Cary is older by a decade) and life-style differences. Ron is a masculine but sensitive man, a gentleman with a tough exterior. Considerate, he makes sure that Cary wears a warm coat and boots, because "it'll be cold by the time we get back." An outdoor man, Ron lives outside town in a greenhouse barn. He embodies the ideal of Thoreau and Emerson, though, as one of his friends says, "He's never read *Walden,* he just lives it." There is no need for Ron to learn from the books; he practices what comes natural and spontaneous to him.

The movie draws explicit comparisons between Cary's and Ron's set of friends. Cary is surrounded with professional and pretentious companions, stuffy types who lack the commonsensical knowledge to lead happy lives. By contrast, Ron's buddies are free-spirited bohemians. His best friend, Mick Anderson, who also runs a tree nursery, used to work for an advertising agency in New York, but resented the constant pressure of "the ulcer circuit," opting instead for a simpler life. Ron served as a role model for Mick once he escaped the Big City and its anxieties. The parties given by Cary's friends stand in sharp opposition to Ron's. Cary's friends live by a rigid etiquette: Sara (Agnes Moorehead) borrows a set of dishes from Cary because she lacks the "right" china. At the country club, people are dressed elegantly; at the Andersons, they wear casual clothes. Cary's friends pretend to be sophisticated but lack finesse. They anxiously wait for Cary to show up and treat Ron as their prey, an object to be ridiculed. Mona, the town's gossip, remarks upon seeing Cary: "There's nothing like red for attracting attention. I suppose that's why so few widows wear it. They'd have to be careful." At the Andersons' everything is improvised: The table, constructed from planks, is covered by a checkered tablecloth. As Michael Stern pointed out,[10] the two sets of people use different drinks. Cary's son is careful in preparing martinis, "the Scott special." By contrast, the ingredients for "the Anderson special," consist of a little bit of this and a little bit of that. Spontaneity, informality, and improvisation mark the behavior of Ron's friends. When Cary first visits the Andersons, Thoreau's *Walden* is placed on the table. Opening the book, she comes across the passage in which he says that "the mass of men live lives of quiet desperation," which is a perfect summation of her life. She continues to read about "different drummers," subconsciously (at this point) concurring with the author's query, "Why should we live in such frantic haste to succeed?"

Ron is juxtaposed with the other men in Cary's life. Howard is just a crass sexist, making a crude pass at Cary. Harvey, Cary's companion, is an elderly gentleman with no sex appeal. Ron, the nature boy, uses not a bottle opener, but his teeth. Unlike Cary's companions, who are other-directed, to use sociologist David Riseman's[11] terminology, Ron and his friends are inner-directed, individuals whose "security comes from inside themselves, and no one can take it away from them." Sirk also juxtaposes the old mill, which Ron renovates for Cary, with her own house. Cary lives in a self-imposed prison, a cage; she is often seen behind closed doors and shut windows. Framed from the outside, Cary looks back, oriented toward her past. By contrast, Ron is often filmed standing *in front* of windows, looking outside with a view of miles ahead; he is future-oriented. Reversing gender-related conventions, it is Ron who approaches the subject of marriage. He also deviates from other normative prescriptions of "masculinity," with his concern for aesthetics, a typically "feminine" pursuit. Ron instructs Cary to defy social conventions, because, in the final account, every person should be his own master. Decision making is considered to be another typically male activity. Telling her how Mick has learned to make decisions for himself, Cary asks: "You want me to be a man?" "Only in that one way," Ron replies, demonstrating a less-rigid view of gender-related behavior; it is clear that in her first marriage, Cary made no decisions.

Everyone objects to Cary's marriage to Ron, though for various reasons. First, there is the issue of class difference. The idea of marrying Ron is appalling to Sara. "A gardener!" she says. "Why doesn't he get himself a money-making occupation?" Cary's two children are also against it. Kay (Gloria Talbott) feels "he won't fit in," and Ned (William Reynolds) favors marrying someone like his father. "There's a certain sense of tradition," Ned says. "Ron's against everything father stood for." Disliking his mother's red dress, Ned charges mercilessly that it is Ron's "handsome set of muscles" that attracts her to him. Under tremendous pressure to "conform," she gives in. But her children are insensitive and hypocrites; ironically, Kay is a social worker. The camera shows the lonely Cary, locked in her room after a dispassionate evening with Harvey, then switches to Kay's first kiss. Kay later misquotes Freud when she tells her mother, "after a certain age, sex becomes incongruous." Moreover, they leave Cary alone on Christmas. Soon Kay announces plans to get married, and Ned breaks the news that if he is not drafted into military service, he will accept a scholarship in Paris. They buy her a television set, a window to the world that will bring, as the salesman puts it, "drama, comedy, life's parade at your fingertips." But the TV set indicates further isolation (not having to go outside) and self-withdrawal rather than a facilitator of culture. Thus, Sirk reverses the conventions of melodramas, showing a bourgeois family in which the children oppress their mother rather than the other way around.[12] He also uses the TV set as an artificial, though unsatisfactory, substitute, for real romances.

Subconsciously Cary knows she has made a mistake and she experiences terrible headaches. The doctor, a benevolent figure who functions as a psychologist rather than a physician, tells her: "Headaches are nature's way of making a protest." Cary's headaches are an individualistic reaction to the town's social ills: rigidity and hypocrisy. Operating as a social worker, he opens her eyes: "Do you expect me to give you a prescription to cure life?" "Forget for a moment I'm a doctor," he tells her, "and let me give you some advice as a friend: 'Marry him!'" (In *Invasion of the Body Snatchers*, the doctor is also asked to forget his profession in order to see a problem more clearly—see discussion below.) At the end, realizing her error, Cary admits, "I let others make *my* decisions," indicating she has internalized Ron's philosophy.

Ideological Summation of a Decade: *Peyton Place*

The quintessential small-town movie of the decade was undoubtedly *Peyton Place* (1957), based on Grace Metallius's best-selling novel. It was not only an important, top-grossing film,[13] but one that led to a sequel, *Return to Peyton Place* (1961) and to a long-running television series. When Americans think of a typical small-town movie, *Peyton Place* is likely to be their first choice. And with good reasons: This melodrama captured better than other films the narrative conventions and value elements of small-town films. It is arguably one of the best small-town films ever made in Hollywood, blending together the thematic and stylistic elements to form a coherent work.

Metallius's novel was scandalous but frank in its revelations about life in a New Hampshire town at the end of the Depression. The secret of the book and film's success was that it dealt with sexual and social taboos, seldom portrayed in a Hollywood film before; the film went one step further than the 1942 shocker *Kings Row.* Just about every controversial issue was touched upon, illegitimacy, rape, murder, suicide, abortion. Fortunately, the book was adapted to the screen by John Michael Hayes, a good writer who did some wonderful scripts for Hitchcock (including *Rear Window*). Hayes actually improved on the book, "laundering" the story and trimming its unnecessary clichés.

The film opens with the arrival of an outsider, Michael Rossi (Lee Philips), the new school principal. Driving through town, the viewers are introduced to some of the characters and the place itself. *Peyton Place* boasts great pictorial beauty—for once CinemaScope really captures the special ambience of a town. Rossi is taking the job from Mrs. Thornton (Mildred Dunnock), the beloved English teacher everyone hoped would assume the position. A charming, considerate man, he makes sure not to threaten too much the school's continuity. At the same time, he has new ideas about education. His liberal philosophy, different from the former rigid system, consists of two credos. First, "to tell the truth as far as we know it. I don't want any teacher making a fairy tale out of it." And second, to "teach a minimum of facts, and a maximum of ideas. Our main job is to teach children how to think—not how to memorize for a few weeks."

The film centers on the lives and times of four family units: the MacKenzies, the Harringtons, the Crosses, and the Pages. For such a large number of characters, it is a tribute to the writer that they are fleshed out in such a manner that, while they remain types, they also have individual attributes. Each character either hides a secret about the past (and later will confess about it) or is subject to some harrowing experience that will transform him or her completely.

The MacKenzies are a one-parent family, headed by Constance (Lana Turner), a young "widow," who has one daughter, Allison (Diane Varsi). If the film has a central character it is Allison, for most of the events are told from her point of view. High-strung, Constance is annoyed by her daughter's daily habit of kissing the portrait of her dead father. It turns out that Constance is a fallen woman, whose adulterous affair with a married man in New York resulted in birth out of the wedlock. Constance is defined by her repressed sexuality. Suppressing her guilt, she is a victim who needs redemption.

The Harringtons are at the top of the class hierarchy. They are the town's big business and upper class. The Crosses are placed at the bottom, living in a shabby shack on the other side of the tracks. But the town likes Selena Cross (Hope Lange) and her hardworking mother, Nellie (Betty Field), who is Constance's maid. Selena's father, Lucas (Arthur Kennedy) is despised, not so much because of his lower class or occupation (the school's janitor), but because he is a drunk and a brute. Lucas is the only town's member who does not believe in the values of formal education and democratic rule.

As in *Picnic*, civilization is too repressive and demanding. The place to express one's biological instincts and true emotions is outdoors, in the open air, free from social pressures and direct observability. Allison experiences her first innocent kiss with the timid Norman Pape (Russ Tamblyn) in their secret meeting place, high on a hill. But not everyone is lucky enough to escape the presence of others. When Rodney Harrington and his girlfriend Betty go swimming (in the nude), they are seen and reported, which precipitates a big scandal. Norman's hysterical mother throws a fit, when someone mistakes Norman and Allison for Rodney and Betty. Nature, as the secret place for adolescents to experiment with their sexuality, features prominently in small-town movies about coming of age. In *Rebel without a Cause* (1955), for example, James Dean, Natalie Wood, and Sal Mineo establish their own nuclear family (with Mineo as their son), acting out adult roles in an isolated and deserted house.

The town's two greatest sins are vicious gossip and hypocrisy. Redemption is thus required not just of its individual residents, but of the town as a collective whole. This is achieved, as in other small-town films, in a collective ritual, a courtroom trial, which brings the membership together. Selena is charged with murdering her stepfather (who had raped her), but it is the town itself, not Selena, who is put on trial and needs to defend itself. It is through awareness and confession that truth could emerge. The town has to learn its lessons in order to reach a new and better equilibrium and a more pragmatic morality. "We've all been prisoners of each other's gossip," says Doc Swain (Lloyd Nolan), the town's moral center. Indeed, the town rejects its previous ways, in which "appearances counted more than feelings." *Peyton Place* is one of the last Hollywood films to make the doctor an honorable citizen, embodying the town's collective conscience.

With all its sensationalistic subplots and devices, *Peyton Place,* like other small-town melodramas, is extremely moralistic and optimistic, express-ing firm belief in the possibility of change, particularly for the youth. Each of the characters transforms, demonstrating they have all learned their lesson. For example, Rodney Harrington, the irresponsible woman-izer, redeems himself when he dies as a war hero in combat. And Norman matures into adulthood, freeing himself once and for all from his monstrous domineering mother. Following Rodney's death, Betty, a young widow, gains acceptance as a full-fledged member of the Har-ringtons. Selena Cross is acquitted at the trial and regains her respect-ability. Allison matures into young womanhood, following a direct confrontation and reconciliation with her mother and a trip to New York. Her commitment to a writing career is now stronger and more realistic. Comparatively speaking, the adults suffer much more than the youngsters. Selena's mother commits suicide (hanging herself up at Constance's house) upon learning about her daughter's rape by her husband. Rodney's father accepts Betty as his daughter-in-law. Constance learns to accept—and express—her sexuality; having exorcised her dis-reputable past, she is now free to get involved with Rossi.

The film deviated from the book significantly.[14] In the film, Rodney Harrington dies as a war hero, but in the book, his father uses his influence to exempt him from military service. Moreover, in the book, Rodney is killed in a car crash, with a woman aboard, after Betty Ander-son becomes pregnant. As for Norman, in the film, he liberates himself from his domineering mother, but in the book, he is discharged from military service because of mental problems.

The Rule of the Patriarch: *The Long, Hot Summer*

A stock character in small-town films of the 1950s is that of the patriarch, the town's boss and/or its owner of business. It is a perfect type to embody dominant, middle-class ideology. A few character actors "spe-cialized" in playing such roles. For instance, Burl Ives played three very similar roles: As Ephraim Cabot in Eugene O'Neill's *Desire under the Elms,* as Rufus Hannassey in *The Big Country,* and, perhaps, best known of all, as Big Daddy in Tennessee Williams's *Cat on a Hot Tin Roof,* all released in 1958. Orson Welles was also cast as a small-town patriarch in *The Long, Hot Summer* (1958), and Eg Begley, as a corrupt politician in Tennessee Williams's *Sweet Bird of Youth* (See chapter 4).

There are three types of paternal figures in Hollywood melodramas of the 1950s. The first type are selfish and domineering patriarchs, usually in the South *(Cat on a Hot Tin Roof, The Long, Hot Summer, Sweet Bird of Youth).* The second type are benevolent patriarchs *(Father of the Bride* or *Written on the Wind).* And the third type are weaklings and passive fathers, dominated by their wives and despised by their sons *(Rebel without a Cause)*. There is a fourth, mixed type: patriarchs who begin as insensitive and domineering but redeem themselves through transformation of personality *(East of Eden, Cat)*.

The narrative structure of these films is based on thematic-ideological conventions that could be summarized in the following way:

1. The health of a strong patriarch is in danger. He is recovering from sickness *(Long)*, going to die *(Cat)*, or dies of heart attack *(Written)*.

2. The patriarch is a widower *(Long, Written, Desire)* or unhappily married *(Cat)*.

3. The patriarch has several children (two boys in *Cat*, a boy and a girl in *Long* and *Written*, three boys in *Desire*).

4. The father dislikes his own child *(Cat)* or children *(Long* and *Written)*.

5. The father favors an outsider, treating him as a surrogate son *(Long* and *Written)*.

6. The biological son is a weakling *(Long)* and/or irresponsible *(Written)* and/or drunk *(Written* and *Cat,* at least initially).

7. The son suffers from sexual problems: he is excessively sexual *(Long)*, inadequate *(Cat)*, or fears sterility *(Written)*.

8. The major ideological function of the younger woman (daughter or daughter-in-law) is to reproduce, to reassure the continuity of the nuclear family. In *Cat,* Maggie's present to Big Daddy's birthday is a (premature) announcement about her pregnancy.

9. The rule of the patriarch (must) continue to prevail through the survival of the family. "I like life so much, I may just live forever," says Varner in *Long.* In *Cat,* Big Daddy is going to die but would like an heir.

In *The Long, Hot Summer,* the antihero Ben Quick (Paul Newman) becomes the hero. The "meanest and lowest creature," Ben is charged with burning barns, but there is no proof of it. Forced to leave town, he is an outsider who needs to begin a new life, not unlike *Picnic*'s hero. The town of Frenchman's Bend is dominated by Varner, a powerful man by virtue of his size, energy, land, and business. A shrewd monster with a gargantuan appetite for life, Varner owns the whole town: the cotton gin, the hardware store, the gas station, and the general store. He introduces himself as "the justice of the peace and election commissioner, a farmer, a moneylender, and a veterinarian."

"Our town is the most nowhere place in the whole state of Mississippi," Eula (Lee Remick), Varner's daughter-in-law, says. "It laces you in as tight as a corset." There is not much to do, or as Eula puts it: "As far as social amusements, there are *none.*" For entertainment, the girls go to Jefferson for shrimp and a movie, but there aren't enough men to go around. The ideal for women, as Agnes says, is to "rush home and get dinner for some big handsome man, and put kids in a bathtub." Clara (Joanne Woodward), Varner's daughter, is a nervous woman and "mighty finicky" about her reputation as a teacher. She is more romantic and optimistic than Agnes, determined to wait "so long as my good looks and sweet temper hold out." Clara feels that "the last, desperate resort is strangers," but "we haven't come to that yet." The film, however, shows otherwise: that there is a great urgency of the town (and the South) in finding strangers to redeem it.

As in other films, one-parent families are the norm and the young protagonists suffer from "parental problems." Ben has never been able to disassociate himself from his infamous barn-burner father, whom he has not seen since he was ten, but still hates. His counterpart, Jody Varner (Tony Franciosa), has also been unable to free himself from his domineering father, and Clara gave up on him when she was nine. Both children feel ambivalent about their father. "I'm all mixed up inside as regards that man," says Jody (bearing a name that is more typically a woman's name). And the virginal Clara knows that her father hates "skinny women and unmarried women" and she is both.

Clara's father has been scaring off all her suitors. The current, Alan Stewart (in *Picnic*, the name of Madge's rich fiancé is also Alan), is a mama's boy; his mother is always concerned he doesn't eat or sleep enough. Slim, weary, and pale, he suffers from an inferiority complex. Going out with Alan is "like eatin' supper with a first cousin." Aware of her loneliness, Clara tells Alan: "Girls get fidgety and talked about and looked at sideways, when they don't have gentleman callers." When this doesn't help, she confronts him more directly: "Do you want me the way a man wants a woman?" But his reply, "I want to help you," disappoints and embarrasses her. Varner is also impatient with Alan: "Do we get the *major* part of your attention?" When Alan explains that his "widow-mother relies on him," Varner bursts out, "Widow, hell! Your old man ain't dead, he just disappeared." Varner is jealous of the Stewarts, because, as Clara says, "quality is the one thing he can't buy, and he knows it." Every conversation between Varner and Clara runs along the same lines; he reminds her that her mother was eighteen when she got married. "Where's my crop?" insists the insensitive father. "What follows me?" Warner wants "a long line with my blood in their veins." "Have you mingled? Or did you keep to your room readin' poetry all this time?" Jabbing his finger at her, he says: "Time, Clara! Time's passin'!" Varner is determined to get some "strong, strappin' men to feed iron into this family's veins." When he mentions Ben, "that big, stud horse," as a candidate, Clara protests he is selling her with no regard for her feeling.

Mistrusting his son's business instincts, Varner tells Jody: "I'm a stonger man than you are still, I'm a better man than you are still"; Jody has heard the same speech ever since he was six years old. A weakling who indulges in sex, Jody is immature and lacks ambition. "I love women, too," says his father, "but I took time out to build this place and leave my mark." It is the kind a business that "you don't *never* give it a rest." "Where do you go looking for it, Poppa," asks Jody helplessly, "if you ain't got it in you?" Upset about the business deal with Ben, Varner puts the latter to test: If he sells the wild horses he will become a partner. Gradually Varner comes to respect Ben, even learns a lesson from him. Varner admits that Ben's "style, brass, and push," are not dissimilar from the way he operates. Indeed, "free as a bird," Ben sees the town as "full of possibilities." With wits, intelligence, and hard work, he progresses from a store clerk to its owner. As his name indicates, Ben Quick is fast and efficient. "One minute we're pickin' him up on Highway 47," says Eula, "and the next he's drinkin' wine out of your momma's old French crystal glasses." As in *Baby Doll*, the Old South is losing its privileged position to the new, upwardly mobile, class. One critic charged the screenwriters for misinterpreting Faulkner's black comedy about materialistic success, turning it instead into "a Horatio Alger bedtime story."[15] True, at the end, it is Ben who instructs Varner in new strategies for conducting successful business operations.

Like *Peyton Place*, the film takes a therapeutic approach to its problems, affirming its belief in direct confrontation. When Mrs. Stewart claims that her boy doesn't need "any traffic" with Varner, he tells her he doesn't want the community to know his daughter has been "jilted" by her "sissy son." Agnes also rebels against her domineering mother, "moving" out of town. She is going to New York, "to study yoga for peace of mind, drink a lot of malted milks to extend my figure, and buy some black underwear to see what happens." At twenty-eight, she is given to anemia and fainting spells, which the family doctor has diagnosed as "purely and simply a case of frustration." When Clara asks Ben for aspirin, he says, "I don't have headaches myself, because I don't have problems." Like Cary's headaches in *All That Heaven Allows*, Agnes's anemia and Clara's headaches *derive* from sexual repression. The film also makes strong associations between fire (burning barns) and sexual desire, a recurrent motif in such films (*Beyond the Forest* and *Splendor in the Grass*). Ben, the sexual stud, is charged with barn burning ("Flame follows him around like a dog!") and, in a weak moment, the sexually hungry Jody sets his father's barn on fire.

Clara thinks Ben is like her father; "one wolf recognizes another." "The world belongs to the meat eaters," says Ben. "If you've got to take it raw, take it raw." He pokes fun at her way of life: "You sit on your side porch with your skinny little friend drinking lemonade—and that's that. You're twenty-three—those are the golden years—and you're being asked to play a waiting game." Ben is beyond gossip, though he is aware that people will talk if Clara marries "a dirt-scratchin,' shiftless, no-good farmer, who just happened by." "Let them talk," he tells Clara. "But you'll wake up mornings smiling." Varner is "a man of purpose," single-mindedly committed to "the survival of the family name," for which purpose he will use "whatever instrument happens to be at hand." "Who says marriages are made in heaven?" Varner tells Ben.

Reflecting the dominant ideology of the 1950s, marriage is also perceived as an economic transaction by Minnie Littlejohn (Angela Lansbury), Varner's mistress. Minnie resents him for keeping her "hidden and put away, like a wool blanket in the summer." Varner has been good to her, she has an Add-a-Pearl necklace, a Zenith radio-TV combination, a Hoover vacuum cleaner, but it is not enough—she wants to get married. Holding that "women have to stand up for themselves," Minnie takes care of the wedding arrangements herself: setting a date, ordering a six-layer cake. In the end, the rule of the patriarch is maintained through the new equilibrium of the three relationships: Eula and Jody achieve a new maturity, and there are two new marriages.

Growing Pains: Tomboys and Misfits—*The Member of the Wedding*

The Member of the Wedding (1953) uses the paradigm of the outsider to its fullest, despite the fact that its characters are all residents of town. This shows that being an outsider is a mental attitude rather than a function of geographical mobility. Each of the three protagonists is an outsider, estranged from his or her surroundings. All three are in a state of anomie, to use Emile Durkheim's concept, marked by normlessness (the lack of norms to prescribe behavior), or situations in which the norms are ambiguous, contradictory, and ill-defined. The film's heroine, Frankie Adams (Julie Harris), is a twelve-year-old tomboy, raised and looked after by Berenice Sadie Brown (Ethel Waters), her black housekeeper. Frankie's mother is dead and her father plays no role in her socialization. A severe, humorless man, he is seldom seen and hardly ever interacts with her. The narrative takes entirely Frankie's (i.e., a child's) point of view, emphasizing that parents are never around when they are needed, and even when around, they lack real understanding of their children.

Frankie's state of mind is conveyed in her narration, which opens the movie: "It happened that green and crazy summer when Frankie was twelve years old. This was the summer when for a long time she had not been a member. She belonged to no club and was a member of nothing in the world. Frankie had become an unjoined person and she was afraid." The film explores in an uncompromising manner Frankie's miserable loneliness. "I have never been so puzzled," is one of Frankie's recurrent sentences, along with "it give me pain just to think about it." Nothing at present pleases Frankie, though her future, as she sees it, also seems bleak. "I wish I had a hundred dollars and never see this town again," she tells Berenice. "I wish I was somebody else except me." She is always worried about one thing or another. "I am so worried about being so tall. You think I'll grow to be a freak?" she asks Berenice in utmost seriousness. She feels that "if I'll be me for the rest of my life, I'll be crazy." Frankie does not even like her name; if it depended on her it would be Jasmin.

The narrative is set in a small (unspecified) Georgia town, during one crucial summer in the life of Frankie, a fiercely lonely misfit, torn between childhood, which no longer satisfies her, and adolescence, which is denied her. Frankie is different from the town's other girls: she is tough and doesn't care about her hair or clothes. She doesn't understand why her brother has brought her a doll; didn't he know she doesn't play with dolls anymore? Told by the girls that she was not elected to the club, she kicks them out of her sight, forbidding them to cross her yard. "I think they've been spreading all over town that I smell bad," she tells Berenice. Sympathizing with her, the cook says, "they are telling big lies about grown-up people too." It takes Berenice, a victim of prejudice and oppression, to explain the "rules of the game." "The whole idea of a club," she says in what is the film's message, "is that members are included and nonmembers are excluded." Throughout the film, Frankie envies her brother, not only for getting married, but for belonging to a larger group. "All people belong to a we, except me," she complains. For Berenice it is the church, for her brother it is the army. Frankie belongs to no club. Her ultimate dream is "to be members of the World! To belong to so many clubs that we can't keep track of them all."

There are no role models in Frankie's life. The only guidance comes from Berenice, who was married four times, the first time at thirteen. In the film's most lyrical scene, Berenice holds the two lonely kids together, Frankie cries on one shoulder and John Henry, Frankie's cousin and neighbor, on the other. For a fleeting moment, a community of misfits is created, an intimate group with a "we" feeling. It's a rare sight, considering the time in which the film was made: black people have seldom served as the moral center in American films. "Why Should I Be Discouraged?" Berenice starts singing, and she is joined by the children, "I sing because I'm happy, I sing because I'm free."

Frankie is contrasted with John Henry (Brandon De Wilde), who occupies a clear status in the social structure. In one of their arguments, Frankie dismisses him as "nothing but a child, entirely young." The other girls are also perceived as "just ugly silly children." She mistreats and abuses John Henry, and only when he dies does she realize how much she has loved him. John Henry has parents but, neglected by them, he spends most of his time at Frankie's. He is lonely too, but he reacts to his loneliness as any normal child would, playing all kinds of games (wearing women's clothes). The film captures well the tantrums and volatile outbursts of Frankie, who is abusive verbally as well as physically. As in many other movies, she is preoccupied with the issue of death; Frankie doesn't believe she will ever die. Frankie feels sadder for Berenice's last beloved husband than for her own mother; she cannot cry for her. Two fateful events change Frankie's life forever: Her brother's wedding and John Henry's death. Indeed, the turning point in Frankie's life is the wedding, with which she is obsessed. "I never believed in love until now," she tells her brother. Shortly after the ceremony, she leaves the house with a suitcase, waiting for the newly married couple in their car's back seat; her father has to drag her from the car, while she is screaming and yelling.

While *Member* has a self-enclosed quality, revealing no clues about its surrounding context, the town serves as a negative reference group. "I swear I'll never come back," says Frankie. Berenice tries to put some sense in her mind. "You're going, but you don't know where." The only outdoor scene in the film occurs when Frankie, running away from home, goes to a bar and encounters a drunken soldier. He too will be glad to leave town; in three days, nobody has said a word to him. Used as an abstract symbol, the town represents a hostile environment: its dark and empty streets makes it seem a ghost town. There are no people, the only sound is that of a couple screaming at each other. At the end, it is Berenice who leaves town. Berenice knows she will never see Frankie again, but she says nothing. As for Frankie, she finally makes some effort to socialize, to belong, striking a friendship with Mary, a new member in town whom she met at the Woolworth's lipstick stand. In the last scene, Frankie is dressed as a girl, not a tomboy, exhibiting more feminine behavior.

This uncharacteristic Hollywood film has one major flaw: the age of Julie Harris, who repeated her stage role. Harris was twice the age of Frankie when she made the movie, and the "cruel" camera, particularly in close-ups, which abound in this film, reveals a young woman instead of a teenager. But it is such a stellar and volatile performance that this credibility gap could be ignored. To director Fred Zinnemann's credit, the film has coherence and integrity, restricting the action to basically one set, the kitchen, and occasionally the backyard, without resorting to the more characteristic device of "opening up" a stage play. In this decidedly indoor movie, the weakest sequence is its one outdoor scene, but it qualifies as a small-town work because of the town's crucial role in shaping the lives of Frankie and Berenice. A demanding film, it boasts an unusually lyrical dialogue, by screenwriters Edna and Edward Anhalt, who altered little of Carson McCuller's book, first adapted to the stage in 1950.

All You Need Is Love: *East of Eden*

John Steinbeck's book, *East of Eden*, was published in 1952,[16] the year *The Member of the Wedding* was released. Elia Kazan's film is a suitable companion piece to *Member*, exploring *male* adolescence. The protagonists of these films share a similar name, Adam. In *Member*, it's Frankie's last name; in *East of Eden*, the patriarch's first name, Adam Trask. There is another link: Julie Harris, the star of *Member*, plays Abra, the girl both boys love. The two films also exhibit similar ideology concerning the "cure" they prescribe for the problems of loneliness, identity formation, and integration into the larger society. The film suffers from excessive theatrical sensibility, stemming from Paul Osborn's career as a playwright and Kazan's as a stage director who uses theatricality in his films. Unlike *Rebel without a Cause* (the other movie James Dean made in 1955), *East of Eden* has not aged well, but it is the film that established Dean as a star.

The narrative begins with a card: "In Northern California, the Santa Lucia Mountains, dark and brooding, stand like a wall between the peaceful agricultural town of Salinas and the rough-and-tumble fishing port of Monterey, fifteen miles away." What connects the town to Monterey is a freight train, used extensively in the story. Set in 1917, just prior to the US entry into World War I, the narrative centers on the Trask family, headed by Adam (Raymond Massey), whose wife Cathy (Jo Van Fleet) has walked out on him years back, leaving him the responsibility of raising two sons: Cal (James Dean) and Aron (Richard Davalos). For years, the patriarch maintains that their mother had died, but when the story begins Cal discovers that Cathy is actually Kate, a madame running a fancy brothel. Later, Cal finds out that a scar on his father's shoulder, which he had explained as a memento of an Indian attack, was caused by his mother's six-gun. Cal has a natural, instinctual rapport with his mother who, at first, rejects him. But, on his second visit, she realizes he is a reflection of her own "wild nature"—she too could not conform to the rigid domesticity demanded by her husband.

The film deals with Cal's desperate search for his roots: renewing the acquaintance with his mother and regaining the love of his father. After some painful experiences, Cal rediscovers the power of family ties and the meaning of romantic love. These two kinds of love, the film says, are needed by every adolescent to grow up as a healthy "normal" person. It is significant that in the first sequence, Cal follows his mother, and in the last, he is in the room of his dying father. For most of the film, however, Cal is alone, isolated from everybody.

For a film pretending to be an epic, it contains a small number of characters. Most of the scenes are theatrical confrontations between two characters (Cal and his mother, Cal and his father), in which revelations are declared and confessions made. The narrative is structured as a melodramatic biblical allegory. Adam Trask is a distant, stern, and self-righteous father, devoting all his attention to Aron, his "good" son. Cal is the "bad" son, often referred to as an animal and compared to his mother Kate, a bad woman running a saloon. (For a film of the 1950s, it is interesting that Kate is not "punished" and does not die, as in the book.) Abra is a good girl, though, she too, by her own admission, has a streak of badness in her. As such, she is the mediator between the two brothers and between Cal and his father. Engaged to Aron, she is clearly in love with Cal. She is the only person Cal can confide in, because being motherless, she has experienced loneliness herself.

Throughout the film, Cal is told he is "nasty, mean, and scary." But he is basically a good, warm, passionate boy, whose entire behavior is motivated by his frustration for not being loved by his father. Jealous of his father's undivided attention to his brother, Cal attempts every possible means to regain his love. Trask's business dream is to refrigerate produce, which can then be transported to the East, for which purpose he bought an icehouse. Cal first attempts to get his father's attention through pragmatic means, by stealing a coal chute to load the produce, but instead of praise he gets reproached. On his father's birthday, he presents him with the money he has saved, but his father reprimands him for profiteering. The spotlight is taken by Aron, when he announces his birthday present: his engagement to Abra.

Despite the fact that most of the film was shot on location, one does not get an overall feel of Salinas as a town. Moreover, important events, such as the breakout of World War I, are treated as external occurrences, experienced by the brothers from the outside. Interestingly, neither brother is idealistic, i.e., collectively oriented—unlike other heroes of small-town movies set in wartime. Aron is a conscientious objector, opposing the war on moral grounds. And Cal perceives the war in pragmatic terms, as an opportunity to go into the beans business, which will help his father.

A major source of tension in town is racism: When the US joins the war, a mob attacks Mr. Albrecht, a German-American and previously a respectable citizen; it is Cal who interferes and thus prevents bloodshed. Sheriff Sam Quinn is a benevolent and liberal figure (like the police officer in *Rebel*), a far cry from the image of authority figures in films of the 1960s and 1970s. The sheriff functions as a sensitive paternal figure, understanding Cal better than his biological father, advising and intervening when he is needed. Sheriff Quinn is the one to confirm Cal's suspicion that Kate is his mother, and to tell him how his father went into a shell after she left him.

The symbols in this film are heavy-handed. For instance, the icehouse could be seen as Adam's cold and emotionally empty life following his wife's abandonment. Interestingly, the romance between Aron and Abra takes place in the icehouse, an enclosed industrial space, signifying emotional chill and lack of intimacy. Watched by Cal, the scene evolves into violence, when he literally attacks the ice, sending huge blocks of it down the chute. Cal's violent act could be interpreted as an act ending his previously icy life, now shattered. By contrast, the romance between Cal and Abra is carried out in nature, in the open fields, or late at night, outside her bedroom in a scene reminiscent of *Romeo and Juliet;* they exchange their first kiss in an amusement park.

East of Eden is an overtly message film: In the next to last scene, Abra explains to the stroke-blighted Adam what needs to be done to "cure" his son's problems. "You have to give him some sign that you love him," she says, "or else he'll never be a man." "It's awful not to be loved," she says. "It makes you cruel." Cal is not a rebellious kid, *all* he wants is to gain the love and respect of his father, for which he is willing to sacrifice himself completely. The film comes to a resolution, when the dying Adam asks Cal to get rid of the nurse: "Don't get anyone else. *You* stay with me. *You* take care of me." Cal, the allegedly weaker son, turns out to be emotionally stronger than his brother. Learning the truth about their mother shatters Aron completely; in a spasm of hysteria he shatters a window with his head.[17] The narrative ends with a role reversal. Cal, the outsider, becomes insider, fully integrated into his family and town. Aron, the former insider, literally becomes an outsider when he enlists in the army (out of despair, not idealism).

Small Towns, Politics, and the Outside World

Pods as Communists: *Invasion of the Body Snatchers*

In the 1950s, a number of science-fiction films used small towns as their settings. Don Siegel's *Invasion of the Body Snatchers* (1956), one of the better of its kind, is set in Santa Mira, California, standing in for every town in America. The narrative's premise is most interesting: A peaceful town is imperceptibly taken over by an alien force. Giant plant pods, products of atomic mutation, turn themselves into replicas of people. The pods turn human beings into faceless, emotionless automatons, incapable of any feeling, be it anger or love. Once again, the image used is that of an initially normal and ordinary town, suddenly thrown out of balance. "At first glance, everything looked the same," the narrator announces. "It wasn't. Something evil had taken possession of the town." The rest of the film explores that "something."

Called back to Santa Mira from a medical conference, Dr. Miles Bonnel (Kevin McCarthy) is greeted at the train station by his nervous nurse Sally. But looking through his clinic's window, everything *looks* to him the same: Wally Everhard is talking someone into buying insurance, Bill Bittner is taking his secretary to lunch. Yet, something strange is going on. In the back of his mind, Miles senses a warning bell: "Sick people who couldn't wait to see me, suddenly were perfectly all right." Later, a boy brought by his grandmother claims that his mother is not his mother; he is reluctant to go home, fearing someone is going to get him. Becky (Dana Wynter), Miles's old flame from high school who is back in town after five years in London, says her cousin Wilma (Virginia Christine) believes that Uncle Ira is not her uncle. "There's something missing," Wilma tells Miles. "There's no emotion. None. Just the pretense of it." Wilma explains that "the words, gestures, tone of voice, everything else is the same, but not the feeling." A general practitioner, Miles believes that "the trouble is inside you!" recommending that she see a psychiatrist. Thus, the first solution to the problem is psychiatric help, with the film acknowledging the increasing popularity of psychiatry in the 1950s. Miles rationalizes his advice to Wilma by saying, "You don't have to be losing your mind to need psychiatric help." But Wilma is firm: "It's a waste of time; there's nothing wrong with me."

As many other films of the decade, *Invasion* deals with three issues: the definition of normal and abormal behavior; the legitimate authority to label behaviors as abnormal or deviant; and the negative effects of conformity, apathy, and complacency. The film suggests that the town's experts and professionals are not to be trusted. The police force, an agency entrusted with the legitimate use of physical force, cannot solve the problem. In fact, when Jack's clone is found, they refuse to call the police, because cops tend to rely too much on logic and dry laws. Psychiatrists are also mistrusted, they too lack the necessary sensitivity or understanding. Psychiatrist Dan Kauffman first diagnoses the situation as a mystery, "It's an epidemic of mass hysteria." Later, when he is summoned by Miles to see Becky's clone (which then disappears), Kauffman refuses to believe. "You saw it only in your mind," he says. "The mind is a strange and wonderful thing; I'm not sure it will ever be able to figure itself out. Everything else maybe, everything but itself." Soon Kauffman himself is converted into one of "them," another soulless pod.

Miles represents the moral center. He is a professional, a doctor, but a general practitioner, not a specialist, thus able to see the problem overall, in its entirety. Moreover, Miles uses his common sense and critical faculties as a responsible individual—not as a professional. When Jack first describes the problem he says: "Would you be able to forget that you're a doctor for a while?" For the duration of the film, Miles forgets his occupational title. The movie advocates independent judgment, common sense, intuition, and self-reliance, and is suspicious of anyone in a position of power or professional expertise. *Invasion,* like Capra's movies of the Depression, singles out the role of an exceptional individual, a charismatic leader, in preventing society from dehumanization, from gradual transformation into an aggregate of unfeeling robots.

The metaphor used to convey mass complacency and conformity is that of sleep. The pods take over human beings when they are not alert, when they are (literally or figuratively) asleep, thus passive. Escaping from town, Miles gives Becky and himself a large dose of pills to stay awake. "We can't close our eyes all night," he tells her, because "we may wake up changed." "Sooner or later," Kauffman tells Miles, "you'll have to go to sleep," i.e., you'll have to conform and join the majority. But Kauffman also reassures him that as soon as he falls asleep, the pods "absorb your minds, your memories, and you're reborn into an untroubled world." The new world will be without love, ambition, grief, or any emotions; "Life will be much simpler and better." Indeed, during their escape, chased by every member in town, Becky cannot stay awake any longer and she falls asleep. "I went to sleep and it happened," says Becky. "A moment of sleep," narrates Miles, and "their bodies were now hosts harboring alien forms of life."

Santa Mira is a typical small town; there is nothing special or distinctive about it (in contrast to 1980s movies, in which small towns exhibit many peculiarities and eccentricities; see chapter 6). The film stresses that what happened in Santa Mira, an average town, can—and will—happen in other towns. In most science-fiction films, the disaster first occurs on a local level, then spreads all over the country. The disaster begins in a small town, moves to bigger regional centers, and finally inflicts the entire nation. Attempting to get assistance, Miles first calls the FBI in Los Angeles, but there is no answer. His call to the governor in Sacramento also fails to go through; all the circuits are busy in both places.

The film unfolds in one long flashback, framed between two brief sequences, a prologue and epilogue, which were imposed by producer

Walter Wanger after the film was shot—against the director's strong objection. Originally, the film was going to end with Miles standing on the highway, trying unsuccessfully to stop the traffic, staring directly at the camera and screaming (at the viewers) "You're next, you're next." But previews indicated that it was alarmingly pessimistic, so a new ending was reshot. In the new version, after considering Miles a "crazy" and "mad" man, the authorities (a good, more reliable psychiatrist) eventually believe in his report and come to the rescue.[18]

Invasion differs from many sci-fi films because there is no immediate confirmation of the hero's report of the "strange" phenomena by other witnesses; the conflict is between *one* individual and the entire community. And unlike other films, *Invasion* shows that the authorities, scientific and political, are neither trustworthy nor competent. Most films reassured their audiences that they were "in good hands," that politicians (or the military) and scientists would come to the rescue when needed. *Invasion*'s ending is so tentative and abrupt that it provides no such reaffirmation, urging instead the need for constant vigilance. In most sci-fi films, the town members eventually organize in a united front to fight the enemy more effectively. However, in *Invasion*, Miles, the insider and moral center, is perceived as an outsider by the town's new moral majority.

The film also works as a nightmarish allegory of mass society, consisting of mindless, feelingless conformists, an interpretation in tune with the mass society critique, which was at its height in the 1950s. Nonetheless, with all the criticism of Santa Mira, there was still intimacy and familiarity—the town's inhabitants know each other by first names—two elements of small-town life that will decline in the 1960s and disappear in the 1970s. Director Don Siegel singled out *Invasion* as his favorite film, because it was "about something, and that's very rare." That the meaning of pods is symbolic was always clear to him: "There are pods—not vegetables from outer space, as in my movie—but real people. Many of my associates are pods, people who have no feeling of love or emotion, who simply exist, breathe, and sleep."[19]

What *Invasion* shares with other science-fiction films of the decade is the notion that the initial threat comes from the outside (another planet). The small-town locale of sci-fi films is thus particularly important, because it usually signals normality, ordinariness, and orderliness. The sci-fi genre peaked in the 1950s as a result of several political reasons. First, there was a renewed interest in outer space. Second, there was fear of the atomic bomb's destructive power. Moreover, because of McCarthy's witch-hunting, filmmakers could not—or feared to—comment directly on current social problems, so they turned to "safer" stories, such as sci-fi and Westerns, using both genres as political allegories. *Invasion* (and the other films of its kind) could be thus enjoyed as "straight" dramas and/or allegories.

Racial Intolerance and Discrimination: *The Lawless* and *Bad Day at Black Rock*

In the late 1940s, a cycle of films examined prejudice and discrimination against ethnic minorities (Jews, blacks, Indians, Hispanics). Some of these films were set in the military (*Home of the Brave,* 1949), others in civilian life. Most narratives took place in urban centers, but a few unfolded in small towns. Kazan's *Pinky* was set in a small Southern town, and *Lost Boundaries* (both in 1949) in a New Hampshire town. Both films dealt with the problems of mulattoes, trying, or forced, to pass as whites, and both protagonists were played by white actors (Jeanne Crain in *Pinky* and Mel Ferrer in *Lost Boundaries*). The two narratives discussed below also provide commentary on the American political process, particularly McCarthyism. Joseph Losey's *The Lawless* (1950) was set in California and dealt with discrimination against Mexican-Americans. The locale of John Sturges's *Bad Day at Black Rock* (1955) was Arizona, focusing on Japanese Americans.

The Lawless (1950) reminded many viewers of *Fury* and *Intruder in the Dust,* because it dealt with a similar theme: mob violence. The context in which *The Lawless* was shown made it all the more relevant: There were riots in Peekskill, New York, precipitated by an advertised performance of Paul Robeson.[20] Set in Santa Marta, in the fruit-growing region of Northern California, it examines a vicious community inflamed by prejudice against Mexican-Americans. The sources of prejudice are never explored, but the film illuminates the *consequences* of such behavior on the victims and their oppressors. In accordance with the conventions of the time, the narrative is explicit and didactic. As the prologue states, it is the story of a town and its people who, "in the grip of blind anger forget their American heritage of tolerance and decency and become the lawless." The problem is never discussed in social structural terms, but is kept safely as a case of discrimination. The migratory workers live in the Sleepy Hollow, the foreign section, that is, the other side of the tracks. In Santa Marta a bridge divides the bad from the good section of town (the script was first titled "The Dividing Line"). But the ghetto is proud of establishing peace and order within its borders. "Tell your readers to look across the tracks," says Sunny Garcia (Gail Russell),[21] a Mexican reporter and unrelenting crusader, "We've erased juvenile delinquency over here." To convey the different life-style of the two sections, director

Losey crosscuts from a Mexican kid using an outdoor shower, to a white kid in a clean bathroom.

The Lawless does not present the Mexican community as a uniformed or undifferentiated group. For example, Paul and Lopo differ in their level of aspiration. Paul is more modest, aiming at owning his land one day, but Lopo believes in changing the community's norms and structure. Members of the two groups meet at a club, ironically called "The Good Fellowship Dance." The community's hatred and anger are brought to the surface when Paul Rodriguez (Lalo Rios) is accused by Joe Ferguson (John Sands), a racist youth with a cool air, of attacking a white girl. The movie shows how the innocent Paul becomes a fugitive after he and his friend, Lopo Chavez (Maurice Jara), are inadvertently involved in a police car accident.[22] Their flight from the police and the ensuing chase precipitate a series of disastrous events. The white press is depicted as callous and sensationalistic, not unlike the press in *They Won't Forget* or *Fury*. "This is the greatest manhunt in the history of this lovely little town," one reporter says. Most of the white residents are hypocritical and duplicitous. Consoling Paul's mother, one woman offers sympathy, "I'm a mother too," but soon after she phones in a vicious report, describing Paul as "mud-covered, sullen . . . a trapped animal."

The only positive characters in the white community are the newspaper's editor Larry Wilder (MacDonald Carey, who played the detective in *Shadow of a Doubt*) and Joe's father, Ed (John Hoyt), the liberal buisnessman. It is interesting that the town's moral mouthpiece is a businessman, a rather unusual convention in small-town films. Ed is exactly the opposite from his son; he has obviously failed in educating him. "I didn't think it could happen here," claims Ed. (Some critics see this passage as commentary on the political witch-hunting of communists in the late 1940s—Losey himself was blacklisted.) Initially, Wilder is not committed, having serious doubts and fears about getting involved. Deeply disenchanted, he instinctively decides to desert: "I'm through with small towns. They're not like I remember them." And it is significant that, only after the mob destroys *his* office, he commits himself to defend the oppressed kid from the lynching mob. Wilder bears the name of many of John Wayne's heroes, but he is more of a Humphry Bogart than a Wayne hero: He is initially hesitant about committing himself to the cause. Still, as in most Capra films, once committed, the leader addresses the masses in powerful speeches, appealing directly to their guilt and shame. But there is a risk: Identifying with the Mexican cause alienates him from the other town members. At the end, he has to start all over again, working for a Chicano newspaper.

Losey builds suspense by the accumulative power of small details about the characters and their social context. By standards of the time, the film was strikingly authentic: Shot on location (including the interior scenes), Losey consulted the photography of Paul Strand and Walker Evans. The manhunt takes place in a rock-filled, desolate landscape, a wasteland outside town, reinforcing visually Paul's sense of isolation and terror. Losey was impressed with the wilderness of rocks and the quality of their sound.[23] The director wanted to show both sides of the American Dream. The nostalgia and good things about small towns are reflected in the sound of distant trains, the sparkle in the air of football games, and the smell of leaves burning at night. However, Hiroshima, the death of President Roosevelt, and the HUAC 1947 investigations disenchanted Losey so much, he wanted to show "the complete unreality of the American Dream."[24] Turning the conventions of Capra's small towns upside down, the film is based on Losey's belief that "the most prejudiced, the most bigoted, the most racist, are always the people from small towns."

Bad Day at Black Rock was one of the rare films to deal with discrimination against Japanese-Americans. The film begins and ends at a railroad station, an abandoned, dilapidated structure. Set in the prairie, with sand dunes rising and falling monotonously, the railroad tracks reach into the horizon. The town of Black Rock is tiny, dismal, and forgotten, surrounded by immutable land; nothing breathes or moves. It is in the middle of nowhere: 32 miles from Sand City, 156 from Phoenix, and 211 from Los Angeles. Isolated, there are no buses or other means of transportation. The whole town is centered on Main Street, a desolate, dirty, and dusty strip. Stylistically, the film begins with a series of long shots; the composition of each has the texture of American primitive painting (Grant Wood). Filmed in CinemaScope, the sweeping vistas of the desert dwarf the town and its inhabitants into midgety proportions.

A robust, one-armed stranger, John Macready (Spencer Tracy) descends from the train. "It's the first time the streamliner stopped here in four years," says the stationmaster. "There must be some mistake." Most of the action takes place at Sam's (Walter Sande) Sanitary Bar and Grill. It is 1945, and Pete, the hotel clerk, claims he has no rooms; they are all filled up with returning soldiers. Wherever Macready turns for assistance, he is rebuffed and needled. The townspeople speculate about the identity of the mysterious stranger who plans to stay "just about twenty-four hours." "He's no salesman," says Doc Velie (Walter Brennan), "that's sure, unless he's peddling dynamite." "He can only mean trouble," says Hector David (Lee Marvin), a vulgar lout. Indeed, Macready's mission is to locate a Japanese farmer, whose son has died in action, to give him a posthumous war medal.

There is no respect for Sheriff Tim Horn (Dean Jagger), the official representative of the law, a boozy guy with bleary eyes. Seen asleep in the lower bunk of the front cell, the sheriff is imprisoned in his own jail;

Macready thought he was a "guest." There is confusion about his role and the status of the law. Told by Reno Smith (Robert Ryan), the actual leader, to do his job, the sheriff asks "What *is* my job?" The diplomaniac sheriff is a weakling, spiritually broken under the strain of conspiracy. The town lacks moral center. The sheriff has lost not only the town's respect, but his self-esteem. Without the rule of the law, it seems as if "the gorillas have taken over." The protagonists' names are ironic. The sheriff boasts an adventurer's name, Tim Horn. The villain is Reno Smith, a name ordinarily associated with good, mid-American values.

It's a nasty town, tormented by hatred and guilt; Smith has infected the whole town with his "bad seed." If the residents are "a little suspicious of strangers," Smith says, "it's a hangover from the Old West." "I thought the tradition of the Old West was hospitality," says Macready. Smith resents the fact that people are always looking for "something" in their community. "To the historian, it's the 'Old West.' To the book writers, it's the 'Wild West.' To the businessman, it's the 'Underdeveloped West.'" Smith wishes all strangers would leave them alone, but Macready's arrival changes everything.

Smith's philosophy is that "a man is as big as the things that make him mad." His biggest problem is how to handle rejection: He tried to join the army the day after "those rats" bombed Pearl Harbor, but he failed the physical. Obsessed with a minority group hatred,[25] the idea that there are loyal Japanese-Americans is "a laugh"; he considers them to be "mad dogs, scum." Smith's reaction to rejection is perverted, using it as an excuse for capturing the unexpectedly valuable land of the Japanese farmer. Komako got there three months before Pearl Harbor, and made wonders with the sterile and barren land, but he was shipped to a relocation center. The town is responsible for burning out his farm and killing him. Nobody even knew Komako had a son, let alone a war hero (who saved Macready's life in Italy).

There is conspiracy in town, ruled by fear and political apathy. At first, even Doc Velie pretends he "doesn't know anything," leading "a quiet, contemplative life." The elderly Velie functions in multiple roles: as notary public, mortician, and veterinarian. "I feel for you," says Doc, "but I'm consumed with apathy. Why should I mix in?" The issue, of course, is that of political involvement. "I try to live right and drink my orange juice every day, but mostly I try to mind my own business, which is something I'd advise you to do." Liz Wirth (Anne Francis), Smith's girl and the only female character, is also afraid to get involved. "I've got to go on living here," she says; "these people are my neighbors, my friends." The film contains that often used phrase in 1950s films,[26] when Liz says, "Maybe I could have been something—a model—but I'm too little and too late, I lack the muscle."

Macready knows "there're not many places like this in America," but, as far as he is concerned, "even one is too many." A man of action, he is determined to perform "one last duty" before he resigns from the "human race." Doc thinks Macready would settle down in Los Angeles, "that hotbed of pomp and vanity," but Macready says he stays out there, because "it's a good jumping-off place—to the Islands, for Mexico, Central America." Undesirable, Macready feels everybody in town would like him "to die quickly, without wasting too much of your time, or silently, without making you feel too uncomfortable, or thankfully, without making your memories of the occasion too unpleasant." But playing on their guilt, he says, "It'll take a *lot* of whiskey to wash out *your* gut." Gradually, Macready forces Doc and Liz to realize that concealing facts makes them just as guilty as committing the crime. Doc is the first to change his mind. "There comes a time, when a man's just got to do something," he tells the sheriff. "There's a difference between clinging to the earth and crawling on it," says Doc, speaking as an existential undertaker.

Neither young nor attractive, Macready is not a conventional Western hero. Defeated, he suffers from the stigma of being crippled. However, he is as silent as a Westerner, a man of action but few words. In his violence, Macready repeats methods he has learned in the army, using commando tactics. In the final showdown, he sets Smith on fire with a blazing gasoline-soaked rag, imitating the army use of napalm. In the film's coda, the town regains its collective conscience, symbolized in Doc's request for the war medal: "We need it, it's something we can maybe build on." "The town is wrecked, just as bad as it was bombed out. Maybe it can come back." "Some towns come back, some don't," says Macready, "it depends on the people," reaffirming populist ideology. In the last shot, having intruded and redeemed Black Rock, the outsider departs. Gathering speed, the train diminishes far into the horizon, and the mysterious stranger turns to his unknown future (a modern version of *Shane*'s hero).

An exercise in sustained suspense, *Bad Day* is a melodrama of retribution that bears resemblance to *High Noon,* though its suspense is tighter. As in *High Noon,* the town is guilt-ridden and literally paralyzed. The relationship between Will Kane (Gary Cooper) and Hadleville is similar to that between Macready and Black Rock. Like Kane, Macready is inner-directed, a man of conscience, an individual pitted against the masses. Both Kane and Macready play on the town's collective guilt, though the former fails. The two heroes are isolated—both are seen walking in empty streets—and both risk their lives for the cause. However, Macready is a more complex character, and unlike Kane, he is not the official representative of the law. Both narratives support individualism and the role of a charismatic leader: In *High* the whole town is condemned; Kane has to fight alone. In *Bad Day*, the residents' guilt torments them and slowly they begin to change. *Bad Day* thus reaffirms the power of reason and the ultimate superiority of democracy.

Conclusion

The postwar era was marked by an increasing trend toward economic and social homogenization. The desirable life-style was suburbanism, and the ultimate role model the "organization man." However, beneath the facade of conformity and homogeneity, there was an underlay of sexual repression and political hysteria that reflected McCarthy's witch-hunting. As a powerful communication industry, transmitting values and norms, Hollywood was a prime target, and McCarthy conducted investigations twice, in 1947 and 1951. America's new status as an international leader and superpower nation, wiped out once and for all the prewar trends of isolationism and independence. These ideological slogans were no longer appropriate.

It was also the last decade in which dominant ideology stressed the notion of America as a melting pot. Until the 1960s, members of ethnic minorities were not only undermined, but were also expected to assimilate passively into mainstream culture, as defined by the white middle class. With the exception of *Salt of the Earth*, (1954) a film about a defiant Mexican-American community, the few films about ethnic minorities all recommended (actually demanded) that their members give up their separate subcultures and adopt white middle-classness, the only sanctioned *American* life-style in the 1950s.

Many films of the decade used Freudian psychology in describing their protagonists' problems and prescribing resolutions for them. Kazan's *East of Eden,* Edward Dmytryk's *Raintree County,* (1957) and the plays by William Inge *(Picnic)* and Tennessee Williams *(Rose Tattoo),* embodied (pseudo) psychoanalytic ideas in their narratives. They were all about loneliness and the need for love—within the boundaries of the family. In *Rebel without a Cause* and *The Wild One,* the youngsters' rebellion is neither political nor social. The former is a melodrama about sensitive kids who, misunderstood and abused by their parents, seek to gain love and respect from their peers. And in the latter, when the leader is asked, "What are you rebelling against?" he replies, "What have you got?"

The conservative ideology and its emphasis on middle-class domesticity was particularly evident in the changes made in transferring stage plays to the big screen; in the process, plays suffered immensely as a result of the strict impositions of the Production Code. The heroine of Tennessee Williams's *The Rose Tattoo* (1955), Serafina Della Rose (Anna

Magnani), is an Italian-born seamstress, transplanted from Sicily to Florida's Gulf Coast. Following the death of her small-time smuggler-husband, she turns into a recluse, keeping his ashes in a gimcrack vase in her shanty parlor. Obsessed with his physical virility, she describes him as a "young bull" (Ben in *The Long, Hot Summer* is also depicted as a stud and bull). Serafina is contrasted with Rosa (Marisa Pavan), her naive teenage daughter, experiencing her first love. At fifteen, Rosa claims she is "ready" for marriage and motherhood. A domineering mother, she forces her daughter to be as recluse and repressed as she is, particularly upon realizing that her husband was unfaithful to her. "I was a peasant," she tells the priest. "I came to him with one dress, but I brought him glory; he was a baron." Refusing to believe that "the man I kept in my heart gave me horns," she is demented by wild grief, and her jealousy turns into fierce possessiveness of her daughter. However, when she meets another truck driver (Burt Lancaster), who has "the body of my husband," she is unable to repress her sexuality anymore.

The film version of *The Rose Tattoo* scaled down the raw sexuality and passion in the original play, lacking Williams's criticism of conventional morality.[27] In the play, as Maurice Yacowar pointed out, it was passion for passion's sake, but in the film, sexual desire is approved of only if it leads to marriage. In the play, Serafina and Alvaro meet by fateful accident, but in the film, Alvaro's sister plots a match between them. In the play, Rosa settles for a night of love; in the film, for domesticity. In the play, Alvaro says, "Sooner or later the innocence of your daughter cannot be respected," which was changed in the film into "Sooner or later, the innocence of your daughter cannot be respected if the family's going to continue."

As in previous decades, the characteristic films of the 1950s contrasted repressive culture with the uninhibited life in nature. However, these conceptual opposites were not framed in narratives about Small Town versus Big City. Rather, the tension between culture and nature prevailed *within* the small town itself: The films compared alternative lifestyles *within* the same town. In each film, the protagonists feel a strong need to escape into nature, withdraw to outdoor places. For example, in *Peyton Place*, it is the hill where Allison and Norman exchange their first innocent kiss. In *All That Heaven Allows*, it is Ron's greenhouse and mill outside town. In *Written on the Wind*, it is the river, where the protagonists used to have picnics as adolescents. In *Rebel without a Cause*, it is the isolated house.

The melodramatic plots of small-town films in the 1950s shared similar narrative structure and thematic conventions. There were always secrets about the protagonists' past that would later be revealed in confessional manner. In addition to *Peyton Place*, other films dealt with illegitimate children and compromising marriages. *A Summer Place* (1959), one of the decade's blockbusters, dealt with a frustrated love, and *The Restless Years* (1959) with illegitimacy concealed from the daughter. Sandra Dee, the most popular teenage star at the time, starred in both films. Sexism was at its most blatant in American films of the 1950s, possibly one of the worst eras for women in Hollywood. *Salt of the Earth* was really an anomaly, an independent production with explicitly feminist consciousness, advocating left-of-center politics. The class conflict, between the miners and their capitalistic managers, changes focus once the women join the men in their strike.

Films in the 1950s still manifested a strong belief in therapeutic approach to personal and social problems. The recommended mode of behavior was direct confrontation, "getting things out in the open," as one character states in *The Long, Hot Summer.* The films stressed the importance of coming to terms with reality—facing the truth was deemed the only way to resolve problems. There was also belief in the patriarchal order and mainstream society. The town as a whole was still effective in asserting "morality" over its individual members. Indeed, most small-town films had clear closures, in the form of resolutions and reconciliations (happy ending).

This trend could be seen in the favorable portrayal of representatives of the law: sheriffs, marshals, policemen. In the James Dean films (*Rebel without a Cause* and *East of Eden*), the sheriff/policeman is more understanding than his biological father, functioning as surrogate father or social worker. In Stanley Kramer's production of *The Wild One* (1954), the first film to deal with juvenile delinquency, a gang of motorcycles (headed by Marlon Brando in a black leather jacket) terrorizes a small (unspecified) town. But like *Rebel,* the cause of their rebellion is diffuse and general and, at the end, they are asked to leave town by a kind and sensitive official. In another Kramer film, *The Defiant Ones* (1958), two escaped convicts, one white (Tony Curtis) and one black (Sidney Poitier), make a symbolic odyssey toward freedom in the Deep South. Chained to each other, their relationship changes from deep hatred to genuine camaraderie. In their flight, they encounter a vicious lynching mob, but are saved by Big Sam (Lon Chaney, Jr.), an upright and fearless man who stands against the mob. The film also contrasts sheriff Max Muller (Theodore Bikel), a humane sheriff with a streak of justice, and the brutish state policeman, in favor of using hunting dogs. The sheriff has to remind the policeman that they are there to capture, not execute, the convicts.

Stylistically, small-town films of the 1950s draw on theatricality and psychological realism, a result of the ascendance of Method Acting as the dominant style in the American theater. A new generation of actors, all graduates of Lee Strasberg's Actors Studio, moved from the Broadway theater to Hollywood in the 1950s. And they all played small-town heroes: James Dean, Montgomery Clift *(A Place in the Sun, Raintree County)*, Marlon Brando *(The Wild One)*, Paul Newman *(The Long, Hot Summer, Cat on a Hot Tin Roof)*. Method Acting was perfectly suitable to the theatrical nature and sensibility of small-town films of the decade, most of which were based on stage plays by Tennessee Williams, Arthur Miller, William Inge, and Lillian Hellman. However, psychological realism and Method Acting have badly dated. Which is the reason why the more stylized films of Douglas Sirk *(All That Heaven Allows* and *Written on the Wind)*, Joseph Losey *(The Lawless)*, and Nicholas Ray *(They Live by Night, Rebel without a Cause)* have held up much better than the work of Daniel Mann *(Come Back, Little Sheba, Rose Tattoo)*, Richard Brooks *(Cat on a Hot Tin Roof)*, or Elia Kazan *(East of Eden)*. The films of Mann, Brooks, and Kazan are interesting today because they feature extraordinary quality in their acting. But despite stylistic variation, thematically, all of these directors (Sirk, Kazan, Losey) satirized middle-class complacency, and warned against latent (or manifest) tendencies toward racism and sexism.

4

• • • • • • • •

The 1960s—
Continuity and Change

Maycomb had recently been told that it had nothing to
fear but fear itself.
—To Kill a Mockingbird

You Are now Leaving the Town of Sparta—Hurry Back!
—In the Heat of the Night

The decade of the 1960s is remembered now for shaping the cultural
sensibilities of the baby boom generation. But it is a rather complex, even
schizophrenic, decade in terms of the culture it produced. The political
events and structural changes that took place in the 1960s altered the
course of the decade from one extreme to another. Indeed, more than
other cultural products, the movies reflected the decade's "split personality." Films made in the early 1960s continued the tradition of the
previous decade, supporting, for the most part, the dominant culture,
whereas films made in the late 1960s (from 1967 on) were more critical
and cynical, expressing countercultural and antiestablishment views.
Unlike other decades, the 1960s thus lack a coherent look or dominant
point of view.

Historically, the most important event of the decade was the election
of John F. Kennedy as president. But sociologically speaking, the decade
began to change around 1963–64. The year of 1963 may be a watershed
year, for it witnessed many significant events: The assassination of President Kennedy, the march on Washington, the publication of Betty
Friedan's landmark book, *The Feminine Mystique,* and the first cohort of
baby boomers graduating from high school. Later in the decade, the
protests at Kent State and Jackson State University, the Free Speech
Movement at Berkeley, the events at Newark and Watts, the Democratic

National Convention in Chicago, all contributed to a new spirit and a new ethos.

The early 1960s movies carried over in theme and tone the attitude of the 1950s small-town films. The culture-lag theory could be used here: Movies tend to lag behind social reality because it takes a long time (at least two years) from the origination of an idea for a film up to its wide release. And the nature of most films is such that they reflect rather than anticipate new trends and new ideas. More specifically, many small-town films in the 1960s were based on 1950s Broadway hits; it took several years to purchase their rights and make their screen versions. This was the case of the screen adaptations of Tennessee Williams and William Inge's plays.

Nostalgic View of Growing Up and Family Life

William Inge's *The Dark at the Top of the Stairs* (1960), transferred to the screen from his Broadway play, depicts a family torn by problems. As other Ingean works, it is set in a small Oklahoma town in the 1920s. The locale and time are not stated explicitly, though hinted through a mention of Valentino's silent *The Sheik* (1921). Each member of the Flood family carries his or her baggage of problems. Rubin Flood (Robert Preston), the father, is a harness salesman whose livelihood is threatened by the automobile. His nagging wife Cora (Dorothy McGuire) is sexually unresponsive. But Rubin is a gentleman, stating with pride: "I never cheated on Cora once since I've been married." Old-fashioned, he also believes that a man should not burden his wife with his problems (even those related to his job). Reenie (Shirley Knight), their shy daughter, is introverted, and Sonny (Robert Eyer), a fearful mother-fixated boy, is unable to protect himself at school. The catalyst of events is Cora's malicious sister, Lottie (Eve Arden), called from the City for a family conference. Her arrival makes things worse by setting up new problems. Like Cora, Lottie is miserable, suffering from a bad marriage; she provides advice she herself should—but does not—follow.

The film lacks subtlety, making every point that was understated in the play too obvious and explicit. And there are additions as well as omissions from the play. The son's sexual awakening—the play's focus—is just one, rather unexplored, element in the film. A new character, the "other woman," Mavis the widow (Angela Lansbury), who did not exist in the play, is introduced in the film. Most scenes are confrontational, as when Rubin tells his wife: "I'm going to see Mavis, I'm going to drink booze, and I'm going to raise any hell I can think of." But his attraction to Mavis is also problematic—she will not go to bed with him.

Lottie is prejudiced against Jews and Catholics, but hers and the town's prejudices are only superficially examined. Reenie is in a state of shock when a Jewish boy she befriends commits suicide because of anti-Semitism. And there is, of course, gossip about Rubin's relationship with Mavis. Like all of Inge's works, the movie is about repression, sexual and emotional, and the urgency to come to terms with the problem. It also deals with the interplay between establishing self-worth and gaining social approval. For instance, fearing the dark at the top of the stairs, Sonny, the mama's boy, learns to defend himself and, at the end, chases the school's bullies. *Dark at the Top* is one of the first movies to deal with male menopause (though not seen as such at the time). Clearly, it is Rubin's last job: With the increasing use of automobiles, there is no demand for harness.

One important link between *Dark at the Top* and two other movies about family life in small towns (*All the Way Home* and *The Music Man* [both in 1962]), was Robert Preston, who played the father in all three: a biological father in the first two, and a surrogate in *The Music Man*. All three movies are sentimental treatments of the American family, and in each Preston plays a sensitive, not stern, father.

James Agee's novel *A Death in the Family* was first adapted to the stage by Tad Mosel, who changed its title to *All the Way Home,* the title of the screen version. As *Dark at the Top,* it is a family drama about the effects of a beloved father's sudden death on his wife and son. The narrative is divided into two parts: the first chronicles the family's life, the second records the impact of his accidental death. The calmness and stability of everyday life is shattered abruptly by the tragic news that the father was killed in a car accident on his way to visit his ill father.

There are explorations into the 1916 Tennessee town, the story's locale. The sounds of arriving and departing trains provide the natural music in town. Fascinated by trains, Rufus likes to stand at a special spot overlooking the railroad tracks and the train station. A lonely kid, with no friends of his age, he is surrounded by adults: parents, uncles, and aunts. Rufus does not like his name because he believes "it's a nigger's name." In the first scene, the father and son watch a Chaplin movie, then take a meandering walk home, stopping to watch shop windows and have a drink at the saloon. The parents' major concern is how to explain to Rufus his mother's pregnancy. "You don't need a minister to tell you how to raise your boy," says the father, when his wife is concerned over: "Suppose he starts making connection between one thing and another." At the end, following her husband's advice, she simply puts her son's hand on her belly.

It is an emotional film, with no drama or conflict, a tactful, reverential ode to the family as a sacred institution. In the first scene, set outdoors, the father tells his son, "It's time to go home." And in the last one, coming to terms with their loss, it is the mother who says, "It's time to go home." The father represents an average man, lacking any special or radiant qualities. He is tender but strong, devoted to his family and yet independent. The film lacks Agee's powerful poetry and subjective style, which probed family life from a child's point of view, stressing the anguish and bereavement of a loss of an idol. Lacking point of view, the passive camera records, instead of illuminating, events. Understated and restrained, the film is bland, but it pays attention to detail, documenting the era through brass-radiatored Model-T Fords, Buster Brown suits, long dresses, Tin Lizzies, and chewing tobacco ads.

The most popular of the Robert Preston small-town trilogy was *The Music Man*, in which he successfully re-created his stage role.[1] Preston plays an outsider, Harold Hill, a charming trickster who persuades the council of River City, Iowa, to organize a boys' band. "Professor" Hill pretends to be a graduate of the Gary Conservatory in Indiana, but is actually a salesman down on his luck. Driven out of town, Hill finds himself aboard a train. Asked "How far are you going, friend?" he says, "Wherever the people are as green as the money." Arriving in River City, Hill encounters in the streets clean-looking and hardworking residents. "What do you do here for excitement?" he asks. "Mind our own business," is one short reply.

Mrs. Sheen (Hermione Gingold) the mayor's wife, rushes to the library to protest the kinds of books her daughter is given. "Keep your dirty books from my daughter," she demands, referring to a book of Persian poetry. Along with the town's respectable matrons, she stages educational American plays, playing the Statue of Liberty (with a torch in her hand), and an Indian. Her husband—mayor doesn't approve of his daughter's Lithuanian suitor, a lower-class man who lives "on the South of town." The other stock characters include a spinsterish librarian, Marian (Shirley Jones), who also teaches piano, and her widow mother, who reproaches her for still being unmarried. "Don't you ever think of the future? He [Hill] maybe your last chance," says the mother. "No girl wants to be an old maid."

Hill functions as a magician, a conman able to convert kids into talented musicians through *faith*. The same function was performed by Burt Lancaster's outsider—con man in *The Rainmaker*. An effective demagogue, Hill preaches that "singing is just sustained talking." Confronted by Marian about his fabricated past, he confesses to his sin. But he also has to face her younger brother (Ron Howard) who, fatherless, relates to him as an authority figure. "Are you a liar? Are you a rotten crook?" asks the kid. "Yes," answers Hill, "but I always think there is a band." The band, real or imagined, is the symbol of hope. At the town's meeting, in which its collective values are tested and reaffirmed, Marian speaks in Hill's favor: "You remember life before he came? After he came, suddenly there were things to do." The outsider, symbolically named Hill, has changed the town completely, restoring faith and bringing excitement to humdrum lives. This outsider, unlike the con man in *The Rainmaker,* stays in town. "For the first time in my life," says Hill, "I got my foot caught in the door," a sentence conveying at once the exposure of his crookedness and intent to settle down.

Directed by Morton Da Costa (who staged the Broadway musical), the film is overliterate, slavishly copying the stage production, with no knowledge or understanding of a *movie* musical. Marion Hargrove's script adheres too much to Meredith Willson's play, and the only redeeming quality is the great music (the showstoppers include: "Seventy-Six Trombones," "Till There Was You," "Gary, Indiana," and "Trouble"). The end result is a photographed play, a nostalgic evocation of what critic Arthur Knight described as "a rustic America as we would like it to have been."[2] However, released in 1962, *The Music Man* was congruent with the optimism of Kennedy's New Frontier.

Love versus Sex: *Splendor in the Grass*

The most powerful small-town film in the early 1960s was undoubtedly Elia Kazan's *Splendor in the Grass.* Made in 1961, from William Inge's original script, it is a typical 1950s film, showing that the beginning of a decade often carries over the themes and ideology of the previous decade. Like *Peyton Place,* it is a summation movie that examines important issues: the pains of growing up, parental authority, adult irresponsibility, social hypocrisy, repressed sexuality, moral and mental breakdown, love and marriage. And unlike *Dark at the Top,* these issues are placed against a specific historical backdrop, conveying a sense of time and place. Kazan's movie bears the scope, intensity, and ambition of an epic film. It has the precision of a clinical case study put under magnifying and scrutinizing glasses.

In the opening sequence, Bud (Warren Beatty, in a stunning film debut) and Wilma Dean, called Deanie (Natalie Wood), are seated in his car, a Model-A Ford roadster with its top down.[3] A long, fervent kiss leaves them breathless; they have to break away from each other to fight for breath. The still of the night makes their passion audible. They are in nature, with the forceful waterfall as background to their desire; water imagery and its sexual connotations prevail in this film. Deanie is dressed in white, suggesting virginal purity, but her dress reveals more than it conceals, thus hinting about the conflict she will experience concerning sexual desire. She begins to protest, though it is clear that she would like to continue. The camera zeroes in on her face, showing *her* reactions. It expresses passion and eagerness for a fulfillment, which both of them want but fear. Bud knows he has gone too far and, deeply upset and humiliated, he jumps out of his car, waiting for his excitement to subside. This one image, showing their passionate, troubled, and puzzled faces, captures the essence of the film and sets the tone of its conflict.

At the center of *Splendor* are two families, the Loomises and the Stampers, situated differentially at the class hierarchy. The Stampers live in a big beautiful house. Ace Stamper (Pat Hingle), another domineering patriarch, is a wealthy man, owning the town's oil wells. Bud is a sensitive kid, but completely uninterested in his father's business, wealth, or prestige. Ginny Stamper (Barbara Loden), Bud's sister, the depraved jazz-age flapper, is a "bad" girl and the black sheep of the family. By contrast, the Loomises live in a small frame building, next to a grocery that Del Loomis (Fred Stewart) owns. The two families are dominated by different figures: the Stampers by the patriarch, whose wife (Joanna Roos) is quiet and passive; the Loomises by the matriarch (Audrey Christie), whose husband is a weakling. Thus, while not one-parent families in the literal sense (as most small-town families are), they are such units figuratively.

It is Mrs. Loomis (no name is given to her) who runs the affairs of the family. "There's big news tonight," she tells her uninterested daughter. "The Stamper oil stocks have gone up fourteen points. If we sold our stocks now, maybe we could send you away to college next year." Mrs. Loomis is disappointed when Deanie says that Bud knows nothing about his father's business. Extremely pragmatic and upwardly mobile, her attentions are single-mindedly focused on her daughter's future, i.e., marriage. There is not one positive adult figure in the whole film. Mrs. Loomis, a neurotic mother, is inadequate as a role model. "Bud could get you into a whole lot of trouble," she warns her daughter. "Boys don't respect a girl they can go all the way with; they always want a nice girl for a wife." "Is it terrible to have those feelings about a boy?" Deanie naively inquires. "No nice girl does," her mother responds abruptly. "Your father never laid a hand on me until we were married! And then I just gave in because a wife has to." Deanie's puritanic mother has never explored or enjoyed her sexuality. She reflects culture's double standard, "A woman doesn't enjoy those things the way a man does," when she says, "A woman just lets her husband come near her in order to have children." In this, she suggests the denial of sexual pleasure, with sex serving instrumental functions for women—the legitimate channel to have a family. Women's obliteration of sexual desire and the priority of motherhood over womanhood have been consistent traits of middle-class culture.

Ace is also concerned with Bud's private behavior, periodically asking him to watch himself with her, and not do "anything you'll be sorry for." Ace's reservations about Deanie have nothing to do with the Loomises' inferior class. "I'm not a snob," he tells Bud, "I got nothing against 'em 'cause they're poor." In fact, Ace and Del Loomis were boys together, and "the only difference between them is that Ace had 'ambition.'" Ace has "a big future planned" for his son: Four years at Yale, then managing his company, which he hopes will merge with one of those big Eastern companies.

The church unifies only superficially the town's diverse residents. Ace attends the services, but invariably falls asleep during the sermons. Outside church, the friendly Ace advises Mr. Loomis to hold onto his stocks, and the two mothers exchange pleasantries; no animosity is sensed. Despite class differences, both families are guilty of hypocrisy and pretentiousness, and both fail in educating their children. This is clear in a Christmas sequence, with crosscutting between the two households. Opening their presents, Deanie's mother wishes Bud's present would "cost a lot less and was a ring," and her father, impatient after four years of courtship, wishes Bud had "a little more gumption." Bud gets from Deanie a soft wool scarf and a pair of socks she had knitted herself. "I guess they couldn't afford a regular present," says Ace.

Ace is contemptuous of his daughter Ginny, making no secrets as to who is his favorite child. Disappointed with her, he informs Bud: "I've got all my hopes pinned on you now, son!" A small-town girl, who moved to the Big City (Chicago), Ginny is perceived as a failure in every way. Sending his wife to bring her back, Ace accuses Mrs. Stamper (no first name for her, either) of spoiling her. Ginny was sent off to a finishing school, where she broke the rules and was kicked out. Next, her mother sent her to the university, where "she goes hog wild and flunks all her courses." Then, she is sent to Art School, where "she ends up with some cake-eater who gets her in trouble so he can marry her." But as soon as her beau learned that her allowance would be cut off, he lost interest in her. Ace describes Ginny as "a headstrong little flapper who wants to have her own way," but he is just as determined to "teach her some discipline." Indeed, when Ginny expresses her wish to go to California and study art, Ace screams, "Art who?" For him, she is "a trollop," an expression that makes his wife shudder.

Ginny thinks they live in "a god-forsaken town." In Chicago, she had friends, but here she's "a freak! people stare at me on the street like I was out of a carnival." "That's because you peroxide your hair and paint your face like an Indian," says her father. Once again, the term *Indian* is used pejoratively; in *Picnic*, Rosemary describes Carter as a "naked Indian." But Ginny is the only member to stand up to her father. "This is the ugliest place in the whole nation," she charges. "Everywhere you look there's an oil well, even on the front lawn. I bet you'd dig a well right here in the living room." Disreputable, Ginny is the major cause of gossip in town. "She is too low for the dogs to bite," says Mrs. Loomis, referring to her abortion. When Deanie protests that "it's all gossip," her mother says, "Every word is true"; she has heard it from Mrs. White-comb who lives right across the street from the Stampers. Ginny is a negative point of reference—the fear mothers have of what might become of their daughters if they "go wild and boy crazy." On New Year's Eve at the Country Club Dance, Ginny gets drunk. Bud dances with her out of pity; no one asks her, even though she is the richest girl in town. "The only place they'll speak to me now is in the dark," says Ginny. "Oh, they're very familiar then."

Deanie is contrasted with Ginny, an unrestrained, amoral woman. They represent two sides of womanhood: purity versus unbridled sexuality, romantic innocence versus carnal lust. Note the similarity in the sound of their names, Deanie and Ginny, and the irony in naming Bud's sluttish sister Virginia, who is anything but virgin. Ginny is evil incarnate: she dances wildly, drinks too much, seduces men. She smokes in public, even outside church. When all four drive to the country, the way Deanie looks at Ginny reveals a complex mixture of feelings: voyeurism, inhibition, but also jealousy. Indeed, once she stops seeing Bud, Deanie begins to take on Ginny's characteristics. She dresses like Ginny, smokes in public and becomes more explicitly seductive. She is a teenager at a crossroads, somewhere along the process of becoming an overtly sexual woman.

Bud and Deanie are the ideal, most desirable, couple at their school, where there are all kinds of girls. There is Juanita (Jan Norris), the school "pickup," who dresses coquettishly and wears too much makeup. And there are Hazel, June, and Kay, who model themselves after Deanie. *All* the girls resent Juanita. "She is disgraceful" says Deanie, protesting the way Bud looks at her. Contrasted with all of them is Angelina (Zohra Lampert), the lower-class girl, who Bud marries at the end. As her name indicates, she is good-hearted and selfless. Most boys in school are no better than Ace; they are products of a sexist culture. "I never look twice at those other girls anymore," states Rusty in the shower room. "Ya take them out and spend good money on 'em and then they expect you to feel satisfied if they kiss you good night."

Like the other classmates, the spinsterish teacher Miss Metcalf (Martine Bartlett) watches Bud and Deanie with admiration, frustration, and envy. What the youngsters study at school feeds their romantic fantasies, with no apparent use or value. "The knights all held a very high regard for womanhood, in fact, they put woman on a pedestal," lectures Miss Metcalf. "Do any of you feel that you are on a pedestal?" All the students think, and some look at Deanie—she is the only one on a pedestal. The school's macho coach likes to bully his players, using sexist language to motivate them: "One day they play like girls, then the next day like they want to kill the whole world."[4]

The adult figures in *Splendor* are of no help; they too are victims of the repressive culture. Bud's father (in the mold of Williams's "Big Daddy") is obtuse, hypocritical, and insensitive, draining any energy and excitement out of his son. When Bud confides in him his sexual frustration, "I feel like I'm going nuts sometimes—like I'm going to come apart," all his father can say is, "What you need for the time being is another type of girl," suggesting he separate between romantic love and sexual gratification. "When I was a boy," Ace recalls, "there was always two kinds of girls, and we boys never mentioned them in the same breath." With his vigorous masculinity and boundless energy, Ace is a domineering patriarch when it concerns his son, but a rather amiable and democratic boss, one who enjoys the company of his men over his wife. He entertains his field workers informally, providing free drinks and oysters, shipped all the way from Baltimore in a refrigerated car. His ambition, that Bud become a football star, is a compensation for his brief career terminated by an accidental fall. "You're running for both of us now," he tells Bud. When Bud falls and Doc Smiley (John McGovern) recommends hospitalization for his pneumonia, Ace promises, "If you pull this boy through there's a bonus waiting for you, a big one—five thousand dollars!" Misunderstood by his father, Bud turns for help to the doctor, but as his name indicates, he is pleasant and smiling—but of no help. "It's hard to advise you," says Smiley, when Bud complains that "everytime we're together, I have to remember . . . *things* . . . a guy can go nuts that way."

Bud is another nature boy who doesn't want to go to college because he knows he is no good. This is unacceptable to his father, whose motto is, "You can do anything you set your mind to" (a recurrent phrase in small-town movies). However, Bud has set his mind on agriculture, and he would like to take over his father's ranch, south of town. "Ranching!" screams the appalled father with strong disapproval. There are two places of escape: by the bank of the river, and Stamper's ranch house, a kind of sporting lodge. After the frustrated experience with Deanie, Bud returns to the river with Juanita, who surrenders to him immediately, but he cannot stand the memory of Deanie and he takes her to a more deserted part of the river. Deanie also returns to the river, but by herself, and, in the film's most controversial scene, she swims in the nude and masturbates. At the ranch house, Ginny is with Glenn, her new working-class beau (from Oklahoma), who works at the Standard filling station.[5] Ginny is the only honest person in the film and the only woman in touch with her libido. "Why don't you take her upstairs," she asks Bud, "and get it out of your system?" She cannot understand; "Why don't you both quit trying to pretend you're so pure and righteous." Full of disdain, Ginny tells Deanie, "He just lets things torment him inside and make him miserable and never does anything about them." There is a powerful scene between the siblings, in which Bud tries to keep Ginny from going out with the next "wrong guy," a married bootlegger. Ferocious, she slaps him hard, bruising his face, then realizing his behavior stems from his own frustration, she softens, feeling sorry for him. As in Vidor's *Beyond the Forest*, the film makes connections between frustrated sexual desire and the constantly churning oil well. Lying in bed, Bud grabs a pillow, as if it were a person, and whispers, "Deanie, Deanie"; in the background, the sound of the oil wells is heard. Placed in similar position in *her* bed, Deanie grabs her teddy bear.

The mortality rate in this moralistic narrative is high: the two "villains" pay for their sins with their lives. Ginny dies in a car accident, a punishment for her loose morality and sexual transgression. She represents a threat to domesticated family life. Ace, her father, a victim of unlimited capitalistic ambitions, commits suicide when the stock market crashes. Both are chastised for immoral, excessive behavior, sexual and economic.

Splendor demonstrates the effects of sexual frustrations on two romantically naive youngsters. Bud epitomizes the conflict between sexual gratification and repression, the tension between obedience to parental authority and the need for rebellion. The effects of sexual abstention are tragic: Deanie suffers a *mental* breakdown; Bud a *moral* breakdown. And despite the fact that her suffering is more overt (she is institutionalized), Bud's pain is no less devastating, his entire world of values is shattered. The film is excellent in portraying Deanie and Bud's dilemmas. What they want, romantic love and sexual fulfillment, not only run against social conventions, but against their *own* beliefs of "proper" behavior. They are victims of overly conformist socialization, perpetuating their victimization by submitting to the coercive norms they themselves suffer from. They are victims, not of fate or circumstances, but of socialization that stresses the wrong ideals. They are also victims of their personalities, too weak to revolt against unnecessary impositions. At the end, their decency and idealistic purity become their own tragedy and it brings them down.

The narrative is framed by Wordsworth's poem, "Ode on Intimations of Immortality," first recited in the classroom, then in the last scene, when Bud and Deanie face each other, after several years apart, for the last time. They are now grown-up, adjusted individuals who have lost their youthful vigor and idealism. Deanie fully understands the real meaning of Wordsworth's poetry: "Though nothing can bring back the hour of splendor in the grass, glory in the flower, we will grieve not, rather find strength in what remains behind."

Unlike other films, the process of growing up is neither glamorized nor sentimentalized. Rather, it is depicted as painful and compromising: The film also shows the need to settle for second bests. Inge's frankness in the treatment of sensitive issues is remarkable, and his two youthful characters are more complex than the protagonists of his other works. Inge succeeds in universalizing from the particular context of Southeast Kansas in the late 1920s. It is a searing, often brutal, exposé of small-town life, emphasizing its criminal narrow-mindedness and rigid culture. *Splendor* evokes a past without being a historical period piece. Indeed, the mores of family life and sexual politics in 1961 were not that different from those prevailing three decades earlier.

Prevalent Small-Town Types: Spinsters

Along with the small-town patriarch, the spinster continued to attract the attention of writers and directors in the 1960s. The decade saw many variations of old maids, though they were enjoying their screen dominance for the last time. It is a screen role that, as a type, has declined, at least in its extreme harshness, treating spinsters as personal and social failures.

The film version of Tennessee Williams's *Summer and Smoke* (1961), was presented thirteen years after the play was written.[6] Set in 1916 in a Mississippi town, it concerns a frustrated spinster, Alma Winemiller (Geraldine Page), and the consequences of her sexual repression.[7] Alma nurses an unrequited love for John Buchanan (Laurence Harvey), the virile next-door neighbor. Under the facade of decorum and gentility, she is burning with desire for the pleasure-seeking John. Spent in futile dreams, Alma's life has been a miss. Caught between a righteous minister-father (Malcolm Atterbury) and insane mother (Una Merkel), she is almost doomed, *almost,* because at the end she transforms. Against the tradition of repressed spinsters, Williams constructed a heroine capable of rebelling against her parents and society's mores. Alma adopts a looser mortality and, in the last scene, picks up a traveling salesman at the town's square.

It is one of the weakest adaptations of a Williams work, stemming from the fact that, as Maurice Yacowar pointed out, it is a stylized play of ideas with an expressionistic setting.[8] Two theoretical forces clash in the play: body, or sensualist orientation, embodied by John, and soul (the heroine's name) or spiritualist orientation. Every character in the movie has its opposite type and embodies an abstract idea. For example, Alma's father is everything that John is not: the two complement each other. To open up the play, director Peter Granville resorts to outdoor activities, band concerts, gambling casinos, and cockfights. But the town is never brought to life and the setting remains an external decor for the psychological study.

In the tradition of small-town adolescents, Alma is the only character to have both parents. John has no mother; Nellie, Alma's student, has no father; and Rosa Gonzales also lacks a mother. But Alma's mother is psychopathic, given to outbursts of malice. Spiteful and addled, she shocks Alma with her kleptomania. Childish, she reveals sensory delight in ice cream. Mrs. Winemiller is a negative role model, a living proof of what might happen to a sexually frustrated housewife, unhappily married to a self-righteous man.

There is also a spinster, albeit a secondary character, in Williams's *Sweet Bird of Youth* (1962), set in St. Cloud, a seamy Gulf Coast town. Aunt Nonnie (Mildred Dunnock) is a victimized and frightened browbeaten woman. She still likes Chance Wayne (Paul Newman), cherishing his love to Heavenly (Shirley Knight), the daughter of Boss Finley (Ed Begley), the corrupt politician. Note the obvious symbolic meanings of names: Alma (soul in Spanish) and Heavenly. The tyrant father has forbidden Heavenly to see Chance, her young lover who has infected her with venereal disease. Instead, he has arranged for her to marry the doctor who sterilized her. The contrast between Chance, who stands for life and adventurism, and the doctor, who brought sterilization, illuminates two types of men and two types of marriages, one based on passion and love, the other on calculation and respect.

Chance comes back to town with a fading movie star, Alexandra Del Lago (Geraldine Page), hoping she will get him a screen test and promote his Hollywood career. A gigolo paid for his sexual services, he is elegantly dressed and drives a white Cadillac convertible. But deviating from conventions of small-town films, Williams does not contrast the small Florida town with the Big City of Hollywood. Sex, drugs, and booze are all integral to Alexandra's (and Hollywood's) life-style, and she is the first to admit, "I was born a monster." However, she is no more monster than Boss Finley; in fact, Alexandra is his female counterpart. Both are calculating and manipulative, relating to people only in terms of what they can get out of them. Still, St. Cloud is more corrupt, vicious, and hypocritical than Hollywood.

Writer-director Richard Brooks turns the townfolk into broad stereotypes. Finley sent Chance out of town with a one-way ticket to New York, telling him, "A town like this has no room for a go-getter, no opportunity for a man who's going places." To get rid of him, Finley sells Chance *his* version of the American Dream: "This is America. Today you're nobody, tomorrow you're somebody." A roughneck, cast in the mold of the Southern demagogue Huey Long, Finley manipulates the mayor, the police, the editor, and an organization called "the Daughters of Dixie" whose support he needs for his reelection campaign. Finley terrorizes those who dare speak against him in public. The house of one such critic, Professor Smith (it is no accident that he is an academic), was invaded by Finley's mob. When the TV reports that the invaders wore masks and tags of "Finley Youth Club," he demands to remove his name from the scandal. Finley has another problem: Miss Lucy (Madeline Sherwood), his mistress, has exposed his sexual impotence. She has written with her lipstick on the ladies' room's mirror that "Boss Finley can't cut the mustard," for which she is deprived of his usual presents.

Fearing censorship, Brooks compromised the play's ending. In the movie, Chance is beaten up (his nose broken), instead of castrated. The whole point of destroying "lover boy's meal ticket," so crucial in the play, thus gets lost in the film. The movie also contains an absurd and implausible resolution: Heavenly defies her father and the two lovers are reunited. Worse yet is the movie's whitewashing of Chance, who, in the play, is much more complex. Brooks distorts the play's meaning, stressing instead the generation gap: the youngsters' innocent love spoiled by the greedy and selfish politician. Still, for an early 1960s movie, it is audacious in dealing straightforwardly with the then taboo issues of drugs, venereal disease, abortion, and degeneracy.

In 1968, Paul Newman switched roles and moved behind the cameras to direct his wife, Joanne Woodward, in *Rachel, Rachel.*[9] Thematically and ideologically, this film also belonged to the 1950s. A sensitive study of repressed life, it bears resemblance to *Summer and Smoke*. But it boasts a modern cinematic sensibility and more accomplished production values; an old story told in a new way. In Stewart Stern's adaptation of *A Jest of God*, Rachel Cameron is a thirty-five-year-old schoolteacher, living with her invalid mother above a funeral home. The narrative spans one crucial summer in Rachel's life, during which she comes to terms with her repressed sexuality and unformed identity. As other screen spinsters, Rachel is trapped between awareness that life is passing her by and lack of courage to break away and make changes.

Rachel experiences her first sexual encounter with Nick (James Olson), a farmer-turned-teacher. She falls in love with him, only to be disillusioned. "I want to say something which I never said before," she tells him. "I am happy. I love you. I want a child." Her desperation shows when she says: "Don't forget to call before the eggs get rotten." Nick lets her believe he is married and deserts her. Later, believing she is pregnant, she tells her friend Calla (Estelle Parsons), "I never thought anything alive could grow in me." "It could be the first decision you have made that you have respect for yourself," Calla tells her. At the hospital, under the fake name of Mrs. James, it turns out to be a false alarm; the symptoms were caused by a cyst.

The film's most interesting sequence is a revivalist meeting, to which she goes with Calla, another middle-aged and lonely teacher, who finds solace to her problems in religious fanaticism. At the meeting, presided over by the town's evangelist (Geraldine Fitzgerald), a glib phony preacher (Terry Kiser) tells his followers: "You're suffering because you can't say what you want." Holding hands, he forces them to express the word love and experience the feeling of it. It proves to be an emotionally shattering experience for Rachel: first, the orgiastic behavior, then a mild seduction by Calla, a latent lesbian.

The film uses many flashbacks—which Rachel narrates—to shed light on her life as a small girl. Rachel is a product of a nagging domineering mother; she is practically her maid, tending to her needs. As many other films, the film celebrates the ordinariness and unsung life of a woman highly aware of her loneliness. In the last scene, Rachel leaves for Oregon, taking her reluctant mother with her. What is awaiting her there? In first-person narration, Rachel says: "Where I'm going anything may happen. Nothing may happen. . . . Maybe I'll marry a widowed man and have children. . . . I may be lonely always. What will happen? What will happen?" The film features an open-ended quality about Rachel's future. Unlike other small-town spinsters, she is neither doomed nor "reformed," an individual lacking any meaningful ties to a larger community.

Nature versus Culture: *The Birds*

The second masterpiece Hitchcock contributed to the output of small-town movies was *The Birds* (1963), a film still underestimated for its brilliant structure, rich ideas, and stylistic virtuosity. The narrative follows closely the three unities of place, time, and action. Unfolding over a period of three days, most of the story takes place at Bodega Bay, California. The story's first part, beginning in a pet shop in San Francisco and ending with the heroine's arrival in town, is a typical Hitchcock romantic comedy of manners. The second part describes the attack of the birds on the town, and the third shows the attack of the birds on the Brenner household and their departure from town. In each of these parts, different ideas and different aspects of the protagonists' personalities are revealed.

The action begins in the City, San Francisco, when Melanie Daniels (Tippi Hedren), a rich socialite, sleekly groomed and exquisitely dressed, meets Mitch Brenner (Rod Taylor), a handsome lawyer, at a bird store. Pretending to work there, Melanie walks with the assuredness of a city dweller, a mischievous grin on her face. Mitch is there to get lovebirds for his sister's birthday. He projects the image of his ideal woman by describing the birds he would like to buy: "not too demonstrative, but not aloof either, a pair that is just 'friendly.'" It turns out they have met in court, when one of Melanie's practical jokes resulted in "the smashing of a plate-glass window." Committed to "the law," Mitch is not "too keen on practical jokes." Mitch put Melanie in her place so that she can see "what it felt like to be on the *other* end of a gag." A woman with no focus in her life, Melanie needs to be restrained. Their first encounter is marked by double entendres that are later developed.

Melanie decides to deliver the birds incognito to Mitch's house in Bodega Bay, an attractive town, surrounded by water and green land. But it is not a known town—Melanie has never heard of it before. Arriving on Saturday morning, the town is booming with activity: fishermen cross the road, old ladies carry shopping bags. The Brenner family is not well integrated in the town: Geographically isolated, their house is on the other side of the bay. The residents do not even know their names. The postal clerk is sure the little girl's name is Alice (another man believes it is Lois), but her name is Cathy (Veronica Cartwright). There is no longer intimacy or knowledge of people, as was the case in small towns (*Invasion of the Body Snatchers*) of previous decades. The Brenners belong to the upper middle class. Mitch is a successful (criminal) lawyer in San Francisco, but he spends his weekends in town, which makes him an insider-outsider.

Annie Hayworth (Suzanne Pleshette), the town's schoolteacher and Mitch's old flame, is also an outsider. She first visited Bodega Bay when Mitch invited her for a weekend. But because of his attachment to his mother Lydia (Jessica Tandy), and lack of passion on his part, their relationship dissolved. Still in love with him, Annie decided to stay in town long after their relationship ended, because she did not want to give up his friendship. Disillusionment about the prospects of a fulfilling life in Bodega Bay may explain Annie's ambivalence toward Melanie. On the verge of entering middle age, she is a woman who is willing to compromise. "I'm an open book," Annie says, but then contradicts herself, "or rather a closed one." Annie is an open and closed book. She is a committed teacher, a bit idealistic. One reason she left San Francisco was boredom, teaching at a private school "little girls in brown beanies." By contrast, the kids at Bodega Bay are thirsty for knowledge. "I haven't got very much, but I'll give them every ounce of it," says Annie. "It makes me want to stay alive for a long time." She is responsible for maintaining order, in and outside the classroom, and later loses her life while protecting Cathy from the birds. Overall, Annie is not the stereotypical schoolteacher—a permanent staple of small-town films. But Annie has to die for ideological reasons: Her presence is a reminder of Mitch's problem of committing himself to one woman. (Hitchcock told Truffaut that her character was "doomed from the beginning.")

Annie provides the most interesting comments about the town. She is first introduced working on her garden; her hair deranged, she is wearing earth-stained gloves. Next to her, Melanie looks completely out of place. "This tilling of the soil can become compulsive," she tells Melanie. "It's a pretty garden," remarks Melanie. "It's something to do in your spare time," says Annie; "there's a lot of spare time in Bodega Bay." Annie knows the town offers little to the casual visitor, unless one is "thrilled by a collection of shacks on a hillside."

The local hangout is "The Tides," a neighborhood restaurant, where women hang out in their house dresses and curlers, and the TV set always shows an old Western. The other crucial information about town is revealed during the birds' attack on its sacred (the school) and strategic (the gas station) institutions. The various reactions to the attack indicate different perspectives to dealing with the problem. One view, held by the ornithologist, Mrs. Bundy (Ethel Griffies), an old woman, dressed bizarrely, is that: "Birds are not aggressive creatures. They bring beauty into the world. It's mankind who makes it difficult." Possessing knowledge about birds, Mrs. Bundy doesn't believe they have "sufficient intelligence" to do such a thing. The other view is held by Jason (Karl Swenson), a drunk, unshaven man, a religious fanatic. "It's the end of the world," he screams, quoting from the Bible. "In all your dwelling places, the cities shall be laid waste." His opinion is so far-out that nobody takes him seriously. The third position, voiced by a well-dressed traveling salesman (Joe Mantell), propagates the use of physical force: "If you ask me, we should wipe them *all* out. World would be better off without them. All they do is make a mess of everything." Hitchcock later makes sure that he is punished with a violent death—his car explodes at the gas station.

But there are more moderate opinions. Al Malone (Malcolm Atterbury) the deputy sheriff, represents the legal authority and his view is based on commonsensical knowledge: "Birds just don't go around *attacking* people without no reason." Plain and of limited intelligence, he is used to giving out speeding tickets or warning drunks. But Malone, and the Santa Rosa police, are not trustworthy. When Mitch suggests making fog with smoke (seagulls get lost in fog), Malone cites the regulations: "There's an ordinance against burning anything in this town." There is also the hysterical woman (Doreen Lang) with her two children, who accuses Melanie of being a witch. "You're evil," she charges, reminding everyone that it all began with Melanie's arrival in town. Irrational and susceptible, she represents the dangerous type of person who spreads vicious rumors and ignites the masses' worst instincts. On the other side of the spectrum are Mitch and Melanie, attempting to apply rational reasoning to the case. However, they gradually realize—as do the viewers—that some issues defy logical analysis, one of the film's major points.

Two images feature prominently in *The Birds,* both imbued with symbolic meanings: The cage and the glass. Early on in the bird store, Melanie opens a cage and a bird flies out. Mitch catches the bird, then says, "Back to your gilded cage, Melanie Daniels." Melanie's careless lifestyle has insulated her from "real" life; she has been in her own insular cage. Later, she is caught in another cage, a telephone booth. The glass suggests the fragility of the social order and the precariousness of human life. The first object Lydia notices when she visits Dan is the broken china in his kitchen. At the Brenners' house, the teacups shake in Lydia's hands, and she later drops a cup. The broken pieces of Lydia's tea set signify the shattering of a stable and protected life.

The paradigm of the outsider is most interestingly used in *The Birds.* Melanie begins as a complete outsider, her arrival in town (similar to that of Uncle Charlie in *Shadow,* or Carter in *Picnic*) changes the lives of its inhabitants. But she gradually becomes an insider, particularly after being accepted by Mitch's mother. Another outsider, though to a lesser extent, is Annie, the schoolteacher; despite the fact that she resides in Bodega Bay, she is lonely and does not really belong. Born in town, Mitch was an insider, but he now visits there only on weekends. Lydia and her daughter Cathy are nominal residents, but they are not well integrated. There is nothing small-town about Lydia; she speaks with the quick tempo of the city dweller. As a group, the Brenners (and Melanie) are insiders fighting for their survival and for maintaining their family against the birds, the outside attackers. This external threat is capable of bringing out the best in the Brenners, overcoming many barriers (the initial animosity between Lydia and Melanie). Under specifiable conditions, outsiders like Melanie can change, acquiring the commitment and courage of insiders.

In the tradition of small-town films, the pattern of single-parent families prevails. The Brenner family is headed by Lydia whose husband died four years ago. Melanie's mother "ditched" her at the age of eleven. Mitch believes that Melanie "needs a mother's care," and, at the end, she gets such care. The film's last image shows the Brenners leaving town: Melanie is held by Lydia. Lydia appears to be a possessive and domineering mother, but she is not. More than afraid of losing her son to another woman, she is afraid of being abandoned. "It's odd how you depend on someone for strength, and how suddenly all the strength is gone, and you're alone." Lydia lacks her husband's natural gift with children. "He really knew the children—he had the knack of being able to enter into their world, of becoming a part of them." Mitch "has always done *exactly* what he wanted to do," which for Lydia is "the mark of a man," but "I wouldn't want to be left alone." Lydia's fragility is suggested by the shaking teacup she is holding in her hands. A lonely woman, she depended on her husband *too* much. "If only your father was here!" screams the hysterical Lydia during the attack.

Hitchcock uses the conventional imagery of the Big City: Cathy believes that most people Mitch knows in San Francisco are "hoods," because he spends "half his day in the detention cells." "In a democracy, *everyone* is entitled to a fair trial," says her mother. Mitch described San Francisco to Cathy as "just an ant hill at the foot of a bridge," and Melanie concurs, "It gets a little hectic at times." A society girl, Melanie has a father who is a publishing tycoon. "She's always mentioned in the columns," says Lydia, recalling a story of how she jumped into that fountain in Rome in the nude. Melanie denies that, claiming she was pushed. The reason why it was mentioned is that the newspaper that ran the story was a rival of her father's paper. Melanie is accused by Mitch of "running with a pretty wild crowd, who didn't much care for propriety or convention or the opinion of others." Melanie has no roots, no bonds to commit her to a career or meaningful life. She does "different things on different days," like taking lessons here and there. She has childish ideas, wanting to buy her old aunt a myna bird that will talk to her.

As in other small-town films, appearances are deceitful. Lydia seems to be possessive and jealous, but she is not. Melanie appears to be self-assured and arrogant, but she is insecure. Possessing the exterior of a sophisticated urban socialite, she is an immature woman who needs to grow up (admittedly, she feels she belongs with "the *other* children"). The changes in Melanie's looks as the story progresses signify a process of maturation, of awakening. In the first scene, Melanie's appearance is meticulous, but in the last, she is bruised, her forehead covered with bandages.

The ideological message of *The Birds,* as Donald Spoto points out, is similar to that of *Shadow of a Doubt;* the fragility of our supposedly orderly world. The film views the universe as a place that must always be guarded against imminent disaster; chaos is around the corner, ready to burst in.[10] As the detective said in *Shadow:* "Sometimes, the world needs a lot of watching. Seems to go crazy every now and then." The birds represent the unpredictable and unacknowledged invisible forces of destruction that cannot be explained or controlled with rational reasoning.[11] Hitchcock shows how the most peaceful setting can turn into the most horribly violent. In *Shadow,* a black smoke is used to signal the arrival of the villain. In *The Birds,* Hitchcock contrasts Lydia's arrival at Dan's farm with her departure, putting smoke in the truck's exhaust to make the road dusty (after Lydia discovers the dead body with the eyes missing).

The birds attack everyone—even children—and everywhere. Dan is attacked at his farm; Melanie on the boat; Cathy and the other kids at school. The birds know no discrimination: chaos is potentially universal. Unlike other films, Hitchcock does not use the birds as punishment against violators of the law. Innocent (children), complacent (Melanie), hardworking teacher (Annie), and farmer (Dan) are all victims of this irrational force. The birds attack the most sacred institutions (school), on the most sacred occasions (Cathy's birthday party). The house, a symbol of security and protection, becomes the birds' target; the Brenners are imprisoned in their own house. The traditional meaning of other symbols is also shattered: Eyeglasses, meant for better vision and greater clarity, get smashed during the birds' attack on the school.

The resolution of *The Birds* is also interesting. Initially, Hitchcock wanted to have a more frightening closure: the Brenners arrive in San Francisco, only to realize that the birds have taken over the Golden Gate Bridge! But in the film, "It looks clear up ahead" is Mitch's last sentence, suggesting hopefulness. The last shot shows the car moving fast into a magnificent sunrise over the hills, while the birds are sitting and waiting. This ending also reaffirms the Brenners' marginal status: Leaving town, they become outsiders.

The Birds combines thematic and stylistic devices of various genres. On one level, it is a suspenseful thriller, but it also contains elements of science fiction *(Invasion of the Body Snatchers)* and horror *(Aliens)* films. On another level, it is a melodrama with several emotional triangles: the troubled nuclear family; the romantic triangle of two women in love with the same man; the emotional bond among three women, representing three generations (Lydia, Melanie, and Cathy). *The Birds* is also a romantic comedy of manners, in the best tradition of the British theater. Hitchcock blends the conventions of these genres masterfully, in a wonderfully paced narrative, making *The Birds* one of the greatest small-town films.

The South: Old and New

Two major movies, *To Kill a Mockingbird* (1962), and *In the Heat of the Night* (1967), explored small-town life in the South. Both dealt with the plight of blacks. Both were nominated for Best Picture, and *In the Heat* won. Both films brought acting accolades to their protagonists: Gregory Peck in *To Kill,* and Rod Steiger in *In the Heat.* More significantly, despite the fact that the two films were made in the same decade, American society had changed considerably between 1962 and 1967.

Father Knows Best: *To Kill a Mockingbird*

To Kill a Mockingbird was based on Harper Lee's novel, which won the 1960 Pulitzer Prize. The excellent script, winning an Oscar Award for Horton Foote, draws sharp characterizations and features poignant dialogue. It tells its story from the point of view of Jean Louise (nicknamed Scout, and played by Mary Badham), a six-year-old girl. It begins with her voice-over narration: "Maycomb (Alabama) was a tired old town, even in 1932, when I first knew it." It was a town where "the day was twenty-four hours long, but it seemed longer. There's no hurry, for there's nowhere to go and nothin' to buy, and no money to buy it with." It is just before dawn when the town is first seen surrounded by cotton farms, pinewood, and hills, and dominated by the Courthouse Square. Maycomb is a poor town: the Depression hit its country folks bad, the farmers the hardest. The importance of movies, as the nation's major entertainment, is conveyed when Dill recounts how his mother entered his picture in the "Beautiful Child Contest" and won five dollars. "She gave the money to me and I went to the picture show twenty times with it."

Atticus Finch (Gregory Peck), a respected, but not prosperous, lawyer, is paid for his services with hickory nuts, because there is no cash to pay with. The town's moral center, he is a young widower, father to two kids, Scout and Jem (Philip Alford). The narrative deals with the growing up of these two and Dill (John Megna), a boy from Meridian, Mississippi, who spends two weeks in town. The Finch kids' mother is dead, and Dill does not have a father. Finch raises his children according to his liberal doctrine: "You never really know a man until you stand in his shoes and walk around in them."

Finch is defending Tom Robinson (Brock Peters), a black man accused of raping a white girl. The trial serves as a collective ritual in which the town's values are tested and reaffirmed. As the narrator says: "Maycomb had recently been told that it had nothing to fear but fear itself." It's a ceremonial occasion for the residents to feel membership in something larger than themselves. All the officials are present at the trial, and people are coming from all over the region. One wagon is loaded with women wearing cotton sunbonnets and dresses with long sleeves. Some men ride horses, others mules. It's the most important event in a long time. "I'm not gonna miss the most excitin' thing that ever happened in this town!" says Jem to her father when he refuses to let her watch the trial.

To Kill combines the traditions of Southern Gothic with the courtroom drama. The elderly Mr. Bradley (Richard Hale), an austere man, is described by the kids as "the meanest man that ever took a breath of life." He keeps his mentally retarded son, Boo (Robert Duvall) chained to a bed, like a dog. Boo even looks like a dog: "His teeth are yellow and rotten, his eyes are popped, and he drools most of the time." The kids believe that Boo "eats raw squirrels and all the cats he can catch." However, attacked by their father's enemy, Bob Ewell (James Anderson), and experiencing real fear for the first time in their lives, they are saved by the one person they dreaded most, Boo. "He gave us two soap dolls," says Scout, "a broken watch and chain, a knife, and our lives." The narrative shows how the children become aware of their *own* prejudices and overcome their fears.

Prejudice, racism, and gossip are rampant. The rigid stratification system is in operation at the courthouse. Reverend Skies, the black Baptist preacher, enters the colored balcony, and four black men, seated in the front row, get up and give their seats. There are no townsfolk on the jury, composed of farmers. Mrs. Henry Lafayette Dubose sits on the front porch in her wheelchair, and Jessie, a black girl, tends to her needs. She keeps a Confederate pistol on her lap under the shawl; the kids say, "She'll kill you quick as look at you." And there is Aunt Stephanie, the stock character of the spinster-gossiper.

Finch's speech (one of the longest in court films) is the centerpiece. He says he has "nothing but pity" for the accused, "a victim of cruel poverty and ignorance." The white woman has committed no crime: "She has merely broken a rigid and time-honored code of our society. A code so severe that whoever breaks it is hounded from our midst as unfit to live with. She did something that in our society is unspeakable. She kissed a black man." Finch blames the state witnesses for being confident that the jury members "would go along with them on the evil assumption that all Negroes lie, all Negroes are basically immoral beings, all Negro men are not to be trusted around our women." It is noteworthy that in 1930, more than half of the states in the Union still outlawed interracial marriages. "It's a sin to kill a mockingbird," Finch concludes, explaining the film's title, "because it didn't do anything but make music for us to enjoy." Cast as a Lincolnesque figure, Finch is the moralistic hero, or as Jem describes him, "a man born to do our unpleasant jobs for us." And even though the jury finds the accused guilty—despite evidence to the contrary—Finch continues to believe "in the integrity of our courts and in the jury system." "In this country," he says, "our courts are great levelers. In our courts, all men are created equal." Heartbroken, Finch has to inform Tom's parents that, breaking loose and running, he was shot by the police.

The children's initiation into the adult world is conveyed effectively. Scout is taught by Calpurnia, the black housekeeper, how to be feminine, how to behave like a lady. The scene in which she wears a dress for the first time bears resemblance to *The Member of the Wedding*'s last scene, in which Frankie, the tomboy, wears a dress. The children learn about poverty, justice, humility, and compassion for other people's problems. They also get to know and respect their father. The narrative's ending, just as its beginning, has a dreamy quality. "The summer that had begun so long ago had ended," says the narrator, "another summer had taken its place, and a fall, and Boo Bradley had come out."

Black Knows Better: *In the Heat of the Night*

Norman Jewison's *In the Heat of the Night*[12] is more of a murder mystery, set in the Deep South, than a small-town film per se. John Ball's novel was adapted to the screen by Stirling Silliphant, who constructed two strong characters. The film begins appropriately enough at the train station—a typical beginning of such films. The air is filled with quiet, country sounds, shattered by the distant blare of a diesel train, whose light is reflected on the surface of the polished rails. The platform is deserted and so are the streets. As the train rolls by, the panning camera reveals a weathered sign: "You are now entering the town of Sparta, Mississippi. Welcome!" The camera zeroes in on the feet of a black passenger, Virgil Tibbs (Sidney Poitier) soon to be arrested as a murder suspect.

Cut to a diner. Sam Wood, a police officer, and his boss, Bill Gillespie (Rod Steiger) are talking to Doc Stewart about a murdered man. "Came all the way from Chicago to build us a factory," says Doc, "to make something out of this town—look what it got him!" Later, at the police station, Gillespie interrogates Tibbs: "What's a Northern colored boy doing down here?" "Waiting for the train," answers Tibbs calmly. "I try to run a clean, safe town—where a man can sneeze and not have his brains beat out," says Gillespie. This first encounter is marked by mutual suspicion and contempt. Tibbs protests the tossing of his wallet, "I earned that money," but Gillespie's bigoted response is: "Colored can't make money like that! Hell, boy, that's more'n *I* make in a whole month." "Down here in Sparta," says Gillespie, "we don't have the problems you got up there. No riots. No mobs running through our streets. Nobody yellin' 'Burn, baby, burn!' We got time to keep the law."

The murdered man's widow (Lee Grant) did not know much about her husband's work, but she "always knew what mattered to him," and building this factory did. She promises to build it on the condition that Tibbs stay on the case. But the town's white racist hoodlums demand to "get rid of the nigger"; at the diner, the cook refuses to serve him food. The blame is finally put on the mayor, who sold out, as Eric Endicott, the victim's prime enemy, says: "When you voted to play his game, uproot this community, turn it into an industrial center, you signed his death warrant." Endicott murdered the new man in town, Colbert, because he knew that the new economic structure would signal his loss of power. As a boss, Endicott used to "sit up on his hill and run this country—until *we* moved in."

As I had previously noted (1987), *In the Heat* was a "male buddy" film depicting the evolution of male camaraderie: the development of friendship and respect between two unlikely candidates. The bigoted police chief Gillespie is relatively new on the job. Lacking the necessary skills to carry out his duties, he needs an expert on the case. Indeed, Tibbs is a brighter and better trained homicide investigator. A cool professional and a gentleman, he even offers to pay for his phone call to his headquarters in Philadelphia. The interaction between the two men must overcome the fact that Tibbs is an educated black from the North. Gillespie is the more provincial and uneducated, living in the rural South (in most films, it's the other way around, with blacks in rural regions). Middle-aged, neither has ever been married, not even "come close to it." "Don't you get a little lonely?" asks Gillespie. "No lonelier than you," says Tibbs. "Don't get smart, black boy, don't pity me!" says Gillespie. But they learn to like and respect each other and, at the end, Gillespie carries Tibb's suitcase to the train station. They part with a handshake, and the camera cuts to the sign at the end of the tracks: "You Are Now Leaving the Town of Sparta—Hurry Back!"

The film explores racial prejudice and the damaging effects of stereotypes—among whites and blacks, representatives of the law and those expected to be protected by it. For example, Sam Wood, a white police officer, has raped a young girl, whom he liked watching in the nude. The movie's soft political message is, as one of its characters says, "Things take time. You can't *legislate* tolerance." Sidney Poitier plays here another morally superior black man, as he did in *To Sir with Love* (1967) and in *Guess Who's Coming to Dinner?* (1968). These three films catapulted Poitier into national stardom, but like the progress blacks made in society, it was too little and too late. And it did not last long: The position of black performers in Hollywood of the 1980s—on-screen and off—is worse than it was in the 1960s.

Worn Clichés or a New Beginning?: *The Chase*

At the time of its release, Arthur Penn's *The Chase* (1966) received mostly negative reviews and subsequently failed at the box office. Bosley Crowther disliked the movie because "everything is intensely overheated" from "the emotional content to the pictorial style." He found the film to be cold, obvious, and a clumsy "attempt to blend a weak but conceivably dramatic theme of civil rights with a whole mess of small-town misbehavior, of the sort that you get in *Peyton Place*."[13] Other conservative critics faulted the movie for being exploitational in language and too graphic in depiction of sex and violence. But reevaluating *The Chase*, Robin Wood describes it as a "seminal work," because "it anticipated many of the major developments that took place in Hollywood in the next decade."[14]

Two writers worked on the script: Lillian Hellman adapted to the screen Horton Foote's book (and later Broadway play). It was Foote's second script of a small-town movie, the first was *To Kill a Mockingbird*.[15] Penn cast major roles with players of New York's Actors Studio (Marlon Brando, Jane Fonda, Janice Rule), but he also used players from the old (Miriam Hopkins) and new (Robert Redford, Angie Dickinson) Hollywood. Known for his meticulous work with actors, Penn assembled one of the best casts in a Hollywood movie. Kennedy's assassination and a real incident in Texas provided the inspiration for the film. The story unfolds in a tawdry Texas town, on a hot Saturday. A melodrama, the narrative paradigm of *The Chase* is that of "the outsider." A white convict, Bubber Reeves (Robert Redford) is on his way back to town to join his wife Anna (Jane Fonda). The task of Sheriff Calder (Marlon Brando) is to arrest the fugitive, but what seems to be a routine assignment turns out to be an ordeal because of the obstacles the town presents. At the end, the revelation that the convict is innocent comes as no surprise.

Unlike other movies, which begin with the outsider's arrival, *The Chase* ends with Bubber's arrival in town. The movie chronicles the effects of Bubber's prospective arrival—talked about and feared, he is seldom shown. For a small-town movie, *The Chase* has an extremely large gallery (about a dozen) of characters. Lacking one major hero, its innovative structure resembles Altman's *Nashville* (1975), another attempt at doing away with one or a few protagonists. Those who perceive it as a conventional genre film—which it is not—charge that it contains *too* many characters, superficially presented. The subtext of *The Chase* is more important than its text: What is implied counts more than what is actually said or shown.

The moral center (though deliberately problematic) is Calder, a sensitive and conscientious sheriff (not unlike Will Kane in *High Noon*). His task is to arrest the fugitive and protect the social order. But unlike Will Kane, Calder is not a conventional hero. There is ambiguity about his status: He is always reminded he owes his position to Val Rogers (E. G. Marshall), the town's richest and most powerful man. Mrs. Reeves (Miriam Hopkins), the fugitive's mother, afraid that they are going to hurt him, offers Calder money. "Isn't my money good enough for you?" she charges when he refuses to accept it. "Val Rogers owns you. He bought you." And if Mrs. Reeves knows, everybody knows, which means the sheriff will never be able to gain the town's respect.

At the same time, Calder is the only person who really cares about blacks' rights. Early on, he tries to save a black man, Lester, from beatings, putting him in the county jail, adjacent to his living quarters. "The people out there are nuts," he tells his wife. "I'm sick of living here. I'm sick of my job." Calder's integrity is not in doubt; what is in question is the effectiveness of his leadership—Lester is later beaten at the jail itself. Here too the movie departs from established conventions: The jail is usually a safe place and out of reach, but in *The Chase*, Rogers invades the "safe" territory, which ironically functions as Calder's private residence. Calder thus lacks control over his public and private domains. He is married to Ruby (Angie Dickinson), a submissive and supportive wife, and, on the surface they enjoy a marital bliss. But there is domestic tension around the issue of children. "I wish we adopted some children," says the wife, revealing that they would like to—but cannot—have a family. Calder also resents the fact that his wife is wearing the dress that Rogers had bought her; he wishes she'd send it back.

Values of dominant culture are probed, particularly those concerning marriage, motherhood, and the nuclear family. Bubber's parents think they have failed as parents. "What did I do wrong?" asks Mrs. Reeves— the perennial question when a child turns out to be different from his parents' expectations. When the sheriff expresses his concern, Mrs. Reeves says with no hesitation: "I don't believe you're sorry." Motherhood is no longer taken for granted as women's ultimate goal. "We never had any children," says an elderly woman to Mrs. Reeves. "It's hard when you don't. . . . It's hard when you do." Most of the action takes place at Sol's Cafe, owned by Anna's stepfather. A morally confused woman, Anna (Jane Fonda) is the center of a sexual triangle. Married to Bubber, she has an affair with Jake Rogers (James Fox), the boss's son. Harsh and contemptuous of Sol, Anna wants out: "You just pay me my mother's part of the business and I'll be out of here in one hour."

The layers of the town's power structure are most visible. At the top of the hierarchy stands Val Rogers, the oil baron and banker, who owns the town. Like other patriarchs (*Cat on a Hot Tin Roof, The Long, Hot Summer*), he is anguished over his weakling, no-good, but *only,* son. The movie deviates from convention, showing Rogers, allegedly the most "respectable," as the town's most vicious person. Rogers controls every aspect of town, its police, economy, and even its education; he announces the construction of a college dormitory for women. It is patriarchal oligarchy at its most extreme.

The town's stratification system is revealed through its social life. It is Saturday night, the big night, and the town boasts parties, set in houses across the street from each other. The poor socialize in Sol's Cafe, the sleazy local bar-motel. The rich people are invited to a celebration of Roger's birthday. Edwin Stuart (Robert Duvall), the bank's vice president, and his wife Emily (Janice Rule) were not asked to the party. Earlier, Emily invites the oil baron for a drink. "Just thought you'd like to see how the lower classes live?" she says, but Rogers questions her, "Are you the lower class?" The adulterous Emily fools around with her husband's colleague, Damon Fuller (Richard Bradford). But jealous, Emily asks Damon about her competitor "How is she in bed?" "I don't carry a computer to bed," says Damon. Jake Rogers is also trapped in a loveless and sexless marriage. Both he and his wife have illicit affairs, about which they talk frankly. Adultery is no longer a secret (as in *Peyton Place* or *The Last Picture Show*). Damon's wife, Mary (Martha Hyer), a cool and boozy blonde, knows her husband is cheating on her. Most men are depicted as macho and sexist; Damon slaps his wife in public when she talks too much about his affairs. And watching Anna dancing, Damon observes: "I like them younger and younger." For Edwin, however, the youths signify his wasted life and lost opportunities: "all the things I wanted to have when I was their age."

As in *In the Heat,* there is racism. The blacks are mistreated and brutally beaten. In the first scene, a black woman forbids her son to get involved with Bubber, propagating segregation: "Let white men take care of white men's problems." The other ethnic minority, the Mexican-American, is in no better position. The Mexican laborers who work for Rogers curse him in front of his son, but he could not care less. Their wives are more hypocritical: a Mexican worker's wife tells Jake she enjoyed seeing his beautiful wife pictured in the newspapers. With no exception, every inhabitant is nasty, mean, intolerant, drunk, or all of the above. Religion is no longer the cement to glue the diverse populace into a tightly knit community; a fanatic woman praying on the street is ridiculed.

The resolution is borrowed from *High Noon,* but goes a number of steps further. Sheriff Calder is not only unable to protect Lester, Bubber (and the town), but unable to protect himself. Brutally beaten, he is helpless. In a manner similar to Will Kane, he leaves town under contempt, except that in *High Noon* viewers were assured that Kane and his wife would settle down somewhere and live peacefully, whereas Sheriff Calder and Ruby drive out of town with no idea of *where* they are going. A representative of the law, Calder becomes at the end an *outsider*, literally and figuratively. Like *High Noon*, which is nominally a Western, but works much better as a political allegory about McCarthyism, the Texas town in *The Chase* is a microcosm of American society circa 1966. Every character represents a recognizable social stratum, and the interpersonal tensions represent conflicts among distinct *social* groups: Parents versus children, legitimate authority versus crime, blacks versus white, rich versus poor, men versus women, dominant culture versus subversive counterculture.

Though using narrative conventions and types from several small-town classics, *The Chase* is innovative.[16] First, it acknowledges the sexual revolution, a term explicitly used in the text. "Do you believe in the sexual revolution?" Emily asks Rogers. As Robin Wood pointed out, the film provides different models of sexual arrangements (monogamy, adultery, triangles). Second, *The Chase* acknowledges the generation gap, along with family and class divisions. Third, the movie conveys the decreasing effectiveness of the legal authority in dealing with crime and violence. Fourth, the issues of civil rights and discrimination against blacks feature prominently in the narrative. Fifth, through the character of Anna, the film provides hints about the new, liberated woman in American society.

The New Countercultural Films

Most critics regard 1967 as a watershed year in the American cinema, one that saw the release of *Bonnie and Clyde* and *The Graduate*. Indeed, by the end of the decade, with Penn's *Alice's Restaurant* and Dennis Hopper's *Easy Rider*, Sam Peckinpah's *The Wild Bunch* and George Roy Hill's *Butch Cassidy and the Sundance Kid* (all in 1969), it was clear that a new film era had begun. *Bonnie and Clyde*, *Alice's Restaurant*, and *Easy Rider* share some similarities. All three made important sociological statements, grounded in their specific historical settings. Though none was a conventional small-town film, as a group, they offered a different view about individual and community in America. All three expressed and thus legitimized the values of countercultural youth. In their style, they combined realistic with mythic elements. Moreover, as a cycle, these movies demonstrated that there was a market for youth-oriented products. *Bonnie and Clyde* and *Easy Rider* enjoyed wide, and *Alice's Restaurant* moderate, commercial appeal.[17]

All three films depict America as a society that has lost its moral center,

174 | Small-Town America in Film

a society no longer sure of its ideology and no longer certain of its future. Breakdown of structure and disintegration of values are the underlying motifs of these films, a society in a state of anomie. Traditional institutions and the mainstay of stability—the nuclear family, legal system, and big business—no longer fulfill effectively their functions. The decline of the patriarchal family, for example, meant that its crucial roles—intimacy, emotional support, source of identity, the "we" feeling— were no longer being met. Following societal attempts to create equivalent structures to the patriarchal family, the American cinema presented two alternatives: collectivist communes (*Easy Rider* and *Alice's Restaurant*) and professional peer groups (*Bonnie and Clyde*).

The first alternative structure to the bourgeois family was the professional peer group. In *Bonnie and Clyde,* the Barrow gang combines different forms of interaction and ties: blood (Clyde and his brother), marital (Clyde's brother and his wife Blanche), romantic (Bonnie and Clyde), and social-professional (Moss and the other members). Providing emotional support, the gang is an intimate primary group, the only meaningful relationship in the members' lives. The film celebrated nihilism and outlawry as a way of life, in defiance of conventional mores and legitimate authority. Bonnie and Clyde are both outsiders, an ex-sharecropper and a waitress (dreaming to become an actress). Unable to assimilate the dominant culture, they devise their own structure and norms. Each member suffers physical and/or psychological stigma. The limping and sexually impotent Clyde tells Bonnie that he's "not much of a lover boy," but makes sure to spell out he "doesn't like boys either." But when his brother asks if Bonnie is the best, Clyde says, "she's even better." Moss is another victimized kid, oppressed and misunderstood by his weird father.

Institutional authority, represented by the law and business world, is depicted as rigid and corrupt. The deputy sheriff is ironically named Homer, a typically small-town name.[18] Rigid and dumb, Homer is ridiculed by Bonnie, who poses for a picture with him. The bureaucratic police are portrayed as mercilessly brutal, using an armored car at the end. Bankers are depicted as greedy, which makes the gang's robberies more sympathetic: Their targets are organizations, not human beings. Until they form the bond, Bonnie and Clyde are alienated from society and from themselves, powerless youths living a meaningless life. The American Dream and its puritanical ethics of hard work are rejected. Accepting the culture's strong emphasis on monetary success, they substitute the acceptable means for achieving success (hard work, formal education) with illegitimate means (crime, violence). In Robert Merton's typology, Bonnie and Clyde's mode of adaptation is that of innovation.

Though innocent, they are not perceived as society's passive victims.

They take their lives into their hands, demanding recognition. Bonnie and Clyde devise unconventional strategies to elevate themselves into legend.[19] When Bonnie writes down poems about their adventures and sends them to the press, Clyde says with pride, "You made me somebody they're gonna remember." The otherwise anonymous and powerless (Riesman's *The Lonely Crowd*) members of mass society are determined to achieve celebrity status and command center stage, if only for a few moments. They are even willing to die for it. These motifs of celebrity-obsession and pathological narcissism will reappear in the cycle of nihilistic movies in the mid-1970s (See chapter 5).

As other films of the Depression, *Bonnie and Clyde* acknowledges the importance of movies as a unifying agent of integration. Bonnie watches with admiration Busby Berkeley's musical, *We're in the Money* (1933), and Moss says he would love to watch films with Myrna Loy. The Barrow gang visits a migrant camp, a commune (in the mold of *The Grapes of Wrath*) and receives a welcome, but it's not an alternative life-style for them. At the same time, they don't reject traditional family bonds. When Bonnie sadly complains, "I have no family," Clyde says, "I'm your family." The narrative also acknowledges the functions fulfilled by kinship, stressing love between parents and children. When Bonnie terribly misses her mama, the ever-responsive Clyde arranges for a meeting with her family in an outdoor picnic. It is one of the film's most emotional scenes, shot in soft focus against blue skies and white clouds, as if it were a pastoral dream. The festive occasion is brought to a halt when Clyde approaches Bonnie's mother, a strong matriarchal figure (like Mother York). "Don't worry, Mother Parker," says Clyde, "when this is all over, Bonnie and I will settle down not three miles from you." "Try to live three miles from me and you'll be dead!" says the weathered-looking woman. Dressed in white Bonnie and Clyde find their deaths in what is possibly the most stylized and most imitated sequence in American films. But artistic innovation aside, their slow-motion death, culminating in an embrace, bears ideological meaning: Defying realism, it is a mythic death, glamorizing the lives of two folk heroes.

Back to Communal Dreams: *Alice's Restaurant*

Inspired by Arlo Guthrie's popular talking-blues ballad, "The Alice's Restaurant Massacree," *Alice's Restaurant* was a cultural summation of a generation, speaking against red-tape bureaucracy and social hypocrisy. An experiment in collectivist life, the film begins by celebrating the virtues of communal life. In Stockbridge, Massachusetts, a surrogate family headed by Alice (Pat Quinn) and Ray Brock (James Broderick) includes hippies, college dropouts, and other "deviants" who cannot conform to mainstream society. The hero is Arlo, son of Woody Guthrie, legendary folk singer, who connects among the film's disjointed episodes. The narrative examines the generation gap between Arlo and his father, particularly their divergent form of political involvement. During the Depression, Woody left his family and committed himself to labor union activism. By contrast, political activism in the late 1960s was marked, not by what one was for, but what one was *against*.

The film takes Arlo's point of view, juxtaposing him against oppressive authority, represented by the college, police, and military. Arlo is kicked out of college because of disciplinary problems, and he is jailed for dumping garbage of a Thanksgiving dinner in an empty lot. His prison record—littering—exempts him from the draft. The film compares Arlo's minor violation (for which he is put in prison), with that of the military (and American government) whose criminality, in its commitment to destruction in Vietnam, is far greater, but there is no penalty for *their* crimes.

Unlike *Bonnie and Clyde*, the police are not described as nasty or mean, just narrow-minded. And as in *Easy Rider*, the established order cannot accept the symbols of the counterculture, mens' long hair and the "confusion" it creates for traditional gender roles. In the film's only violent scene, Arlo is hurled by rednecks through a window, after harrassment about his hair (and masculinity). However, unlike *Easy Rider*, wherein women feature poorly, the central figure of *Alice's Restaurant* is Alice, a quasi-feminist heroine. Cowriter Venable Herndon perceives Alice as "the personification of the *anima* figure Jung speaks of, the clan matriarch, the sacred mother of the subconscious."[20] By standards of 1960s heroines, Alice is more in control and, though she engages in cooking (traditionally a female endeavor), she does it *by choice*.

Alice and Ray experiment with alternate family structures. Older than the other members, they are caught in between the old bourgeois order (monogamy and nuclear family) and the new one (free-spirited sexuality). Alice is sexually attracted to the much younger Shelly (with whom she has an affair), but the imposition of the monogamous code is confining and creates strain. The movie describes the commune's problems while establishing itself in a deconsecrated church. For instance, religious rituals are replaced with secular celebrations, the Thanksgiving dinner and the second wedding of Ray and Alice. These rituals are meant to increase the members' integration into the group. There is also a new collective ritual: The bell tolls whenever Alice and Ray are making love. The commune is located in a deconsecrated church, but, as an alternative structure it lacks the equivalent strength of religious values to integrate the membership. The commune's values are not binding enough, and the members' commitment lacks the strength to make it durable.

In mode of adaptation, the commune members are rebellious, to use Merton's schema. However, despite attempts to withdraw from the oppressive adult order, the latter keeps impinging on their lives. Arlo is an insider-outsider, never completely committed to the cooperative way of life. His lack of belongingness derives from necessity (his father's terminal illness), but also choice (his career as a singer). He moves back and forth between the commune and New York City. Contrasted with the commune's free love is a Greenwich Village night club, in which a middle-aged proprietor makes a pass at Arlo. And there are also advances by a girl who wants to sleep with Arlo, because she is sure he will be famous one day!

At the end, the commune breaks up. Ray, like other screen heroes, believes that a farm in Vermont would solve the problem. "If we'd a just had a real place," he says, "we'da all still been together . . . without buggin' each other . . . we'd all be some kind of family." Ray is a dreamer who has not lost his naïvete, but he too understands the strain between private and collective life. He envisions a (utopian) commune, "where everybody can have his own house, and we could all see each other when we wanted to." Ray aims at reconciling the tension of individualism and cooperativism, private ownership and shared life. But he is aware of the value contradiction: a monogamous "bourgeois" marriage versus free-spirited sex. Ray becomes hostile, begging the members to stay, but to no avail.

As in other small-town films, the movie portrays different forms of death, natural and accidental, ordinary and ritualistic. Self-destructive, Shelly dies of drug abuse while riding his motorcycle. For his funeral, they use the church car, and the service is performed to Joni Mitchell's heartbreaking rendition of "Songs of Aging Children." Woody Guthrie dies at the hospital, of a rare disease of the nervous system. Nonetheless, the main causer of death is the army, attacked for its "official" policy of destruction in Vietnam. (In his physical, Arlo screams at a military doctor, "I wanna kill!" expressing what the army actually does in Vietnam.)

In the film's last scene, Alice, wearing her white wedding gown, stands alone in front of the church. The camera moves back, observing Alice at an increasingly bigger distance. The panning forward, while zooming backward, conveys the uncertainty about Alice's status; she is out of focus. Isolated from her immediate surroundings, Alice is in the process of becoming a mythic figure. But the ending also connotes loneliness (physical and emotional) and uncertainty about Ray and Alice's marriage. *Alice's* presents a nonglamorous view of communal life: the hardships of alternative life-style. Significantly, the commune dissolves as a result of *inside* pressures: Excessive use of drugs and lack of powerful norms to regulate behavior. The movie ends on a note of disillusionment, not unlike the ending of *Easy Rider.*

From West to East in Search of America: *Easy Rider*

Wyatt (Peter Fonda) and Billy (Dennis Hopper), the protagonists of *Easy Rider* (1969) were new screen protagonists: Hippies on motorcycles in search of "America." Their names resonate with numerous Westerns about Wyatt Earp and Billy the Kid. However, instead of "Young Man Go West!" Wyatt and Billy ride from West to East. What is left of the Old West's ethos are two outlaws who make enough money from drugs (sold to a capitalist in Los Angeles), to cover for a fun trip to New Orleans's Mardi Gras. Drug dealing is not regarded as more deviant than the activities carried out daily in the business world. For Billy, "dope peddling" is no worse "than the Wall Street tycoon spending eighty percent of his time cheating the government." They are not young, but adhere to the cult of youthfulness, hedonism without any responsibility, familial or marital. A road movie, *Easy Rider* begins as a hymn to the openness and vastness of the American land, and ends as a tragic vision of the American Dream. Billy and Wyatt are contrasted with the "straight" world, the bigoted rednecks who cannot tolerate their looks (long hair), ideals (spontaneity, freedom) and culture (rock music).

In an early scene, they stop to repair a flat tire at a poor rancher's house. Crosscutting, the film conveys the two contrasting life-styles: the rancher's horse and their motorcycle. Surrounded by a huge family at dinner time, Wyatt tells the rancher: "It's not every man who can live off the land, you know, doing his own thing his own time. You should be proud." But he is not terribly convincing and it is clear that it is not a life-style for him and Billy. Later, visiting a commune, the two express interest and respect, but basically cannot adopt this collectivist life-style. "You know, this could be the right place," says one member, urging them to stay because "time's running out." But Billy wants to go, and the inarticulate Wyatt says, almost apologetically, "I'm hip about time, but I just gotta go." But where they are going and what their goals are remain unclear. The movie celebrates romantic individualism, but also presents a warning: excessive (irresponsible) individualism might have negative effects. The scene at the commune is indeed ambiguous. At first, it appears as a fascinating way of life, reminiscent of the back-to-the-soil movement during the Depression—the sequence is romanticized through the use of soft-focus camera. But like *Alice,* the film also suggests the problems of living in communes. It's a hard life, and the film does not attempt to glorify it.

The film's most intriguing character is George Hanson (Jack Nicholson), a boozy and disenchanted small-town lawyer, a semiestablishment figure. "You know, this used to be a helluva country," says Hanson. "I can't understand what's gone wrong with it." "All we represent to them," says Billy, "is somebody who needs a haircut," but Hanson knows better. "What you represent to them is freedom," and it is freedom that scares the bigots. At the end, all three find their death: Hanson is brutally murdered, and Wyatt and Billy are blown off the road. Neither insiders nor outsiders, Billy and Wyatt belong to no group.[21] *Easy Rider* portrays the counterculture, but is sensitive enough to suggest that it might not work as a viable life-style. In this context, the meaning of the statement "We blew it" is really ambiguous: is it meant as a summation of the countercultural generation, or just of Billy and Wyatt?

Conclusion

Movies about small towns in the 1960s were more innovative, thematically and stylistically, than those of previous decades. The new movies reflected the breakdown of the studio system as well as the fragmentation of American society. The most characteristic, often the best, movies of the decade dealt with the decline of the Old West and the breakdown of the old morality as a result of the political assassinations, the civil rights movement, the Vietnam War, and other structural developments. The new freedom, on- and offscreen, produced two kinds of narratives. One group stressed the irreconcilable generation gap between parents and children. The other focused on the decline of legitimate authority in society.

The first theme was most effectively used in Martin Ritt's *Hud* (1963), a transitional film between the more naive films of the early 1960s and the more cynical ones later. The Production Code was bent, allowing such words as "son of a bitch" and "bastard" to be heard for the first time onscreen. The language used in this film was so unprecedented that it helped to bring down the Production Code. It starred Paul Newman, as an immoral Texas rancher, "a white Cadillac cowboy." Antiheroic and self-aggrandizing, Hud is a hedonistic womanizer, disregarding others' rights. However, the pragmatic Hud understands that Texas's economic future is in oil, not cattle. When his cattle contract "foot-and-mouth" disease, he wants to sell them, but his father is appalled by the very suggestion of "passing on bad stuff to my neighbors," calling his son "an unprincipled man." "You don't give a damn," charges the old man. "You don't value nothing. You live just for yourself."

The antagonism between father and son is mutual, not unlike the conflict in *Rebel without a Cause* and *East of Eden.* "My mama loved me," says Hud, "but she died." In contrast to Hud, the father is an old Western-type rancher, who spurns the lure of oil, clinging to the traditional values. The old man believes in taking a moral stance, making decisions about "what's right and what's wrong." Hud's nephew Lon (Brandon De Wilde) stands between the two men, first idolizing Hud, then switching to the father's side. The turning point is when the drunken Hud assaults Alma (Patricia Neal), their housekeeper. A cynic, hard-bitten slattern, Alma has lived the hard way, but somehow retained her dignity and compassion. When she accuses Hud of being a "cold-blooded bastard," he charges back, "You're not young anymore, what are you saving it for?" "I've done my time with one cold-blooded bastard," says Alma, "I'm not looking for another." Alma's gambler-husband left her stranded in New Mexico. At the end, the old man dies, Alma leaves in disgust, and Hud is left alone. The symmetrical narrative begins with Lon's (the outsider) arrival and ends with his departure.

The countercultural movies of the late 1960s shared in common a cynical view of legitimate authority. In *Bonnie and Clyde,* a policeman is captured and ridiculed, and in *Easy Rider,* the view is harsher; Wyatt and Billy are cold-bloodedly shot down by roughnecks. In their style too, the new movies discouraged viewers from emotional identification with the story and/or characters; distanced detachment became the operative mode. In *Alice's,* for example, instead of a direct shot of Arlo, he is often observed through a window, a framing device that promotes viewers' detachment.[22] The three countercultural films attacked similar targets—conformity, rigidity, materialism, consumerism, and oppressive authority. Disillusionment is their dominant motif. All three attempted to redefine the American ethos of success but in their search for America the heroes of *Easy Rider* found nothing but hostility, prejudice, and bigotry.

American society in the late 1960s was similar in some respect to that in the early 1930s.[23] The only difference is that the Great Depression was precipitated by a major economic crisis, whereas in the 1960s, the crisis was political (severe erosion of the legitimate authority). The Johnson administration enjoyed its lowest prestige in 1967, the height of the Vietnam War. *Bonnie and Clyde* was released just months before the antiwar march in Washington, DC. However, in both eras there was loss of faith in the traditional values of the American Dream. As Andrew Bergman noted, the cycle of gangster films in the 1960s was similar to the cycle of the 1930s. *I Am a Fugitive from a Chain Gang* (in 1932, with Paul Muni) offers many analogies with Martin Ritt's *Cool Hand Luke* (in 1967, with Paul Newman). And Clyde's outlaw was not that different from the heroes of *Little Caesar* (Edward G. Robinson). *The Public Enemy* (James Cagney), or *Scarface* (Paul Muni), all made in 1931–32.

Moreover, in films in the late 1960s, small-town folks are no longer portrayed as idealistic or superior to City folks. In John Schlesinger's *Midnight Cowboy* (1969), Joe Buck (Jon Voight) is a small-town stud, an immature fool who believes he can use his traditional (Texan) values in the Big City. Attractive, Joe is convinced he is the answer to the prayers of lonely, love-starved women. But he is amoral (more than immoral), his image of the city is based on delusion, a product of watching too much television. In New York, Joe is even lonelier than other city folks. In the final account, he is just another loser, a misfit who cannot adapt to urban life. As in *Hud,* what is left of the Old West in *Midnight Cowboy* is a cowboy outfit and a set of empty platitudes. In the film's last image, Joe is on a bus to sunny Florida with another misfit, Ratso Rizzo, a Times Square derelict (Dustin Hoffman), but the sickly Ratso dies in his arms. *Midnight Cowboy* is merciless in its view of the farmboy-hustler *and* the Big City. New York is seen as a jungle populated by deviants: hookers, lonely homosexuals, and other misifts. For once, there are no major ideological differences between City and Country.

1950s

23. Mr. Banks (Spencer Tracy) wakes up after a nightmare (about his failure and inadequacy as a father) in Vincente Minnelli's *Father of the Bride* (1950). The Production Code required that even married people sleep in separate beds, thus his wife (Joan Bennett) had to express her concern from afar. (Courtesy of The Museum of Modern Art/Film Stills Archive)

24. Hollywood's ultimate suburban portraiture—embodied in a barbecue party—in Martin Ritt's *No Down Payment* (1957). Jean (Patricia Owens), the film's most desirable woman, is surrounded by three different types of men: The host (Pat Hingle, right), her husband–engineer (Jeffrey Hunter, center) and their Tennessee hillbilly neighbor (Cameron Mitchell). (Courtesy of The Museum of Modern Art/Film Stills Archive)

25. In Laslo Benedek's *The Wild One* (1953), Hollywood's first film about juvenile delinquency, a gang of motorcyclists (led by Marlon Brando), wearing black leather coats, terrorizes a small town. (Courtesy of The Museum of Modern Art/Film Stills Archive)

26. The sexually repressed teacher–spinster (Rosalind Russell) attacks the outsider–stud (William Holden) in *Picnic* (1955), voicing some of the harshest words in a small-town film: "You won't stay young forever . . . did ya ever think that? What'll become of you then? (Courtesy of The Museum of Modern Art/Film Stills Archive)

27 and 28. Images of different life-styles are conveyed in two parties in Douglas Sirk's melodrama *All That Heaven Allows* (1955). Elegant and formal, the first party is given by Cary's (Jane Wyman) pretentious friends (27); the second, informal and cozy party by Ron's (Rock Hudson) spontaneous companions. Note the checkered tablecloth (Hollywood's sign of working class) and Ron's opening the wine bottle with his teeth. (Both courtesy of The Museum of Modern Art/Film Stills Archive)

29. A moment before the first kiss between two misunderstood and fatherless youngsters, Norman (Russ Tamblyn) and Allison (Diane Varsi), in *Peyton Place* (1957), the most popular small-town film of the decade. As in other films, the scene is significantly set in nature, on a hill. (Courtesy of The Museum of Modern Art/Film Stills Archive)

30. A gathering of a squabbling Southern dynasty in Martin Ritt's *The Long, Hot Summer* (1958). It is headed by the patriarch (Orson Welles, smoking a cigar, right), and includes Lee Remick, Anthony Franciosa, Paul Newman, and Joanne Woodward. It is no coincidence that both children (Franciosa and Woodward) are standing and watching their father in anger. (Courtesy of The Museum of Modern Art/Film Stills Archive)

31. Fred Zinnemann's *The Member of the Wedding* (1953) features an odd community of three misfits: The black housekeeper (Ethel Waters, sitting), the tomboy–adolescent (Julie Harris), and her neighbor–cousin (Brandon De Wilde). (Courtesy of The Museum of Modern Art/Film Stills Archive)

32. Generation gap: Father (Raymond Massey) and son (James Dean) fight and reconcile in Elia Kazan's *East of Eden* (1955). (Courtesy of The Museum of Modern Art/Film Stills Archive)

33. The doctor (Kevin McCarthy), the only "sane" person, and his sweetheart (Dana Wynter), escape from Santa Mira, a town of conformists (in the shape of green pods) in Don Siegel's political allegory, *Invasion of the Body Snatchers* (1956). (Courtesy of The Museum of Modern Art/Film Stills Archive)

34. John Sturges captured the myth of the stranger–outsider–redeemer, the one-armed World War II vet (Spencer Tracy) visiting a malignant and racist town, in *Bad Day at Black Rock* (1955), pitting him against the vast horizon— and the town's bigots. (Courtesy of The Museum of Modern Art/Film Stills Archive)

1960s

35. Following a nervous breakdown and separation, the now mature and disenchanted former lovers, Warren Beatty and Natalie Wood, meet for the last
time in *Splendor in the Grass* (1961). (Courtesy of The Museum of Modern
Art/Film Stills Archive)

36. Two repressed teachers in Paul Newman's elegiac *Rachel, Rachel* (1968): A latent lesbian (Estelle Parsons, center) and the mother-dominated eponymous heroine (Joanne Woodward, right). The bird cage is a metaphor of the emotional state of both women. (Courtesy of The Museum of Modern Art/Film Stills Archive)

37. Escaping from the birds' attack: The town's teacher (Suzanne Pleshette, left) and the city girl (Tippi Hedren, right) in Hitchcock's *The Birds* (1963). In composition, this frame is complementary to the town's image in *Invasion of the Body Snatchers* (picture 33). (Courtesy of The Museum of Modern Art/Film Stills Archive)

38. Gregory Peck, as a Lincolnesque lawyer–figure, defends a black man (Brock Peters) accused of raping a white woman in the court drama, *To Kill a Mockingbird* (1962), scripted by Oscar-winner Horton Foote. (Courtesy of The Museum of Modern Art/Film Stills Archive)

39. An alternative life-style during the tumultuous decade of the 1960s was return to the soil. One of the most interesting aspects of the youth-oriented *Easy Rider* (1969) was the depiction of communal rituals and ceremonies, such as praying and singing. (Courtesy of The Museum of Modern Art/Film Stills Archive)

1970s

40. The last scene of Peter Bogdanovich's brilliant evocation of small-town life in 1951, *The Last Picture Show* (1971): The desperate youngster (Timothy Buttons) and the frustrated housewife (Cloris Leachman) hold hands. The breakdown of their affair is also the breakdown of the community. (Courtesy of The Museum of Modern Art/Film Stills Archive)

41. A typical night in town: Car-cruising in *American Graffiti* (1973), wherein most of the interaction takes place within or between cars. (Courtesy of The Museum of Modern Art/Film Stills Archive)

42. Back to nature in *Jeremiah Johnson* (1972): Disgusted with civilization, the mythic hero (Robert Redford) goes back to the wilderness. (Courtesy of The Museum of Modern Art/Film Stills Archive)

43. Most of Steven Spielberg's *The Sugarland Express* (1974) is set on the road, where hundreds of assorted cars are attempting to arrest a fugitive couple. (Courtesy of The Museum of Modern Art/Film Stills Archive)

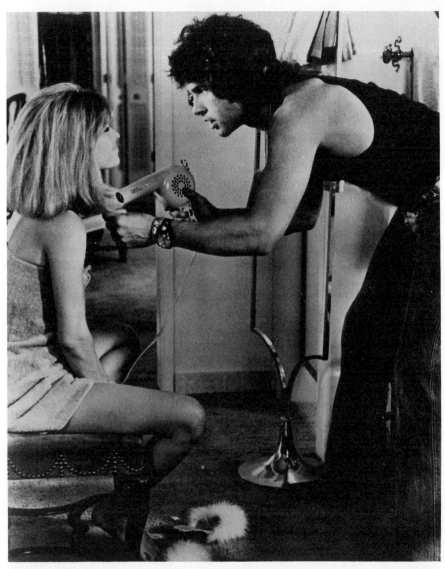

44. A "small-town" Casanova at work: George (Warren Beatty) blows his former girl's (Julie Christie) hair in a suggestive scene from *Shampoo* (1975), a film set in the incestuous community of glamorous Beverly Hills. (Courtesy of The Museum of Modern Art/Film Stills Archive)

45. Not many movies have used the supermarket, a typical woman's domain and the essence of suburbia's consumerism, as a locale. The last scene of *The Stepford Wives* (1975) is set at a supermarket, where the housewives–robots shop and socialize (at the center, Katharine Ross). (Courtesy of The Museum of Modern Art/Film Stills Archive)

46. A moment of calm relaxation and camaraderie for the four working-class youngsters in *Breaking Away* (1979), a film that turned losers into winners, using sports and classical music in its background. (Courtesy of The Museum of Modern Art/Film Stills Archive)

LA BANDE
DES QUATRE

© 1979 20 th Century Fox tous droits réservés

47. On their way to the wedding, the couple meet in the middle of the road, in Jonathan Demme's still unrecognized charmer, *Citizens Band* (1977). (Courtesy of The Museum of Modern Art/Film Stills Archive)

1980s

48. Voyeurism in a small town: In David Lynch's *Blue Velvet* (1986), an adolescent (Kyle MacLachlan) secretly observes a horrifying scene, the kind of which previous screen heroes could not even dream about. (Courtesy of The Museum of Modern Art/Film Stills Archive)

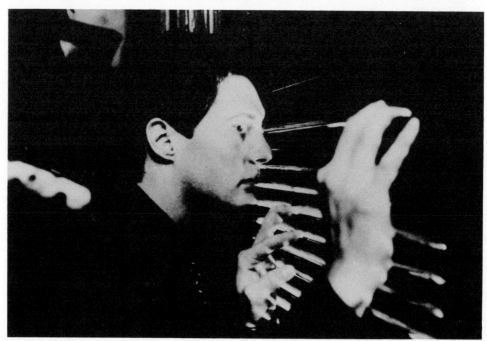

49. Jessica Lange played a modern Mother Earth, a farmer–leader, in *Country* (1984), a film which celebrated the myth of "the land" by casting a woman in a traditionally male role. (Courtesy of The Museum of Modern Art/Film Stills Archive)

50. Nostalgia without tears—the very last moment of adolescence and innocence in *Racing with the Moon* (1984). The two buddies, Sean Penn (left) and Nicolas Cage (right), chase after the departing train that will take them to military service—and adulthood. (Courtesy of The Museum of Modern Art/Film Stills Archive)

51. In Robert Zemeckis's blockbuster *Back to the Future* (1985), there is a significant role reversal: Father George McFly (Crispin Glover, right) takes notes from his son Marty (Michael J. Fox) on how to court his future wife and son's mother. (Courtesy of The Museum of Modern Art/Film Stills Archive)

52. At the center of Rob Reiner's *Stand By Me* (1986) are four male adolescents, who set out on an important mission that will forever change their lives: Wil Wheaton (left), River Phoenix (second from left), Jerry O'Connell (pointing), and Corey Feldman (right). (Courtesy of The Museum of Modern Art/Film Stills Archive)

5

• • • • • • • •

The 1970s—
Nostalgia and Irony

I guess the town can get along without us till Monday.
—*The Last Picture Show*

I can't sit still. I always feel like I should be somewhere
else.

—*Bound for Glory*

The 1970s were not a strong decade for films about small-town life,
qualitatively or quantitatively, particularly in comparison with the decade
of the 1980s, one of the richest in small-town imagery. The decade began
with *The Last Picture Show* (1971), one of the best and most commercial
small-town works. However, this brilliant movie lacked the more distinctive themes of the 1970s. It was there on its own, a product of Peter
Bogdanovich's aesthetics rather than its social or historical milieu; the
film had more to do with the director's knowledge of Hollywood's genres
than with the surrounding political setting. If a pessimistic, rather cynical, evocation of small-town life marked the beginnning of the decade, a
completely different mood marked the small-town film that closed it, the
cheerful and uplifting *Breaking Away* (1979), which prepared the ground
for the typical ambience of 1980s movies.

In the 1970s, small-town films perpetuated dominant myths, old and
new, in American culture. As James Monaco observed, the prevalent
myths were a strange mixture of nostalgia, paranoia, and revenge,[1] all
reflective of the collective psyche during the Vietnam War and the
Watergate scandal, the two major events of the decade. And while
nostalgia was by no means a new trend, paranoia and revenge were. The
three motifs showed Americans to be alienated from their political and
social system, described in film after film as corrupt and ineffectual.

182

Nostalgia produced such small-town films as George Lucas's *American Graffiti* (1973) or James Bridges's *September 30, 1955* (1978). Fear and paranoia resulted in a cycle of disaster films (*Airport* and its sequels; *The Poseidon Adventure, Earthquake, The Towering Inferno, Jaws*) and political thrillers (*Three Days of The Condor, All the President's Men*). The theme of revenge permeated right-wing films (*Dirty Harry, Death Wish* and their sequels), all violent narratives in which the protagonists' sentiments were crude, but their response was effective to an increasingly violent society and less-effective government. But the motif of revenge crossed over many genres and could also be found in horror movies set in small towns (*Carrie, Halloween*) or in the country (*Jeremiah Johnson*).

Another prevalent trend of the 1970s was the male buddie film, which began with *Easy Rider*. These movies of celebrated male heroism and male friendship, excluding women completely from their narratives. Most of the decade (up to 1977) will be remembered as the worst years for women in the American cinema, on-screen and off. A wide gap existed between the economic and occupational roles of women in society and their symbolic or cultural treatment in film. Significantly, the most negative screen portrayals, which either *trivialized* women's domestic roles and/or *condemned* career women, occurred in the late 1960s and early 1970s—just when women were beginning to leave their mark in the social structure (See conclusion).

Nostalgia: *The Last Picture Show* and *American Graffiti*

Few people could anticipate the critical and commercial success of *The Last Picture Show*, a film nominated for the Best Picture Oscar, winning acting accolades for two of its distinguished performances.[2] The narrative begins with an impressive long shot of Anarene, Texas, in a cold morning in 1951. It is dawn, and except for the old white Nash, which belongs to the night watchman, the square is deserted. Wind blows the curling dust down the empty Main Street, and the camera pans across the Royal Theater (the picture show), a laundromat, a dinky beauty parlor, and a grocery store. Sonny Crawford (Timothy Bottoms), the film's hero and moral conscience, struggles with the choke of his black Chevrolet pickup, but to no avail.

Most of the action takes place either in the pool hall or the town's café. Shabby, the pool hall has a counter, a small candy case, and a green Dr. Pepper machine. Sam the Lion (Ben Johnson), the pool hall's owner, is an aging cowboy. Run-down on the outside, the café has a sign that does not hang straight and much of its paint is peeling off. But the interior is clean and cozy, with bright linoleum, red leathered booths, several stools, and a shiny jukebox, which is constantly playing. People tend to let their steam off in this café. For example, Sonny complains to the tough waitress Genevieve (Eileen Brennan), "Ain't nobody to go with in this town." Genevieve's role is crucial: She connects among the various characters, and also provides commentary on their actions. It is Genevieve who observes that Anarene is so small it is impossible to sneeze without all the inhabitants offering a handkerchief.

Another prevalent sight is the local Picture Show that, due to the increasing popularity of television, is losing its customers by the day. Sonny has missed the newsreel and the film has already begun, so Miss Mosey charges him only thirty cents. Sonny is in the moviehouse not so much to see the film, *Father of the Bride,* but to meet Charlene Duggs (Sharon Taggart), his girlfriend of one year. Hugging and kissing, Charlene reminds him it is their anniversary: "We been going steady a year tonight." "Seems like a lot longer," says Sonny. Disappointed that he did not bring a present, she says: "You can give me a dollar; that's what it cost me and Marlene (her sister) for the show." They then move to his car, where she lifts her sweater, and he unhooks her bra. But he is bored; they have done it too many times and now he wants to do "*something* different." Charlene is furious, "You cheapskate! You never even given me a present an' now you want to go right ahead and get me pregnant." Outraged, Sonny says, "My God, it was just my hand!" "Mommy told me how that old stuff goes—we'll have plenty a time for that when we get married." Charlene thinks Sonny "ain't good-looking enough," and he also has no ducktail, referring to Van Johnson's style, a popular movie star at that time.

As in other films, one-parent families characterize many of the youngsters. Sam the Lion is a widower, living with Billy, his only son who is mute and retarded. "You and Duane," says Genevieve, "both in boardinghouse, him with a mother, you with a father." It "don't seem right" to her, but then, on a second thought, she admits, "I'm no one to talk. I never got on with Mama—still don't." Bitter and frustrated, Genevieve is one among many inhabitants for whom the town offers no future. When Sonny suggests that Genevieve quit her job and make her husband go to work, she says: "Honey, we got four thousand dollars worth of doctor bills to pay—I'll probably be making cheeseburgers for your grandkids."

The town's students are not particularly bright, lacking intellectual horizons and open-mindedness. When the English teacher wonders if they are interested in John Keats, Joe Bob remarks that "it's silly of all the *poets* to want to be somethin' besides what the Lord made 'em," because "it's criticizing the Lord. "At the gym, Herman the coach is determined to make his lazy students "real men." "Run, you little piss-ants," he says. "Tough it out! You gotta be *men*, like the rest of us—If y'all didn't jack off so much maybe some of you could stay in shape." A macho man,

Herman is rude and sexist. Asking Sonny to take his wife to a doctor, he notes, "You know women, always something wrong with 'em."

The town's class structure is very visible. Jacy Farrow (Cybill Shepherd), the prettiest and richest girl in town, is driving a convertible. In Jacy's bedroom, there is a big picture of herself as "Football Queen" and stuffed animals on her bed. Jacy reads a movie magazine, the kind of escapist reading that girls her age find fascinating. The relationship between Jacy's mother, Lois (Ellen Burstyn) and her daughter is in the tradition of *Peyton Place*, except it's more cynical. Allison MacKenzie was an agreeable, honest girl, whereas Jacy is mean and bitchy. Constance MacKenzie was repressed, but Lois is beyond that, a bitter forty-year-old woman, who feels her happy days are over. "I'd just hate to see you marry Duane," says Lois. "You wouldn't be rich anymore, and in about two months he'd quit flattering you." "You married Daddy when he was poor," says the defiant Jacy, "and *he* got rich, didn't he?" Quick to answer, Lois says, "I *scared* your Daddy into getting rich." What was left unsaid or implied in previous films, becomes overt in this movie. "You're rich and you're miserable," Jacy tells her mother. "I sure don't want to be like you." Viewers know, however, that she will turn out to be just like her mother. A practical woman, Lois suggests Jacy go to the doctor to "arrange something so you won't have to worry about babies." But it is Jacy who is hypocritical. "It's a sin, isn't it?" she says, "unless you're married." Lois is extremely matter-of-fact, and she wants to demystify the magic of sex. "Don't be mealymouthed," she says. "If you slept with Duane a few times you'd see there isn't anything magic about him, and then we can send you to a good school." There is another reversal of conventions: Unlike Allison MacKenzie, Jacy does not want to leave town, she just wants to go to Wichita Falls. But her mother does not give in. "Everything's flat and empty here," she says, "and there's nothing to do." Finally, she warns: "Jus' remember, beautiful, everything gets old if you do it often enough." Disenchanted with her own marriage, she advises her daughter: "If you want to find out about monotony real quick, marry Duane." Lois's view of marriage is shared by the other inhabitants. "Is bein' married always so miserable?" Sonny asks Sam. "Oh, not necessarily," Sam replies, "just about eighty percent of the time."

In contrast to the Farrows, the Poppers live in an ugly house. The kitchen is small and messy; the breakfast dishes have not been washed nor has the table been cleared. A plain, drab woman, Ruth Popper (Cloris Leachman) is Lois's age, but looks much older. Like Lois, however, she is confined in a bad marriage, lacking any self-worth. Getting back from the doctor, she asks Sonny to come in, "if you can stand me for a few more minutes," admitting she is "scared to be alone." At the

Christmas dance, when she complains to her husband that she doesn't feel well, he retorts, "Hell, you never feel well." *Scare* is a word Ruth uses repeatedly. Upon consummating her relationship with the much younger Sonny, she apologizes for crying. "I was just scared," says Ruth, "I could never do this." She reached a point in her life, where "I can't do *anything* without crying about it." She is the type of woman "who wasn't brought up to leave a husband, or maybe I was just scared to." She married Herman because she was young and thought "hairy-chested football coaches were about it." Petrified, she fears that if he finds out "he'll shoot us," for "he's always glad to have an excuse to use his deer rifle."

The youngsters like Billy, but once in a while they play cruel jokes on him. "What we *oughta* do," says Duane, "is buy Billy a piece of ass." "We oughtn't let 'im die a virgin." observes Leroy. "Momma says idiot kids don't live long anyway." This irritates Sonny, who cares about Billy more than the other boys. "He ain't no idiot kid," he says angrily, "he just don't talk." They thus take Billy to a prostitute and force him to have sex with her. Furious, Sam, a surrogate father and role model to the boys, kicks them out.

No future to look forward to and no exciting present to live in, the town's residents spend a lot of time talking about their pasts. "I'm just as sentimental as the next fella when it comes to old times," Sam tells Sonny. He ruminates nostaligcally about the time he used to own this land, and how the country has changed since then. The first time he saw it, there wasn't a mesquite tree on it, or a prickly pear neither. Sam's great love was Lois, as she later tells Sonny: "If it hadn't been for him, I'd have missed it—whatever it is." "I'd have been one of those Amity types that think bridge is the best thing life has to offer." Living in her past memories, Lois feels Sam was "the only man I ever met who knew what I was worth."

The film shows the ambivalent attitude most residents feel toward their town. "I'm sick of this town," says Duane to Sonny. "Why don't we jus' take off an' go someplace?" Sonny concurs, "I guess the town can get along without us till Monday." "If I was young enough to bounce that far I'd go with you," says Sam. Duane later leaves town, but he does not go to a Big City, just to Odessa, another town, where "the roughnecks say you can get a job anytime."

Sam is the town's moral center; when he dies (of stroke), a whole life-style disappears with him. "He had his own way of doin' things," says Andy. "It's a wonder somebody don't steal the town," says Duane, when the café is closed after his death. Sam owns the town's three cultural centers (the pool hall, the café, and the picture show). An ex-farmer, he continued to live as a cowboy, committed to the Old West's code of ethics.

Sam is the last vestige of the cowboy-gentleman, a homespun phi-losopher in the mold of Will Rogers, only more handsome.

The Last Picture Show draws no explicit comparisons with life in the Big City. Still, Lester Marlow, who invites Jacy to a midnight swimming party in the nude, lives in Wichita Falls, and he is a little more sophisticated than the youngsters of Anarene. And Jacy and Duane go to the Wichita Falls Motel to consummate their relationship, but, under pressure, Du-ane, the macho boy, cannot perform. "I might have *known* you couldn't do it," says the merciless Jacy. "Now I'll *never* get not to be a virgin." More important than her passion or joy, is "What'll we tell everybody?" Their classmates are outside the motel, sitting in their cars waiting to hear a firsthand report about "the event." Embarrassed by the whole experi-ence, Jacy threatens Duane, "You better not tell one soul! Just pretend it was *wonderful*." Later, when they go back to the motel and do it, she is disappointed, "Oh, quit prissing, I don't think you did it right, anyway." Jacy and her mother are sexually involved with the same man, but Jacy's sex with him is also unsatisfactory. After Duane leaves town, Jacy dates (and marries) Sonny, which upsets Duane, despite the fact that he does not live there anymore. "Don't make no difference," says Duane, "I'll *always* live here," indicating that no matter where one goes, spending the formative years in Anarene, the town will always continue to be the frame of reference. Sonny does not show much respect for him either. "The only reason Jacy went with you long as she did," he says, "was 'cause you was in the backfield, and I was in the goddamn line!" Enraged, Duane hits Sonny with a bottle on his eye.

The alternative to living in Anarene is going to the army; it is 1951 and the Korean War is on, though the war is not a big issue. "You wanna go over to Korea and get yourself killed," says Genevieve. She thinks he is "a lot better off stayin' with Ruth Popper." Shocked, Sonny asks, "Does *everybody* know about that?" Almost everybody: Their illicit affair has become public knowledge. "Hadn't you heard about them?" Lois asks Jacy. "Been goin' on about six months."

In the film's last scene, Sonny visits Ruth. No longer involved, they sit in the kitchen, holding hands with a sad expression on their faces. This image dissolves and is superimposed on a tracking shot of the deserted town. *The Last Picture Show* ends just as it began, only more depres-singly—a result of what the viewers know about the town. Main Street is empty, and so is the square; only the stark telephone poles are there. The wind blows, raising the dust, and the picture show is closed.

As was shown, death is a recurrent motif in small-town movies, and *Picture Show* shows a variety of deaths—accidental, sudden, and unex-pected. Sam dies suddenly (of a stroke), with no warning. His son Billy dies in a car accident; he is run over by a truck. Duane is likely to die in combat in Korea. In addition to actual death, there is spiritual death of practically every individual and the town as a whole. In adapting Larry McMurtry's book to the screen, Bogdanovich (and McMurtry) changed the two movies screened at the picture show. In the book, it's *The Kid from Texas,* an Audie Murphy vehicle, which Duane watches the night before going to Korea. In the movie, it is Howard Hawks's epic Western, *Red River.* The charismatic figure of John Wayne, who was then at the height of his popularity, dwarfs the lives of Sonny and Duane even more. A 1948 release, it is not clear if *Red River* is playing in Anarene for the first time. The second movie used is *Father of the Bride* (1950), instead of *Storm Warning* (1950), a melodrama about an oversexed Ku Klux Klan killer in the South, starring Doris Day and Ronald Reagan. Charlene may fantasize about Elizabeth Taylor, while carrying on with Sonny, and the contrast between the world's most beautiful women and Charlene is ironic and bitter. The kind of magazines people read indicates their wish to be somewhere else; Genevieve reads *Ladies Home Journal.* The movies they see also feed their fantasies about idealized life-styles. The gap between their everyday lives and the culture they consume underlines even more their futility and frustration.

In a similar vein to many small-town works set around the 1900s— which explore the impact of technological change (the automobile) on small-town life—Bogdanovich strategically located his narrative in 1951, when television was spreading in America, on the verge of becoming the most popular form of entertainment. As an innovation, television was more important than the invention of the automobile, because it brought "the outside reality" into the living room, thus changing leisure from a collective to a privatized experience. Because of TV, people went less to the movies and the collective aspect of moviegoing, sitting in the dark surrounded by a large and anonymous public, was lost. But television also exposed an extremely diverse population to the *same* contents, thus serving as a homogenizing experience, at least superficially. The result was that small communities lost their distinctive life-styles, becoming more and more similar. *The Last Picture Show* shows the gradual decay and death of community life (Toennis's gemeinschaft), lamenting the loss of intimacy and declining integration.

If *The Last Picture Show* presents a gloomy portrait of small-town life during the early advent of television, *American Graffiti* (1973) moves the setting forward by a decade, to 1962, when television had already established itself as the mainstay of American culture. However, as far as youths were concerned the relevant medium is radio and the music is rock; radio is shown to be their whole lifetime. *American Graffiti* is only nominally set in 1962, for the icons and symbols used are of the late 1950s. Take, for example, the cars: some girls cruise in a Studebaker; Steve drives a white '58 Chevy; and Laurie a '58 Edsel. The songs are also of the late 1950s: in the opening scene, at Mel's Drive In, we hear "Rock Around the Clock," then Del Shannon's "Runaway." There is also music by the Platters, the Beach Boys, Flash Cadillac and the Continental Kids. The movie stars emulated are Connie Stevens and Sandra Dee for the girls, and (the myth of) James Dean and Elvis Presley for the boys.

There is saturation of mass media, and their influence is pervasive; the kids' dialogue makes many references to pop culture. Debbie tells one boy he is like the Lone Ranger, and Curt falls in love with a girl from *Citizen Kane*. The recurrent audiovisual motif is a blast of rock music, coming from an endless stream of cars cruising around the block in Modesto, a small town in Northern California. The car cruising takes the form of a modern dance piece, in which the relations among dancers (cars in the film) form, shift, separate, and reform—either by logic or by chance.

Modesto's moral center is not a type like Sam the Lion, an old-time moralist, but Wolfman Jack, the disc jockey, whose show unifies the town's kids. Indeed, the disc jockey, as a profession and the town's moral focus, provides a new cultural symbol in youth films.[3] Wolfman interacts with each member separately, and each youngster perceives him in a different way. He serves as a secret friend to each one of them. Wolfman is not seen much, but his presence is felt through the music he chooses for them to listen to. "The Wolfman been everywhere and he seen everything," people say in admiration, "he got so many stories, so many memories." As the community's expressive leader, Wolfman later arranges for a (telephone) interview between Curt and the unknown blonde he falls in love with, thus helping fulfill latent dreams. The music in *American Graffiti* suggests that all the kids, no matter where they are, *are* listening to the same radio program. The offscreen music performs narrative and ideological functions, cementing the otherwise episodic structure and interweaving the adolescents' crisscrossing paths.

Modesto is a self-contained entity; there are no excursions out of town. The action itself is confined to one long hot summer night, from sunset to sunrise, during which the adolescence of four male youngsters comes to a dramatic end. Modesto is the kind of town that changes image and personality; the alternation of day and night sequences captures this variable quality. During the day, one sees on main street a line of used-car-lots, small shops, department stores, and greasy spoons. At night, one sees the flashing, neon-lighted signs, and an endless parade of cars, some customized, others lowered. The town looks much more "glamorous" at night; Haskell Wexler's excellent cinematography emphasizes the town's dazzing kaleidoscopic features at night.

The narrative's real star is not human, but an object—the car and the life-style it embodies. These adolescents don't seek nature to regain their emotional balance, solve their identity crises, or make love. The car is a symbolic substitute for nature, providing emotional security, physical protection, and comfortable environment. It serves as a metaphor to America's innocence and naïveté in the early 1960s, when isolationism in foreign politics was still strong. Significantly, most of the interaction in *American Graffiti* takes place through the cars' windows, but it is rich communication, including exchange of provocations, flirtatious remarks, and insults. A convenient shield, the car's window is the only window to the real, outside world. Director George Lucas described his film as "a metaphor of what we once had and lost." The movie presents that era's complacency and apathy, along with its political naïveté and insularity. Instead of making explicit statements about the past's superiority to the present, the nostalgia is put in historical perspective, allowing viewers to decide for themselves their attitude toward those years. This is one portrait of America's past, *American Graffiti* seems to say, and it is up to the viewers to determine how this particular past has shaped—or led to—the present.

The four protagonists are high-school graduates at a turning point. Their crucial dilemma is staying in town or going to college. Curt (Richard Dreyfuss) and Steve (Ron Howard) are about to go to college, but Curt is hesitant about it. "I was thinking I might wait a year," he tells Steve, "go to the city." As in other movies, the kids are aware of the town's possibilities and limitations. "You can't back out now!" says Steve. "We are finally getting out of this turkey town, and now you want to crawl back into your cell." The radio station's manager concurs with Steve: "No offense to your hometown here, but this place ain't exactly the hub of the universe." The manager's frustration derives from his realization that "there's a whole big beautiful world out there . . . and here I sit sucking popsicles."

Different types are represented by the four youngsters. Attractive and pleasant, Steve serves as his class's president. Curt is the bright, inquisitive intellectual; winning a prestigious fellowship assures him that he would go to college. Less handsome, Terry the Toad (Charlie Martin Smith), is a follower; worshipping Steve, he gets to use his grand Impala. John Milner (Paul LeMat)is a negative reference figure: at twenty-two, he is still immature, emulating James Dean. He drives a yellow '32 Ford deuce coupe, puffs on a Camel, with his butch haircut molded on the sides into a ducktail. John is the simpleton, anti-intellectual type, unimpressed with college. "You probably think you're a big shot," he tells Steve, "but you're still a punk." The champion of drag racing, John considers himself a ladies' gentleman.

The conversations carried on by the youngsters may sound trivial—to adult viewers—but are important to them. At the girls' lavatory, Laurie (Cindy Williams) is worried because Steve is going away. Her friend Peg Fuller is sure she will forget him in a week; if she is elected senior queen, she will have many admirers. "Remember what happened to Evelyn Chelnick when Mike went into the marines?" says Peg, trying to cheer Laurie up. "She had a nervous breakdown and was acting so wacky she got run over by a bus!" At the same time, at the boys' lavatory, the guys work as intensely on their coiffures as the girls do, smoothing their ducktails, primping their glossy waterfalls, and waxing their crew cuts to stand stiff. After teasing a classmate for using a pimple cream, Steve applies it on his neck. Eddie is surprised to hear about Steve and Laurie's "arrangement." "We're still going together," says Steve, "but we can date other people"; it is clear, however, this was *his* idea. To make him jealous, Laurie goes with a hot-rodder, but at the end they are reunited after an accident. The drag race in *American Graffiti* lacks the consequential effects of a similar race in *Rebel without a Cause,* though the Modesto youngsters have probably learned about such races from the James Dean movie.

Focusing on four boys, *American Graffiti* takes an exclusively male point of view. If the movie were made a few years later, it would have had to include stronger female parts. The girls in the film exist as romantic interests for the boys, lacking personalities of their own. Still the movie shows different types of girls: Laurie is compared with Debbie in the way they relate to love and sex. Laurie's ideal is to have a monogamous relationship, whereas Debbie is more pragmatic.

The narrative ends with Curt's departure to college out East. His plane takes off while the sound track plays "Good Night Sweetheart." What were the options of small-town kids at the time: go to college, run away to the Big City, or stay in town and live a complacent and stifling life. However, with all his ambition to pursue his studies, Curt's departure from town conveys the price, the loss of intimate friendships he will never experience again.[4] But he also knows that if he stays in town, his life would have turned out worse. The fate of the four friends is printed on-screen, and it is shocking because it violates the former nostalgic and pleasant mood. The viewers are suddenly thrown off balance, from a fantasy-dream to a newsreel. The cards tell that John Milner was killed by a drunk driver, in 1964. Terry Fields was reported missing in action in Vietnam, in 1965. Steve Bolander is an insurance agent in Modesto. And Curt Henderson is a successful writer who went to Canada (because of the draft). Feminist critics pointed out the narrative's sexist bias, charging that the filmmakers obviously did not find it necessary to report what has happened to its female characters.

Anarchy and Disillusionment: Twisted Views of Rural Life

In the 1970s, small-town and rural life were depicted more harshly than in any previous decade. Three critical treatments, sharing similar thematics, appeared at the same time, two marking stunning film debuts: Steven Spielberg's *Sugarland Express* (1973) and Terence Malick's *Badlands* (1974); the third was Robert Altman's *Thieves Like Us* (1974). Two other movies also dealt with anarchy and reflected disillusionment with American society: *Jeremiah Johnson* (1972) and *Paper Moon* (1973). Despite diversity of styles and variety of settings, all five films were reactions to their immediate political surroundings.

Anarchy and Back to Nature: *Jeremiah Johnson*

The contradictory attitudes of nostalgia and cynicism were well captured in Sydney Pollack's *Jeremiah Johnson* (1972), a film that became a blockbuster because of Robert Redford's stardom—despite risky subject matter. Disillusioned with society, the movie's eponymous hero turns his back on civilization and goes back to nature, as if he were following Thoreau's scriptures in *Walden*. A narrator sets the film's mythic tone, informing that "nobody knows where he comes from," and that Jeremiah "said good-bye to whatever life was there below." The word *below* signifies both location, below the mountains, and values, inferior life. Pollack (with cinematographer Andrew Callaghan) frames Utah's vast lands in a way that dwarfs Jeremiah against the forceful magnitude of nature.

Jeremiah is a dropout, a retreatist (to use Merton's typology) a man who rejects society's goals and prescribed means to achieve them. Withdrawing into the past of the Western frontier, the film chronicles in detail his initial inexperience in fighting nature and the Indians. Jeremiah's first winter is near fatal, until he meets another "professional" mountaineer who provides him with the basic tools for survival. "Keep your nose to the wind and your eye to the skyline," advises Bear Clau, who also instructs him how to skin a bear, sleep on coals, hunt, trap, and deal—or avoid—the Indians. His solitude is interrupted by an Indian massacre of a settler's family, leaving a crazed wife and a mute boy as survivors. The film seizes the tension between Jeremiah's need for complete solitude *and* for human relationship. Indeed, he becomes the surrogate father of the boy (after his mother kills herself) and, with his new Indian wife, establishes some sort of family life.

In addition to the disenchantment with society, the other motif is revenge. When the Crows slaughter his wife and boy, as a result of invading their sacred burial ground, Jeremiah goes on a revenge rampage. The film suggests that even a peaceful man could be forced to become a killer, and that one can never escape completely "civilization's" contamination. Unlike most Westerns, it does not present the Indians as an undistinguished mass, acknowledging Indian feuds and differentiating the Flatheads from the Crows. However, the ending, in which Jeremiah encounters an Indian on a white horse, is ambiguous. They exchange looks that convey the complex relationship between the white man and the Indian: love-hate, respect-contempt. Initially, Pollack envisioned an ending in which Jeremiah freezes to death, a more logical resolution. But Redford opted for a more ambivalent ending, claiming that the viewers should make up their own minds.

Jeremiah Johnson contains elements of the myth Leslie Fiedler (1972) describes as "Good Companions in the Wilderness," the meeting between the white fur trapper in the wilderness and the Indian warrior. This myth's power is in its ability to contain the misogyny of the American male, hopes of reconciliation with the Indians, and retreat from the pressures of civilization itself. Jeremiah is a mysterious figure when the narrative begins and remains an enigma at its end. An abstract type, a symbol of wildlife, he must have struck chords with younger audiences.[5] The film also sends contradictory messages, both right- and left-wing: It imparts disgust with the white establishment and desire for peaceful life in nature, but also shows that savagery and violence are universal elements, in the City as well as nature.

Anarchy and Sentimentality: *Paper Moon*

Bogdanovich's *Paper Moon* was yet another example of a work by a director preoccupied with Hollywood's classic genres. It was inspired by *Little Miss Marker* (1934), a Shirley Temple vehicle, in which the child star won out over an opportunist. It is once again in black and white (cinematography by Laszlo Kovac), an homage to Gregg Toland's work in *The Grapes of Wrath*. Like *The Last Picture Show,* this film was at once an evocation of a specific time and place and a commentary on it though, unlike the 1971 film, did neither well. Set in rural Kansas and Missouri during the Depression (circa 1936), it concerns the growing affection between Moses (Ryan O'Neal), a con artist, and Addie (Tatum O'Neal), who may or may not be his illegitimate daughter.

The most controversial aspect of *Paper Moon* was the portrayal of Addie, a far cry from Shirley Temple, Margaret O'Brien, and other Hollywood child-stars. Addie is a precocious nine-year-old girl who manipulates Moses in the best way possible. Tough in attitude and behavior, she swears, using foul language. In her leisure, Addie stays in bed, lights herself a cigarette, and listens to the radio. Completely adaptable to changing conditions, Addie saves Moses several times. Moses sells the Bible to bereaved widows, whose names he takes from obituaries. Highly intuitive, Addie sets the price for the sale: When she senses it's a rich man's house, the price goes up. Addie has no moral scruples and is not above cheating: She embarrasses a cashier in a department store, implying she gave a twenty- (actually five-) dollar bill.

The narrative consists of two major and two secondary characters. In the second part, Moses befriends a floozie (Madeline Kahn) and her maid, a black girl. Unlike other films, *Paper Moon* at least acknowledges the presence and subjugation of blacks in the 1930s. When Addie asks the black girl, "Why don't you quit?" she says her mother had forced her to become a maid, believing that "the white woman would be good to her." As soon as Moses's attention centers on the floozie, Addie sees to it that she falls from grace. At first, she refuses to give her the front seat of the car. Then, she schemes for a gentleman caller, a hotel's clerk, to visit her and makes sure she is caught by Moses. In one of the film's better-written scenes, Addie confronts Moses. She is upset that "they don't work anymore," that they waste their money on clothes and nice hotels. Protesting, she demands that Moses get rid of his flame. At first, the floozie tries to pacify Addie with a child's talk, "I'll let you put on my earrings," or "I'll teach you how to put on a makeup." But a tomboy, Addie could not care less about these frivolous matters. What changes Addie's mind is her touching speech, culminating in the sentence, "In any case the affair won't last long . . . it's hard times."

The period details in this film are quite impressive: the old cars, the fascination with new models, the old popular radio programs featuring Jack Benny, Fibber McGee, and others. Manipulative and mechanically plotted, the film's strategy is so cynical and detached that it is devoid of any genuine feeling. This makes its sentimental resolution and doubtful morality not only sudden but unearned. Moses delivers Addie to her aunt in St. Clouds, but stealing on the run is more appealing than settling down to normality and getting an education, as other children of her age. Moses also has second thoughts and he finally takes her back. *Paper Moon* features anarchic philosophy with a twisted view of childhood, one that could be just as unhealthy and harmful as growing up within a suffocating milieu; education and domesticity are rejected. Glamorizing deviance and legitimizing Addie's status as an outsider—a child-monster—the narrative fails to provide a clue as to how Addie is going to make the inevitable transition from childhood to maturity and womanhood.

Anarchy as Lack of Control: *The Sugarland Express*

Anarchism as an attitude was also manifest in *Sugarland Express* (1973), based on an actual 1969 incident, when an escaped convict, Robert Samuel Dent, and his wife, Ila Faye, drove across Texas to reclaim their child from its adoptive parents. The account of the three hundred mile

chase commanded the attention of the entire state, with television playing a major role in the formation of public opinion. In the film, Lou Jean
Poplin (Goldie Hawn), an impulsive and desperate woman (who has also
served a sentence), visits her husband Clovis (William Atherton) at a
Texas prerelease prison farm, where he is waiting out the final months of
a one-year term for petty larceny. Strong-willed, she threatens to leave
him unless he escapes and helps her reclaim their infant son, about to be
given out for adoption; the State Child Welfare Board has determined
they are unfit. They get a ride with an elderly couple, but the slow pace
of their old rickety Buick attracts the attention of a Highway Patrol
officer. Soon official alarms are out and roadblocks set up. Most of the
narrative, describing the plan to stop the fugitive couple, is set on the
road, with impressive shots of traffic jams on highways and intersections.
At one point, the pursuing caravan is swelled to two-hundred assorted
cars. Thousands of people are waiting on the streets to show their
sympathy for the couple's rebellious defiance.

Sugarland Express stresses the crucial role of the news media in covering this event and in making instant celebrities out of hoodlums. The
press is held responsible for making the Poplins' story arouse curiosity
and receive sympathy. The media create and exploit the public's fascination with criminals, an issue already explored in *Bonnie and Clyde*. But the
police force is also guilty: in Louisiana, two opportunistic cops believe
this is *their* chance to break in the new patrol car, have some fun, and
achieve celebrity status for themselves. Captain Tanner (Ben Johnson, in
a role similar to Sam the Lion in *Last Picture Show*) stands out as a
conscientious police chief, struggling to avoid bloodshed at all costs. With
eighteen years of service, he boasts no killing to his name. He is a man of
principle, with an inner ethic code, as well as a man of action. The chase
draws all kinds of weird, glory hunters hoping to promote their own
visibility. For example, a celebrity-hungry owner of a chicken stand offers
the couple free food if they give themselves up at *his* place. Other
supporters carry stickers that say: "Register Communists, not guns." The
couple is showered with good wishes and presents (baby clothes and
toys) in every town they pass through. But these thrill seekers present an
obstacle to the police's law enforcement. There is a horrifying shot of a
terrified kid, knocked backwards by his rifle's power; the chase brings
out unbridled exhilaration and the worst of mob behavior, susceptible to
violence and destruction. Another shot shows a teddy bear run over, as if
signifying the end of innocence for children, comparing them with the
hunters and their guns.

Technology figures prominently, with every act becoming more deper-
sonalized: Most communications take place within cars or via two-way
radios. Captain Tanner uses Lou Jean's father to persuade his daughter

to give up her foolish scheme, but instead, he gets angry and scolds her. The film shows, as Pauline Kael pointed out, the effects of the mass media on people, the way they look (pink curlers), their eccentric hobbies (the woman collects gold stamps at service stations), but without putting them down.[6] Neither film nor characters display any humanity. The protagonists are antiheroic and small-minded, unable to see beyond their immediate interests. They set off events they don't know how to pursue, events that later take control of them. *Sugarland Express* is imbued with a sense of fatalism—people acting according to biological instincts, lacking awareness and control over what they are doing. Of the two protagonists, it is the woman who masterminds the scheme, though without much brains. In the end, she is also responsible for her husband's death by a sniper. The movie is ambiguous in portraying Lou Jean's maternal needs. At times, one gets the impression that the couple is out to get their son out of revenge; at other times, the feeling is of a long-suffering mother. The couple is portrayed as desperate, but not really dangerous. Their defiance with prison records and their anti-establishment attitudes were in tune with the alienation of many Americans from their government in 1973 and 1974, during the Watergate crisis. The movie is strong in suggesting the origins of mob behavior, a crowd going out of control. Starting as a small incident, the crisis grows out of any proportion. The police force, in charge of controlling the situation, is devoid of effective power. Everyone in the film is helpless and ineffectual; the crisis seems to follow its own logic. By implication, American society is viewed as a system without any regulative norms or coercive power; a society on the loose, with no moral center or binding collective conscience.

Unlike the protagonists of *Bonnie and Clyde,* who are the stuff of modern myths, Lou Jean and Clovis can ignite the masses' imagination only for seconds, until the next media celebrities assume their place. Bonnie and Clyde had at least some control over their lives; Lou Jean and Clovis have none. But like *Bonnie and Clyde, Sugarland Express* is a disguised Western: the fugitives stand in for the solitary Westerners (what has remained of them), and the procession of police cars is a modern, technological version of the posse in classic Westerns.

Anarchy and Alienation: *Badlands*

Terence Malick's *Badlands* bears some similarity to *Bonne and Clyde, Sugarland Express,* and *Jeremiah Johnson,* though its thematic approach and stylistics are different. Loosely based on the real-life killers Charles Starkweather and Carol Fugate, it is a fictionalized account of the rootlessness of two youngsters, Kit Carruthers (Martin Sheen), a twenty-five-year-old garbage collector, and Holly Sargis (Sissy Spacek), a fifteen-year-old girl. Like *Bonnie*, it's a ballad, or folktale, but unlike *Bonnie*, it lacks romanticism and doesn't mythologize its heroes. Like *Jeremiah Johnson*, most of the narrative is set far from civilization, in the wide plains of North Dakota and Montana. And like *Sugarland Express,* at its center is a fugitive couple, defying society's norms. Compared with all three movies, however, *Badlands* is the most formal and self-conscious endeavor. The film does not take a definite approach toward its characters (or the society in which they live), and unlike *Paper Moon*, it discourages the audience from exhibiting sympathy for the characters. The viewers are distanced by a cold film, whose protagonists are themselves devoid of human feelings. *Badlands* is framed by Holly's voice-over narration and its aesthetics is that of stylized, formal tableaux.

Set in 1960, *Badlands* is a chilling exposé of alienation as a state of self-estrangement and aimlessness. Holly's mother has died when she was young and she now lives with her working-class father. Kit has no family, friends, or any meaningful bond. He is engaged in one of the most meaningless and humiliating jobs possible: garbage collection. Spotting the bored Holly, a child-woman, with her long beautiful hair and sexy shorts, he falls for her. Their courtship is depicted through walks along the tree-sided streets and the river. A gentleman, Kit does not immediately demand to consummate their relationship. But once they have sex (in the woods), both look disappointed. Kit walks away, and Holly is bewildered and disenchanted; her knowledge is totally drawn from confessional magazines. "Did it go the way it's supposed to?" she asks Kit. "Is that all there is to it?" And with a sigh of relief, "I'm glad it's over." It is the only time they engage in sex. They think they are in love, but their relationship fails to show it. In fact, Holly says early on that Kit is in the wrong line of work and from the wrong side of the tracks, and she wonders what her husband would be like. Both are incapable of emotions toward each other and other people. In his murder spree, it is not clear if Kit holds on to Holly because he loves her, or because he needs a witness, an audience to appreciate and applaud; he tells Holly he doesn't want to die without a girl shrieking for him.

Her domineering father forbids her from seeing Kit and, upon finding out that she has deceived him, he shoots her dog in cold blood. As a further punishment, he forces her to take more music lessons on a clarinet. A brute, he tells Kit straightforwardly that he is not good enough for his daughter. Kit kills her father in front of Holly, buries his body in the basement and sets the whole house on fire. The blaze is shown in a stunning montage, with the camera lingering on every object burnt, while the sound track plays "Satie." The horror of the deed is deflated and diffused by the æsthetic style, as if director were saying there is beauty in the most horrendous act.

On the run, the couple starts a new life, living in nature on minimal subsistence. Wearing a jeans suit and white T-shirt, Kit bears strong resemblance to James Dean, of which he is aware; everybody in the film tells him so. A modern version of Hemingway's White Hunter or Jeremiah Johnson, Kit lives outdoors, in a tree house, instructing Holly how to shoot, cut wood, fish—in short how to live in the wilderness. Like Jeremiah, his goal is to be a mountaineer in Canada. "We have become sensitive to the rhythms of the logs," says Holly in her voice-over narration. It is not, however, an idyllic life. Kit lacks an appreciation of the beautiful vistas around them: Reflecting the Cold War mentality, he tells Holly that if the Commies would drop the atomic bomb they might as well start in Rapid City. Containing few characters, most of the narrative juxtaposes the couple against the big skies and the vast, barren lands of the Great Plains.

After weeks of complete isolation, their "first taste of civilization," as Holly says, is the sight of a train. Gradually Holly loses interest in Kit and their life, telling him she feels "like an animal." She surrenders, and after several posses and chases, he is in captivity too. Arrested in Montana, the police officer is disappointed to realize that Kit "is no bigger than I'm." The policemen are amiable, not vicious or mean (like in *Bonnie and Clyde*) and Kit shares with them secrets and jokes. Asked by a cop if he likes people, all Kit can say is, "I guess they're OK." Still perplexed, the cop asks, "Why did you do it?" "I don't know," says Kit, "I always wanted to be a criminal . . . just not this big a one." The law officers are indifferent: Smiling at his answers, they show neither indignation nor anger. A similar syndrome of alienation and aimlessness is depicted in *River's Edge*, wherein a high-school youngster kills for no apparent reason (chapter 6). In both films, moral emptiness is viewed as an inevitable by-product of mass society and its vulgar culture.

The dysfunctional role of the media is depicted in a manner similar to *Bonnie* and *Sugarland Express*. The media's thirst for sensationalism confers status on the criminals, turning them into instant celebrities; the stories make Kit a bigger-than-life figure. And as in *Sugarland Express*, the townspeople are eager to get any story or souvenir from Kit, be it his watch, pen, or a piece of candy. Full of contradictions, Kit is not counter-cultural in the mold of *Easy Rider*'s protagonists. He does not defy institutional authority per se. For example, he likes orderliness and dislikes litter; he shoots a football because it is "excess baggage." Kit also shows respect for Holly's education, insisting that she take her books with her so that she will not "fall behind." Holly is an innocent victim, satiated by stories fleshed out by film magazines and dime novels. At the end, Holly rehabilitates, marries a lawyer, and settles down to domesticity. Kit, however, is carried in a helicopter to his execution, but even now, he registers no emotions; life and death are equally meaningless for him.

Anarchy and Romanticism: *Thieves Like Us*

In the highly original *Thieves Like Us* (1974), Altman continues his concern of reworking the conventions of Hollywood's genre films, in this case as a response to *They Live by Night* (1948) and *Bonnie and Clyde*.[7] But unlike *Bonnie*, *Thieves* is neither nostalgic nor mythic; there is no attempt to glorify the protagonists as heroes. And unlike *They Live*, which uses the stylistic of film noir, it is neither sad nor depressing, using instead irony with comic relief. Shifting the locale to Mississippi, it is a tale of three bank robbers, set against the context of Depression America. The film abounds with icons of popular culture, the most important of which is Coca-Cola. In almost every scene, there is a bottle of Coke; even the state penitentiary has advertisement signs. Altman suggests that Coke was one of the few unifying objects in an increasingly diversified society. The drink was affordable by every class, and, being new, appealed to everyone. But drinking Coca-Cola (and, by the same token, going to the movies, or listening to the radio) establishes only a superficial equality among the classes. Coca-Cola, and pop culture, thus functions as opium to the masses, diverting their attention from their real class interests.

The male camaraderie in *Thieves Like Us* is also superficial, created under circumstantial pressures rather than genuine need for sharing interests.[8] The three criminals are so different that their attempt to create a primary group is bound to fail. The protagonist is Bowie (Keith Carradine), a twenty-three-year old man, whose father died when he was young. Joining a carnival, he began his criminal career at sixteen when he participated in a holdup, for which he served seven years in prison. When the film begins, Bowie, like Joe in *Fury*, converses in the most natural way with a dog. "Do you belong to someone, or are you a thief like me?" pointing out the meaning of the title (we are all thieves). A loner, Bowie is unable to abide by society's norms, but also unable to create a meaningful bond with the bank robbers or with Keechie (Shelley Duvall), his girl. Keechie is a kindred (lonely) soul who, unlike Bonnie, lacks the looks or glamour; she is a plain, ordinary girl, a victim of society.

Bowie is a (born) loser, but he is a good kid, driven into crime by circumstances; he is neither a countercultural rebel nor a crazed killer. "It was him or me," Bowie explains the motivation for a murder based on self-defense. He still maintains his simplicity and straightforward approach. In fact, initially he cannot rob a bank because he doesn't know how. Not committed to crime is a way of life, he would like to conform to society's rules. He is an outsider who, given the choice, would like to become an insider, reform, and go straight. At heart, Bowie is a romantic fool, a gentleman, addressing Keechie as "Miss." He is surprised she has had no men in her life: "You never had one, even to walk you to church?" "You think I should?" she asks. Their romance is thus *first* love for both. When he gives her a watch, she doesn't know how to wear it. Their passion is consummated during a radio broadcast of the "most celebrated love story." As they make love, the line from *Romeo and Juliet,* "thus did Romeo and Juliet consummate their first interview by falling madly in love with each other," is heard. It is an ironic comment: Both are products of mass culture, reflected in radio soaps. "You are not supposed to do it so often," she says, and it is clear she has read it in a confessional magazine. They are grown-up children, who continue to talk like children. "Do you like me a whole lot?" she asks. Driving to an isolated house, where they will enact out their marriage, sharing a household together (similar to *They Live by Night* and *Rebel without a Cause*), Keechie listens to "American Housewives Commercial for Refrigerator, Queen of Kitchen" on the radio.

By contrast, Bowie's two mates are outsiders, professional criminals. An aging robber, T-Dub (Bert Remsen) is reckless, boasting about his track record, "this will be my thirty-sixth bank robbery." Chicamaw (John Schuck), the third partner, is a heavy drinker and near psychopath who takes pleasure at rehearsing robberies with children. Bowie is not part of it, observing Chicamaw's games from his room, thus becoming a self-reflexive viewer of his own activities. Most of the robberies are not shown on screen: The camera keeps the viewers outside the banks, at a distance. The only robbery shown is the last one, shot from a high angle. As they are forced to kill a teller, President Roosevelt delivers a radio speech about the importance of security and peace and the government's commitment to these values.

Bowie's strong need to belong first drives him to his male friends, though unlike *Bonnie,* the gang does not function as a surrogate family. He then switches his emotional involvement to Keechie, trying to establish a household with her, which turns out to be a futile effort as well. Coming back from the robbery, Keechie charges: "You lied to me, liar. It was me or them. You took them." The two groups cannot coexist in harmony, and he drifts back and forth. At this point, he belongs to the male group out of obligation, and it is too late to establish a union with Keechie.

The ending is most revealing, lending significance to the narrative and the film's approach. Arriving at the Grapes Motor Hotel, Bowie and Keechie are greeted by children who play with firecrackers. They do not know that Mattie (Louise Fletcher), T-Dub's sister-in-law, will betray Bowie. The film uses children the way Westerns *(High Noon)* have: they play with fire, foretelling to the audience that a bloody and dangerous scene is soon to follow. She is in bed, and he voices his dreams about a better future, living on a farm. Standing behind a screen door, drinking Coca-Cola, Keechie watches how Bowie gets mowed down; her screams are shown in slow motion. The film draws a parallel between the police shooting the shack to pieces (in a long sequence) and Keechie smashing the Coke bottle; both the windows and glass bottle are shattered to smithereens.

Both *They Live* and *Bonnie* end with the death of their protagonists, but here Altman is also innovative. Bowie's is not a heroic or ritualistic death (as in *Bonnie*); he is reduced to a body bag. In the final scene, the pregnant Keechie is at the train station. While waiting, the evangelist Father Coughlin delivers an impassioned Resurrection speech to farmers and laborers about the need to bear their burdens in silence. Keechie has no money and no ticket, and while bearing her grief within her, she talks to a woman who is seating next to her, drinking Coke. "The child will not be named after his father," she says, assuring that Bowie's death is not going to be mythologized. This stands in sharp opposition to endings in which the protagonists march into history *(Young Mr. Lincoln)* or myth *(Bonnie)*. Later, Keechie merges with the masses, climbing up a staircase; she is now an ordinary woman, one of a large and faceless crowd.

Thieves Like Us offers a realistic feel of the Southern countryside during the Depression: the dreary gas stations, the churches, the banks, the Grapes Motor Hotel. However, the narrative's most innovative element is its sound track and the way it is interrelated with the story. At times, the characters listen to the radio: There are long montages that show every member pursuing his interests *while* listening to the radio. In fact, Bowie is so distracted by the radio that he has a car accident. The second, and more interesting, use of the radio is to let it provide ironic commentary on the protagonists. For example, when Bowie first meets Keechie, the radio plays a "Firestone" commercial, and when the three rob a bank, the radio plays *Gangbusters,* a popular show in the 1930s. When the couple makes love, Altman uses a soap-opera version of *Romeo and Juliet.* In this sense, the protagonists are never alone; the radio is always on.

In its clarity of vision and controlled artistic execution *Thieves Like Us* stands out. Its style is relaxed and casual, in sharp departure from *Bonnie* and *Badlands.*[9] The film is successful in both telling a story and commenting on it, by distancing the characters from their actions, and by distancing the viewers from the characters. In *Thieves Like Us*, the protagonists possess self-reflexivity, whereas in *Badlands* they show little awareness of what they are doing. With the exception of *Paper Moon*, all the aforementioned films employed similar strategies: distancing viewers from the narratives. Andrew Sarris described *Thieves* as "another carefully composed exercise in chilling disenchantment,"[10] a strategy that may account for their failure at the box office—unlike the enormous success of *Bonnie*, which encouraged audiences to *identify* with its two heroes. Of the five films about anarchy, *Badlands* is the most self-conscious, though *Thieves* is the most original, narratively and stylistically.

Suburbia as Small Town: *Shampoo*

The portrayal of suburbia in the 1970s (*Shampoo, Jaws, The Stepford Wives*, all in 1975) approximates that of small-town: There is not much difference in the two respective life-styles. This similarity is explicit in the narrative and, sometimes, in the visual look. "*Shampoo* is sort of *Our Town*," said coscreenwriter Robert Towne. "It's Grover's Corners 1968, only it's Beverly Hills." Indeed, Beverly Hills is portrayed as a self-contained community, isolated from its surroundings geographically and culturally, boasting a distinctive way of life. Yet this audacious film is anything but a reworking of old conventions. For one thing, no small-town film has a glamorous hairdresser as its protagonist. Warren Beatty (producer, cowriter, and star) takes a profession that is stereotypically homosexual, and not only turns it straight but makes the hero a womanizer, a modern-day Casanova.

George (Beatty), a charming hairdresser, works in a popular parlor, but he also makes house calls to his rich clients. There are three "women-clients" in his life, all favoring his sexual prowess. Felicia (Lee Grant), a middle-aged married woman; Jill (Goldie Hawn), his girl, who wants to marry him; and Jackie (Julie Christie), his old girl, a confused woman who is the mistress of Lester (Jack Warden), a rich businessman and Felicia's husband. He brings excitement to their lives and understands their "unique" problems like no other man. And there is a fourth girl, Lorna (Carrie Fisher), Felicia's alienated, mother-hating daughter. In the film's most outrageous scene, George is seduced by her. Their conversation begins with a series of disagreeable questions: "Are you gay? Are you making it with my mother?" Then, showing no inhibitions, she asks, "Do you want to fuck?" Few films have dared *show* a man sexually involved with a mother and her daughter (*The Graduate* was an exception), but what is interesting is that when Felicia finds out George went to bed with Lorna, instead of being furious, she becomes even more passionate.

George is basically a small-town hero who, instead of wanting to own his land, wants to own his beauty salon. Dressed in tight blue jeans and a black leather coat, he rides his motorcycle from assignation to assignation. George carries his hair dryer in his hand, in a (phallic) manner reminiscent of the way Clyde and other Westerners hold their guns; the hair dryer *is* George's gun. As in small-town movies, the characters are incestuously interrelated in complicated networks of relationships. For example, Lester, a modern version of the shyster lawyer, is a dishonest businessman who drives around in a Rolls Royce, constantly tuning to business reports from Wall Street. A married man, he keeps Jackie as a mistress, but Jackie was George's girl, and she is a close friend of Jill, his fiancée.

There is no distinction between behavior in the workplace and in privacy. "I never know when you're working and when you aren't working," says Jill. George is working (screwing) all the time. The film abounds with double entendres. Lester wonders: "How did you get into . . . that line of work?" or "Felicia says you're very interested in your shop." But George is up for a comeuppance, he is a naive, even foolish, Don Juan, who is bound to fail. At the end, he is deserted by all the women. Realizing that it is Jackie he really loves, he proposes to her, but it is too late, and she leaves him alone, on the top of a hill overlooking Beverly Hills. In the film's last shot, George is isolated, standing on a hill with no place to go and no goal to pursue.

Set on Election Day, November 4, 1968, *Shampoo* draws analogies between private and political life at this juncture of time and place. Beatty said the movie was meant to be "about the intermingling of political and sexual hypocrisy."[11] contrasting sexual with political mores. For example, most sexual encounters occur in public spaces: Their participants are either being observed and/or caught by others. By contrast, the political process (important decision making) is carried out in privacy, behind closed doors. The film's central sequence is a political banquet, with the television commenting on Nixon's sweeping win, but nobody pays attention; Jackie performs fellatio on George under the table. The film provides severe condemnation of the materialistic and superficial way of life in Los Angeles, the last frontier—it is all surface and name dropping, but no substance.

Typically of Los Angeles, the protagonists' professions are related to the "glamour" industries: George is a hairdresser and Jill a model. The preoccupation with hairstyles signifies ultra concern with physical appearances. The overindulgence in sex becomes a commercial commodity; none of the characters seems to enjoy it. It's a calculating, cold sex, with no emotions and no pretense of romance or courtship. In fact, very few sexual encounters are climaxed; the participants are often caught—by the wrong people—with their clothes down. During the party, when George and Jackie go to an empty house to make love, they are caught by Lester and Jill. George runs after Jill to explain, but by the time he is back, Jackie is gone. George is eager to please, never for a moment giving an account to himself of who he is. People become slaves to their private life (sex) at the expense of getting involved emotionally or politically. No character talks about or understands politics. *Shampoo* is about whoring, in sex and in politics, and the price of doing it. Made in 1975, a year after Nixon's resignation over the Watergate scandal, the film suggests that Nixon's hypocrisy and cheating were similar to those in Americans' everyday lives. The protagonists' lack of concern with larger issues than themselves accounts for the fact that Nixon was elected in the first place. The television set is on most of the time, but it is not enough, one has to watch and be alert, otherwise it is just a blur of images and sounds.

Class and Mobility: *Breaking Away*

The most accomplished small-town movie in the 1970s, *Breaking Away* (1979), paved the way for the next decade. Its best achievement was Steve Tesich's original script,[12] winning a well-deserved Oscar Award. The film shows sensitivity to American "peculiarities," despite the fact that it was written by an immigrant of Yugoslav descent and directed by an Englishman, Peter Yates. Set in Bloomington, Indiana, it contains some motifs of Booth Tarkington's (*Alice Adams*) work.

Four young guys walk toward the camera on a narrow dirt road, surrounded by thick vegegation—the sound track plays the melodic "O' Bury Me Not on the Lone Prairie." The abandoned quarry dwarfs the teenagers, who have to climb over rocks—a symbol of the obstacles they have to surmount because of their inferior background. It is a beautiful spot in nature, a huge pool of water with cliffs on three sides, a place where the four friends spend a lot of time together, their favorite hangout. The major issue is what to do after graduation from high school. "My dad says Jesus never went further than fifty miles from his home," says Cyril (Daniel Stern). "And look what happened to him," Mike (Dennis Quaid) quips. Cyril will "kinda miss school," but there is also a sense of relief; "It's the first time nobody's going to ask us to write a theme about how we spent our summer." Still a kid, Cyril joins the kids playing basketball; he got "depressed as hell when my athlete's foot and jock itch went away." Cyril was sure he would get a basketball scholarship, but did not. He suffers from inferiority complex, perpetuated by his father, who is "real understanding" only when he fails. Cyril's dad bought him a guitar because he was sure he would never learn to play it.

By contrast, Dave (Dennis Christopher), the film's hero, is planning to take the college entrance exam; he is "just curious to see if I can pass." Moocher's father is in Chicago, so he has the option of moving to Chicago, where there's a lot more jobs.

The four guys are members of a cohesive primary group. Delighted that he no longer works for the A&P, Mike says, "Aren't you glad we got fired." "We didn't get fired," Moocher corrects him. "You got fired. We quit." "One for all and all for one," exclaims Mike with pride, hoping his friends would continue "to stick together." But there is still sexual segregation. Moocher is the only one who goes steady with Nancy (Amy Wright), soon to become his fiancée. The whole thing is a secret, without his mates' knowledge. Moocher experiences a conflict between commitment to his male camaraderie and romantic interest. Nancy left her home, but she moved to an apartment only five blocks away from her folks. Her aspiration level is as low as the boys': If she keeps up the good work, she will become a head cashier.

The film contrasts this working-class group with the richer college kids, who describe the poor as "dumb-ass cutters, goddamn rednecks, retards." The only thing the two groups share in common—and fight over—is territory: both groups like to swim at the quarry hole. Mike hates those "bastards," because, "they've got indoor pools and outdoor pools on the campus, but they still got to come here." "It's my goddamn quarry!" says Mike; Cyril sings the theme of *Exodus:* "This hole! This quarry hole is mine!" The group resolves that if the college kids invade their territory, they will go to their campus and raise hell—which they later do.

The college kids reside on a nice street, "Fraternity Row," in enormous houses surrounded by neat lawns. The modern structures stand in sharp opposition to the other side of town, where the cutters live. The students are engaged in upper-class pursuits: sunbathing in fashionable suits, washing their expensive cars, listening to transistor radios, playing Frisbee. "Going to college must do something to girls' tits," says Cyril. "Just look at them campussies and sororititties." "They've got it made," says Moocher. But Dave sees inverse correlation between riches and happiness, reminding them that the Italians, his role models for now, are poor but happy.

Dave's father, Mr. Blase (Paul Dooley), is worried about his son. "He wanted a year with those bums, so I gave him a year, but what's he going to do?" Evelyn (Barbara Barrie), his more relaxed wife, believes he should go to college. "Why should he go to college?" asks the father. "I didn't. When I was nineteen, I was working in the quarries ten hours a day." But now most quarries have shut down and there are no jobs. He wants his son to come home "tired from looking [for a job]. He's never tired." Mr. Blase believes his son is "too stupid" to go to college, besides he is afraid that, once in college, Dave will thumb his diploma at him. "He is worthless, I could die of shame everytime I see him."

In other films, families fight with their kids, demanding they live at home, but not here. Dave's commitment to home derives from his belief that "Italian families stay together." Moreover, Dave thinks his parents should have another kid. He is more for conventional family values than his folks are. On his first date with the rich Katherine (Robyn Douglas), she tells him she doesn't miss her parents and that she went "as far as I could to get away from them." Dave puts her to tears when he says, "but *they* miss you." Dave is romantic, sending flowers to Katherine. When her rich boy friend, Rod (Hart Bochner) demands to know if "Dave has gotten into you?" she slaps him. But like Moocher, Rod is more concerned whether anyone saw him get hit by a woman than by the act itself.

Admiring the Italian racers, Dave becomes obsessed with their lifestyle. He pretends he is Italian ever since he won that Italian bike. His room is an Italian museum, with posters of Italian racers, Italian movies, Italian racing magazines. His favorite singer is Enrico Gimondi singing Neapolitan Favorites, and his cat's name is Fellini. Using an Italian phrase book, he converses in Italian. His father is appalled by the sight of his son shaving his legs. Sick and tired of sautéed zucchini and fetuccini, he wants "some American food." "Try not to become Italian on us," says Dave's mother. "Your father's quite Protestant." "He was a normal pumpkin pie," an elderly lady observes upon seeing Dave biking and singing in Italian. "Now look at him. His poor parents."

Dave's father used to be a stonecutter, working for the college buildings. When he visits the Quarry Shop, he avoids stepping into the limestone dust with his polished shoes. He is glad to be back, but he keeps a little distance, to show how far he has come in life. Indeed, the old-time cutters think he looks like "a government safety inspector," or "a union organizer." However, when the younger cutters don't recognize him, he is offended. The scene captures beautifully the nuances of class structure and distinctions in small towns. In *Breaking Away,* the father has lost his camaraderie and support group; he no longer belongs! A used-car salesman, his lot contains all kinds of cars: "Campus Cars," "Graduate School Special," "English Major," "Homecoming Queen." "I sold one of my worst cars to one of them today," he pokes fun at the college kids; occasionally, he is not very honest. The film thus offers cynical observation about upward mobility: Is being a car salesman a better job than a cutter, a job that at least requires specialized skills?

Though neither frustrated nor bitter, Dave's mother dreams of going to exciting places. She carries a passport, just in case, but she has never been outside of Indiana. The protagonists, veterans and youngsters, display a healthier attitude toward sex than their counterparts in similar films. Dave's mother orchestrates a seduction scene with the right music and candles, and even casual stripping. While Dave courts Katherine by singing, his mother seduces his father with Italian music. Every act follows with a counteract: When she removes the flower from her hair, he reciprocates by ripping the pencil case out of his pocket.

The highway sign states: "Welcome to Bloomington—Home of Indiana University." "It's campus everything," says Mike. "I feel like some Indian reservation surrounded by Disneyland." "What gets me," he continues, is "reading in the papers how some hotshot kid is the new star on the college team." "Every year there'll be a new one and it's never going to be me." Mike's brother *broke away* from his class, he is a cop; Mike calls him "pussycop." A loud protest follows the university president's announcement to include in the contest a local team from the town. "Most of you will only spend four years here, but to a lot of us Bloomington is our home, and I don't like the way you are behaving in my town." Rod believes "they're not good enough," and, interestingly, a black student "forgets" *his* minority status and says, "The whole thing reeks of tokenism."

The film's title works on many levels. At its most literal, it refers to the moment in bicycle racing when one cyclist bursts out of the pack. At a more symbolic level, it describes that crucial moment in life (as a race), when an individual has to forego soothing and comforting primary relationships and enter into the "real" unknown world. Dave's father has broken away from the cutters, and Dave needs to break away from his family and close-knit friends. Katherine has broken away from her family. *Breaking Away* is a coming-of-age picture, replete with rites of passage and initiation into adulthood. The film depicts those precious last moments of "irresponsible" adolescence. It is set in the last summer of adolescence, just prior to the beginning of the inevitably disillusioning adulthood. But the film itself breaks away from stereotypical settings and characters. Familiar issues of small-town movies are presented in a new setting.[13] The class conflict is not depicted as a bitter struggle, and unlike most American movies, this one shows that sexuality does not have to end in middle age. Though somehow resentful and defeated, the losers become winners, if only for one brief moment—when they win the race.

The cutters are the real outsiders, and in their own town. Highly aware of their social origins, they display an acute sense of class consciousness; unlike the pretentious Alice Adams, they know their limitations. The nominal outsiders are the college kids, invading town from all over the country and dominating it for a couple of years. Paradoxically, it is the college kids who contribute to the town's prestige and national visibility. Each of the four guys represents a different attitude toward life. Some are losers, willing to admit, at eighteen, their defeat. Says Mike: "I'll just be Mike twenty-year-old. Mike thirty-year-old. Old man Mike. But the college kids will never get old, out of shape, 'cause new ones come every year. And they'll keep caling us 'cutters.'" "To them it's a dirty word," says Dave, "but to me it'll just be something else I never got a chance to be." Mike used to be a leader but, embittered about his failure to become a college athlete, he knows that his glory as a star quarterback is over; nothing ahead of him could be as exciting as that. A compromiser, Moocher sees the solution in marriage, willing to take any job that will enable him to marry a girl of his own class. No mobility for him either. Cyril is the cynical type, resigned to play the failure his parents always believed he would be.

Dave, the only future-oriented member, will amount to something. A romantic dreamer, he is also the loyal friend, committed to values of family and camaraderie. He too is disillusioned at the end with his Italian subculture: In his first race with them, the Italians cruelly mistreat him. Dave accepts his working-class background, even grows to be proud of it. Stripping the walls of Italian memorabilia, Dave calls his father "Dad," instead of Papa. A Capraesque hero, Dave is capable of transforming himself, of moving beyond his immediate circumstances, of forging a new identity. Spunk, intelligence, energy, generosity, and idealism prove to be invaluable assets in his case.

The film has no consideration of ethnic barriers; there are few blacks, for example. The narrative stresses that there is still greater mobility in the United States than other countries. But while the class system is more open, three of the four kids will not improve on their initial status, thus perpetuating the built-in inequality. The film also endorses democratic values, such as free play and competition. At the end, the obnoxious and rich Rod must acknowledge the cutters' special qualities and their win. In turning its protagonists into winners, albeit in a more plausible manner from the underdog of *Rocky*, *Breaking Away* set the characteristic tone of other films of the 1980s.

Conclusion

In the 1970s, films about small-town life have become more self-conscious. In addition to telling their stories, each film also provided commentary about other small-town *movies*. This trend was inevitable: The body of small-town films has become so extensive and awareness of the filmmaking processes so acute that young filmmakers who chose to direct small-town narratives familiarized themselves with the thematic and stylistic conventions of previous films. As was noted, the genres used for exploring small-town life changed from one era to another. For example, in the 1950s many sci-fi films were set in small towns. In the 1970s, the resurgence of the horror film exploited small towns as a locale for all kinds of horror. The horror film cycle included Brian De Palma's *Carrie* (1976) and reached its commercial popularity with *Halloween* (1978).

Carrie's eponymous heroine (Sissy Spacek) is on one level a stock character: a misfit who comes of age and discovers her sexuality under the most terrifying conditions. An early scene shows the totally unprepared Carrie experiencing her first menstruation at the gym; her friends react as if she were a freak. "Help me," she screams in desperation, but her friends laugh, and it takes her teacher to pull her out of hysterics. Fatherless, she lives with her crazed, fanatically religious, mother (Piper Laurie), who perceives herself as a virgin damaged by sex. Shy and sexually inhibited, Carrie's main desire is to gain acceptance by her peers; she is unloved at home and ridiculed at school. However, the second part of the narrative turns into a slash horror film, another revenge story, thus fitting into the decade's dominant theme of vengeance. Carrie's telekinetic powers are used against her classmates and mother. In her retaliation, kitchen knives whizz through space, piercing her mother's body until she looks like a crucified saint.

Nostalgia, the other prevalent motif, did not always pay off. Hal Ashby's *Bound for Glory* (1976) made with an eye for the bicentennial, failed dismally at the box office. Episodic in structure, the narrative concerns the myth of Woody Guthrie, the great folk singer and union organizer. Message-oriented, without any attempt to speak to contemporary viewers, *Bound for Glory* chronicles the life of an ordinary individual who becomes extraordinary. It begins in a small impoverished Texas town, where Woody works as a sign painter, and ends with his CBS Radio contract in New York, focusing on his labor agitation and politicization of radio programs. The film shows, however, the tension between public and family life, and between show-business career and political commitment. Woody succeeds as a public leader, but fails as a family man. When his suffering wife complains, "You're always tryin' to fix the world, but you don't care nothin' 'bout your family," his response is mythic, "I can't sit still. I always feel like I should be somewhere else."

In the mid-1970s, Hollywood produced a cycle of films about paranoia and political corruption—all in the context of the Watergate scandal and its aftermath (Nixon's resignation). Prominent among this group was Spielberg's *Jaws* (1975), a well-made thriller, which also works as a political allegory. Like *Invasion of the Body Snatchers*, a peaceful Long Island community, ironically named Amity, is terrorized by a mammoth shark. What starts as a dream—spending a day in the sun and swimming out in the ocean—turns out to be a collective nightmare. But instead of unifying the community against the external threat, the danger brings out the worst of its "respectable" citizens (similar to *High Noon*). Concerned with the residents' safety, Chief Brody (Roy Scheider) decides to shut down the beaches, but the corrupt mayor worries about its damaging effects on summer tourism, the town's livelihood. Planning a cover-up, the mayor first attempts to persuade the residents that "it's all psychological." "You yell 'shark,'" he says, "and we've got panic on our hands on the Fourth of July." Immoral, the other professionals are also not trustworthy. The coroner is willing to change his diagnosis and claim the victim's cause of death was a boat.

As in other small-town films, nature, here the calm blue ocean, is presented as an unknown and unpredictable elemental force. Three men set out in an open boat to pursue the shark. Hooper (Richard Dreyfuss), is an intellectual scientist of rich background, a shark expert who wears glasses. Quint (Robert Shaw), a working-class man, is obsessed with sharks because of his past. And Brodie, the married police chief, functions as the moral center: a man who left the Big City (New York) because he wanted a quieter and simpler life. Rational, his heroism is not the bravura kind; he admits he is scared and doesn't like to swim. Conforming to the popular "male buddy" genre, the three men develop an intimate camaraderie. At first, the macho man pokes fun at the expert, calling him "a college boy," but gradually they learn to respect and enjoy each other's company. The three men sing, "Show Me the Way to Go Home," an ironic rendition, because none of them is the domesticated type. Reversing conventions of screen heroism, the action hero is devoured by the shark. Ideologically, the film rejects left-wing (propagated by experts) and right-wing (the macho fighter) politics, opting for a centrist position.

Christopher Lasch has defined the 1970s as a decade embodying the culture of narcissism, a culture that worships instant celebrity in a society obsessed with electronic images. Films of the 1970s expressed this obsession, particularly the cycle of crime films set in the rural South *(Badlands, Sugarland Express, Thieves Like Us)*. The protagonists of these narratives are motivated by a ruthless pursuit of media visibility and mass recognizability. That they lack substance and deserve no celebrity status is beside the point: They all want to see their pictures in the newspaper or, better, television. Narcissism, an indication of both self-absorption and insecurity, is at the center of these narratives. Their protagonists are desperate for reaction of the media *(Bonnie and Clyde)* and/or live audience *(Badlands)* to their deeds. They behave as if there are always viewers to their actions, which emphasizes even more the need for perpetually performing and being "on."[14]

The most typical films of the decade described the influence of the mass media (radio, film, and television) on small-town life, acknowledging the role of popular culture in shaping the lives of Americans. *Sugarland Express* and *Thieves* show the sensationalism of provincial newspapers (particularly during the Depression), exploiting crime stories to their fullest. People consume escapist fare (soap operas, gangster stories, commercials), to divert their attention from their dreary reality. Moreover, the characters of these films like to read about their exploits in the newspapers. It is unclear to what extent the media make their consumers more alienated from their surroundings, but media exposure is all-pervasive. The analogy to the present is clear: American society has become a mass, highly stratified, society and the immense power of the mass media on everyday life cannot be ignored anymore. As Richard Shickel has observed, only celebrity power—taking the form of common idols but no common ideals—now offers Americans a sense of community.

It is no accident that, with the exception of *Sugarland Express,* women function as witnesses, passive bystanders, to men's heroics—real or fake. The limited, stereotypical portrayal of women in small-town and country films of the 1970s shows that Hollywood was out of touch with reality, ignoring the progress women were beginning to make in the social structure. Indeed, the cinematic images of women were not up-to-date: a culture lag[15] prevailed between society's material conditions and its symbolic representations. It would not be an exaggeration to claim that, from the late 1960s to the late 1970s, there was ideological backlash in Hollywood, manifested in three ways. First, there was a paucity of screen roles for women, particularly leading roles.[16] Second, as I previously pointed out, (1987) men dominated Hollywood not only quantitatively, but also qualitatively. The typical, big-budgeted movies were action-adventures, focusing on male friendships and male courage. The major movies of the decade usually featured two male stars in the leading roles, with few, or no women, in their narratives. Among the Oscar-nominated and/or blockbuster films were: *In the Heat of the Night* (1967), starring Rod Steiger and Sidney Poitier; *Midnight Cowboy* (1969), with Jon Voight and Dustin Hoffman; *Butch Cassidy and the Sundance Kid* (1969), with Paul Newman and Robert Redford; *Patton* (1970), with George C. Scott and Karl Malden; *The French Connection* (1971), with Gene Hackman and Roy Scheider; *Deliverance* (1972), with Jon Voight and Burt Reynolds; *The Godfather,* Parts I and II (1972, 1974), with an all-male cast, Marlon Brando, Robert De Niro, Robert Duvall, and Al Pacino; *The Sting* (1973), with Paul Newman and Robert Redford; *The Towering Inferno* (1974), with Paul Newman and Steve McQueen; *Dog Day Afternoon* (1975), with Al Pacino and Chris Sarandon; *Jaws* (1975), with Richard Dreyfuss, Roy

Scheider, and Robert Shaw; and *All the President's Men* (1976), with Robert Redford and Dustin Hoffman. Finally, most of the box-office stars in the 1970s were men. Between 1970 and 1976, Barbra Streisand was the only woman among the ten box-office stars who had the largest drawing power. And the biggest names in the industry were stars with a strong and tough "macho" image, such as Steve McQueen, Clint Eastwood, Lee Marvin, Charles Bronson, Robert De Niro, and Al Pacino.

6

• • • • • • • •

The 1980s—
Eccentricity
and Self-Consciousness

Beg, borrow, or steal, but, by God, you hang on to this land.
—*Country*

The landslide victory of Ronald Reagan in 1980 and the defeat of liberal candidates and causes were interpreted by some as an indication that American society was shifting into a more conservative mood. These critics suggested that in their reaction against the cultural and political liberalism of the 1960s, Americans were turning toward more traditional roles, institutions, and ideologies. The new conservative mood was seen as a counterreaction to the rising divorce rates, increasing number of working women, the me generation and its cult of intimacy, sexual promiscuity, and other social problems. The pursuit of the good old days—that may have never existed—became another myth.[1] The resurgence of a neoconservative and patriotic mood, epitomized by the Reagan administration also resulted in the production of films that strongly reaffirmed traditional virtues associated with small towns, such as honesty, integrity, commitment to the land, and the centrality of the nuclear family (*Places in the Heart* and *Country* are good examples).

Country-and-western music, the fastest growing industry over the last decade, was also discovered by Hollywood, and one could find country music and/or country music themes in big-studio, big-budget films. For example, *The Electric Horseman* (1979), starring Jane Fonda and Robert Redford, featured country singer Willie Nelson on the sound track and in a small role. *Coal Miner's Daughter* (1980), a biographical picture about Loretta Lynn's rise to stardom, turned out to be a blockbuster and an Oscar-winning film.[2] Country-and-western music came of age in the

1980s, a far cry from a film like *Five Easy Pieces* (1970), in which Jack Nicholson threatened to melt his girlfriend's records of Tammy Wynette "down into hair spray," if she played them again. Country-and-western music used a new organic beat, which made people feel close to each other, this at a time when people were tired of dancing to disco music, where one dances virtually by oneself.[3] The new popularity of Western music was also reflected in new trends of fashion: a combination of cowboy boots and Ralph Lauren Western wear. These films expressed nostalgic reaffirmation of tradition and patriotism—in reaction to international problems that beset American politics at the time.

Of all six decades, the 1980s have been characterized by the production of the largest, richest, and most diverse film output about small towns. After a decade of ignoring rural America and its small towns, the American cinema seemed to have rediscovered the potentialities of such settings and locales. The resurgence of small-town and country themes was influenced by a new generation of writers who burst into or made their mark in the cultural scene. Veteran writer Horton Foote had written the script for *To Kill a Mockingbird* and the play upon which the screen version of *The Chase* was based. In the 1980s, Foote continued to enrich the tradition of small-town explorations, producing an impressive body of work for the stage *(The Widow Clare)*, screen *(The Trip to Bountiful)*, and television (the miniseries based on the film *1918*). Sam Shepard (arguably America's foremost playwright), has devoted his entire career to the exploration of rural settings and characters. Many of his plays (and films) are set in the Mohave Desert: *Fool for Love* (1983). Beth Henley's work has also been exclusively situated in small towns: *Crimes of the Heart* and *Nobody's Fool* (both in 1986) and *Miss Firecracker* (1989). The demise of the studio system and the fragmentation of the old Hollywood made the independent cinema a viable mode of filmmaking. The height of the independent movement was in the 1980s, with several movies exploring rural settings *(Heartland,* 1980; *Stacking,* 1987; *Rachel's River,* 1989).

The Eccentricities of Small Towns

In the 1980s, small-town America is not a barren land; there is new life and energy, and even bizarre and mischievous characters. In 1986 alone, at least four movies celebrated the idiosyncrasies of small towns and the eccentricities of their inhabitants: Jonathan Demme's *Something Wild;* David Byrne's *True Stories;* David Lynch's *Blue Velvet;* Bruce Beresford's *Crimes of the Heart.* In most of these films, there is *seemingly* a moral and emotional vacuum, if one's look is confined to the exterior of small towns. In actuality, however, these movies showed a huge reserve of energy and imagination hidden beneath a most ordinary facade. However, unlike other decades, in the 1980s, there is not much organized community life. Individuals are rather left to their own devices. But, as Janet Maslin pointed out, Main Street still exists as a set of values that demands conformity; "in those ways, Main Street will never change."[4] The new narratives stress more than their old counterparts the individual's need to separate and distinguish himself from mainstream mores. The individual's relationship with community remains the urgent and essential issue it has always been, but it has become more difficult and problematic.

A young generation of talented directors began working in the 1970s, including some of the brightest filmmakers the American cinema has ever had: Woody Allen, Martin Scorsese, Jonathan Demme, Steven Spielberg, George Lucas, David Lynch. Despite various educational backgrounds, each has been endowed with a cinematic vision of his own, charting his narrative and thematic territory. Of the aforementioned directors, Demme contributed the most to probing small-town and rural life, complementing in many ways Scorsese's exploration of the "urban nightmare" *(Mean Streets, Taxi Driver, After Hours)*, and Allen's bittersweet view of Manhattan *(Manhattan, Hannah and Her Sisters)*.

A Jonathan Demme Trilogy

Initially released as *Citizens Band, Handle with Care* (1977) failed at the box office twice. The movie would have been more successful had it been released earlier (in the late 1960s), or later (in the 1980s), but in the context of the 1970s, it was an orphan. The second title, *Handle with Care*, was less successful than the original, which at least did justice to the film's concerns. *Handle with Care* resonates more meaning when examined in relation to Demme's later works, *Melvin and Howard* (1980) and *Something Wild* (1986).

Based on original screenplay by Paul Brickman, it explores the social psychology of CB radio operators in mid-America. Set in a small (unidentified) California town, it is a community of eccentric individuals who share love, actually obsession, to talk into the air. A folk comedy, composed of loosely tied vignettes, it is a quirky study of half-a-dozen characters. Its premise is Freudian, juxtaposing the individual's unrepressed ids with their socially shaped selves. *Handle with Care* shows how CB radios enable people to express their sexual fantasies to strangers in a manner they would not dare in personal, face-to-face, interactions. It also shows that, under certain circumstances, strangers could truly transform themselves—here with the assistance of CB radios—into a close-knit community. The film thus demonstrates the paradox of a mass medium (radio), which at once separates and unifies, a medium that helps maintain anonymity and at the same time make people feel they belong to a larger community.

Three triangles are at the center of the narrative. The first consists of Spider (Paul LeMat), his father Papa Thermodyne (Robert C. Blossom), a drunken bum, and his brother Dean (Bruce McGill). The second triangle is made of the brothers and Pam (Candy Clark), the girl they both like. The Angels compose the third triangle: Chrome Angel (Charles Napier), a truck driver, Dallas Angel (Ann Wedgeworth), and Portland Angel (Marcia Rodd). The two women meet accidentally on a bus, only to realize they are married to the same man, Chrome, a con man.

As in *American Graffiti,* it is a community of individuals who spend as much time in their cars as anywhere else, but there is a basic difference: they are in their car by themselves and talking into the airwaves fulfills subconscious desires. The protagonists' public names are all icons of popular culture: Spider, Electra, Warlock, Cochise, Hot Coffee, Chrome Angel, Smilin' Jack, the Red Baron. The radio helps them unleash their most hidden sexual fantasies. For instance, Electra (Pam's name), otherwise an ordinary girl, breathes into the air outrageous sexual words that overexcite a man so much he reaches orgasm in his truck. Chrome Angel, also listening to her, piles up a rig and finds himself in an accident.

Spider, the film's hero, named Blane, is by profession a mechanic, running a CB repair shop. He is a self-styled crusader, cutting off the wavebands of people who violate the FCC regulations. A number of parasites make his "enemy list": a redneck Fascist obsessed with Communism; a priest, who sees great danger in America's increasing secularization; and an old man, most interested in reminiscing about the past. There is no communication between the father, a retired truck driver, and Spider. At one point, failing to wake his father, Spider walks to the other room and calls him on the radio transmitter; the old man immediately wakes up! In fact, he comes to life *only* when he uses the CB.

But the radio also helps integrate the community. In the film's climax, an old man is lost in the woods during torrential rains. With no exception, every member in town, is searching for him, and the CB proves to be most useful. In mood, this sequence in the forest bears resemblance to *A Midsummer Night's Dream.* The image of strangers, holding hands together, conveys the notion of individuals participating in a collective, quasi-religious, ritual. The film's eccentrics could be descendants of Preston Sturges (*Miracle* or *Hail*), though the style is decidedly different. Demme's "touch" is lighter and less frenzied than Sturges's. The casting of Paul LeMat and Candy Clark, both of *American Graffiti* fame, suggests some continuity. If in the Lucas film, cars were the adolescents' dominant means of interaction, in Demme's, radios replace cars. But they fulfill a similar function: they define their protagonists' space and connect between their private and public lives. Still, *Handle with Care* is a more original work than *American Graffiti,* defying genre conventions and established types.

Melvin and Howard, singled out by the National Society of Film Critics as the best film of 1980, was more commercially successful. If *Handle* is a fable, a folk comedy, *Melvin* is both more poetic and lyric. One critic was so excited about the film that he described it as "painting a vision of America as robust and generous as Walt Whitman's."[5] The picture is distinguished by Bo Goldman's high-quality writing, winning the Oscar Award for original screenplay.

The narrative begins with an unlikely, most bizarre, meeting, in the Nevada desert, between one of America's richest man, Howard Hughes (Jason Robards), and one of its poorest, Melvin Dummar (Paul LeMat). Driving his junk-laden pickup truck, Melvin finds Hughes on the ground, thrown from his motorcycle. White-haired and long-bearded, Hughes looks like a crazed prophet, a sage of ancient times. Trying to cheer him up, Melvin talks nonstop, sings "Santa's Souped-up Sleigh," and even persuades Hughes to sing with him "Bye Bye Blackbird." Melvin wishes for a better job, at an airplane factory like McDonnell Douglas or Hughes. "What a shame," the old man remarks casually, "I might have done something. I'm Howard Hughes." Upon reaching Las Vegas, Melvin drops Hughes at the Sands Hotel and gives him his change, a quarter. This unlikely encounter is magical, not only because of Jason Robards's great performance, but because the two men interact on *equal* terms and the media-created, monstrous Hughes emerges as a human being. This encounter also indicates the American democratic-egalitarian spirit, reflecting Melvin's (and the film's) optimistic view of the possibility of establishing meaningful rapport with people who differ in status or class.

Melvin returns to Gabbs, Nevada, to his trailer-home, where he lives with Lynda (Mary Steenburgen) and their daughter Darcy (Elizabeth Cheshire). In the morning, Lynda wakes up to the sound of repossession men, hauling away Melvin's truck and his new motorcycle. She calls her boyfriend, Clark Taylor (Chip Taylor) for help, and leaves Melvin. But in Reno, Taylor walks out on the bruised and battered Lynda in a low-rent motel. Tracking Lynda down, Melvin finds her dancing in a sleazy Reno go-go club. Assaulting the stage with her suitcases and causing disorder, Lynda is fired. Her second job is as a waitress in a topless joint. This time Melvin is impatient and, with divorce papers in hand, he is granted custody of their daughter.

In the next scene, a very pregnant Lynda is at her mother's, calling

Melvin. Softened, he asks her to remarry him at the Silver Bell Wedding Chapel in Las Vegas. Broke, with a thirty-nine-dollar ceremony, Melvin ignores his doubts over the identity of the father of Lynda's baby. Later, Lynda leaves him for the second time, criticizing his ridiculous purchase of a Cadillac and a huge motorboat (which is on land!). Melvin listens to her, protesting only when she says they are poor: "Broke maybe, but not poor." Still, Lynda is determined to leave, and her last sentence to him is "C'est la vie," which neither he nor *she* understands. "What's that?" asks Melvin? "French," says Lynda, "I used to dream of becoming a French interpreter." This shocks Melvin: "You don't speak French!" but Lynda has the last word, "I told you, it was a dream!"

Melvin and Howard was billed as a romantic comedy, "a fiction based on fact," but as writer Goldman said, "Whether Melvin was telling the truth or not never really concerned me." And director Demme concurred, "the film is about what if Melvin was telling the truth."6 According to the film, Hughes's will was mysteriously left at Melvin's gas station, but it was contested and eventually declared a forgery. The central, most illuminating, scene is a TV game show. The movie captures better than other films the obsession with winning jackpots and prizes. What is left of the elusive American Dream of hard work and success is the unrealistic belief, of the middle and lower-middle classes, in sharing the national spotlight and appearing on TV, if only for seconds. In this sequence, the film is wryly perceptive about the quality of mid-American life. Melvin's fantasies are to be rich (winning in a game show) but also creative (writing a hit song). Vulnerable, he is also humble and generous: He is genuinely happy for those who win; perhaps the next time it will be him. "Look at it this way," he tells his jealous daughter Darcy, "the friendly skies, look, look how happy she is!" Modeled after "Let's Make a Deal," the film's "Easy Street" has a smooth host, Wally (Mr. Love) Williams, with a soothing voice, who functions as a priest, or pastor, in this collective ritual. A modern version of Capra's "little man," TV does not represent mass, anonymous, and impersonal culture. On the contrary, for Melvin (and his likes) TV game shows offer a bond with millions of anonymous strangers, united by their love of the medium and fantasy to win.

Demme demonstrates a most perceptive eye for the offbeat in rural America, particularly the characters' fantasies and interpretations of the American Dream. The film does not condescend to its outrageously eccentric protagonists. To each his own—let them dream—the film says, if it helps them survive the day. Melvin is a quintessential American hero: innocent, naive, idealistic, not very bright (though not dumb either), kindhearted, trusting and, above all, generous. The film offers a bittersweet commentary about chasing the American Dream of monetary success and upward mobility, about the constant attempt to rise above one's limitations—but also the inevitable fall back. The characters are not fully aware of their class origins, nor do they see their backgrounds as obstacles; optimistic and naive, they feel they may overcome them one day. It's a far cry from those small-town films wherein individuals from the other side of the tracks are doomed forever—unless they go to war or leave town. In Demme's film, individuals are ever hopeful and never defeated—despite facing one crisis after another. The Melvins of the film will always find employment and always be romantically attached. Contrary to what F. Scott Fitzgerald said, there are second chapters in their lives. Indeed, after a second divorce from Lynda, Melvin marries Bonnie (Pamela Reed), a pragmatic woman, and manages a gas station. Melvin's occupations are innovative for a protagonist in American films: He first works in a factory, then at a dairy, winning the title "Milkman of the Month."

Something Wild (1986), the third of the "Demme trilogy," cashed in on a new screen type in the 1980s: the Yuppie. Once again, at the center of the narrative is an unlikely pair: Charlie Driggs (Jeff Daniels), an uptight Wall Street tax accountant, and Lulu Hankel (Melanie Griffith), a sexy and reckless woman. They meet in a downtown Manhattan luncheonette, when Lulu spots Charlie beating a check. Confronting him outside, she offers him a ride to his office, but instead takes him to a sleazy motel in New Jersey. Newly appointed vice president of a big consultant firm, he protests he has meetings to attend, reports to write, calls to return. Besides, his wife and children are waiting for him in his suburban house. Ignoring his protests, she stops at a liquor store to pick up some Scotch and cleans out the cash register. At the motel, she handcuffs him to the bedpost, rips his clothes, and makes love to him in a manner he has never experienced before.

The two characters could not be more different, that is, initially—before Charlie reveals *his* hidden secrets and dark spots. Under seemingly divergent uniforms, the two turn out to be kindred souls. Charlie starts out as an ultraconservative guy, wearing a starched shirt and a suit, the 1980s version of "The Man in the Gray Flannel Suit." Wearing a kinky little black outfit, Lulu dons a Louise Brooks page-boy wig; Lulu is Brooks's best-known screen role. Her real name, Audrey, also seems to be drawn from movie lore, perhaps Audrey Hepburn, whose role as Holly Golightly in *Breakfast at Tiffany's* Audrey slightly resembles. In this and other aspects, Demme shows how pop culture has become a new, secular religion, permeating every aspect of life.

After a most surprising beginning, the film changes tone, evolving into a "road comedy": the couple drives from lower Manhattan to New Jersey, Pennsylvania, Virginia, and back to suburban New York. Lulu takes Charlie to her mother's small-town home and introduces him as her husband. Then off to a tenth high-school reunion, titled "76 Revisited," a joyful occasion that turns into a nightmare when Audrey's ex-husband, the psychotic Ray Sinclair (Ray Liotta) shows up. From then on, the film goes downhill, turning into a thriller, with the two men desperately vying to get Audrey.

However, Demme's offbeat tone in *Something Wild* is similar to his comedies, though the mix of genres is disquieting. In parts, the movie is a 1980s version of a Depression screwball comedy, *It Happened One Night*, albeit with role reversal. Instead of Clark Gable's Peter Warne, an aggressive, boozy, sexual, and self-centered newspaperman, there is Audrey, as the unemployed and sexual aggressor. And instead of traveling from the country to the city (from Florida to New York), the couple drives from the city to the country. Demme keeps things moving at such high-energy pace that the film's flaws become apparent only when it is over.

The narrative shares similar themes with Martin Scorsese's *After Hours* (1985), a more coherent film, and David Lynch's *Blue Velvet* (1986), a film boasting a stronger directorial vision. Like other "Yuppie Angst" movies (*Desperately Seeking Susan* and *Lost in America*, both 1985; *Into the Night*, 1986), *Something Wild* suggests that appearances are deceptive: nothing is what it appears to be, and no one should be trusted for who they say they are. Charlie and Lulu, initially opposite characters, turn out to be similar. *After Hours* and *Something Wild* complement each other in some respects: the Scorsese film is about one nightmarish experience in New York's Soho; Demme's is its rural counterpart. In both films, the hero is a square, successful professional, an upright and uptight ass. "I'm a rebel," says Charlie, "I just channeled my rebellion into the mainstream." By this time, however, Lulu's transformation has gone into the opposite direction, showing signs of domesticity. "What are you gonna do now that you've seen how the other one lives—the other half of you?" In this sentence, the film's message, bearing resemblance to *Shadow of a Doubt*, becomes too obvious. But unlike *After Hours*, wherein the hero goes back to "normal life" at the end of his ordeal, Charlie undergoes a radical transformation, and his future is in doubt.

One element in *Something Wild* that went unnoticed by critics is its concern with ethnic America. The three protagonists are all white, but the background is heavily populated with blacks: Baptist Church members, musicians, waiters, gas attendants, and hitchhikers. No clear clues are provided about the meaning of their conspicuous presence. It may be an ironic commentary on Reagan's policies, with their "white supremacy" overtones, reminding viewers that, despite greater visibility, ethnic minorities are still oppressed and, for the most part, at the bottom of the hierarchy. Or perhaps the movie is saying that Charlie, a liar (he has no wife or children) and a privileged (upper-middle-class) citizen, is no better than the black characters—despite a facade of respectability, education, and professionalism.

Something Wild also shows that crime, violence, and psychosis are no longer the exclusive territory of urban life; rural America has its own share of ills. Like *Blue Velvet,* one of the best small-town films of the decade, there is a role reversal: a female protagonist is sexually aggressive with a more innocent WASP male. In *Something,* Lulu's sexual practices (handcuffs, fellatio) and her transgressive desires shock the Yuppie hero. But in both, the narrative transforms, i.e., restores, these women into more traditional roles (in *Blue Velvet,* the "bad" girl is actually a good mother). Like *Something Wild, Blue Velvet*'s theme was inspired by a popular song, Bobby Vinton's hit of the 1960s. Finally, as in Demme's film, *Blue Velvet* concerns the delicate balance between the normal and abnormal, a theme that goes back to Hitchcock's *Shadow of a Doubt,* but it is given a different interpretation and presented in a new form.

The Normal and the Abnormal: *Blue Velvet*

In *Blue Velvet*'s Lumberstone, social time is measured by nature: The radio station announces, "At the sound of the falling tree, it's 9:30." It is the kind of town "that knows how much wood a woodchuck chucks." The film features a brilliant beginning: the camera pans slowly across a clean white picket fence, with red roses in front of it. It is a beautiful day with blue skies, and there are pleasant sounds of birds chirping and a faint sprinkler. Clean-uniformed policemen smile as they outstretch their arms and let children cross the street safely. A bright red fire engine is moving slowly down the street; the firemen are also smiling. Yellow tulips sway in a warm afternoon breeze, as the sprinkler goes around shooting water. The whole sequence has a dreamy, surrealistic, quality. The camera suddenly cuts to under the grass and ominous sounds come up as black insects are crawling and scratching in the darkness. This powerful image sets the film's tone, announcing its thematic concern: the dialectic duality of beautiful surfaces and the horrible things that lurk underneath.

Dressed in khaki trousers, canvas shoes, straw hat, and dark glasses, Mr. Beaumont (Jack Harvey) is watering his grass with a hose, but he is suddenly hit with a seizure and falls to the ground. The water shoots crazily onto the driveway and his car. At the same time, Mrs. Beaumont (Priscilla Pointer), is curled up on the couch, smoking a cigarette and enjoying her daytime soap. The precariousness of human life, the sudden eruption of violence, a seizure, in the most peaceful of settings, is jarring. Shortly after, Jeffrey Beaumont (Kyle MacLachlan) is called back home from college. He has to work at his father's business, a hardware store. At the hospital, the father is concerned because Jeffrey has never seen him with his teeth out; once again, the theme of appearances versus reality.

Walking down the dirt road in a vacant field, Jeffrey finds a human ear, covered with ants racing frantically around it. A good boy, he reports the incident to detective J. D. Williams (George Dickerson) who asks Jeffrey not to discuss the incident with anyone. But understanding that Jeffrey is "real curious," the detective says, "I was the same when I was your age, that's what got me into this business." The coroner says he doesn't "recall anything coming in minus an ear," suspecting the person might still be alive. A close-up of the ear, in a mortician's dish, reveals a rare view of the crevices around the dark hole.

A small community, people know each other in Lumberstone. Mrs. Williams (Hope Lange) knows Jeffrey's mother from church. Her daughter, Sandy (Laura Dern), a high-school senior, remembers Jeffrey as "pretty popular" from school. All of Jeffrey's old friends are gone (to college?), and lonely, he strikes a friendship with Sandy. Sandy arouses his curiosity when she tells him about a woman who has been under surveillance. He decides to spy on her. "There are opportunities in life for gaining knowledge and experience," says Jeffrey, and in some cases "it's necessary to take a risk." This provides "justification" for his proposition to sneak in and observe the mysterious woman. Still a child, Sandy thinks his idea sounds like "a good daydream," but doing it is "too weird, too dangerous."

He excites her and she cancels a date with Mike: "There's a game tonight and he'll never miss me." Jeffrey is contrasted with Sandy's beau, a big football player. Mike is straight and rational, with no spontaneity in his life. Taking vitamins, he says: "The body is like a machine. Everything has got to stay in perfect tune for perfect health." Mike drinks water, but no beer. He takes no coffee, and refuses blueberry pie and ice cream because they contain too many calories. He is a young man, unwilling to take any risks.

Dorothy Vallens (Isabella Rossellini), a beautiful woman with round figure and full red lips, sings at the "Slow Club," a sleazy nightclub on the outskirts of town, surrounded by a trash-strewn parking lot. There is also the "Barbary Coast," a corner bar with a back room with naked girls. Both clubs are set apart from Main Street. Dorothy delivers a slow version of "Blue Moon" and Bobby Vinton's "Blue Velvet." Sneaking into her apartment, Jeffrey finds an empty child's room; a small pointed hat with a propeller on top is on the bed post. He observes Dorothy put on a record, "For Your Precious Love" (which makes her cry), then undress and shower, wearing a blue-velvet robe. Caught, she demands to know, "How many times have you sneaked into girls' apartments and watched them undress?" There is an expression of disbelief when he says, "never before." "Get undressed," she commands, "I want to see *you*." She pulls his underpants down to his knees, holding a knife to his genitals. It's a rare occurrence in American films for a woman to command (or even wish) a man to undress. This scene is powerful because it conveys a sense of what women may have experienced when told by men to undress. Now, it's a role reversal: An intense female gaze at Jeffrey's genitals.

Jeffrey's sexual naïveté is juxtaposed with the villain's, Frank Booth (Dennis Hopper), a brute endowed with raw sexuality ("I'll fuck anything that moves"). Frank has kidnapped Dorothy's husband and son and now abuses her sexually. Stocky with a burr haircut, Frank wears an old black jacket, blue jeans, and boots. "Mommy, Baby wants to fuck," he says while looking at Dorothy's crotch and wearing a mask for the canister filled with helium. He sucks and bites the velvet coming out of her mouth, while pinching her breasts. Slugging her in the face, he reaches a climax in his pants. Later, Jeffrey suffers the ultimate degradation when Frank smears lipstick on his face and kisses him on the lips.

"You can hit me too, if you want to," Dorothy tells Jeffrey. They start making love, then, carried away, he throws her head back against the wall, and slaps her in the face. Dorothy is not crazy ("I know the difference between right and wrong"), just a masochistic victim; she smiles through the pain. In most small-town (and other American) films, the attitude toward sex is hygienic, often childish. In this film, however, sex is not only erotic, but shown as an act of risk and adventurism. Their lovemaking is accompanied by images of flames and sounds of roaring beasts (the association of sexual desire with fire is a recurrent motif). Lynch's innovative touch is in film's visuals: The images are at once hallucinatory (with a dreamy quality) and realistic. For example, Lynch shows the sight of blood in close-up, and records the sound of huge cells moving. There are extreme close-ups of termites: Aunt Barbara, an absentminded woman with thick glasses, pinches a termite and looks at it, then leaves it for Jeffrey to observe. The narrative follows the logic of a bad dream, a nightmare, dealing with the unconscious and unaccountable fantasies, what may be considered in mainstream culture sheer perversity.

As many small-town films, *Blue Velvet* is about coming of age, the transition from adolescence to adulthood, though the rites of passage are not ordinary (Norman and Allison's innocent kiss on a hill or Rodney and Betty's swim in the nude in *Peyton Place*). Here, the daring sexual initiation is carried out by a mature woman and there are no inhibitions. The films offers the shock of recognition and catharsis too, containing the most eroticized energy to be displayed on the American screen.

And as other small-town narratives, social order must be restored. Jeffrey's mother says at one point, "You just can't stay out half the night and carry on, there's got to be some order." The theme of unspeakable horror lurking beneath seemingly ordinary life is expressed by Sandy, "It's a strange world," and Jeffrey, "Why is there so much trouble in the world?" Sandy recounts a dream in which "the world was dark because there weren't any robins," but "all of a sudden, thousands of robins flew down and brought the blinding light of love." Indeed, like *Shadow of a Doubt,* the narrative reaffirms that "love would be the only thing that would make any difference," but "until the robins come there is trouble." Through direct and actual experience, Jeffrey learns the rewards of living a clean and safe life. Similar to the protagonist of *Something Wild,* the narrative uses the motif of the double: Jeffrey has a clean, neat, wholesome look but also curiosity and an urge for adventurism. Earlier, at the college dance, hiding behind a furnace, Jeffrey is intrigued by the sight of a student trying to rape his girl friend. It takes some time until he takes action and interferes—the allure of voyeurism is one of the film's important issues. The film's worldview is childish, perhaps intentionally so, seen from an adolescent's point of view. Jeffrey explores the dark side of his own personality. "I'm seeing something that was always hidden," says Jeffrey. "I'm involved in a mystery, I'm learning." The film shows both the allure of the unknown and the horror of it once encountered.

Sandy's adolescent status is clearer: Younger than Jeffrey, she still sees the world in black and white. "I don't know if you're a detective or a pervert," she tells Jeffrey; he is actually both. Note than when a robin arrives on the kitchen window, it has an insect in its beak. Sandy represents the naïve belief in a good world and decent life. The ideological distinction between Sandy and Dorothy is also visual: the blond versus the dark-haired look.[7] Like most small-town films of the decade, there is no moral center. The town is run by drug dealers, and the police are also implicated. Detective Gordon is involved in crime, and it's not clear how much detective Williams knows. "It's over now," he tells Jeffrey, but unlike films of previous decades, the viewers are not certain that the crime and corruption are resolved. At the film's coda, the narrative shifts back from the subconscious to the conscious, and from below to above ground, stressing the need for ordinary life, that is, normal love and sex. The restoration of order and the relegation of Dorothy to normal motherhood (in the last scene, she is seen with her son) are at best precarious, if not fragile.

Eccentricity for Eccentricity's Sake

Using eccentric personalities, situated in seemingly ordinary and plain locales, is also the premise of *Crimes of the Heart*, written by Beth Henley, and David Byrne's *True Stories* (both in 1986), cowritten by Byrne, Henley, and Stephen Tobolowsky. The sensibility of *Crimes of the Heart* remains theatrical, despite attempts to "open up" the play. One never finds out how people live in Hazlehurst, Mississippi, but it offers vivid personalities: three Chekhovian sisters. Lenny MacGarth (Diane Keaton), the oldest, is a modern version of the small-town spinster. Her problem (supposedly a secret), a shrunken ovary, which in past movies would have been a subject of gossip behind her back, is now discussed in the open, as if they were talking about her hairdo. Lenny loved Billy Boy, the horse, ever since she was a kid; now it has been struck by lightning. She throws a tantrum over a candy box her sister Meg has opened and eaten. Lenny, the family's black sheep, has grown bitter, but not entirely devoid of humor and self-awareness.

Meg MacGarth (Jessica Lange) is the small-town girl whose acting ambitions have carried her to Los Angeles, but instead of working in the film industry, she is working for a dog food manufacturer. *Her* open secret is a nervous breakdown. Life in the Big City has made her harsh, but she is now in control of her feelings. Meg's homecoming provides the film's few contrasts between Small Town and Big City. Babe MacGarth (Sissy Spacek), the youngest and least bright of the three, likes to paint black dots on her toenails. Motivated by instincts, not reason, she has shot her husband in the stomach, because she did not like "his stinking looks." But after shooting him, she offers him, in the tradition of Southern hospitality, a glass of iced lemonade. Babe is a child-bride (a bit like Tennessee Williams's heroine in *Baby Doll*). Unlike other Southern heroines, neither Babe nor her sisters are sexually repressed or racially biased. Meg has had an affair with a married man (without being punished for it), and Babe with a fifteen-year-old black kid.

In line with many small-town protagonists, the three sisters have no parents; their mother committed suicide, taking the cat with her. The only family members are Old Granddaddy, now in the hospital suffering a stroke, and their cousin, Chick Boyle (Tess Harper), a gossipy and shrewish type, disliked by the three women. The narrative spends much time with this family reunion: the sisters reminisce about their childhood, leaf through scrapbooks, share sexual secrets about their lovers. They are actually three faces of the same person, three sides of femininity: shyness and asexuality (Lenny), ripeness and overt sexuality (Meg), and childishness and naïve sexuality (Babe). Each of the sisters has one big confessional scene, following the theatrical conventions of such intimate plays. Under different circumstances, the naughtiness and crazed behavior of the sisters would be offensive, but here, as the title suggests, they are presented as all heart and feeling. The sisters' eccentricities are genuine. For example, Babe is preoccupied with the media coverage of the case. Her frame of reference is her mother's suicide, which received national attention in the *National Enquirer*. Married to a prominent politician, she is now concerned that her story will be covered only locally.

Similar narrative logic, carried to more schematic extreme, distinguishes *True Stories,* a glorification of the commonplace and kitsch. The characters derive from human interest stories in tabloid newspapers. They are put together in a format that features a narrator, observing the citizenry of Virgil, a small Texas town. *True Stories* pays homage to the boundless spirit and imaginative life-styles that such small towns—and America—inspire. The formal occasion for the celebration is Virgil's celebration of the state sesquicentennial.

Symmetric, the film opens and closes with the same image: a single figure (Byrne, the narrator), in Stetson and string tie, drives a fire-engine red convertible against a flat and barren horizon. The austere landscape makes the characters and their houses stand out even more. The narrator performs the function of the druggist in *Our Town,* wandering through town, observing its habits. But unlike the narrator of *Our Town,* who encounters the commonplace, Byrne does not cease to be surprised by what he sees. Taking the liberty of free commentary, he makes comic asides, distancing himself from the narrative. Following a montage of the encapsulated history of Texas, the viewers get to know the people, not flesh-and-blood, but cardboard icons of popular culture. Consider some of the types: The Cute Woman (loosely based on a TV show hostess who likes to paint pictures of puppies), the Computer Guy, the Lying Woman, (who claims to have written half of Elvis Presley's songs), the Lazy Woman (a television addict, who never gets out of bed), the Visionary Businessman, the Innocent (in constant search for love).

"I was attracted to the characters," Byrne said, "because they had their own eccentricities, but they weren't ashamed of them."[8] None of the characters in *True Stories* is alienated, lost, or guilty—a major difference from eccentric characters in movies of previous decades. In the past, individuals usually felt ashamed of their eccentricities and tried to get rid of them or keep them as secret—if they were perceived as obstacles to their integration into mainstream society. In films of the 1980s, America has a Main Street, but it's looser and less confining, permitting the existence of alternative life-styles that may not be condoned by dominant culture. Byrne's film is an "appreciation of people and things," a tribute to "openness and willingness to see things differently, to try things, to experiment."[9] *True Stories* is a democratic celebration of the unique qualities that make the most ordinary and bland appear special and extraordinary. Indeed, the centerpiece is the climactic "Celebration of Specialness," consisting of more than 130 unusual talent acts: disco-dancing goldfish, glass harmonica players, yodelers, precision dance teams, the Tyler Junior College Apache Belles, etc. The fashion show at a shopping mall is staged with a life-sized wedding cake, living grass suits, trompe l'oeil brick wall suits, and local clubs with matching uniforms.

The problem of this film is that it is not about Virgil, or small towns, or even Texas, but about pop culture, as reflected by television and consumerism. Byrne wanted to show that "there are a lot of places like Virgil—the way people live, the places they work and the kind of community they experience when new industry is taking over." But, as one critic noted, the film reflects Byrne's "distinctly postmodern sensibility," showing "high-tech cum postcard America, well-stocked supermarket shelves, tract houses under the sky, rat-a-tat-tat TV channel zapping."[10] Cinematographer Ed Luckmann was influenced by Ken Graves and Michael Payne's *American Snapshots*. With its sensibility of a snapshot, the film's aesthetics mixes the styles of "the corner drugstore, the Bauhaus concept of functional imagery, and Japanese calligraphy."[11] Visually, it is a ninety-minute music-video, bringing back the glories of montage, fast cutting and editing.

Women in the Country

As was shown, the male-dominated Hollywood did not reflect the progress women were making in the economic and occupational marketplace. There was actually an ideological backlash, on- and off-screen (See chapter 5). The change in the screen roles allotted to women occurred in the late 1970s, a whole decade after the emergence of the women's movement. In the following decade, for the first time in history, female screen roles surpassed men's in their diversity, variability, and challenge. The resurrection of the "women's film" in the 1980s included narratives set in the country or small towns. Martin Scorsese's *Alice Doesn't Live Here Anymore* (1974) is considered to be a turning point, because it was the first major film in a long time to feature a strong role for a woman. Ellen Burstyn, who won the Best Actress Oscar for it, was instrumental in bringing the project to the screen.

Thematically, however, *Alice* was compromising and far from the feminist film it had intended to be. Its eponymous heroine is a recent young widow, struggling to launch a new life for her and her adolescent son. Victimized by her husband, a truck driver who had taken her for granted as mother and wife, she is shocked—but also relieved—when he gets killed in a highway accident. *Alice* offered a new screen heroine: feisty, sarcastic, even self-mocking. In her portrayal, Burstyn combined elements of Katharine Hepburn's force of will, Shirley MacLaine's gaminelike vulnerability, and Barbra Streisand's zaniness.[12] Alice meets two men: Ben (Harvey Keitel), a married man, who assaults her physically, and David (Kris Kristofferson), a peaceful farmer, who functions like a knight in a fairy tale; he is everything a woman could hope for, downright unreal—even using the word "please" when he talks to her. But at the end, she becomes dependent again, settling into what seems to be a second complacent relationship, albeit with a more sensitive man. Dreaming about Robert Redford, Alice actually gets a prince. A road comedy, *Alice* was set in the countryside, a less-familiar territory in American films: Alice drives a station wagon from New Mexico to Arizona, then back to her hometown in Monterey, California. The landscape includes motels, diners, drive-in restaurants, gas stations, rest areas, all icons of country life, used effectively by Jonathan Demme in his 1980s comedies *(Melvin and Howard, Something Wild)*. The popular success of *Alice* showed that there was interest in women's stories and that they were commercially viable.

Gaining Consciousness: *Norma Rae*

The film that was specifically inspired by *The Grapes of Wrath* was Martin Ritt's *Norma Rae*, a fictionalized account of Crystal Lee Sutton, a textile worker turned labor activist, living in a Baptist town in the Deep South. Set in the summer of 1978, the narrative begins with the arrival of an outsider in what appears to be a dormant town. His arrival sets in motion events that will forever change the town and its workers. The film is original in its use of the outsider: Reuben Warshowsky (Ron Liebman) is a Jewish labor organizer from New York. Dressed in tennis shoes, blue jeans, and a T-shirt, he projects the nervous, intellectual energy associated with Jewish culture and the Big City. The narrative pays attention to the social context within which he struggles to unionize the workers. The textile mill is the major source of employment, thus the inhabitants *depend* on it for their livelihood. Reuben has to fight against rigid capitalistic management, racism (the white workers fear the blacks will take over), closed-minded religious leaders, and, most important of all, victimized workers, either unaware of their exploitation or passively accepting it. The plant looks like a battlefield, full of jolting, nerve-shattering machines, whose deafening noise produces ceaseless trembling vibrations. The enormous space is filled with rows of old wooden looms. There are no windows and no sunlight, only blank brick walls. The mill suggests a prison, a closed, timeless world, in which the workers do not—and cannot—think. They cannot even hear what people are saying.

In the first sequence, Norma Rae (Sally Field) realizes that her mother, Leona Witchard (Barbara Baxley), has not heard what she had said twice.

She rushes her to the doctor to examine her hearing. At first, the cool Dr. Watson dismisses the case's seriousness, "It happens all the time." His advice is to find another job. "What other job?" screams Norma. "In this town, this is the *only* job." "You're nothing to any of 'em," she tells her mother—and herself. Indeed, the workers are vastly exploited: They are overworked and underpaid. Lunch breaks are too short. A sign in the dining room instructs: "Give your chair to a spinner, they only have fifteen minutes." As other workers, Leona shows traces of beauty gone; she works with her face buried in a spiderweb of threads. Norma's father, Vernon Witchard (Pat Hingle), doing backbreaking stoop labor, later dies on the job. In the film's most emotional scene, Norma grabs a piece of cardboard, scrawls in large letters UNION, gets on a table, and holds the sign. At first, the workers are bewildered, then slowly, one by one, they shut down their machines. The deafening noise gradually turns into a meaningful silence.

Innovative, the film provides a new type of screen heroine, occupying an important place in the gallery of uniquely American heroines, Alice Adams, Frankie Adams, Alice Hyatt. A thirty-one-year-old widow, Norma Rae is the mother of two children, one illegitimate, the other born shortly before her husband died. Norma strikes a unique friendship with Reuben. The two protagonists could not have been more different, though they are not social types. A leftist intellectual, Reuben is engaged to a Harvard University labor lawyer. His favorite leisure activities include poetry (Dylan Thomas), Chinese food, and the Metropolitan Opera. By contrast, Norma has never traveled and has not read much. In fact, she has never met a Jew, thus initially possessing similar stereotypes about Jews as the other town's inhabitants. "I heard you all have horns," she says. "What makes you different?" Reuben answers in one word, "History." However, they share in common true grit and strength to recognize a good cause and fight for it—which is more important for their friendship than similar backgrounds. *Norma Rae*, like *Melvin and Howard*, epitomizes the democratic ethos, the potentially open quality of American life.

By standards of classic American films, Norma Rae is a woman of loose morality. In an early scene, she is in a motel with a married man. Once a week, she is taken out and gets, as he describes it, "a big steak, pralines, and sex." When Norma tells him "there's a lot of gossip," and that she has decided to terminate their affair, he slaps her in the face, reminding her, "You're here to make *me* feel good." But in sharp deviation from conventions, Norma is neither condemned for her promiscuous sexuality, nor for giving birth out of wedlock. "Did you get married?" asks Reuben. "He didn't bother," Norma replies. As for her husband, he died in a barroom brawl, six months after her second child was born.

Norma Rae also stands out in choosing *not* to sentimentalize the town, despite its many social ills. There is racism against blacks, xenophobia, anti-Semitism, sexism, religious fanaticism. For example, upon arrival, Reuben is accused by Norma's father of being a "crook, agitator, and Communist." When Norma is promoted to a supervising job, her family and friends show overt resentment, suspecting she might side now with the management. Her father says he does not "like to be pushed" by his own daughter, and the other workers refuse to talk to her. Disgusted, she quits her job and goes back to work on the floor. Nor does the film idealize New York's union leaders, who reproach Reuben for using a woman with such a "low reputation." They may be committed to unionism and other causes, but when it comes to interpersonal relationships, they too possess rigid stereotypes. Fearing a woman like Norma might give the union a bad name, they demand that he cease to use her; he defiantly refuses.

Courtship and marriage are far from glamorized. In Norma's life, being married is just one status and not the most important one. The proposal of Sonny Webster (Beau Bridges), who works in a gas station, is one of the most original and unsentimental in American films. "I don't owe a nickel in this town," he says. "I can fix anything electrical. I'm all right after my first cup of coffee." Having said what he considers basic, he proceeds: "I turn my paycheck the minute I get it. And I come straight home from work and I stay there." Norma, too, is matter-of-fact. She asks Sonny to kiss her, because "if that's all right, then everything else will be."

Nature is represented by the lake, where Norma and Sonny spend a relaxed day in the country. It is also the place where Norma and Reuben go swimming. There are two refreshing points about this sequence. First, they don't make love and the scene is devoid of any romanticism or eroticism. Second, Reuben and Norma are not observed by others and there is no gossip.[13] Norma spends more time with Reuben than with her husband, a good, trusting man. At first, Sonny complains that she has neglected her domestic chores: cooking, washing, ironing. He is also envious that, when taken to jail and has only one phone call to make, she calls Reuben, not him. Expressing his resentment to Reuben, the latter sums up Norma's personality in three brief sentences: "She stood on the table. She's a free woman. You can either accept her or not." In a fit of jealousy, Sonny confronts his wife, suspecting she might be unfaithful to him. Here too, Norma Rae deviates from other screen heroines: she has not slept with Reuben, but admits "he's in my mind." As a mother, Norma is not the self-sacrificing type. "I'm a jailbird," she tells her children. "I'm not perfect. I make mistakes." "You're gonna hear many things about me, but you're going to hear them from *me* first." She then tells her children the truth about their respective fathers.

The closure of *Norma Rae* is remarkably consistent, standing in opposition to more conventional Hollywood endings. Norma and Reuben part with a respectful handshake rather than the clichéd embrace or kiss. And even though there are still differences between them, they part as *equals, both* having benefited from the friendship. Reuben has changed Norma's life, which is now richer; she is much more politically aware. But Reuben thanks Norma for her stamina, companionship, and commitment to the cause. The closest Reuben comes to expressing personal interest is in saying, "I enjoyed looking at your shining hair." Norma has gained self-respect and self-discovery of resources she has always had in her, but had to be revealed. Norma is now a new woman, with a new consciousness.

Robert Ray claims that "ideologically, *The Grapes of Wrath* and *Norma Rae* are virtually the same movie, regardless of their superficial differences: male hero versus female hero, right-wing (John Ford) versus left-wing director (blacklisted Martin Ritt), farm work versus city work. According to his interpretation, "both films propose that political problems can only be solved by messianic, individualistic leaders." However, individualism is a long-enduring attribute (myth) of most American films, particularly the social problem films. Ray oversimplifies the comparison between the movies, stating that both "portray workers as powerless, lazy, and fearful." In Ray's view, *Norma Rae* "*seems* different because it employs the standard Hollywood strategy of assimilating (and co-opting) a fashionably dissident *topos* potentially threatening to the prevailing ideology—in this case, feminism, defused by having Norma Rae appear dependent on the male labor organizer."[14] But by American films' standards, Norma *is* a feminist heroine, demonstrating that an uneducated but resilient woman could acquire political consciousness (the first necessary step in any protest movement) and could also introduce normative and structural changes. Feminist critics have argued that Norma gains consciousness with the assistance of a man, implying that without a man she would never have changed. But under the circumstances in which she lives, is it possible for Norma Rae to change without the assistance of a male outsider? Could change have originated in town by any of the local residents, male or female? For a Hollywood film of 1979, *Norma Rae* made a new statement about gender roles and politics.

Farming: A New Screen Occupation for Women

Set in 1910, Richard Pearce's *Heartland* (1979) tells the story of Elinore Randall (Conchata Ferrell), a young widow who moves out West to take a job as a housekeeper on a ranch. Unlike other films of this cycle, casting a newcomer, who did not look like an actress, contributed to the film's authenticity. A big-boned, wide-hipped woman, Ferrell's looks are ordinary. Based on diaries of a real pioneer, the film examines the challenges and hardships of frontier life, celebrating the American spirit of fierce independence. The narrative propagates long-enduring myths: Elinore would like to own her own ranch, because, as she puts it, "all my life I've been working for somebody else." Refreshingly though, there are not many speeches, or much dialogue. The movie is at its best when it is speechless; for long stretches of time, the strong visuals convey the narrative without the need of words.

Heartland begins with the arrival of Elinore in a train crammed with people. Her harsh employer, Clyde Stewart (Rip Torn), is a man of few words. At first, their interaction is restricted to work: She commits herself to give "a full day's work for a full day's pay." But she ends up working more than she did back in Denver, where "I've always had my Sundays free." The film records her daily routines: cleaning, cooking, sewing, milking, and sometimes reading *(Dryland Homesteading)* or playing dominoes. The other women are just as tough as Elinore. Grandma (Lilia Skala) arrives on a horse, wearing a cowboy hat. "You don't play with these winters," Grandma warns Elinore, recalling how her baby froze to death one winter. In addition to brutal storms (the painful sight of a half-dead horse, left out in the blizzard), there is also lack of food, and the men are leaving. "It's not your fault," says the indomitable Elinore. "We'll start all over again." Women in *Heartland* do their equal share, but they don't get the same recognition men do.

Emotions are vastly understated, but they are there. For example, when Clyde proposes to Elinore, it's a brief and unsentimental proposal. At the wedding, (shot with many real-life residents), she wears her apron and work boots. Later that night, they are in bed, but they are shown sleeping, holding hands. Pregnant, she waits as he goes to fetch a midwife from another farm, but a storm prevents him from returning in time and she gives birth alone. Like Grandma, Elinore loses her baby. "At least we have the chicken," she tells Clyde half seriously, half humorously. An ultrarealistic film, it celebrates the passionate attachment to the wild outdoors. Nature is not used as a background or external decoration, but as a major character. And unlike other movies, nature is not contrasted with culture. In *Heartland,* nature is culture; there is no life outside or beyond nature. The film abounds with matter-of-fact scenes, showing in graphic detail pigs slaughtered, cattle skinned, cows giving birth. And the very last image, a shot of a sunny day, reaffirms Clyde and Elinore's commitment to the land. In style and emotional power, the stark realism of *Heartland* bears the same kind of lyrical effects as *The Southerner.*

A Farm Trilogy: *Places in the Heart, Country,* and *The River*

Three movies in 1984 described farming from the point of view of women: *Places in the Heart,* starring Sally Field, *Country,* featuring Jessica Lange, and *The River,* with Sissy Spacek. The appearance of three movies about farm life in one year, as if suddenly the farmers' plight was the most important issue on the national agenda, was probably a coincidence. What was not a coincidence, though, was the fact that all three featured strong heroines. In the 1980s, every major actress in Hollywood sought "substantial," preferably moralistic, screenplays. After two decades of underrepresentation and stereotypical casting, the American cinema finally offered more and better roles for women than for men. Though different in style, the three movies share similar narrative structure. Their thematic conventions could be summarized in the following schematic way:

1. A crisis disrupts the stability of family life, forcing the woman to take charge.
2. The woman proves to be stronger and more committed to the cause than the man.
3. The husband is not around when most needed.
4. The woman is first and foremost a mother, then a wife.
5. The children are put to a test; there is an intergenerational conflict.
6. The struggle is against nature (storms, floods, barren land)
7. The struggle is also against human elements (governmental bureaucracy).
8. The banks threaten to foreclose the farm; bankers as representatives of big business are negatively portrayed.
9. The politicians either don't care and/or are ineffectual.
10. The values of country life are superior to the Big City.
11. The narrative contains a clear closure, a resolution in which the immediate problem is resolved.
12. The woman gains (more) self and political consciousness.
13. The husband comes back and the unity of the nuclear family is restored.

Country was the least sentimental of the three films, even though it, too, dealt more with the myth of farming than its realities. It was inspired by newspaper articles about farmers' economic hardships in the Midwest, between 1981 and 1983. Though Reagan was in power, the film attacks the farm policies set by the Carter administration, particularly the embargo on sales to the Soviet Union. A tornado during corn harvest destroys the crops, and with the FMHA (Federal Farmers Home Administration) calling in on short notice their loans, the farmers face bankruptcy and the loss of their land.

Tom McMullen (Matt Clark), the county representative of FMHA, charges that "something is wrong with the way you're doing things." The Ivys have four hundred thousand dollars worth of assets, but they are not making a decent living. "Low prices and 14 percent interest don't help," says Jewell (Jessica Lange). Carrying too much loan debt, McMullen sees two ways out: "a fairy godmother to help you catch these loans up," or, "you're going to have to partially liquidate." Gil (Sam Shepard) claims that McMullen "can't look at it short-term," that farming is "a way of life, we may have several bad years, but it always comes back." Thus, one of the conflicts is the difference between farming as a career (a way of making a living) and farming as a way of life. For McMullen "it's business, and if you don't look at it that way, you're behind the times." But the unfeeling McMullen is dismissed: He is "a college boy who knows nothing but numbers." The narrative thus perpetuates the myth of the superiority of pragmatic experience over formal education (from books).

There is also a domestic conflict. A proud and stubborn man, Gil doesn't want "everybody knowing our business," wishing to "keep our troubles to ourselves." "That kinda pride'll kill you quicker'n a gun," says Otis (Wilford Brimley), Jewell's father. Worse yet, Gil won't let Jewell get a job. "I'm not gonna have my wife waiting on tables for tips." The tension between romantic individualism and organized collectivism is expressed in the intergenerational conflict. Otis is in favor of the Depression's collectivism: "You get your neighbors, share your equipment, trade your labor." "Beg, borrow, or steal," he says, "but, by God, you hang on to this land." An old-fashioned farmer, Otis stands for continuity: "The land was yours, just like it was mine after it was my daddy's. Just like it'll be your children's, when their time comes." "Our blood goes deep as the roots of that tree in this ground, and ain't nobody can yank us with a piece of paper." Watching his father plow behind his mules, Otis determined to never leave the place; he never did, except for fighting overseas during World War II.

The bank's president, Walter Logan, is a cold-blooded bureaucrat, who also subscribes to farming as big and modern corporate business. "We're part of a chain now," he says. "Numbers have to support any loans we make." Gil is for a personal approach, missing the times "when the bank used to loan money on the man, not the numbers." This illustrates the organizational dilemma of impersonal bureaucracy versus personal relationships between officials and customers. Jewell tells the banker she "would rather be a thief than do what you do for a living." The farmers' problems are seen as the fault of governmental policies. Gil was encouraged to expand, adopting wholeheartedly Carter's slogan, "We're gonna feed the world!" but, soon after, the government put embargoes on foreign sales. McMullen refuses to take responsibility, claiming: "The FMHA doesn't set government policy." And he concludes: "You're a has-been, all you little farmers." The scene is depressing: In Allison, a town with population of 2,064 people, signs of Out of Business are common, along with mass sales of farm implements: tractors, combines, plows, cultivators.

At the end, Jewell is in favor of taking action, "We gotta do something." "I don't know how to work harder," Gil says. "I don't know how to beat those goddamn pencil pushers neither." Under pressure, he collapses emotionally: he starts drinking heavily, gets nasty and abusive with his children, and finally walks out on them. Collective action, organized by Jewell, is the only viable solution: In the film's climax, the farmers rebel against the government-sponsored auction. But the film can't conceal the cracks in the mythology of farming and "the land." "We're maybe the first generation in the country," says a farm wife, "who don't necessarily believe life's gonna be better for our children than it was for us."

An earth mother figure (a modern Ma Joad), Jewell holds the family together. Throughout the film, an emphasis is placed on the centrality of the nuclear family in providing love, support, and unity. The film begins, appropriately enough, in the kitchen, which is the setting of many subsequent scenes. Jewell holds Missy, her ten-month-old daughter, on her hip and at the same time cooks hamburgers. Relationships between Jewell and Gil, and among the children, are natural and spontaneous: There is bickering, competition for attention, and sensitivity to marital strife between parents. The film closely observes the routine lives of farmers. The most effective scenes are those the least self-conscious, without the platitudes—for example, the sight of Jewell rounding up sheep that are taken away to settle a debt. Filmed in Iowa, with many real-life farmers, *Country*'s style is decidedly realistic. While the myths are grounded in specific reality, the film's messages overwhelm in their heavy-handedness. At the end, it is unclear who the real "villains" are. Is the film against Carter and/or Reagan's farm policies? Moreover, Gil's character remains an enigma. Accused of being a bad farmer, the film never asks to what extent the charge is valid. With all the attention to details, *Country* continued to perpetuate prevalent myths in American culture: The symbolic importance of "the land" and farmers.

These myths have been so powerful and enduring that, even if they contradict logical reasoning, they were still maintained. In *The River*, a rich farmer, Joe Wade, pressures a state senator to build a dam to irrigate his massive land. He hires farmers to break up the levee Tom Garvee (a modern version of Tom Joad of *The Grapes of Wrath?*) has built to protect his land. But in the end, they switch allegiance and help Tom. There is no doubt that Wade is right, but he is portrayed as a greedy villain. Stylistically, the emotionally rousing sequence, in which Tom and his friends protect his land (i.e., stubborn dignity) from flood, reminds one of Vidor's ditch sequence in *Our Daily Bread*. As in *Country*, *The River* shows farming to be a matter of life-style and a symbol of dignity, not a rational and profitable enterprise. Once again, in the contest between reality and mythology, the latter wins triumphantly.

Places in the Heart was the most commercially popular of the three movies, grossing in domestic rentals over sixteen million dollars; *Country* and *The River*, each about four million. The first to be released, *Places* was a prestige production: both director Robert Benton and star Sally Field are previous Oscar winners. But its greater success could be attributed to the fact that it was safely set in the past, during the Depression. Its stylistics also indicated that Benton meant it as an evocation of myth, a personal film memory, rather than a social problem film (as *Country*, in the manner of a "living newspaper" and hard-edged journalism). Sentimental, *Places* was an ode to humanity and celebration of togetherness; the community headed by the widow consists of society's weakest elements: children, a black man, and a blind. As such, it was less overtly political than the other two farm movies. Unlike *Places*, *Country* showed that hard work is not enough to save the land from foreclosure. Made with utmost restraint, the film also denies Jessica Lange the customary close-ups, a star's reverential treatment. Still, the creators were nervous about the film's criticism of the Reagan policies in an election year: *Country* opened in early October, one month prior to the elections. The producers allegedly refused benefit showings for social causes to avoid further politicization of the film, insisting the villain was not "the Reagan Administration, but monolithic bureaucracy and government apathy."[15]

Time Warp Machines: Back to the Past and Back to the Future

The most popular film of 1985, *Back to the Future*, is undoubtedly the most commercial small-town film ever made. As is the case with other blockbusters, technical (special effects) and artistic (production values) distinction explains only in part its immense success. Thematically, *Back to the Future* touched a special chord in the American collective (un)consciousness: Its unusual appeal may have derived from its value-assumptions. For example, the failure of many kids to believe that their parents were once young like them. Or children's wishful thinking that they are brighter and more knowing than their parents were at their age. At the same time, children would also like to believe their parents were smart and strong, at least not dumb. And if in actuality children cannot choose their parents, they can *fantasize about* their parents being *different. Back to the Future* cashes in on a universal (Freudian) wish fulfillment: children's power to choose their parents and transform them into ideal role models.

Back to the Future was not the only film to deal with this fantasy: Concerned with similar issues *Peggy Sue Got Married* (1986) was dubbed in Hollywood "Back to the Future for Adults." Both films examine small-town life from two time perspectives: past and present. Both are comedies in the vein of Capra *(It's a Wonderful Life),* borrowing from the master central motifs. The two movies also share similar setting, California: *Back* is set in 1955, and *Peggy Sue* in 1960. The age of their protagonists is also the same: in *Back,* Marty is seventeen; in *Peggy Sue,* the heroine goes back from forty-three to eighteen.

Marty McFly (Michael J. Fox), *Back's* hero-student is a media-minded kid, owning all the recent electronic tools and toys, including a cordless telephone. The walls of his room are covered with posters of rock stars and cars. Marty arrives at school on a skateboard, wearing mirrored Porsche sunglasses and listening to a Walkman. Late, Marty is confronted by the principal, Mr. Strickland (Donald Pleasance), a stern, humorless disciplinarian. "You've got a real attitude problem," says Mr. Strickland. "You're a slacker. You've got aptitude, but you don't apply yourself." The one thing Marty hates hearing is that he is like his father, but the principal says: "Your father was a slacker too, and look where it got him: Nowhere!" Worse yet, his girl Suzy tells him that, according to her shrink, "All of our emotional anxieties are a direct result of the influence our parents had in our childhood." "In that case," says Marty, "you can kiss me off right now."

Marty's balding father, George (Crispin Glover), age forty-seven, wears an old suit, probably bought at Sears. A passive, defeated man, he can't make any decisions. "If I wait around for him to make a decision," Marty observes, "I'll be collecting social security." "My shrink says a lot of parents are sexually repressed," Suzy says. "That's an understatement," Marty replies. "If you listen to her [his mother], I must be living proof of immaculate conception." George is the butt of everyone's jokes, and, lacking self-esteem, he laughs at himself. Biff Tannen (Thomas F. Wilson), a lout who wears gold chains and pinky rings, screams at George for lending him a car without warning it had a blind spot. He hits George on the chin, grabs his money, and walks out on him.

Marty's mother Lorraine (Lea Thompson) is her husband's age, sloppy, overweight, and a bit alcoholic. They have two other children: Dave, twenty-two, the eldest, who wears a McDonald's uniform, and Linda, nineteen, who wears too much makeup. A 1950s family, the McFlys dine on meat loaf, Kraft macaroni and cheese, Bird's Eye mixed vegetables, and French's instant mashed potatoes. Lorraine doesn't like Suzy on "morality" grounds. "Any girl who calls up a boy," she says, "well, girls just shouldn't do that." And she advises Linda: "It's terrible, girls chasing boys. Boys won't respect you. They'll think you're cheap." "It'll just happen," she consoles her daughter, "like the way I met your father." But, outspoken, Linda thinks it was stupid that Grandpa hit her father with his car, and, besides, she does not understand "what Dad was doing in the middle of the street." "Bird watching," says the mother. "Our story was love at first sight." This scene contrasts sharply with what Marty learns later: that his father was a Peeping Tom, and his mother, a sexual aggressor.

The McFlys are victims of suburban stagnation and easy, but uninspired, life. What was the suburban dream of the 1950s has turned into a nightmare in the 1980s. Marty's house is situated in a development called "Lyon Estates," a row of monotonous houses. The suburban strip includes McDonald's, Dunkin' Donuts, Kentucky Fried Chicken, and other chains. There is one exception, the house of the lunatic Dr. Emmett Brown (Christopher Lloyd), an old Victorian house in the midst of the homogenous buildings. Doc is the last vestige of individualism when it comes to living quarters and personality. Wearing a white sanitation suit, he is proud of his dog, a huge St. Bernard, named Einstein. Doc's car, a sleek, stainless steel Delorean, has been remodeled, looking like a toy from *Star Wars*. At precisely eighty-eight miles per hour, an atomic reaction is triggered, precipitating a miniature nuclear explosion. The Lybians sold Doc the plutonium for his car-machine in exchange for his commitment to construct a nuclear plant. Caught by terrorists at the shopping mall, Marty jumps into Doc's car, and through magic is transplanted into another world.

Marty lands in an unknown country: the Peabody farm. Its owners believe his car is a flying saucer from outer space, a reference to a popular phobia in the 1950s. Marty finds himself on a two-lane highway, on which a lit billboard proudly states: "Step into the Future with the All-New 1955 Studebaker." It is Saturday morning, November 5, 1955. Tuning in to the radio, Marty listens to a commercial advertising "the best value in the forty-eight states," and to Perry Como singing "Papa Loves Mambo." President Eisenhower has just announced he would seek reelection. "Holy shit, 1955," claims Marty, "I haven't even been born yet!" Looking around, Marty sees the Lyon Monument, but the vast ground is clear and there are lots without homes. A billboard depicts an artist's rendition of the American Dream: an idyllic brick home, nestled between magnificent oak trees, with a family of four standing beside their Cadillac. "Live in the Home of Tomorrow, Today!" it says in big letters, promising this "dream project" to be completed by the winter. "I can hardly wait," utters Marty, knowing exactly how it would look. In 1955, the Elmdale Central Business District is booming; it is a vibrant commercial center. The buildings are clean and freshly painted, and the local moviehouse is playing *Cattle Queen of Montana*, starring Barbara Stanwyck and Ronald Reagan. The town's homes evoke a pleasant feeling: big front porches and white picket fences.

Entering the local café, Marty is struck by the menu: Hamburger for twenty-five cents, Chocolate Soda for fifteen! "Gimmy a Tab," says Marty. "Kid," says the impatient Lou, "I can't give you the tab unless you order something." Marty's next question is even more perplexing: "Have you got any Sweet'N Low?" Suspicious, Lou asks for the money, but is shocked to be handed a twenty-dollar bill: "What do you think this is, a bank?" At school, the punky Biff torments his father, the class's nerd, about getting his homework done on time. And he plays the same old joke, telling George his shoe is untied, so that when he looks down, he can hit him in the chin. "What do you let that asshole walk all over you for?" asks Marty. "What can I do?" says George. "He's bigger than me." "Once a wimp, always a wimp," Marty remarks to himself.

Marty is shocked to realize that his father is a Peeping Tom. Watching a naked girl with his binoculars from up in a tree, the branch breaks and George tumbles into the street just as a car is approaching. "Dad, look out," cries Marty, knocking his father out of the path; the car hits him. Characteristic of his father, instead of helping Marty, he leaves him there unconscious. Taken to Lorraine's bedroom, Marty awakes up in bed wearing no pants. "They seemed a little tight, so I took them off," she explains, calling him Calvin, because that is the name (Calvin Klein) on his underwear. At dinner, Lorraine's family is watching TV—Jackie Gleason in the classic episode "Man from Space" from *The Honeymooners*. Lorraine is excited about "our first TV set," a brand new Dumont model, but, unimpressed, Marty tells her, "We have six of 'em." "You must be rich," says Lorraine. It makes no sense to them when Marty claims to have seen this episode on a rerun. But more shocking to Marty is Lorraine's insistence that he spend the night there, putting her hand on his leg.

At school, Mr. Strickland not only looks the same, but sounds the same, lecturing George about being a slacker. At the cafeteria, Marty sees how Biff and his friends humiliate his father, making him step on splattered mess and slip, showered by his own food. In a role reversal, it's

Marty who instructs his father how to court Lorraine. But when Marty suggests to Lorraine that she go out with George, she is bewildered: "Me, hit it off with that chicken? Are you kidding? He's not my type. You're more my type, because you stood up for him. I think a man should be strong so he can protect the woman he loves." Like George's hysteria in *It's a Wonderful Life,* Marty panics, knowing that if his parents will not go out to the dance together, he will never be born!

Against great odds, Marty fulfills children's ultimate fantasy to control the fate of their parents and supervise their own birth. Moreover, Marty transforms his parents from losers to winners. It's in this motif that *Back* is grounded in its immediate ideological context: Reagan's obsessive stress on economic success, upward mobility, and good family life. Indeed, in the last scene, George and Lorraine are dressed in their tennis outfits, carrying themselves with confidence and self-importance. They project the image of a happily married couple. When Marty protests that he cannot go to the lake tonight because the car is wrecked, his father corrects him, "There's nothing wrong with my car, Biff is out there waxing it right now." In another role reversal, Biff is diligently waxing a new Lincoln Continental. A uniformed maid brings French toast, as George is talking about his new house and new car. The movie also transforms the black helper at Lou's café into an ambitious politician running for mayor.

Doc Brown performs an interesting function in the narrative, reversing the conventions of small-town doctors. He is at once an insider and an outsider, a child and adult, dumb and extremely bright, Marty's real friend but also a big brother who provides guidance. In its upbeat philosophy, *Back* shows children's wishful desire to redefine their reality. It reflects the (subconscious) desire of children to play an active part in bringing their parents together and in their own conception. For an American film, the narrative comes amazingly close to portraying incest between Marty and his mother, which would have threatened his own birth. Ideologically, it's no longer father knows best, but son knows better—an indication of parents' increasing loss of authority in the 1980s. The film takes the youths' point of view, placing them center stage: *They* instruct their parents how to stand up to their enemies, court, and make love. But with all its energy and optimism, the movie cannot conceal the fact that in 1985, the town lacks a moral center, playing no collective role in the lives of its dwellers. In fact, there is no town anymore, but rather every individual for himself or herself, with no involvement in communal life.

Peggy Sue Got Married was also based on a universal fantasy, posing an existential question: Given the opportunity to relive one's life, what changes would one introduce? It is a bright idea, built on the seductive thought of many adults, "Knowing what I know now, if I had the chance to do it all over again, I'd sure do things a lot differently." Who could resist the opportunity to relive the past with the present's knowledge? *Peggy Sue* deals with the periodic need of individuals to reassess their lives and reestablish their self-worth.[16]

Peggy Sue (Kathleen Turner) is a middle-aged woman on the brink of divorce. Charlie Bodell (Nicolas Cage), the only man she ever dated, got her pregnant at eighteen. He had singing ambitions, but not much talent. Now, he is a "Crazy Eddie" type, an appliance store owner with TV commercials like: "Hi, I'm Crazy Charlie, and I'm not just smashing TVs, I'm smashing prices! I've got the lowest prices in town." Her daughter Beth tries to console her, "Lots of people are separated and divorced." "Not from the guy with the lowest price in town," says Peggy Sue. Preparing for her twenty-fifth school reunion, Peggy Sue sports a late 1950s "flip" and wears her prom dress. "In all that time, haven't you at least tried another hairstyle?" asks her friend Carol. "I just did it for the reunion," says Peggy Sue. "I thought it would be fun." Carol thinks Peggy Sue should have left town years ago, as she did. "It's not so bad," says Peggy Sue. "I have two wonderful kids, my own business." But it *is* bad: she is facing a severe midlife crisis.

At the reunion, one learns about Peggy Sue's schoolmates, a "representative" mixture of types. Madeline Hutton and Arthur Naggle were high-school sweethearts who married right after graduation; a "polyester couple," they are still together. Maddy wishes she could wear Peggy Sue's dress, but she lacks "the nerve and the figure." Carol Heath and Walter Getz were also high-school steadies, but they went their separate ways. A successful dentist and still a good dancer, Getz's slogan is "taps and caps." "How does it feel to have missed the sexual revolution?" asks Beverly into the mike. Beverly has done well for herself, "graduating from the school gossip to a broadcast bitch." Richard Norvik, the class's genius, is a "fucking millionaire whose fucking computers put many out of business."

The committee has decided to choose the two people who best represent the spirit of Buchanan High, Class of 1960. Everyone is sure about the male choice, Richard, he has earned "fame and fortune and the respect of this country's scientific and business communities." But it's a surprise when Peggy Sue is selected. Indeed, the excitement and heat prove to be too much and she faints, waking up at her senior year. Grounded by her father, Jack Kelcher (Don Murray), a traditional father-husband, she protests: "I don't wanna go to my room. I wanna play. I wanna import Japanese cars. I wanna go to Hollywood and make love to Marlon Brando while he's still gorgeous." Her mother, Evelyn (Barbara Harris), is a submissive wife, a victim of patriarchal marriage without knowing it. "Peggy Sue, you know what a penis is," she tells her daughter. "Stay away from it!" In the car, when Peggy Sue wants to "go all the way," Charlie is shocked. "Jeez," he says, "that's a guy's line"; a girl was not supposed to talk in such a way back in 1960.

Peggy Sue sports a ponytail and wears bobby socks and pedal pushers. In class, she shocks her teacher when she announces: "I happen to know that in the future I will never have the slightest use for algebra, and I speak from experience." Given the power to fantasize about what she was denied as a teenager, she goes to bed with the class's beatnik poet, drinks a stiff whiskey, and even uses foul language ("you machoschmuck"). In the film's most emotional scene, Peggy Sue exercises many children's wish and visits her grandparents, who died when she was young. Grandmother Elizabeth tells her that "being young can be just as confusing as being old," and Grandpa Barney says that "if I had a chance to do it all again, I'd take better care of my teeth."

However, the gimmick—the viewers know Peggy Sue is adult, but the characters believe she is one of them—does not work: Kathleen Turner looks ridiculous, a mature woman in a tight dress. The film fails to establish any recognizable reality, 1960 or 1985. Lacking concern for narrative time, Peggy Sue looks too old to have a mother like Barbara Harris, and too young to have a twenty-two-year-old daughter. The film also suffers from structural weaknesses and a superimposed happy ending, tacked on by the studio after the film was shot. The reconciliation between Peggy Sue and Charlie lacks credibility, a pat resolution and compromise that make the tale's resonance pointless.

Sloppily directed, only the opening and closing sequences are visually satisfactory. In both, Peggy Sue sits in front of her mirror, and the camera gradually pulls back. The tension between the two spaces, her real self and reflection in the mirror, are used as symbols of her present and past. In this symmetrical beginning and ending, her daughter is present, a possible reminder of the family's centrality; the value of family unit is stressed over personal fulfillment. Preaching sacrifice and resignation, the film is conservative in its ideology, favoring marriage (it's not clear whether the philandering Charlie will ever change) over divorce, and family life over singlehood. But the resolution also suggests that Peggy Sue is incapable of applying the knowledge of her past to the present. Accumulated knowledge, based on actual experience, does not necessarily lead to action or change, when strong feelings are concerned. In the final battle, heart wins over head.

Containing a richer emotional texture than *Back to the Future*, *Peggy Sue* shows a similar role reversal: Like Marty, Peggy Sue's grown-up daughter assumes emotional responsibility for her parents. In both films, the children are more mature (and have more control) than their parents.

But unlike *Back,* Peggy Sue travels backward to her *own* past, and she is not given magical powers of transformation (Marty changed his parents from losers to winners). A Capraesque heroine, Peggy Sue, like George Bailey in *It's a Wonderful Life,* is given the chance to go back to her past and erase her destiny. But, unlike George, who never doubted his love for Mary, Peggy Sue continues to have doubts about her marriage and is uncertain that a brighter future is ahead of her. Suffused with sentimentality, *Peggy Sue* is about survival and patient endurance, placing emphasis on the preciousness of the most mundane moments in life: breakfast with family, love among siblings. Unlike other American movies, *Peggy Sue* embodies a fatalistic philosophy: one can't change one's fate and, given the choice, most people are likely to make the same decisions and repeat the same "mistakes." Increasing awareness does not necessarily result in making different decisions, because decisions are also based on subconscious emotions and instincts. It is a sad, melancholy movie, recommending people to come to terms with—and make the best out of—their lives.

Two Visions of Coming of Age: *Stand by Me* and *River's Edge*

Rob Reiner's *Stand by Me* (1986) and Tim Hunter's *River's Edge* (1987) feature male protagonists (children in the former, adolescents in the latter), and in both, the issue of death figures prominently. But if *Stand by Me* is suffused with the magic of childhood, *River's Edge* presents in a detached style the cruel side of growing up. *Stand by Me,* the less disturbing and more conventional of the two, is based on Stephen King's autobiographical novella, *The Body.*[17] The narrative is framed in a long flashback, introduced by its adult hero, Gordie (Richard Dreyfuss), now a middle-aged writer: "I never had any friends later on like the ones I had when I was twelve. Jesus, does anyone?" Cashing in on nostalgia, this framing device distances the story and characters from the viewers, putting them in a more objectified reality.

Set in the summer of 1959, the film centers on one extraordinary weekend in the lives of four friends, a weekend that at once epitomizes the magic of childhood and signals its inevitable end. At the edge of Castle Rock, a woody town in Oregon.[18] Gordie Lachance (Wil Wheaton) is about to begin a two-day trek into the heartland of the nearby forest. A town of 1,281 people, Castle Rock is, for Gordie, "the whole world." Gordie plays a penny card game with his buddies, Chris Chambers (River Phoenix), thirteen, and Teddy Duchamp (Corey Feldman), twelve. For several days, there has been a radio report about a boy who disappeared when he went hunting for blueberries in the woods. Vern Tessio (Jerry O'Connell) tells them that he overheard an awesome secret: His brother and his friends have stumbled upon the body of the missing boy. Their pact is *not* to report their discovery to the authorities, because the body was found while they were driving a stolen car. Vern immediately excites his friends, wishing to be the first to get credit for the heroic deed that, in a town like Castle Rock, will make them instant heroes.

Each of the four friends has a stigma, an attribute that makes him not only different but disreputable. Gordie is haunted by the death of his older brother Denny, a star athlete and the family's pride. He believes he will never fill Denny's shoes. Insecure, Gordie feels inadequate, his greatest asset is his inclination to tell stories; he is a natural-born writer. A year older (at this age every month counts), Chris functions as the instrumental and expressive leader, protecting the group from outsiders and regulating tensions among members. But Chris is also a victim, abused by his alcoholic father. He is convinced the town will never let him rise above his family's low status. Teddy also carries wounds, his stigma derives from thick glasses and disfigured ear, a product of his abusive father, a World War II hero. He would dodge trucks and trains to gain the love he has never been given at home. Overweight and scared of his own shadow, Vern is an outcast whose desperate ambition is not to be ridiculed (or called "chicken"). To gain acceptance as an insider, he is willing to pass any test of endurance and prove he can overcome any fear.

The film shows how these individual weaknesses are overcome in a group context. How primary relationships—the social support, intimacy, the "we" feeling, the protectiveness of the group from the "outside" world—function as a safety valve in counterbalancing personal problems. Only when they are *together*, their problems are manageable, if not curable. The film depicts a series of tests, rites of passage, the children have to pass as individuals and group members. For example, they test their fate as they attempt a shortcut over a high river-spanning bridge, with a locomotive engine at their heels. It is thus far the scariest and most adventurous moment in their lives. At night, sitting around a bonfire, they tell stories, which are shown in flashback. The fat kid recounts a revenge tale—how he participated in a pie-eating contest, at the end of which he vomited over a contestant's face. Another kid tells how he returned the money he had stolen to his teacher, but she bought a dress with it. Gordie has nightmares about Denny's funeral in which his father says, "It should have been you."

The kids are aware of their class and intellectual differences. There is also conflict between them and the older hoodlums, who wear tattoos, drive fast, and knock down mailboxes. Confronting these outsiders, they feel "it ain't fair, we were the first," but neither group gets credit for finding the body. References to popular culture in 1959 abound in the movie. There is music of the period (the title song), and the boys speculate about Annette Funicello's breasts. At the end of this fateful trip, their lives are no longer the same. "We'd only been gone two days," the narrator says, "but somehow the town seemed different, smaller." For each kid, the trip is a self-revelatory odyssey. Two of the four, Teddy and Vern, are destined to stay in Castle Rock, as they say, "We are never going to get out of this town." In similar manner to *American Graffiti*, viewers are informed that Teddy tried to get into the army, but had bad eyes. Gordie became a successful writer. Chris went to college and became a lawyer, but he was stabbed while standing in line in a restaurant; once again, accidental death is a prevalent motif in small-town films.

Though based on a real incident in Northern California, *River's Edge* reveals no information about its specific locale. The narrative reverses the conflict in *Stand by Me:* Here, the heroes are high-school students, and the bullies younger children. Moreover, the discovery of the body is not a climactic, shocking experience, but the point of departure. Both films show the fascination of seeing a dead body for the first time. A recurrent question in both films is: "Do you want to see a dead body?" However, this question bears different meanings and has different effects on the protagonists of *River's Edge*.

The narrative begins at the river, only this time nature is the scene of two crimes. It is not the place small-town heroes flee to relax from the turmoil of their lives, and it is not a place to swim on a hot day. It is the reverse: The river looks muddy and unappealing. Tim (Joshua Miller), a young boy, stands on a bridge and slowly drops his sister's doll into the water. Across the bridge, another crime has taken place. Samson, nicknamed John (Daniel Roebeck), is staring calmly at the nude body of his girl, Jamie, whom he had murdered on a whim. An association is established between the murdered girl and the drowned doll: Which of the two acts is meaner, and which has left more impact on its doer?

The place soon becomes a tourists' sight: John takes his friends to see Jamie's body. They stand transfixed by the horrible sight, but no one moves or calls the police. Worse yet, none shows any emotional reaction; they are not outraged. John neither regrets nor apologizes for his crime. Lacking any feelings, he coolly explains that Jamie "upset" him; he killed her without much thinking. A disturbing film, *River's Edge* has a nightmarish quality of a collective fear—adolescence, that cherished and eagerly awaited phase of life, turns out to be confusing and vacant. Unlike most teenage sex comedies of the 1980s, this one doesn't glamorize youth. Rather, it presents a bleak picture of coming of age, a time of boredom and waste, with no sense of direction or moral support. The film provides no explanation for the teenagers' state of anomie, though it gives some clues.

Like other films, *River's Edge* presents a gallery of types. Layne (Crispin Glover) is the group's leader, a high-strung, pill-popping guy, who believes that protection of the group's spirit is the ultimate goal. Perceiving group loyalty as a sacred value, he is convinced that it is their duty to cover up the murder. Layne reasons that Jamie is already dead, so nothing can be done about it, but John is still alive and needs help. The narrative offers a clinical case study of a leader who gradually loses his power over his followers. Wearing a black ski cap over his long hair, he looks menacing. Layne would use any argument to persuade his mates of the validity of such values as loyalty and friendship. "Why do you suppose the Russians are gearing up to take us over?" he challenges Matt, expressing his disgust with weak Americans.

Contrasted with Layne is Matt (Keanu Reaves), the only member who defies Layne and goes to the police, though it takes him time to do it. Matt is basically no different from the other members: he smokes dope, skips school, and even "steals" Layne's girl (under her initiative, but he sees no problem with it). Director Hunter said he was intrigued by the moral paradox inherent in the situation of a bad guy standing for loyalty, and the good guy as a stool pigeon, "betraying" his friends. Matt is more sympathetic than the others, but decidedly not a hero. At the police station, asked why it took him so long to report, he replies, "I don't know." "How do you feel about it?" the cop inquires. "Nothing," Matt says with disturbing honesty.

Clarissa (Ione Skye Leitch) is also unable to filter her feelings. "I cried when that guy died in *Brian's Song*" (a TV movie), she says. "You'd figure I'd at least be able to cry for someone I hung around with." This suggests the greater impact of TV melodramas than real-life events on human behavior. Unlike other teenage films, the group is neither cohesive nor united. Social encounters are not based on primary or intimate relationships, and the friendships lack substance and meaning. However, what *River's Edge* shares with other youth films is its attitude toward adult figures, presented as irresponsible and indifferent. Living empty and meaningless lives, the kids are literally left to their own devices. The few adults in the film fail as role models. Matt's father has disappeared; his mother lives with a brute who doesn't care about her kids. Though a nurse (an ironic occupation in terms of her selfishness and insensitivity), she cares more about her dope than her children. The kids don't like her lover and there is always quarrelling or fighting in the house. The movie fails to show one evening in which the family spends time together; home is a place to be only when there is nothing better to do. The hippie generation is also ridiculed. Its representative, the schoolteacher, tries to excite his apathetic students with his activism ("We took to the streets and made a difference"), but he is perceived by them as a freak, a caricature.

Matt's twelve-year-old brother, Tim, is desperate to gain acceptance as a member of Matt's group. The film draws a parallel between Tim, who murdered his sister's doll, and John, who murdered his girl. Judging by their motivation and reaction, there are no significant differences between the two. The image of a doll is used in another context: there is the inflatable doll, kept by the psychotic Feck (Dennis Hopper) as a reminder of the girl *he* had murdered. Ironically, the only adult who possesses some humanity is Feck, but he has paid a price, losing his mind. A crazed loner, he genuinely regrets his deed. Here the movie reverses conventions, showing in its comparison of the two murderers that the older member at least feels *something;* his counterpart, John, is incapable of any feeling. Asking John, "Did you love her?" Feck is outraged by John's response, "She was O.K." Feck is also the chief supplier of the group's drugs, which are taken as given; the narrative makes no issue of the drugs. The problem posed by the film is: Assuming that kids do grow up in amoral surroundings, a drug-oriented culture, and anomie, do these factors really justify, or explain, their vacant and immoral behavior?

Conclusion

The decade's movies expanded the gallery of small-town heroes and especially heroines. There was a wider representation of class (with several working-class protagonists), geographical region, and a "return" to farmers and farming after decades of neglect. The greatest contribution of the 1980s to the small-town mythology has been the inclusion of *women*—a new element in a mythology that has been almost exclusively confined to men. As I have previously shown (1987), what was common to the new heroines was their transformation from ordinariness to extraordinariness. At the beginnings of the narrative, they are ordinary, even plain, but by potential strength, circumstances, and necessity, they become extraordinary.

At the center of *Resurrection* (1980)[19] is Edna McCauley (Ellen Burstyn), a working-class woman, whose husband dies in a car accident. Paralyzed from the waist down, she returns to her home in rural Kansas. She soon discovers she possesses a mysterious healing power, thus becoming the inspirational-spiritual leader of the community. Like *Norma Rae* and the farm trilogy, *Resurrection* stresses that Edna is an ordinary, uneducated woman—not a saint—who becomes extraordinary through magical powers. The narrative fuses new feminist ideas with old and sentimental conventions. It contains a Freudian conflict between Edna and her terse father: they have been alienated ever since he forced her to have an abortion that left her sterile. The film's antifundamentalist statement (some inhabitants believe she is a force of evil) was also relevant in 1980, when the fundamentalist movement was rising in popularity. It also contrasts Edna's humanistic healing powers with the City's (Los Angeles) scientific establishment, which tries, but cannot, explain her powers rationally. Accepting her strength as mysterious, *Resurrection* emphasizes values associated with small-town folks: inner strength and self-reliance.

Nita Longley (Sissy Spacek), the young divorcée of *Raggedy Man* (1981), is a switchboard operator who lives in the office with her two young sons. Upwardly mobile, she practices typing, aspiring for a better job. She pleads with the company's manager for a job transfer, reminding him that "this was supposed to be a stepping-stone." "There is war going on," he keeps saying, which means she is "frozen." There is no separation between work and leisure, people awake her at all times of the day and night; for better or worse, Nita is the communication center in town. But one day, Teddy Roebuck (Eric Roberts), a sensitive sailor, stops by, and a tender romance ensues. The kids immediately relate to him as their surrogate father. But the town's residents are of the malevolent and gossipy types. A chattery customer stops by to pay his telephone bill; the next day, the whole town knows about Nita's affair. Worse yet, the Triplett brothers, who have an eye on Nita, harass her two boys.

Like *Something Wild*, *Raggedy Man* is an incoherent text, mixing elements from other films without integrating them into a congruous story. Specifically, it borrows from *To Kill a Mockingbird* the strange character of Boo, here Bailey (Sam Shepard), Nita's ex-husband who is supposed to have joined the army, but is actually in town watching over his family. The film also lifts from *Halloween* and *Wait until Dark* the notion of a sexually harassed woman, helplessly trapped in her own home. Attempting to reconstruct life in a small town (Gregory, Texas) in the 1940s, the film lacks a consistent point of view, combining nostalgia with cynicism. The misconceived ending is also unsatisfactory: Nita leaves town for San Antonio; on the bus her kids talk about Teddy (a hint that they may reunite).

Heart like a Wheel (1983) further expanded the range of roles allotted to women, chronicling the career of Shirley Muldowney (Bonnie Bedelia), the only race driver, male or female, to have won the National Hot Rod Association World Championship for three times. This film challenges male-dominated society and its ingrained sexism. A working-class woman, Muldowney competes in one of the most male-dominated establishments, the world of drag racing. The narrative traces twenty-five years of her life, from her adoration of her country singer–father through an ill-fated marriage to an unambitious auto mechanic. It documents her battles for the drag-racing crown with bureaucratic officials and biased news media (all Big City ills). And like *Alice* and *Norma Rae's* heroines, Muldowney offers a new definition of motherhood, through the unorthodox education she gives her son, who later joins her crew.

The protagonist of Mike Nichols's *Silkwood* is another ordinary, but unconventional woman: Karen Silkwood (Meryl Streep), the nuclear plant worker, who died in 1974 under mysterious circumstances (on her way to meet a *New York Times* journalist with a confidential report). Working as a lab technician at Kerr-McGee nuclear plant in Cimarron, Oklahoma, Karen is a distraught, even-selfish mother, who has left her three children in Texas. Imperfect and reckless, she is flighty, free-living, devil-may-care woman (she defiantly bares a breast in front of her male workers). But like Norma Rae, Karen is capable of changing and, exposed to poison, she transforms from a careless woman to one with an acute political awareness; a worthy individual capable of thinking for herself. Through strength of character, Karen becomes a heroine, though in her personal life she continues to be "nontraditional," a woman with "loose" morality.

In addition to the focus on women in small-town narratives, the 1980s were marked by two other trends. First, an abundance of comedies, set in small towns or in the country, featuring eccentric characters (*Baby Boom, Housekeeping, Raising Arizona, Roxanne, The Witches of Eastwick,* all in 1987; *Big Business, Bagdad Cafe,* both in 1988; *Miss Firecracker,* 1989). And second, an attempt to evoke straightforwardly episodes of the American past. For example, some films re-created the coming of age in small towns during World War II (*Raggedy Man,* 1981; *Racing with the Moon,* 1984), while others dealt with male pursuits such as sports (*All the Right Moves,* 1983; *The Natural,* 1984; *Hoosiers,* 1986; *Field of Dreams,* 1989). What characterizes these movies is a simple, old-fashioned, narrative structure and a set of nostalgic values.

For example, in *Racing with the Moon,* the chief protagonists are the train and the railroad tracks. The narrative follows the friendship of two youngsters during the last six weeks prior to their enlistment in the marines. In the last scene, racing for the departing train, the boys grab onto the railing of the last car, then turn and wave goodbye. The transition from childhood into adulthood is dramatically captured in this brief moment of farewell to town—and their innocence. Like *Raggedy Man,* the screenplay is both predictable and anachronistic, confusing conventions of past and present. The obligatory scene of swimming in the nude and passionate lovemaking is not likely to have occurred in 1942. Shot in the rugged coast of Mendocino, a locale used by other small-town films (*East of Eden, The Russians Are Coming,* and *Summer of '42*), the recurrent image is that of youngsters walking in the open fields. The town is not seen as stifling, but its inhabitants use nature to establish their identities and examine their relationships. An idyllic evocation of coming of age, *Racing with the Moon* (and other movies of the 1980s) featured a different kind of nostalgia, one that praised traditional values, but without the previous sentimentality.

Conclusion

The transmission of attitudes and images about small towns (and other social phenomena) has been particularly effective through *films,* because of their characteristics as a medium: Rapid transmission (the same message is watched by many at the same time), mass orientation (the message is targeted toward a large and heterogeneous audience), and public nature (in theory, the contents of film is open to all).[1] This book focused on the cinematic treatment of small towns, because movies have been the primary source of entertainment in the United States up to the 1950s, and an important form (following television's lead), since then. Small-town films were examined in four terms: *Cultural texts,* narrative paradigms, thematic conventions, prevalent issues, recurrent conflicts and characters; *Art forms,* formal attributes and artistic conventions of style; *Ideological constructs,* meanings and normative definitions (of gender roles, for example); and *Mass-marketed products,* entertainment products for the large public.

The Small Town and the Big City as Ideological Constructs

Small-Town America is an ideological construct that has been culturally conditioned and shaped. The influence of the "outside reality" (demographic trends) on this construct has been selective: Artists choose elements from reality and rearrange them to fit a model (often a myth) they hold about a social phenomenon. The links between actual small towns and their cinematic images are therefore indirect and complex. Indeed, even when the reality of small towns contradicted their corresponding literary or cinematic myths, filmmakers have ignored or underplayed (consciously and unconsciously) this reality and held onto their schemes. It is therefore important to understand the narrative, ideological, and stylistic *conventions* of small-town portraiture, because the cinematic myths of small towns have reflected mental attitudes and a climate of ideas rather than their actual positions.

251

As an image, the ideological construction of Small-Town America is no different from that of the Big City. One cannot draw simple or direct references from the reality of cities to their corresponding images, because artists often express viewers' latent and unarticulated attitudes. Like towns, actual cities, have their individual histories (plagued, bombed, moved, expanded), but the associations of the City as an image, "reflect attitudes which appear to have changed little since the beginning of Western culture."[2] The mythic resonances of both the Small Town and the Big City have not changed much, despite historical differences and structural changes. However, the mythology of the Small Town is a distinctly American creation, hence the concept Small-Town America, in contrast to the mythology of the Big City, a construct shared by many Western societies.

The activation of *specific* (and not others) Small Town and Big City myths, at *certain* (and not others) historical times, calls for an explanation. Up to the late 1950s, roughly the age of the studio system and Classic Hollywood Cinema, there were significant differences between the mythology of the Small Town and the Big City. The portrayal of small towns tended to be favorable, with most films indicating ideological preference for the values associated with such a life-style. However, from the 1960s on, the difference between the cinematic imagery of the Small Town and the Big City has subsided. For example, no longer is the City depicted as the exclusive domain of solitude, isolation, or crime. Individuals in small towns can be just as isolated and estranged from their communities as their City counterparts. In films of the New American Cinema (from the 1960s on), small towns have been depicted as fragmented communities, lacking moral gravity and coercive power over their individuals. With no organized collective life, individuals in small towns are left to their own devices, lacking meaningful bonds with friends, neighbors, and the town as a whole. In these films, individuals are no longer required to sacrifice their personal interests for the town's collective goals and values.

In its portrayal of country and rural life the American cinema has also displayed strong ideological biases. For example, despite the fact that statistically more Americans are blue-collar workers than farmers, films have continuously given preference to farmers. The dramatic decline in the proportion of farmers in the occupational structure (from 37.5 percent in 1900, to 21 percent in 1930, to 11.8 percent in 1950, to 2.8 percent in 1980)[3] has not affected film mythology. In the 1980s, the American cinema has been more preoccupied with farmers than industrial workers. The only new trend in the cinematic portrayal of farmers has been the inclusion of women *(Country, Places in the Heart, The River)*, but the values embodied in rural films featuring women have been the same. This coherent depiction is based on ideological reasons: Glorification of the farmer has prevailed in American culture from the Jeffersonian era and its antiurban bias. Moreover, if the portrayal of small towns has somehow changed over the years, the cinematic imagery of farmers has remained the same. In thematics and ideology, the farmers of *The Yearling* (1946), *Shane* (1953), and *Oklahoma!* (1955) are no different from those in *Cimarron* (1931) or *State Fair* (1933). And the treatment of female farmers in *Country* or *Places in the Heart* has been similar to that of their male counterparts in *Sergeant York* and *The Grapes of Wrath*, forty years earlier.

The narrative and stylistic imagery of the Big City have also been consistent, at least from the beginning of the sound era. King Vidor's *The Crowd* (1928), John Ford's *Arrowsmith* (1931), Merian C. Cooper's *King Kong* (1933), and William Wellman's *Nothing Sacred* (1937) have defined forever the visual imagery of the City in American films. For example, the use of long shots and high angles in filming the city's architecture, has ideologically resulted in the "dwarfing" of "anonymous and faceless crowds," pitting them against the City's magnitude, loneliness, impersonality, and anonymity. In film noir, usually set at night, the City seems to be even more menacing. Booming with activity and energy during the day, the City's streets are shown to be empty and deserted at night (often wet, rain-swept, and foggy). Walking down the streets, individuals appear as shadowy figures in constant danger. The typical settings of such narratives are "low-life" locales: shabby offices of private eyes, sleazy saloons, sinister cocktail lounges, third-rate hotels. The City's seedy bars are usually neon-lighted, reflected in windows. The protagonists often live in basement tenements, in which their small rooms are dominated by mirrors and nightlamps; the shades are pulled down.[4] This imagery (Bette Davis walking alone in the streets of Chicago in *Beyond the Forest*) stands in diametric opposition to the romantic image of adolescents walking in the open fields in small-town movies *(Peyton Place, Stand by Me, Racing with the Moon)*.

Yet the imagery of Small Town is no more of an ideological construction than the contents of other communications. Herbert Gans[5] showed that even "hard news" does not limit itself to reality judgments, containing instead many value statements. Though expected to show dispassionate detachment in their work, journalists cannot proceed without using social values. The prevailing values in news (like those in small-town films), are neither the journalists' nor distinctive to the news. Rather, they are values shared by the sources from which journalists obtained their information, which explains why and how they have influenced every form of popular culture, including films. However, the two media may differ: Values in the news are often implicit or latent, whereas in films they tend to be explicit and overt. Based for the most part on fictional sources, films' narratives have greater freedom in approaching their subject matters. But similarly to films, the news media *assume* an ideological consensus about values, which in reality may or may not exist. Moreover, many news stories are about *violation* of values, in the same way that small-town films have dealt with *deviation* from norms. Both kinds of stories fulfill the function of collective reaffirmation of mores. The punishment of violators, in films and the news, calls attention to the existence and strength of the norm.

Gans found six underlying values in American news: Ethnocentrism, altruistic democracy, responsible capitalism, small-town pastoralism, individualism, and moderatism. Most of these values have also underlined the narrative structure of small-town films. Small-town pastoralism is the specification of two more general values: The desirability of nature and smallness per se. Like American films, news stories have contained strong rural, anti-industrial values, favoring small towns over other types of settlement. And conversely, the Big City in news stories has usually signaled social problems: racial conflict, poverty, crime, violence, homelessness, unemployment. Anything Big (cities, industry, government) is perceived as a threat. As was shown in Capra's films, bigness implies inhuman and impersonal life, thus a threat to individual freedom. The ideal organization (in *Meet John Doe*) is a grass-roots association on a "human scale," though the precise specifications of this scale remain vague.

Similarly to their portraiture in American films, suburbs have not been deemed newsworthy—despite the fact that over one-third of the population resides in them. In addition to statistical underrepresentation, suburbanism has usually received bad press. In films and the news, suburbs have been viewed as breeding grounds of homogeneity, blandness, and boredom. Significantly, as Gans noted, coverage of the suburbs has increased in the news, because they began to suffer from "typically urban" problems (crime, drugs) and continued to protect themselves against the "invasion" of ethnic minorities. By contrast, the youth movement into rural Pennsylvania, California, and Vermont received *extensive* and *favorable* treatment in the news—and in films of the 1960s and 1970s. Extensive economic growth has been perceived as a serious danger to communal life. Pastoral values are more romantic, and stories about the deaths of small towns—as a result of economic development and expanding suburbs—have been suffused with sentimentality. Small-town pastoralism also calls attention to the threat of new technology (automation, computerization), which might endanger individual life. The introduction of automobiles, and later television, has been perceived in both films and the news, as robbing people of their humanity, intimacy, friendliness, and neighborliness. Small-town films (and news stories) have continued to celebrate the old technology, lamenting the passing of the life-style associated with it. For example, narratives *(The Last Picture Show)* have lamented the decline of moviegoing as collective entertainment. Moreover, industrial mills, once the object of criticism due to their exploitation of workers *(Peyton Place, Splendor in the Grass)*, have changed their meanings and come to signify a time of unity when, despite class distinctions, the town's members at least interacted with each other and shared belongingness to the same community. Finally, small-town pastoralism is interrelated with respect for tradition. In films and news stories, tradition has been valued because it is a known, pre-dictable, and orderly entity. Tradition provides for continuity of the established order—any change is perceived as a potential threat to stability.

Social-Historical Variation in the Imagery of Small Towns

Using a social-historical framework, the book showed that in every decade, different film genres were used to explore small-town life. In the 1930s, comedy was a prevalent genre; in the 1940s, serious dramas and war films; in the 1950s, melodramas and the "women's film"; in the 1960s, melodramas, but also innovative (nongenre) films; in the 1970s, horror films; and in the 1980s, comedy dominated again the production of small-town films. Within the generally favorable attitude of film (and dominant culture) toward small towns, there have been variability in concept and diversity in image. Culturally conditioned, in each of the six decades under consideration, small-town films have embodied different symbols and projected different meanings. The political and ideological conditioning of small-town products becomes evident when a group of typical films, made in the same decade, are examined and compared. As Barbara Deming noted, a social pattern emerges, "a plight more general . . . a condition that transcends the literal situation dramatized by any single film."[6] The claim that every film is unique, sui generis, and should be examined in its own right, is thus countered by the sociologist's trend of analyzing a group of films in terms of their recurrent narrative structures, thematic concerns, and stylistic devices.

During the Depression, one of the solutions to the nation's social and economic problems was "the return to the soil." Most films praised uncritically the virtues of small towns and country life *(State Fair)*, though only a few *(Our Daily Bread)* proposed the establishment of agricultural communes. Indeed, within the context of dominant ideology, Vidor's critical views of urbanization and industrialization made him suspicious of propagating Communist ideas. By contrast, Capra's populist films *(Mr. Deeds, Mr. Smith)* were more successful and characteristic. They drew sharp contrasts between the values of the Small Town and the Big City, condemning the latter's corruption, greed, and impersonality.

A darker, more ambiguous, portraiture of small towns marked the films of the 1940s—despite the fact that the country was at war. The stylistics of film noir was used to convey a bleaker vision of small towns. Even Capra's upbeat and sentimental *Wonderful Life* contains a darker sequence: Life in Bedford Falls without George Bailey. This nightmarish imagery was often subconscious, operating beneath the films' surfaces, but it was there for viewers who wanted to see. The heroes of some 1940s films *(Best Years of Our Lives)* are "products of deep crisis of faith," each mourning "a vision of happiness which eludes him."[7] But in the final account, Capra's optimistic belief in the community and its values is unmistakable and unshaken. Continuing the tradition of the Depression, Capra envisions a rather integrated community, composed of individuals who sacrifice for one another and for the town as a whole.

In the 1950s, however, the ideological attitude toward small towns began to change and movies became more critical in their portrayal. Ordinary life in small towns was depicted as emotionally stifling *(All That Heaven Allows)*, intellectually suffocating *(Peyton Place)*, and sexually repressive *(Picnic)*. But despite such strains, narrative texts of the decade still advocated the centrality of patriarchal ideology, described by Robin Wood as: "The organization of sexual difference within the patriarchal order, a project whose ultimate objective must be the subordination of female desire to male desire and the construction or reinforcement of a patriarchally determined normality, embodied by the heterosexual couple."[8] At the same time, most of these movies could not conceal their ideological strains and their resolutions (happy endings) were not always convincing. Still, up to the late 1950s, Main Street was more than a row of offices and stores. Small towns boasted communal pride and concern for moral virtues—marked by a moral center, or collective conscience, which was often demonstrated in lengthy trial sequences *(Young Mr. Lincoln, Peyton Place, To Kill a Mockingbird)*. Order and stability in small-town films were typically represented by policemen, politicians, and other service professionals (doctors). With the possible exception of *Kings Row* and *Invasion of the Body Snatchers,* until the late 1950s, classic narratives embodied strong, almost irrational, belief in the possibility of healing and the restorative power of doctors and psychiatrists.

In the 1960s, however, as a result of the political assassinations, the Vietnam War, and the social protest movements (the women, the blacks, the students), the dominant culture—which had always been defined by white, middle-class men—was challenged and questions raised about its validity as the only sanctioned life-style. Some critics, such as Noam Chomsky *(American Power and the Mandarins)* and Philip Slater *(The Pursuit of Loneliness),* believed that many of the country's problems stemmed from its strong (unrealistic) belief in technology and scientific knowledge. Indeed, in films of the last two decades, there is no communal life and no attempt to integrate individuals into the town as a whole. Individuals are more likely to be on their own, and Main Street exists as an abstract set of vague values. Individuals in such films *(Crimes of the Heart)* insist on—and succeed in—separating themselves from the town's mores. The town (and, by implication, American society) no longer possesses the moral authority to demand unqualified sacrifice from its people. The gradual decline and disintegration of community life in America were expressed in *The Chase, Alice's Restaurant, Easy Rider.* These films dealt with imminent or actual breakdown, showing that the old patriarchal order and capitalistic system do not effectively function anymore. Disintegration appeared on every level of society, from the most micro (individual) to the most macro (society) unit.[9] The motifs of disenchantment and disintegration were expressed in individuals' loss of control, over themselves and others. Protagonists of small-town films have gradually lost their sense of identity and worth, with no sense of direction.

The dominant myths of nostalgia, paranoia, and revenge appeared in small-town films of the 1970s. All three themes expressed elements of collective consciousness and the national psyche, particularly the increasing alienation from the political and legal institutions. Political authority in such films was depicted as corrupt and ineffectual in solving society's problems. Moreover, the preoccupation with achieving celebrity status prevailed in every type of film: small-town *(Crimes of the Heart),* rural *(Bonnie and Clyde, The Sugarland Express),* and urban (Martin Scorsese's two great films, *Taxi Driver* and *King of Comedy).* These movies showed the cynical, but true, facts that criminality and outlawry *can* get their practitioners instant celebrity.[10]

In the 1980s, with the resurgence of a neoconservative and patriotic mood, epitomized by the Reagan and Bush administrations, many small-town films have been marked by nostalgia and reaffirmation of virtues associated with small towns, such as commitment to the land and strong family life *(Country, The River).* The decade saw films that resorted to the simpler old times *(Places in the Heart, Field of Dreams)* and traditional values *(Hoosiers)* as consoling and reassuring myths. However, in the 1980s, films have been marked by contradictory trends: A strange combination of cynicism, irony, and nostalgia. These contradictions in values resulted in the production of compromising *(Resurrection, Baby Boom)* and incoherent *(Raggedy Man, Racing with the Moon)* texts.

Distinctive Thematics and Stylistics of Small-Town Films

Stylistically, the transition from studio-made to on-location shooting had a tremendous influence on the look and feel of films. Up to the late 1940s, most small-town films were shot on the studio lot, which meant that the town was rarely shown in its entirety. On-location shooting, color cinematography, CinemaScope and other devices have changed the look of Small Town. For example, the typical beginning of a small-town film was an establishing (tracking) shot of the town, often from the point of view of an outsider *(Peyton Place)*, or a bird's-eye view *(All That Heaven Allows)*. According to conventions, it became customary to begin a film with a pan across town (often an aerial shot) or of Main Street, which conveyed rapidly and effectively the town's size, location, territorial boundaries, "nature" sights (lake, river, hill), train station, and stratification system (the other side of the tracks). The visual look of small-town films has also been determined by ideological considerations. For example, in the 1940s, several films *(Kings Row, The Magnificent Ambersons, Shadow of a Doubt)* borrowed stylistic codes from film noir. And Peter Bogdanovich shot his small-town *(The Last Picture Show)* and country *(Paper Moon)* films in stylized black and white, deviating from the norm of color cinematography, to convey a bleaker vision.

Most small-town films were based on the fiction of male writers, made by male filmmakers. With no exception, all eighty films analyzed in this book have been directed by men. The gender of small-town protagonists also shows extraordinary preeminence of *male* characters: About one-half have been men, one-fourth women, and the rest both men and women. The three strongest decades for women in small-town films, either as sole protagonists or members of teams, have been the 1930s, 1950s, and 1980s, but there are significant differences among the decades. Most female protagonists in the 1950s are contained in melodramas (Douglas Sirk's *Written on the Wind* and *All That Heaven Allows*, the plays-films by Tennessee Williams and William Inge), whereas in the 1930s and 1980s, the range of screen roles allotted to women is much wider, appearing in every genre, comedies, dramas, social problem films. The second difference concerns the woman's role and her ideological meaning in the narrative. In the 1950s, the typical closure of films restored women to patriarchy, relegating them to domesticity. In the classic narratives, potential danger awaits an unmarried woman; singlehood means vulnerability, loneliness, and danger, physical and emotional. By contrast, the 1980s are more similar to the 1930s in that women are either equal to, or even stronger than, men (the "farm trilogy").

While there has been greater representation of social class, most small-town narratives have been about, or have taken the point of view of, *white* protagonists, reflecting American society (and Hollywood's) neglect of ethnic minorities. With the exception of *The Member of the Wedding*, in which the black housekeeper provides the moral center, in most films, there are either no black characters or they play secondary, highly stereotypical, roles. Other ethnic minorities (Hispanic, Asian, and Jewish) have also been underrepresented. Even films that acknowledged America's ethnic minorities, demanded that their members conformed to dominant *white* culture.

For example, in thematic mode, *A Medal for Benny* (1945) is similar to Capra's "little and plain folk," except it deals with California's "Paisanos," of mixed Hispanic and Indian blood. Benny, the dead War hero, was an outcast, chased out of town by the police. People believe he had disappeared, but he has actually joined the military and died in action. Charley Martini (J. Carrol Naish), his father, says in a ceremony honoring his son: "I don't talk so good . . . but maybe it is good for the country that she must depend for life on all kinds of people like my son." His speech echoes the way Hollywood—and dominant culture—wished Americans would feel about their sons' sacrifice. Reflecting the diversity of American society, ethnic heterogeneity is not viewed as a sign of fragmentation, or a problem, but as a melting pot. However, in the name of integration into white middle-class values, the *Paisanos* are denied their distinctive culture; they must assimilate to gain legitimacy and respectability. Viewed from today's perspective, the film is sentimental and condescending to ethnic minorities, but it reveals ideological strains that could not be reconciled. For example, Charley's landlord threatens to evict him because he cannot meet his payments, and the bank's rude officers turn down his loan application. Not beyond immoral conceits, the politicians exploit the occasion, abusing Charley's trust and nobility. "This medal is going to do for Pantera what the quintuplet did for Canada," says one. "You get the glory, we get the gravy," says another. Concluding at the train station, with a big farewell for another "nonconformist" going to the army, the film shows that, under the "right circumstances" (War), the "little Paisanos," outsiders by ethnicity, can be molded into insiders.

One of the most enduring myths in small-town films has been the portrayal of politicians and politics as a process. Professional politicians have seldom been heroes in the American cinema, but with the progress of time, their cinematic images have deteriorated considerably. It is no coincidence that charismatic leaders in small-town movies are recruited from the masses (in Capra's films) and from remote rural places *(Young Mr. Lincoln, Sergeant York)*. But small-town narratives have chronicled a transition from the righteous and moralistic heroes of *Young Mr. Lincoln* and *Mr. Smith*, through the benevolent sheriffs of *East of Eden* and *The Defiant Ones*, through the ineffectual sheriff in *Bad Day at Black Rock* and the confused sheriff in *The Chase*, all the way to the politicians' loss of authority and prestige in *Bonnie and Clyde*, *Badlands*, *The Sugarland Express*, and *Jaws*.

The best small-town narratives have contained dialectical conflicts, through which ideological-mythic resolutions are explicitly provided. Such films have dealt with the delicate balance between the normal and abnormal, order and disorder. The normal and familiar life functions as the starting point for an understanding of the deviant and unfamiliar. And forays into the abnormal and chaotic render meaningful and reassert the power of the normal and orderly. These narratives *(Blue Velvet, Something Wild)* use the strategy of defamiliarization, displacing the commonplace to reveal submerged patterns of meanings in life. Small-town films have warned against the ever-present threat of chaos, demanding that order be guarded (and chaos prevented) by the routines of everyday life. The omnipresence of violence, simmering beneath the facade of a quiet and decent life, and the delicate balance between the bizarre and the ordinary has preoccupied filmmakers from Hitchcock *(Shadow of a Doubt)* to David Lynch *(Blue Velvet)*. Moreover, unlike many Western films, wherein the thematic problem is the coming of civilization (law and order) to the frontier, in the typical small-town films, law and order have already been established and the problem is one of *too much* law and order. Life, in fact, has become so institutionalized and norms so rigid that they suffocate individuality, creativity, and freedom *(Picnic, All That Heaven Allows)*.

To illustrate the thematic concern of the duplicity of human nature, small-town films have used the stylistic device of *mirrors*. "All of us, actors and spectators alike," Christopher Lasch has observed, "live surrounded by mirrors. In them, we seek reassurance of our capacity to captivate and impress others, anxiously searching out blemishes that might detract from the appearances that we intend to project."[11] The use of mirrors is both literal *(Alice Adams, Peggy Sue)* and metaphoric *(All That Heaven Allows, Bonnie and Clyde, Badlands)*. Mirrors in small-town films are employed to show subjective, often distorted, reality (the way the protagonists would like to see themselves), as well as a more objective reality (the way they are forced to perceive themselves by others). But looking at themselves in the mirror also indicates the protagonists' strong yearning for reaffirmation that they exist and that they will be remembered in—*and* after—their lifetime. The need "to be somebody" and, by implication the fear of losing one's identity, has been one of the most recurrent motifs in small-town films, from Alice Adams to Clyde Barrow. The difference, though, between small-town protagonists of the 1930s and the 1970s is the latter's greater status anxiety (or desperation) and willingness to resort to illegitimate means in order "to be somebody."

The most interesting films have used the narrative paradigm of the outsider. Some outsiders *(Blue Velvet, Something Wild)* leave a familiar world and enter an unfamiliar one, then return to the familiar on their own, completely transformed by the experience. They move into (and out of) what Victor Turner (1969) has called the "liminal," that period or position at the center of the ritual process, which is outside the constraints of the normal and the routine.[12] Outsiders often know and feel the pain of being out of sync in towns where conformity reigns supreme *(Peyton Place, Crimes of the Heart).* Georg Simmel's essay on "the stranger" helps to understand the distinctive qualities of the outsider in small-town films.[13] The outsider represents a combination of nearness and distance in relation to the surrounding world. He is not just a wanderer, "who comes today and goes tomorrow," but a person "who comes today and stays tomorrow" *(Peyton Place).* His position is determined by the fact that initially he does not belong to any particular spatial group and that he may leave again *(Picnic).* Not *fully* integrated, the outsider is assigned a role that other members cannot play: Because of his partial involvement, he can see the situation more objectively. The outsider is called on as a confidant; confidences are given to him because they are less consequential. The outsider is likely to be a better judge between conflicting parties, because he is not tied to either of the contenders. Unbound by "commitments which could prejudice his perception, understanding, and evaluation of the given, he is the ideal intermediary in the traffic of goods and emotions."[14] The outsider is what he is, through his relations with others who assign him a particular position and expect him to act out his assigned role.

The dichotomy between the sacred and the profane, based on Durkheim's theory, has marked many small-town narratives. The profane, the ordinary, mundane, and unremarkable, differ from the sacred, the exceptional, the awesome, and the ritualized. In such films, it is often the contrast between the domestic, taken-for-granted world and the unreachable, inaccessible world. Durkheim was aware that secular objects can assume sacred meanings, and that despite secularization, there will always be distinction between sacred and profane because members of society need to have such distinctions. However, because there is considerable space between the sacred and the profane, small-town films point to the significant boundaries between the two domains, indicating the crucial events (or symbols) of each.[15] The rituals that acknowledge the transition from the profane to the sacred have included: Births, marriages, deaths, initiation into groups (rites of passage), the treatment of outsiders—strangers. These events are marked by a set of standardized, though significant, actions that identify the seriousness of the distinction and the awe with which the passage across it is held.

More specifically, small-town narratives have been preoccupied with depicting the sociocultural effects of technological innovations on both towns and their individual members. Films have portrayed the invention of automobiles *(The Magnificent Ambersons, Our Town, The Dark at the Top of the Stairs);* the discovery of oil *(Giant, Hud);* the popularity of radio *(Paper Moon, Thieves Like Us)* and movies *(Bonnie and Clyde)* during the Depression; the coming of television *(The Last Picture Show)* and the popularity of TV game shows *(Melvin and Howard);* cars and rock 'n' roll music *(American Graffiti),* and even CB radios *(Handle with Care).* The concern with technological changes is interrelated with personal changes. Small-town narratives take place in strategic times of their protagonists' lives. Some films have been situated during holidays: Christmas *(Dr. Bull, All That Heaven Allows),* New Year's *(Splendor in the Grass),* Halloween *(Meet Me in St. Louis, Halloween).* Others have occurred during collective celebrations, such as Labor Day *(Picnic),* Fourth of July *(Young Mr. Lincoln, Summer and Smoke).* For Durkheim, a society is formed and shaped by bringing itself to consciousness through collective representation, which it then externalizes and worships. The festive occasions in small-town works, religious or secular, military or civilian, are turning points in which individuals are particularly vulnerable, reassessing their self-worth and establishing their identities and relation to their communities.

The loss of innocence and naïveté (the rosebud of *Citizen Kane),* and the corresponding disillusionment and disenchantment have also been distinctive of small-town films. In *Young Mr. Lincoln,* the loss consists of the hero's love for Ann Rutledge (captured in Lincoln's walks along the river). *The Magnificent Ambersons* and *Kings Row,* both set at the turn of the century, lament a bygone era and its disappearing life-style. In *Written on the Wind,* the protagonists' picnics at the river symbolize their happier times as youngsters. *Racing with the Moon* cherished the naïveté of the country during World War II, and *American Graffiti* its innocence before President Kennedy's assassination. *Stand by Me* celebrates the uniquely intimate friendships one has during adolescence, the kind of bonds unlikely to prevail in later life.

Related to loss is the issue of death, though death in small-town movies contrasts sharply with the more heroic-ritualized death in Westerns. Most deaths tend to be accidental or sudden, and thus unheroic. And unlike the sacrificial death in war dramas, heroes of small-town movies do not typically die heroically, for a cause. Rather, they are victims of circumstances over which they lack control. In *The Last Picture Show*, Billy dies in a car accident. In *American Graffiti*, one youngster is missing in action in Vietnam, the other is hit by a drunk driver. In *Stand by Me*, Chris is stabbed while standing in line in a restaurant. In films of the 1970s, the protagonists are shot or executed by the police. With the exception of Bonnie and Clyde's mythic end (in slow motion), the death of other petty criminals *(Thieves Like Us, Badlands, The Sugarland Express)* is unglamorous and just as meaningless as their lives.

Finally, a large number of small-town protagonists are orphans *(Mr. Deeds, Fury, The Miracle of Morgan's Creek)*, and the most prevalent family structure is the single-parent family *(Kings Row, East of Eden, Picnic, Peyton Place)*. Even when adolescents belong to whole families, the inner tensions make the structure less harmonious and less supportive than expected or desired to be. One typical family unit is headed by a domineering mother and a weakling father *(Rebel without a Cause)*. Being an orphan (or having one parent) in these films is socially, rather than biologically, significant. In *The Member of the Wedding*, Frankie Adams has a father, but he plays no role in her socialization; her only meaningful bond is with her black housekeeper who functions as her surrogate mother. Indeed, the significant others (and role models) in the maturation of adolescents are usually *not* members of their biological families. In *The Last Picture Show*, Sam the Lion serves as surrogate father to all the male adolescents, most of whom belong to one-parent families.

The *inadequacy* and malfunctioning of the nuclear family (single or two-parent) has been a dominant motif in small-town films: the *family* is often a malignant structure.[16] In *The Magnificent Ambersons*, the family is insulated from the outside world, and in *Shadow of a Doubt*, unable to deal effectively with its members' problems. The attitude toward the family is at best ambivalent: It can be supportive but, more often than not, is repressive. The family generates problems, personal and social, and does not contain individual needs; instead of managing tensions, the family nurtures them. Most families are one-parent, metaphorically if not literally. The fathers may be dead *(The Miracle of Morgan's Creek, Hail the Conquering Hero)*, absent *(The Member of the Wedding)* or weak *(Shadow of a Doubt, Rebel without a Cause)*. The mothers may be aggressive *(Rebel)*, domineering *(The Long Hot Summer)*, neurotic *(The Birds)*, demented *(Summer and Smoke)*, repressed *(Peyton Place, Picnic)*, and repressive *(The Rose Tattoo)*.

Yet, with all their criticism of the family and town, most films are optimistic concerning the future of their protagonists, particularly children. Beginning with *Our Daily Bread*, continuing with Capra's political comedies and, at present, Jonathan Demme's folk comedies, small-town narratives express strong belief in a better, more fulfilling, and less inhibiting future. Longfellow Deeds, Mr. Smith, John Doe, Cal Trasky, and Marty McFly have all assumed mythic proportions and become icons of popular culture because they embody uniquely American values. Alice Adams, Allison MacKenzie, Frankie Adams, Alice Hyatt, Norma Rae, and Peggy Sue have become legendary heroines for the same reason. As was demonstrated in my (1990) study, the most frequent cultural qualities of these heroes and heroines have been: *Individualism*, the belief in the power of a single charismatic person (male or female) as a leader; *common sense*, knowledge based on experience of the everyday life rather than formal schooling; *pragmatism*, orientation to life that is realistic and down-to-earth; *resourcefulness*, the ability to mobilize necessary resources needed to accomplish goals, be they collective (political, public) or domestic (family, home); *self-assurance*, strong belief in one's powers to survive and even improve on one's life; *determination*, the capacity to fight for one's values against all odds; *control* over one's fate—the belief that, in the final account, one is a master of one's life; and *optimism*, a strong orientation, according to which life in the future can be better and more fulfilling, and willingness to defer immediate rewards for the achievement of more important goals in the future. These cultural orientations have been basic American values and integral to dominant culture, going beyond small-town narratives. This is another way of saying that, along with Westerns, narratives about small towns have been uniquely *American* films.

Small-Town Movies by Decade*

1930s

The Crowd	1928	*The Farmer Takes a Wife*	1955
Sunrise	1928	*Steamboat 'Round the Bend*	1935
City Girl	1930	*Way Down East*	1935
Arrowsmith	1931	*Come and Get It*	1936
The Mouthpiece	1932	*The Country Doctor* (series)	1936
Dr. Bull	1933	*Reunion*	1936
The Life of Jimmy Dolan	1933	*Five of a Kind*	1938
Little Women	1933	*Dodsworth*	1936
Little Women	1949	*Fury*	1936
One Man's Journey	1933	*Mr. Deeds Goes to Town*	1936
State Fair	1933	*Theodora Goes Wild*	1936
State Fair	1945	*These Three*	1936
State Fair	1962	*Winterset*	1936
The Stranger's Return	1933	*The Andy Hardy Family*	1937
This Day and Age	1933	*A Family Affair*	1937
Babbitt	1934	*I Met My Love Again*	1937
It's a Gift	1934	*You're Only Young Once*	1938
Judge Priest	1934	*Judge Hardy's Children*	1938
Our Daily Bread	1934	*Love Finds Andy Hardy*	1938
The World Moves On	1934	*The Hardys Ride High*	1939
You're Telling Me	1934	*Andy Hardy Gets Spring Fever*	1939
Ah, Wilderness	1935	*Judge Hardy and Son*	1939
Alice Adams	1935	*Andy Hardy Meets Debutante*	1940
Dr. Socrates	1935	*Andy Hardy's Private Secretary*	1940
The Farmer Takes a Wife	1935	*Life Begins for Andy Hardy*	1941

---

*This list also includes films that are set in the big city or suburbia, but draw comparisons with small towns.

The Courtship of Andy Hardy	1941
Andy Hardy's Double Life	1942
Andy Hardy's Blonde Trouble	1944
Love Laughs at Andy Hardy	1946
Andy Hardy Comes Home	1958
Interns Can't Take Money (became Dr. Kildare series)	1937
Lost Horizon	1937
Nothing Sacred	1937
Stella Dallas	1937
I Met My Love Again	1937
Mr. Dodd Takes the Air	1937
They Won't Forget	1937
Blondie (series)	1938–49
Blondie Meets the Boss	1939
Blondie Takes a Vacation	1939
Blondie Brings Up Baby	1939
Blondie on a Budget	1940
Blondie Has Servant Trouble	1940
Blondie Plays Cupid	1940
Blondie Goes Latin	1941
Blondie in Society	1941
Blondie Goes to College	1942
Blondie For Victory	1942
Blondie's Lucky Day	1946
Blondie's Holiday	1947
Blondie Knows Best	1947
Blondie's Reward	1948
Blondie's Secret	1949
Blondie's Big Deal	1949
Blondie Hits the Jackpot	1949
Four Daughters	1938
Kentucky	1938
A Man to Remember	1938
Mother Carey's Chicken	1938
Nancy Drew (series)	1938–39
Of Human Hearts	1938
Young Dr. Kildare (first official entry)	1938
Dr. Kildare's Strange Case	1940
Dr. Kildare Goes Home	1940
Dr. Kildare's Crisis	1940
Dr. Kildare's Wedding Day	1941

Dr. Kildare's Victory	1942
Calling Dr. Gillespie	1942
Dark Delusion	1947
Dr. Christian	1939
Gone with the Wind	1939
Henry Aldrich (series)	1939–41
Mr. Smith Goes to Washington	1939
Of Mice and Men	1939
Young Mr. Lincoln	1939

1940s

Abe Lincoln in Illinois	1940
An Angel from Texas	1940
The Grapes of Wrath	1940
Our Town	1940
Primrose Path	1940
All That Money Can Buy	1941
Among the Living	1941
Cheers for Miss Bishop	1941
How Green Was My Valley	1941
The Little Foxes	1941
The Man Who Came to Dinner	1941
Meet John Doe	1941
Nice Girl?	1941
The Penalty	1941
Remember the Day	1941
Sergeant York	1941
Swamp Water	1941
Tobacco Road	1941
Kings Row	1942
The Magnificent Ambersons	1942
The Talk of the Town	1942
Crime Doctor	1943
Happy Land	1943
The Human Comedy	1943
Johnny Come Lately	1943
The Ox-Bow Incident	1943
Shadow of a Doubt	1943
Step Down to Terror (remake)	1958
The Eve of St. Mark	1944
The Fighting Sullivans	1944
Hail the Conquering Hero	1944
Johnny Comes Lately	1943

The Miracle of Morgan's Creek	1944
Meet Me in St. Louis	1944
Since You Went Away	1944
A Medal for Benny	1945
Our Vines Have Tender Grapes	1945
The Southerner	1945
State Fair	1945
The Best Years of Our Lives	1946
It's a Wonderful Life	1946
The Killers	1946
The Postman Always Rings Twice	1946
The Stranger	1946
Till the End of Times	1946
The Yearling	1946
The Egg and I	1947
The Farmer's Daughter	1947
Gentleman's Agreement	1947
Johnny Belinda	1947
Magic Town	1947
The Romance of Rosy Ridge	1947
All My Sons	1948
Good Sam	1948
June Bride	1948
Mr. Blandings Builds His Dream House	1948
Sitting Pretty	1948
The Walls of Jericho	1948
All the King's Men	1949
Beyond the Forest	1949
Flamingo Road	1949
Intruder in the Dust	1949
The Lawless	1949
A Letter to Three Wives	1949
Lost Boundaries	1949
Ma and Pa Kettle (series)	1949

1950s

Father of the Bride	1950
Father's Little Dividend (sequel)	1951
The File on Thelma Jordan	1950
The Jackpot	1950
Kiss Tomorrow Goodbye	1950

Storm Warning	1950
Our Very Own	1950
Outrage	1950
I Want You	1951
A Place in the Sun	1951
The Whistle at Eaton Falls	1951
Aaron Slick from Punkin Crick	1952
Come Back, Little Sheba	1952
The Member of the Wedding	1952
Wait 'Till the Sun Shines, Nellie	1952
Young Man with Ideas	1952
The Actress	1953
The Affairs of Dobie Gillis	1953
The Farmer Takes a Wife	1953
It Happens Every Thursday	1953
Salt of the Earth	1953
Small Town Girl	1953
War of the Worlds	1953
The Wild One	1953
All That Heaven Allows	1955
Bad Day at Black Rock	1955
East of Eden	1955
Good Morning, Miss Dove	1955
Picnic	1955
The Rose Tattoo	1955
Baby Doll	1956
Bigger than Life	1956
Bus Stop	1956
Friendly Persuasion	1956
Giant	1956
Invasion of the Body Snatchers	1956
Invasion of the Body Snatchers (remake)	1978
The Kettles in the Ozarks	1956
The Rainmaker	1956
Tea and Sympathy	1956
Written on the Wind	1956
The Kettles on Old MacDonald's Farm	1957
No Down Payment	1957
Old Yeller	1957
Peyton Place	1957
Return to Peyton Place	1961
Raintree County	1957

The Blob	1958		*The Killers*	1964
Beware! The Blob (sequel)	1971		*The Unsinkable Molly Brown*	1964
Cat on a Hot Tin Roof	1958		*Bus Riley's Back in Town*	1965
The Defiant Ones	1958		*Shenandoah*	1965
Desire under the Elms	1958		*The Chase*	1966
Doctor in the Village	1958		*Follow the Boys*	1966
The Goddess	1958		*The Russians Are Coming, The Russians Are Coming*	1966
Home Before Dark	1958			
Hot Spell	1958			
The Long, Hot Summer	1958		*Hurry Sundown*	1967
Rally 'Round the Flag, Boys!	1958		*In the Heat of the Night*	1967
The Restless Years	1958		*This Property Is Condemned*	1967
Some Came Running	1958		*Rachel, Rachel*	1968
Anatomy of a Murder	1959		*The Heart Is a Lonely Hunter*	1968
It Happened to Jane	1959			
A Summer Place	1959		*Alice's Restaurant*	1969
			Easy Rider	1969
			The Gypsy Moth	1969
1960s			*Homer*	1969
			The Learning Tree	1969
The Dark at the Top of the Stairs	1960		*Last Summer*	1969
			Midnight Cowboy	1969
Elmer Gantry	1960			
The Fugitive Kind	1960			
Inherit the Wind	1960		**1970s**	
The Sundowners	1960			
The Sound and the Fury	1960		*Five Easy Pieces*	1970
Wild River	1960		*I Walk the Line*	1970
Return to Peyton Place (sequel)	1961		*The Last of the Mobile Hot Shots*	1970
The Second Time Around	1961		*Red Sky at Morning*	1970
Splendor in the Grass	1961		*Beware! The Blob*	1971
Summer and Smoke	1961		*Klute*	1971
All Fall Down	1962		*The Last Picture Show*	1971
The Chapman Report	1962		*The Liberation of L. B. Jones*	1970
The Music Man	1962			
State Fair	1962		*No Drums, No Bugles*	1971
Sweet Bird of Youth	1962		*T. R. Baskin*	1971
To Kill a Mockingbird	1962		*Deliverance*	1972
All the Way Home	1963		*The Emigrants*	1972
The Birds	1963		*Fat City*	1972
Hud	1963		*Jeremiah Johnson*	1972
Lilies of the Field	1963		*Sounder*	1972
Papa's Delicate Condition	1963		*Part 2, Sounder* (sequel)	1974
Baby, the Rain Must Fall	1964		*The All-American Boy*	1973

American Graffiti	1973	Heartland	1981
The Last Detail	1973	Honky Tonk Freeway	1981
Necromancy	1973	On Golden Pond	1981
Paper Moon	1973	The Postman Always Rings	1981
The Sugarland Express	1973	Twice	
Alice Doesn't Live Here	1974	Prom Night	1981
Anymore		Raggedy Man	1981
Badlands	1974	Vernon Florida	1981
The Greatest Gift	1974	Come Back to the Five and	1982
Harlan County, U.S.A.	1974	Dime, Jimmy Dean	
Thieves Like Us	1974	Jimmy Dean	
Jaws	1975	E.T.	1982
Nashville	1975	First Blood	1982
Shampoo	1975	Liar's Moon	1982
Smile	1975	The Loveless	1982
The Stepford Wives	1975	Silent Rage	1982
Baby Blue Marine	1976	All the Right Moves	1983
Bound for Glory	1976	Americana	1983
Carrie	1976	The Big Chill	1983
Moving Violation	1976	Cross Creek	1983
Nashville Girl	1976	Fool for Love	1983
Close Encounters of the	1977	Heart Like a Wheel	1983
Third Kind		Racing with the Moon	1983
Handle with Care (Citizens	1977	Silkwood	1983
Band)		Tender Mercies	1983
Heroes	1977	Country	1984
Slap Shot	1977	Falling in Love	1984
The Turning Point	1977	Finders, Keepers	1984
The Buddy Holly Story	1978	Grandview, U.S.A.	1984
Days of Heaven	1978	Gremlins	1984
The Deer Hunter	1978	Last Night at the Alamo	1984
Halloween	1978	Paris, Texas	1984
September 30, 1955	1978	Places in the Heart	1984
Breaking Away	1979	Racing with the Moon	1984
The Electric Horseman	1979	Red Dawn	1984
More American Graffiti	1979	The River	1984
Norma Rae	1979	A Soldier's Story	1984
		Alamo Bay	1985
		Back to the Future	1985
1980s		Blood Simple	1985
Coal Miner's Daughter	1980	The Color Purple	1985
Honeysuckle Rose	1980	The Emerald Forest	1985
Melvin and Howard	1980	Flash of Green	1985
Resurrection	1980	Lost in America	1985
Four Friends	1981	Murphy's Romance	1985
Ghost Story	1981	1918	1985
Hard Country	1981	Sweet Dreams	1985

The Trip to Bountiful	1985	*River's Edge*	1987
Witness	1985	*Roxanne*	1987
At Close Range	1986	*The Witches of Eastwick*	1987
Blue Velvet	1986	*Bagdad Cafe*	1988
Crimes of the Heart	1986	*Big Business*	1988
Crocodile Dundee	1986	*Everybody's All American*	1988
Hard Choices	1986	*Kansas*	1988
Hoosiers	1986	*Miles from Home*	1988
Nobody's Fool	1986	*Mystic Pizza*	1988
On Valentine's Day	1986	*1969*	1988
Peggy Sue Got Married	1986	*Rachel River*	1988
Pretty in Pink	1986	*Stacking*	1988
Something Wild	1986	*Sweet Heart's Dance*	1988
Stand By Me	1986	*Tiger Warsaw*	1988
Sweet Liberty	1986	*Back to the Future, Part II*	1989
True Stories	1986	*The 'Burbs*	1989
Violets Are Blue	1986	*Field of Dreams*	1989
Baby Boom	1987	*In Country*	1989
Fatal Attraction	1987	*Miss Firecracker*	1989
Housekeeping	1987	*Staying Together*	1989
Near Dark	1987	*Stanley & Iris*	1990
Raising Arizona	1987	*Back to the Future, Part III*	1990

Notes

Introduction

1. For a history of small towns in America, see Lingeman (1980); for sociological studies see Stein (1964), Warner (1949, 1963), Vidich and Bensman (1963).
2. Thomas O'Connor, "Martin Ritt," *New York Times*, January 12, 1986.
3. Kracauer (1966), p. 5.
4. Ibid., p. 5.
5. Bergman (1971), pp. xiii–xv.
6. Kracauer (1966), p. 12.
7. Maltby (1983), p. 10.
8. See Gans (1957).
9. Ray (1985), pp. 11, 249,
10. Lévi-Strauss (1985), p. 122; quoted in Silverstone (1988), p. 27.
11. See analysis of Lévi-Strauss in Silverstone (1988), pp. 27–28.
12. For analysis of myths in film and literature, see McConnell (1979), pp. 3–8.
13. Frye (1957).
14. Ray (1985), p. 249.
15. Monaco (1981), p. 293.
16. Saussure (1966), p. 117.
17. This point draws on Berger's analysis of semiology (1982), pp. 29–31.
18. A sign is an icon if its significance depends on some resemblance between the signifier and signified; it is an index, if there is real (causal) connection between the sign and what it signifies; and it is a symbol if the significance depends on social conventions (arbitrary decisions that must be learned).
19. Barthes (1967), p. 95.
20. Hall (1973), p. 2.
21. Burgelin (1972), p. 319.
22. See Braudy's (1976) analysis of genre conventions.
23. Wilde (1973), p. 86.
24. See Nisbet's (1966) discussion of the sociological tradition in terms of thematic paradigms based on moral issues.
25. Wood (1986), p. 245.
26. Ibid., p. 163.

271

Chapter 1: The 1930s—Idealism and Optimism

1. Most of John Steinbeck's novels were adapted to the screen, though the best film versions were Lewis Milestone's *Of Men and Mice* (1939) and John Ford's *The Grapes of Wrath* (1940). See discussion of Steinbeck's *East of Eden* (1955) in chapter 3.
2. Jacobs (1968), p. 516.
3. In 1950, they amounted to 11.8 percent of the population, and in 1980, to 2.8 percent (Gilbert and Khal, 1987, p. 70).
4. July 31, 1935, quoted in Shindler (1979), p. 130.
5. See Bergman (1971), pp. 70–71.
6. *State Fair* has been remade twice as a musical by Twentieth Century-Fox, though the first version is still the best. The 1945 film, directed by Walter Lang, boasted a rousing score by Richard Rodgers and Oscar Hammerstein II, and starred Charles Winninger, Fay Bainter, Jeanne Crain, and Dick Haymes. The film was extremely popular at the box office. In 1962, another (duller) version, directed by Jose Ferrer, featured in its cast Alice Faye (in her comeback role), and Charles Winninger, who recreated his 1945 role. A younger generation of stars, including Pat Boone, Ann-Margret, Bobby Darin, and Pamela Tiffin, decorated the film. The 1962 musical moved the story to Texas, but was sentimental and condescending to country life.
7. January 27, 1933.
8. Prior to *Our Daily Bread*, Vidor made another agrarian romance, *The Stranger's Return* (1933), a little-known film, based on Phil Stong's screenplay. Conventional, it is the story of a young City woman (Miriam Hopkins), recently separated from her husband, who goes to her grandfather's farm, where she finds her roots and true love, a college graduate turned farmer (Franchot Tone).
9. Vidor (1954), p. 152.
10. Ibid., p. 153.
11. Christensen (1987), p. 37.
12. Vidor (1954), p. 155.
13. Maltby (1983), p. 158.
14. One of the few directors to examine these alternative lifestyles was Arthur Penn, in *Alice's Restaurant* (See chapter 4).
15. Sarris (1968), pp. 117–19.
16. October 4, 1934.
17. October 4, 1934.
18. Lessons of a similar kind would be learned by the blacklisted filmmakers of *Salt of the Earth* (1953), another anti-establishment and independent film.
19. Daryl F. Zanuck, of Twentieth Century-Fox proposed to make a film about Dr. Dafoe, the famous Canadian physician who made history when he delivered the Dionne Quintuplets. Dr. Dafoe was awarded the Order of the British Empire and became a celebrity overnight, but few people knew that his life had been quite tough, practicing medicine in a godforsaken place, Moosetown, a small lumber town. Three movies, all starring Jean Hersholt as Dr. Dafoe

(called in the film John Luke) exploited the Dionne Quintuplets episode. The first (and best), *The Country Doctor* (1936), chronicles Dr. Luke's fight over the issue of building a new hospital. The enormous success of *The Country Doctor* series motivated a rival studio, RKO, to make its own series, *Dr. Christian*, also starring Jean Hersholt, thus making him the most popular doctor in Hollywood's history. The series was first aired on the radio, in 1937, and it outlived the popularity of the film series, running until 1953. Set in Rivers End, Minnesota, six movies were made, beginning with *Meet Dr. Christian* (1937). In the 1950s, *Dr. Christian* was made into a popular television series, starring MacDonald Carey.

20. The other two were: *Dr. Bull* and *The Prisoner of Shark Island*.
21. Lewis refused the 1926 Pulitzer in literature, because of the prize's alleged advocacy of novels that represented "the wholesome atmosphere" of American life and the "highest standard" of American manners.
22. Gallagher (1986), p. 76.
23. In Hitchcock's *Suspicion* (1941), Lina (Joan Fontaine) also refers to her husband (Cary Grant) as a baby.
24. Gallagher (1986), p. 94.
25. A similar idea appears in Spielberg's *Jaws* (1975). See discussion in chapter 5.
26. See discussion of Ford's heroes in Stowell (1986), pp. 5–6.
27. In Ford's Western, *Stagecoach*, Doc Boone is a social outcast, run out of town because of his drinking problem, but he redeems himself when he helps Mrs. Mallory give birth.
28. Cukor's version was the second of three films. The first was a silent (1919) film, and the third (1948) made by MGM and directed by Mervyn LeRoy as a sentimental Christmas card. It starred: June Allyson, Elizabeth Taylor, Janet Leigh, and Margaret O'Brien. In 1978, a television adaptation featured Dorothy McGuire as Marmee and Greer Garson as Aunt March.
29. *Alice Adams* was previously filmed in 1923 with Florence Vidor in the title role.
30. See Goffman's (1959) theory of the presentation of self in social life.
31. *New York Times*, September 17, 1976.
32. See discussion of *All That Heaven Allows* in chapter 3.
33. Maltby (1983), p. 159.
34. Howard Barnes, November 13, 1936.
35. Frank Nugent, November 13, 1936.
36. Harvey (1987), p. 224.
37. Roffman and Purdy (1981), p. 166.
38. D. W. C. *New York Times*, June 14, 1936.
39. Ott (1979), p. 173.
40. Nondiegetic insert consists of a shot cut into a sequence, showing objects which are outside the space of the narrative (Bordwell and Thompson, 1986, p. 384).
41. Frank Nugent, June 7, 1936.
42. Silver and Ward (1979), p. 110.
43. Christensen (1987), p. 38.
44. Sarris (1969), pp 86–87.
45. Julius J. Epstein and Leonore Coffee's script was based on Fannie Hurst's

Cosmopolitan magazine story, *Sister Act;* the film's original title was *Because of a Man.*

46. Sennett (1971), p. 141.

47. *Daughters Courageous* was followed with *Four Wives* (1939) and *Four Mothers* (1941). In 1955, cashing in on Doris Day's popularity, a musical remake of *Four Daughters*, titled *Young at Heart*, was released, starring Frank Sinatra.

48. Four writers contributed to the screenplay, though it bears the signature of Ben Hecht.

49. Roffman and Purdy (1981), pp 57–58.

50. In the musical *Wizard of Oz* (1939), Scarecrow and Tin Man are also in favor of collective, group support, longing for a populist alliance between farmers and workers.

51. *Village Voice,* June 1, 1972.

52. Brown (1970), p. 60.

53. Kerbel (1975), p. 10.

54. For a systematic analysis of screen images of American stars, see Levy (1988), pp. 100–130.

Chapter 2: The 1940s—Ambivalence and Cynicism

1. Deming (1969), p. 6. For a good discussion of her book, see Roffman and Purdy (1981), p. 268.

2. The New York Drama Critics Award was given that year to another work set in rural America, the stage adaptation of John Steinbeck's *Of Mice and Men.*

3. *New York Times,* December 20, 1987.

4. Quoted in Smith (1966), p. 216.

5. Quoted in Truffaut (1985), p. 153.

6. Ibid., p. 152.

7. Some see in the organist Wilder's alter ego. A closeted homosexual, Wilder also had a drinking problem.

8. See a good discussion of this issue in Spoto (1976), pp. 136–43.

9. Tim Holt bears a strong physical resemblance to Orson Welles; he is a thinner, younger, and more attractive version of the director.

10. Tennessee Williams expressed similar feelings about the deterioration of the Old South in *Baby Doll,* and William Faulkner in his stories, made into *The Long, Hot Summer.* See chapter 3.

11. See discussion in Bordwell and Thompson (1986), pp. 244–45.

12. It was based on Victor Trivas's story and Anthony Veiller's script; John Huston and Welles received no credit for their work.

13. Bazin (1978), p. 14.

14. Andrew Sarris, *Village Voice,* November 11, 1986.

15. Nominated for the Best Picture Oscar, it grossed over two million dollars in domestic rentals (equivalent of 22 million dollars at present).

16. David Platt, *Daily Worker,* February 6, 1942.

17. Two films in the 1980s, *Back to the Future* and *Peggy Sue Got Married,* dealt with similar concerns (See chapter 6).

18. Plastic products signify the same meaning in Mike Nichols's *The Graduate* (1967).

19. Glass in small-town films signifies fragility and vulnerability. See discussion of *All That Heaven Allows* and *The Birds* in chapters 3 and 4, respectively.
20. The following point is taken from Ray's (1985) excellent analysis of the film, pp. 198–99.
21. It's ironic that Lionel Barrymore, usually associated with good-hearted heroes (*Grand Hotel, David Copperfield*, Judge Hardy in *A Family Affair*, the first of the Andy Hardy series), plays such an outrageous villain.
22. See a discussion of these films in Levy (1987), pp. 137–38.
23. *New York Times*, July 4, 1941.
24. In John Ford's *The Searchers* (1956), the Bible and the Gun also symbolize the two tools of American ideology of expansion.
25. O. L. Guernsey, *New York Herald Tribune*, August 27, 1945.
26. A. W., *New York Times*, August 27, 1945.
27. The script, consisting of brief scenes (titled "Devers," "Daisy's coat," "The Possum," "Spring," and ending with "The Storm"), was singled out as one of the year's best screenplays.
28. Silver and Ward (1981), p. 331.
29. *New York Times*, January 20, 1944.
30. Quoted in Harvey (1987), p. 617.
31. Ibid., p. 637.
32. The film was based on Stuart Engstrand's novel, adapted to the screen by Leonore Coffee.
33. This line is used by Martha in Edward Albee's *Who's Afraid of Virginia Woolf?* except that Martha can't remember the specific movie it came from.
34. Mary Ann Doane (1987), pp. 64–65.
35. See discussion in Quart and Auster (1984), pp. 18–20.
36. Ray (1985), pp. 183–96.
37. In *Meet Me in St. Louis* (1944), an otherwise upbeat slice of Americana, there are also dark undertones that threaten to undermine the unity of the nuclear family.

Chapter 3: The 1950s—Conformity and Repression

1. For details of the distribution of the American population in cities and suburbs, see Denisoff and Wahrman (1975) and Robertson (1977).
2. For a discussion of this issue, see Donaldson (1969).
3. Many classic Westerns have employed this narrative structure, some in a mythical-religious way. In *Shane* (1953), for example, the outsider (Alan Ladd) is a former gunfighter, defending a family of homesteaders. He rides into town in the film's beginning and departs at its end, after redeeming it from evil.
4. The play, which won the George Jean Nathan Award, opened on Broadway on February 15, 1951 and ran for 190 performances.
5. Tennessee Williams used the same type of man in *Sweet Bird of Youth* (See chapter 4).
6. Molly Haskell (1974) suggests that Inge and Williams, two homosexual

playwrights, were expressing their own (subconscious) fear of aging through their female protagonists.

7. Wood (1975), p. 162.

8. The trend to portray suburbs as small towns also prevailed in the 1970s (see discussion of *Shampoo* and *Jaws* in chapter 5).

9. Kirby, a popular name of masculine heroes, was used in several John Wayne war and Western films (See Levy, 1988).

10. Stern (1979), p. 115.

11. In *The Lonely Crowd* (1950), David Riesman et al. distinguished among three types of character: tradition-directed, inner-directed, and other-directed.

12. For a good discussion of this genre, see Schatz (1981), pp. 245–60.

13. The success of *Peyton Place* was immense, grossing in domestic rentals over eleven million dollars. The film was nominated for nine Oscars, though won none; the awards went to David Lean's *The Bridge on the River Kwai*, its competitor in the Oscar contest (See Levy, 1990).

14. The following discussion draws on MacKinnon (1984), pp. 38–39.

15. Kawin (1977), p. 53.

16. In his screen adaptation, Paul Osborn focused on one part of the weighty novel.

17. Once again, as in *All That Heaven Allows*, glass is used to reflect a fragile mental state of mind.

18. There is a problem though: if one pays close attention to the film's beginning, before the flashback begins, one notices that Miles is by himself. Thus, the sequence in which Miles escapes town with Becky looses some of its suspense, because viewers may remember that Becky is not with Miles at the end.

19. Don Siegel's speech at a 1980 tribute to his work at the University of Southern California, Production File of *Invasion* at the American Film Institute.

20. Ottoson (1981), p. 103.

21. As was the custom at the time, she is played by a white actress.

22. The producers imposed the melodramatic elements of rape and the police car going up in flames—against Losey's wish.

23. Hirsch (1980), p. 39.

24. Ciment (1985), p. 96.

25. Robert Ryan played a similar role, a vicious racist, in *Crossfire* (1947).

26. Marlon Brando said the same thing to his brother (Rod Steiger) in the famous cab scene in Kazan's *On the Waterfront* (1954).

27. My analysis draws on Yacowar (1977), pp. 27–28.

Chapter 4: The 1960s—Continuity and Change

1. Opening on Broadway on December 19, 1957, *The Music Man* achieved a record with 883 performances.

2. *Saturday Review*, August 1962.

3. Peter Bogdanovich's *The Last Picture Show* (1971) featured a similar beginning (see chapter 5).

4. Almost the same words are uttered by the macho coach in *The Last Picture Show* (see chapter 5).
5. In Douglas Sirk's *Written on the Wind,* the nymphomaniac daughter (Dorothy Malone) also picks up her working-class studs at the gas station.
6. In 1952, Jose Quintero directed a landmark stage production, famous for establishing Geraldine Page as a foremost stage actress.
7. Interestingly, in 1961, another film revolved around a spinster (Deborah Kerr), *The Innocents,* based on Henry James's book *The Turn of the Screw.*
8. Yacowar (1977), pp. 67–70.
9. It marked Paul Newman's directorial debut, for which he received the New York Film Critics Circle Award; Joanne Woodward received the Circle's acting award and was nominated for a Best Actress Oscar.
10. Spoto (1976), p. 385.
11. Ibid., p. 388.
12. There were a number of (inferior) sequels, with Poitier playing the same role, *They Call Me Mr. Tibbs!* (1970) and *The Organization* (1971). In 1988, it was made into a television series, under the same title.
13. *New York Times,* February 19, 1966.
14. Wood (1986), p. 11. *The Chase* preceded Penn's masterpiece, *Bonnie and Clyde* (1967), and is also one of the few small-town movies in the 1960s, two good reasons for its inclusion.
15. In the 1980s, Horton Foote wrote about small towns more than any writer, producing an impressive body of work for the stage, screen, and television.
16. The following discussion is indebted to Wood's (1986) analysis of the film, pp. 11–25.
17. According to *Variety's* figures, *Bonnie and Clyde* grossed in domestic rentals 22 million dollars, *Easy Rider* 19, and *Alice's Restaurant* 6.
18. It was the name of Mickey Rooney's small-town hero in *The Human Comedy* (1943), and Harold Russell's war veteran in *The Best Years of Our Lives* (1946). In 1970, John Trent directed *Homer,* a film about a small-town youngster during the Vietnam War.
19. For a good discussion of this point, see Cagin and Dray (1984), p. 23.
20. Quoted in Monaco (1981), p. 251.
21. Cagin and Dray (1984), p. 70. For an interesting interpretation of the film's ending, see p. 73.
22. Kolker (1988), p. 58
23. This point draws on Bergman (1971), pp. 170–71.

Chapter 5: The 1970s—Nostalgia and Irony

1. See Monaco (1981), pp. 280–94.
2. The winners were Cloris Leachman and Ben Johnson, both in the supporting categories. Ellen Burstyn was singled out by the New York Film Critics Circle.
3. Jack Nicholson played a disc jockey in Bob Rafelson's youth-oriented film, *The King of Marvin Gardens* (1972).

4. In *Stand By Me* (1986), Richard Dreyfuss played another writer who, looking back on his life, realizes he never had the same intimate friendships as those of his youth (See chapter 6).
5. *Jeremiah Johnson* demonstrated the problem of casting a movie star in such role. Clearly, this film could not have been made without Redford's bankable stature, but his handsome looks and established screen image, as an urban and suave man, worked against the simplicity and primitiveness of the character he had to play.
6. *New Yorker,* March 18, 1974.
7. His literary source, Edward Anderson's 1937 novel of the same title, was adapted to the screen by Joan Tewksbury. Nicholas Ray's celebrated film noir, *They Live by Night,* was based on the same book.
8. For a systematic discussion of the notion of individual and community in this, as well as other Altman films, see Kolker (1988), pp. 335–39.
9. Pauline Kael, *New Yorker,* February 4, 1974.
10. *Village Voice,* April 4, 1974.
11. Quoted in Christensen (1987), p. 143.
12. An immigrant from Yugoslavia, Tesich made a semi-autobiographical film: He graduated from Indiana University and raced in the Little 500 race, winning the 1962 championship.
13. Arthur Schlesinger, *Saturday Review,* October 13, 1979.
14. On the issue of narcissism and media obsession, see Gabbard and Gabbard (1987), pp. 189–225.
15. See discussion of the concept in Ogburn (1922).
16. Studies (Greenberg et al., 1980) about the portrayal of gender in television documented that men have outnumbered women in every type of program. The paucity of women's roles in American film has been chronicled by Monaco (1981, pp. 91–98) and Levy (1987, pp. 201–4).

Chapter 6: The 1980s—Eccentricity and Self-Consciousness

1. See discussion in Kennison (1980).
2. Other movies set in the country and/or dealing with country music were: *Urban Cowboy, Honeysuckle Rose,* and *Hard Country* (all in 1980); *The Best Little Whorehouse in Texas* (1982); *Tender Mercies* (1983).
3. Phil Patton, *New York Times,* March 9, 1980.
4. Janet Maslin, *New York Times,* December 21, 1986.
5. Michael Sragow, *Rolling Stone,* March 19, 1981.
6. Production Notes for *Melvin and Howard,* library of the Academy of Motion Picture Arts and Sciences (AMPAS).
7. This contrast is similar to the one between Grace Kelly's blond Amish wife and Katy Jurado's Mexican saloon girl in *High Noon* (1952).
8. Production Notes for *True Stories,* library of AMPAS.
9. Director Jonathan Demme, who made the concert film *Stop Making Sense* (1986), said in an interview: "This is brand new. If anybody can bring cinema narrative out of the bog it's in, it's David Byrne." Production Notes for *True Stories.*

10. J. Hobberman, *Village Voice*, October 14, 1986.
11. Interview in Production Notes for *True Stories*.
12. Frank Rich, *New Times*, 1975.
13. One almost expects the swimming scene to follow the conventions (sensationalism, gossip) of a similar scene in *Peyton Place* (1957). The violation of these expectations makes the scene all the more pleasurable.
14. Ray (1985), p. 18.
15. Christensen (1987), p. 166.
16. The screenplay, written by Jerry Leichtling and wife Arlene Sarner before *Back to the Future*, wanted to demonstrate "a recognition that we alone are responsible for our destiny." Production Notes for *Peggy Sue Got Married*, AMPAS.
17. The novella was deftly adapted to the screen by Raynold Gideon and Bruce A. Evans.
18. The film was shot in Brownsville, Oregon, standing in for Castle Rock, Maine. The railroad sequence was filmed in the Mount Shasta area in California.
19. Scripted by Lewis John Carlino, it was commissioned by actress Ellen Burstyn for herself.

Conclusion

1. See Wright (1986), pp. 6–8.
2. Pike (1981), p. x.
3. Gilbert and Kahl (1987), p. 70.
4. Quart and Auster (1984), pp. 23–24.
5. The following discussion is based on Gans (1979), pp. 48–50.
6. Deming (1969), p. 6, quoted in Roffman and Purdy (1981), p. 268.
7. Ibid.
8. Wood (1986), p. 245.
9. Ibid., p. 29.
10. In *Taxi Driver* (1976), Travis's craziness is interpreted as heroism by the press, and in *King of Comedy* (1983), even though Rupert is jailed, his crime (kidnapping a popular talk show host) turns him into a celebrity.
11. Lasch (1979), p. 2.
12. See discussion of Turner's thesis in Silverstone (1988).
13. The following discussion draws on Coser's summary of Simmel (1971), pp. 182–83.
14. Ibid., p. 183.
15. See Van Gennep, A. (1960).
16. For a portrayal of the family in the work of American directors, see Gallagher (1983).

Select Bibliography

Appelbaum, Richard. *Size, Growth and U.S. Cities.* New York: Praeger, 1978.

Barber, Benjamin R. and Michael J. Gargas McGrath, eds, *The Artist and Political Vision.* New Jersey: Transaction, 1982.

Barthes, Roland. *Elements in Semiology.* London: Jonathan Cape, 1967.

————. *Mythologies.* New York: Hill and Wang, 1972.

Baxter, John. *King Vidor.* New York: Simon and Schuster, 1976.

Bazin, Andre. *Orson Welles: A Critical View.* New York: Harper and Row, 1978.

Berger, Arthur Asa. *Media Analysis Technique.* California: Sage, 1982.

Bergman, Andrew. *We're in the Money: Depression America and Its Films.* New York: New York University Press, 1971.

Bordwell, David and Kristin Thompson. *Film Art.* New York: Knopf, 1986.

————. *The World in a Frame.* New York: Doubleday, 1976.

Braudy, Leo. *The World in a Frame.* New York: Doubleday, 1976.

————. "Genre: The Conventions of Connection." In Mast and Cohen (1979), pp. 443–68.

Brown, William R. *Imagemaker: Will Rogers and the American Dream.* Columbia: University of Missouri Press, 1970.

Burgelin, O. "Structuralist Analysis and Mass Communication." In D. McQuail (1972).

Cahnman, Werner L. (ed.). *The Sociology of Ferdinand Toennies.* Chicago: University of Chicago Press, 1971.

Cagin, Seth and Philip Dray. *Hollywood Films of the Seventies.* New York: Harper and Row, 1984.

Cahiers du Cinema, "John Ford's Young Mr. Lincoln," in Nichols (1976), pp. 493–529.

Carey, James W. (ed.). *Media, Myths, and Narratives.* California: Sage, 1988.

Christensen, Terry. *Reel Politics: American Political Movies from "Birth of the Nation" to "Platoon."* New York: Blackswell, 1987.

Ciment, Michel. *Conversations with Losey.* New York: Methuen, 1985.

Cook, David M. and Graig G. Swager. *The Small Town in American Literature.* New York: Harper and Row, 1977.

Coser, Lewis. *Masters of Sociological Thought.* New York: Harcourt, Brace, 1971.

Deming, Barbara. *Running Away from Myself: A Portrait of America Drawn from the Films of the 1940s.* New York: Grossman, 1969.

280

Denisoff, Serge R. and Robert Wharman. *Introduction to Sociology.* New York: Macmillan, 1983.

Dickstein, Morris. "Frank Capra: Politics and Film." in Barber and McGarth (1982), pp. 317–33.

Doane, Mary Ann. *The Desire to Desire.* Bloomington: Indiana University Press, 1987.

Donaldson, Scott. *The Suburban Myth.* New York: Columbia University Press, 1969.

Durkheim, Emile. *The Elementary Forms of Religious Life.* New York: Free Press, (1912) 1965.

Elshtain, Jean Bethke, "Our Town Reconsidered: Reflections on the Small Town in American Literature," in Yanarella and Sigelman (1988), pp. 115–36.

Fiedler, Leslie. *Love and Death in the American Novel.* New York: Dell, 1969.

———. *The Return of the Vanishing American.* London: Paladin, 1972.

Fine, David M. *The City, the Immigrant, and American Fiction, 1880–1920.* Methuchen, NJ: Scarecrow, 1977.

Frye, Northrop. *Anatomy of Criticism.* Princeton: Princeton University Press, 1957.

———. *Fables of identity.* New York: Harcourt, Brace and World, 1963.

Gallagher, Tag. "Looking Homeward in Vina—the Family in American Film." *Mosaic,* 16 (1983), pp. 71–82.

Gallagher, Tag. *John Ford.* Berkeley: University of California Press, 1986.

Gans, Herbert. "The Creator-Audience Relationship in the Mass Media." in Rosenberg and White (1957), pp. 315–24.

———. "The Rise of the Problem Film." *Social Problems* (1964), pp. 327–36.

———. *Deciding What's News.* New York: Random House, 1979.

Goffman, E. *Gender Advertisements.* New York: Harper and Row, 1976.

Gombrich, E. H. *Art and Illusion.* Princeton: Princeton University Press, 1961.

Gornick, V. and B. Morgan. *Women in Sexist Society: Studies in Power and Powerlessness.* New York: Basic Books, 1971.

Grant, B. (ed.). *Film Genre.* Methuchen, NJ: Scarecrow, 1977.

Greenberg, B. et al. *Life on Television: Content Analysis of U.S. TV Drama.* Norwood, NJ: Ablex, 1980.

Gurevitch, Michael et al. (eds.). *Culture, Society, and the Media.* New York: Methuen, 1982.

Hall, John. *The Sociology of Literature.* New York: Longman, 1979.

Hall, Stewart, "Encoding and Decoding in the Television Discourse," CCS Occasional Paper, 1973, quoted in Woollacott, 1982.

Harvey, James. *Romantic Comedy in Hollywood.* New York: Knopf, 1987.

Haskell, Molly. *From Reverence to Rape.* New York: Holt, Rinehart, and Winston, 1974.

Hirsch, Foster. *Joseph Losey.* Boston: Twayne, 1980.

Jackson, Kenneth L. *Crabgrass Frontier: The Suburbanization of the United States.* New York: Columbia University Press, 1985.

Jacobs, Lewis. *The Rise of the American Film.* New York: Teachers College Press, 1968.

Jarvie, I. C. *Movies and Society.* New York: Basic Books, 1970.

Kasen, Jill H. "Whither the Self-made man? *Social Problems* 28 (1980), pp. 131–48.

Kawin, Bruce F. *Faulkner and Film.* New York: Ungar, 1977.

Kazin, Alfred. *A Writer's America: Landscape in America.* Knopf, 1988.

Kerbel, Michael. *Henry Fonda*. New York: Pyramid, 1975.

Kirby, Jack Temple. *Rural Worlds Lost: The American South, 1920–1960*. Louisiana State University Press, 1987.

Klapp, O. *Heroes, Villains, and Fools*. Englewood Cliffs, NJ: Prentice Hall, 1962.

Kolker, Robert P. *A Cinema of Loneliness*. New York: Oxford University Press, 1988.

Kracauer, Siegfried. *From Caligari to Hitler*. Princeton: Princeton University Press, (1947), 1966.

Kuhn, A. *Women's Pictures: Feminism and Cinema*. Boston: Routledge and Kegan Paul, 1982.

Landau, Jon. "I Fought the Law and the Law Won." *Rolling Stone,* May 9, 1974.

Lerner, Max. *America as Civilization*. New York: Simon and Schuster, 1957.

Levi-Strauss, Claude. *Structural Anthropology*. New York: Doubleday, 1967.

———. *The Raw and the Cooked: Volume 1. Introduction to the Science of Mythology*. London: Jonathan Cape, 1969.

———. *The View from Afar*. New York: Basil Blackwell, 1985.

Levy, Emanuel. *And the Winner Is: The History and Politics of the Oscar Award*. N.Y.: Ungar, 1987 (new expanded edition, Continuum, 1990).

———. *John Wayne: Prophet of the American Way of Life*. New Jersey: Scarecrow, 1988.

———. "The Democratic Elite: America's Movie Stars." *Qualitative Sociology,* 12 (1989), pp. 29–54.

———. "Stage, Sex, and Suffering: Images of Women in American Films." *Empirical Studies of the Arts* 8 (1990), pp. 53–76.

———. "Social Attributes of American Movie Stardom." *Media, Culture, and Society* (1990), pp. 247–67.

Lingeman, Richard. *Small Town America*. Boston: Houghton Mifflin, 1980.

McConnell, Frank. *Storytelling and Mythmaking*. New York: Oxford University Press, 1973.

McElvaine, Robert S. *The End of the Conservative Era: Liberalism after Reagan*. New York: Arbor House, 1987.

McQuail, Dennis (ed.). *The Sociology of Mass Communications*. London: Penguin, 1972.

MacKinnon, Kenneth. *Hollywood's Small Towns*. New Jersey: Scarecrow Press, 1984.

Maltby, Richard. *Harmless Entertainment*. New Jersey: Scarecrow Press, 1983.

Marling, Karal Ann. *The Colossus of Roads. Myth and Symbol Along the American Highway*. Minneapolis: University of Minnesota Press, 1984.

Mascotti, Louis H. and Jeffrey K. Hadden (eds.). *Suburbia in Transition. New York Times,* 1974.

Mast, Gerald and Marshall Cohen (eds.). *Film Theory and Criticism*. New York: Oxford University Press, 1979.

Mellen, J. *The Big Bad Wolves: Masculinity in the American Film*. New York: Pantheon, 1977.

Merton, Robert K. *Social Theory and Social Structure*. New York: Free Press, 1957.

Metz, Christian. *Film Language: A Semiotics of Cinema*. New York: Oxford University Press, 1974.

Millichap, Joseph R. *Steinbeck and Film*. New York: Ungar, 1983.

Mohl, Raymond A. and James F. Richardson (eds.). *Cities in American History*. Belmont, California: n.p., 1973.

Monaco, James. *How to Read a Film.* New York: Oxford University Press, 1977.
———. *American Film Now.* New York: New American Library, 1981.
Monkkonen, Eric. H. *America Becomes Urban.* Berkeley: University of California Press, 1988.
Mumford, Lewis. *The City in History.* N.Y.: Harcourt, Brace and World, 1961.
———. *The Culture of Cities.* New York: Harcourt Brace Jovanovich, 1970.
Nichols, Bill (ed.). *Movies and Methods.* Berkeley: University of California Press, 1976.
———. *Ideology and Image.* Bloomington: Indiana University Press, 1981.
Nimmo, Dan and James E. Combs. *Subliminal Politics: Myths and Mythmakers in America.* New Jersey: Prentice Hall, 1980.
Nisbet, Robert. *The Sociological Tradition.* New York: Basic Books, 1966.
O'Connor, Carol. "Sorting Out the Suburbs: Patterns of Land Use, Class, and Culture." *American Quarterly* 37 (1985), pp. 382–94.
Ogburn, William F. *Social Change.* New York: Huebsch, 1922.
Ott, Fredrick W. *The Films of Fritz Lang.* Secaucus, NJ: Citadel, 1979.
Ottoson, Robert. *A Reference Guide to the American Film Noir.* New Jersey: Scarecrow Press, 1981.
Park, Marlene and Gerald E. Markowitz. *Democratic Vistas: Post Offices and Public Art in the New Deal.* Philadelphia: Temple University Press, 1984.
Park, Robert, et al. *The City.* Chicago: University of Chicago Press, (1925), 1967.
Patton, Phil. "Country Movies Are in Tune with the New Patriotism." *New York Times,* March 9, 1980.
Paul, Rodman W. *The Far West and the Great Plains in Transition, 1859–1900.* New York: Harper and Row, 1988.
Perin, Constance. *Belonging in America.* Madison: University of Wisconsin Press, 1988.
Phillips, Kevin P. *Post-Conservative America.* New York: Random House 1982.
Pike, Burton. *The Image of the City in Modern Literature.* Princeton: Princeton University Press, 1981.
Powers, John. "Bleak Chic." *American Film,* March 1987, pp. 46–51.
Propp, Vladimir. *Morphology of the Folktale.* Austin: University of Texas Press, 1973.
Quart, Leonard and Albert Auster. *American Film and Society Since 1945.* New York: Praeger, 1988.
Raphael, Ray. *The Men from the Boys: Rites of Passage in Male America.* Lincoln: University of Nebraska Press, 1988.
Ray, Robert B. *A Certain Tendency of the Hollywood Cinema.* Princeton: Princeton University Press, 1985.
Riesman, David et al. *The Lonely Crowd.* New York: Doubleday, 1950.
Robertson, Ian. *Sociology.* New York: Worth, 1987.
Roffman, Peter and Jim Purdy. *The Hollywood Social Problem Film.* Bloomington: Indiana University Press, 1981.
Rosen, M. *Popcorn Venus: Women, Movies, and the American Dream.* New York: Coward, McCann, and Geoghegan, 1973.
Rosenberg, Bernard and David Manning White (eds.). *Mass Culture.* New York: Free Press, 1957.

Sallach, D. "Class Domination and Ideological Hegemony." *The Sociological Quarterly*, 15 (1974), pp. 38–50.

Sarris, Andrew. *The American Cinema: Directors and Directions*. New York: Dutton, 1968.

———. *The John Ford Movie Mystery*. Bloomington: Indiana University Press, 1975.

Saussure, Ferdinand de. *Course in General Linguistics*. New York: McGraw-Hill, 1966.

Schatz, Thomas. *Hollywood Genres*. Philadelphia: Temple University Press, 1981.

Schickel, Richard. *Intimate Strangers: The Culture of Celebrity*. New York: Doubleday, 1985.

Schwab, Jim. *Raising Less Corn and More Hell: Midwestern Farmers Speak Out*. Urbana: University of Illinois Press, 1988.

Sennett, Ted. *Warner Brothers Presents*. New York: Arlington, 1971.

Silver, Alain and Elizabeth Ward (eds.). *Film Noir*. Woodstock, NY: Overlook, 1979.

Silverstone, Roger. "Television and Culture," in J. W. Carey (1988), pp. 20–47.

Simmel, Georg, "The Stranger," In Wolff (1955), pp. 402–8.

Smith, Page. *As a City upon a Hill*. New York: Knopf, 1966.

Spoto, Donald. *The Art of Alfred Hitchcock*. New York: Doubleday, 1976.

Stein, Maurice R. *The Eclipse of Community*. New York: Harper and Row, 1964.

Stern. Michael. *Douglas Sirk*. Boston: Twayne, 1979.

Stowell, Peter. *John Ford*. Boston: Twayne, 1986.

Strange, Mary. *Family Farming: A New Economic Vision*. Lincoln: University of Nebraska Press, 1988.

Toennies, Ferdinand. *Community and Society—Gemeinschaft and Gesellschaft*. Translated and edited by Charles P. Loomis. Michigan: Michigan State University Press, 1957.

Tott, Susan. *Blooming: A Small Town Girlhood*. Boston: Little, Brown, 1981.

Truffaut, Francois. *Hitchcock*. (revised edition). New York: Simon and Schuster, 1984.

Tuchman, Gay, Arlene. K. Daniels, and J. Benet (eds.). *Hearth and Home: Images of Women in the Mass Media*. New York: Oxford University Press, 1978.

Veblen, Thorstein, "The Country Town," in Dorfman (1934).

Vidich, Arthur I. and Joseph Bensman. *Small Town in Mass Society*. Princeton: Princeton University Press, 1968.

Vidor, King. *A Tree Is a Tree*. New York: Longmans and Green, 1954.

Warner, Lloyd M. *Democracy in Jonesville*. N.p.: 1949.

———. *Yankee City*. New Haven: Yale University Press, 1963.

Warner, Sam Bass Jr. *Streetcar Suburbs*. Cambridge: Harvard University Press, 1969.

Weber, Max. *The City*. Trans and edited by Don Martindale and Gertrud Neuwirth. New York: Free Press, 1958.

Weinstein, Michael A. *The Wilderness and the City: American Classical Philosophy as a Moral Quest*. Amherst: University of Massachusetts Press, 1982.

White, Morton and Lucia White. *The Intellectual versus the City: From Thomas Jefferson to Frank Lloyd Wright*. New York: New American Library, 1962.

Wilde, Oscar. *"De Profundis" and Other Writings*. London: Penguin, 1973.

Wirth, Louis, "Urbanism as a Way of Life," *American Journal of Sociology*, 44 (1938), pp. 3–24.

Wood, Michael. *America in the Dark*. New York: Basic Books, 1975.

Wood, Robin. *Hollywood from Vietnam to Reagan*. New York: Columbia University Press, 1986.

Wolff, Kurt H. (ed.). *The Sociology of Georg Simmel*. New York: Free Press, 1955.

Woollacott, Janet, "Messages and Meanings," in Gurevitch et al. (1982).

Wright, Will. *Sixguns and Society: A Structural Study of the Western*. Berkeley: University of California Press, 1975.

Yacowar, Maurice. *Tennessee Williams and Film*. New York: Ungar, 1977.

Yanarella, Ernest J. and Lee Sigelman (eds.). *Political Mythology and Popular Fiction*. Westport, CT: Greenwood Press, 1988.

Index